Behavior Disorders

Theory and Practice

MARGARET CECIL COLEMAN
The University of Texas at Austin

Prentice-Hall, Inc., Englewood Cliffs, New Jersey 07632

Library of Congress Cataloging in Publication Data

Coleman, Margaret Cecil.
  Behavior disorders.

  Includes bibliographical references and index.
  1. Problem children—Education.   2. Deviant
behavior.   3. Child psychopathology.   4. Community
and school.   I. Title.
LC4801.C58 1986   371.93   85-3702
ISBN 0-13-071770-3

Editorial/production supervision and
interior design: Kate Kelly/Debbie Ford
Cover design: Wanda Lubelska Design
Manufacturing buyer: Barbara Kelly Kittle

Printed in the United States of America

10   9   8   7   6   5   4   3   2   1

ISBN 0-13-071770-3   01

Prentice-Hall International (UK) Limited, *London*
Prentice-Hall of Australia Pty. Limited, *Sydney*
Editora Prentice-Hall do Brasil, Ltda., *Rio de Janeiro*
Prentice-Hall Canada Inc., *Toronto*
Prentice-Hall Hispanoamericana, S.A., *Mexico*
Prentice-Hall of India Private Limited, *New Delhi*
Prentice-Hall of Japan, Inc., *Tokyo*
Prentice-Hall of Southeast Asia Pte. Ltd., *Singapore*
Whitehall Books Limited, *Wellington, New Zealand*

Dedicated to my parents,
Noah B. and Jeanette Sharpe Cecil

Contents

eight

Ecological Programming: Home and Community

nine

Adolescents

ten

Severe Behavior Disorders

References

Index

Foreword

This text *BEHAVIOR DISORDERS: THEORY AND PRACTICE* by Margaret Coleman should perhaps be titled THEORY *INTO* PRACTICE since its focus is on translating the best thinking and technological innovations into practical strategies for use by teachers and other professionals in understanding, identifying and intervening with the behavior disordered school-age population. I think the book succeeds very well in achieving this goal and it would be desirable if more texts shared such a focus in the behavior disorders area.

One of our most salient and frequently occurring failures in providing for the needs of educators in the behavior disorders area is the development, validation and replication of intervention procedures which produce high-magnitude treatment effects but which are not adapted to the requirements of school settings and the social agents who must implement them. These strategies have relatively low ecological validity in terms of their utility and practical application. Scholars and researchers who develop such strategies are often not interested in doing the laborious work necessary to adapt them for effective use by school professionals in a range of educational settings. This book bridges the gap between theory and practice very effectively.

Books such as this, written by a professional who thoroughly understands schools, the behavior disordered population and the technologies of assessment and intervention, are extremely valuable and in very short supply. This book contains state of the art information that is immediately useable by teachers and other professionals who either work in or relate to the school setting. It is well written and the content is highly relevant to the daily tasks that educators face in coping with the needs of behavior disordered students. I particularly appreciate the resource materials that are provided for the reader's convenience at the end of chapters and the information on working with parents and community agencies.

If I were writing an introductory text on behavior disorders, this is the kind of book that I would try to produce. It addresses very important topics in the behavior disorders area (severe behavior disorders, adolescents, identification) in a comprehensive fashion; it develops a thorough profile of the behavioral attributes of the BD population and provides a variety of perspectives for the reader's use in understanding causal factors relating to the etiology of behavior disorders.

The author admits an ecological bias in conceptualizing issues and approaches relating to this population. I have come to fully appreciate this frame of reference in the past five years and believe that it has great utility in guiding program practices in responding to the needs of BD pupils. The joint focus of behavioral ecology on both person and setting-specific factors and its emphasis upon achieving a satisfactory person-environment fit has powerful face validity. I share the author's enthusiasm for this approach.

I highly recommend this text. It is a powerful resource guide and provides useful, relevant information for the practitioner working with the behavior disordered population. It is a most substantive contribution to the field. I wish there were more texts like it available. The author is to be commended for producing such a high quality product for educational consumers.

Hill M. Walker
Professor, Division of
Special Education and
Rehabilitation
University of Oregon

Preface

It has always been perplexing to me that, as college students, we were supposed to read research and theory (which we found boring and practically useless, but necessary to pass courses) and somehow translate it into practice. It seemed to me that our mission was to find a transitional link between theory and what we should do in the schools. This introductory text is an effort to provide part of the missing link by integrating theory and practice into a useful text for teachers. I have attempted to show how various theories of deviant behavior are applied in school settings, and, in each chapter, I have tried to keep the focus on the teacher and the teacher's concerns.

The first two chapters of this text provide groundwork for understanding the concept of behavior disorders and the history of educational services for the behavior disordered student. Chapters 3 and 4 describe five theoretical models of disturbance—biophysical, psychodynamic, behavioral, sociological, and ecological. Although my bias toward an ecological approach to working with the behavior disordered surfaces in many chapters, I have tried to maintain a balance of theoretical perspectives by discussing the application of each model to educational settings. Chapters 5 through 7 address specific competencies that are needed to work with behavior disordered students, such as arranging an environment conducive to learning, individualizing instruction, and managing problem behavior while providing emotional support. The last three chapters focus on special issues: working with parents and community agencies, dealing with the behavior disordered adolescent, and teaching the severely disordered.

The book is intended as an introduction to behavior disorders. The methods and "how-to" chapters are not intended to be comprehensive; rather, it is hoped that the information provided will make teachers aware of the options and alternatives that are available to them in the classroom. The supplementary readings at the end of each chapter (which as a student, I used to ignore) were carefully selected to offer either additional, specific information or to stimulate further discussion and thinking on a significant topic. It is hoped that my readers will make better use of these readings than I was accustomed to doing.

I have many people to thank for their assistance and encouragement on this project. Special thanks are extended to John Knowles for his constant support throughout the writing. Jim Gilliam and Rich Simpson read the majority of the manuscript and offered valuable suggestions for improvement. Dona Stallworth and Jim Gilliam made contributions to the text by writing vignettes based on their experiences with behavior disordered students. Linda Brown offered not only excellent critiques and editorial assistance but also provided the much-needed push to get started and the encouragement to finish. Thanks, Brownie. Appreciation is extended to other colleagues, too numerous to list, who read single chapters and provided feedback.

Deborah Hirsch, the typist, deserves a special note of thanks for fast and extremely efficient service. And last, thanks to my friends and colleagues at the University of Texas who accommodated me when my door was shut and my time was short.

M.C. Coleman

Reality

Why live a life of disgrace
when you think people love you
and it ain't true or that
they love you and they don't.
I guess you live in dreams
and wonders when you think
the world is pink and flowers,
when you see the reality in the world
is full of black and hate.
There is no love in one.
I try to see dreams but
reality would always come by black
and no love for anything or anyone.
I don't know why I was born—
by love or mistake,
hate toward Dad or his last name.
I hope years pass by fast.
Later I can get married, have kids.
But I'm dreaming again—
But it's better if I dream
In a dark room or out of space
But not in a black world.

Isela M.

Feelings

My feelings aren't an open book.
In fact, I usually don't know what they are.
I feel so mean, cold-blooded, unreasonable
        at times;
But yet, I can be a sweet, soft dove.
I guess the hardest question I've ever heard
                is
        How are you feeling?
I mean, how am I feeling? At times I just
        can't tell.

Kelly D.

one

Definition
and Identification

Defining Behavior Disorders:
  Concepts, Characteristics,
  and a Definition

Identification Procedures:
  Tests, Team Meetings, and
  Roles

---

orientation

"Along with the hazards of street crime, drunk driving, and Christmas shopping is that of defining what is meant by 'emotional disturbance' . . . Emotion is nonrational, nonlinear, and so far has been pretty elusive to being pinned down by precise prose" (Bower, 1982, pp. 55–56). Eli Bower uses humor to describe what is in reality a very complex and frustrating problem for all professionals who work with behavior disordered students. Although federal regulations have provided some direction for definition and evaluation, the identification procedures for these students are complicated by many factors, including differences among professionals in terminology, training, and adherence to theoretical models. As teachers, you should be aware of your own personal and professional biases and be prepared to take an active role in the identification process.

OVERVIEW

This chapter explores a number of issues in the process of defining behavior disorders and identifying students as behavior disordered. Three basic questions are addressed:

(1) *How is disordered behavior defined?* The difficulties in defining deviance and the need for a definition are explored. The federal definition is presented and reviewed.

(2) *What are the characteristics of behavior disordered students?* Research on characteristics of disordered behavior, prevalence, and sex ratio is presented. A typical case example is described.

(3) *How are the behavior disordered identified?* Legal requirements for identification procedures are outlined. Advantages and disadvantages of instrumentation

1

and the decision-making process are highlighted. The chapter concludes by defining the optimum role of the special education teacher in identification.

HOW IS DISORDERED BEHAVIOR DEFINED?

Since its appearance more than 50 years ago, *emotional disturbance* has been an umbrella term for such varied conditions as schizophrenia, autism, psychosomatic disorders, phobias, withdrawal, depression, anxiety, elective mutism, aggression and a host of other pathologies. This variation in terminology reflects concepts that are unique to particular professions or theoretical positions. Although educators have made great strides in other areas, the field continues to be plagued by a lack of consensus on definition and terminology. The next section of this chapter is devoted to clarification of several factors that contribute to the difficulties in defining disturbance.

Factors Influencing Concepts of Deviance

A number of interrelated factors influence personal and professional decisions concerning which behaviors are acceptable and which behaviors are unacceptable. Among these factors are:

(1)   variation in individuals' tolerance ranges for behavior
(2)   differences in the theoretical models from which professionals operate
(3)   differences in terminology associated with emotional problems
(4)   sociological parameters of behavior.

Tolerance ranges.   Everyone has preferences for certain types of behavior and aversions to other types. Teachers also differ radically in their opinions of what is acceptable in the classroom, and it is not unusual for teachers to prefer teaching certain types of students. Although the literature consistently reports teacher preference for students who are characterized as passive or conforming (Helton & Oakland, 1977; Silberman, 1969, 1971), and unfavorable teacher attitudes toward aggressive students (Algozzine, 1977; Coleman & Gilliam, 1983; Rich, 1979; Walker & Buckley, 1973, 1974), individual teachers' tolerance ranges as well as their reactions to specific individuals vary widely. For example, dependent behavior may elicit sympathy and concern from one teacher, no reaction from another, and a negative attitude from a teacher who places a premium on independence and self-initiation. Teachers' potential for interaction with students has been found to be a function of their tolerance level for behaviors exhibited by those students (Algozzine & Curran, 1979).

Hewett and Taylor (1980) hypothesize that teachers have two general ranges of tolerance, one for academic differences and one for behavioral differences. They further propose that the tolerance for academic differences is much broader: if a student falls within the expected range for behavior, then she is more likely to be maintained in the regular classroom despite serious academic problems. Other researchers have found that behavioral and academic expectations are interactive: if a teacher has low behavioral expectations for a student, then cognitive or academic expectations will also be lowered (Good & Grouws, 1972; Gordon & Thomas, 1967). One study revealed that teachers' perceptions of their students' reading abilities were more closely related to ratings of classroom behavior than to actual reading achievement or performance on reading tests (Brown & Sherbenou, 1981). While the exact relationship between academic and behavioral expectations remains unspecified, it is clear that teachers do react differently to various types of behavior exhibited in the classroom. This state of affairs led Algozzine (1977) to question whether emotionally disturbed students are not best described as "disturbing" rather than "disturbed."

Theoretical models.   A second factor influencing concepts of deviance is the number of conflicting theories of how emotions and emotional problems develop. Each theory of emotional disturbance has unique terminology, identification procedures, and a preferred mode of treatment. Although many classification schemes for theories of deviant behavior have been developed, perhaps the one most widely accepted by educators was proposed by Rhodes and Tracy (1974), who grouped the numerous theories of emotional disturbance under five major conceptual models. These will be presented in Chapters 3 and 4. While there are some common elements, each model promotes a different view of definition, etiology, identification procedures, and intervention methods.

All professionals, whether they articulate it or not, operate from beliefs that are based on one or more of these models. Personal perceptions of deviance and subsequent decisions about definition and identification are heavily influenced by such theoretical beliefs. These beliefs depend, in part, on the theoretical and philosophical persuasion of the training program from which an individual graduates. Physicians, psychologists, and educators emerge from a wide variety of training programs that emphasize different theoretical views, diagnostic tools, and treatment procedures. These theoretical orientations are further reinforced in the work setting. A multidisciplinary team charged with making decisions about an individual student may represent several theoretical stances and thus may view the student in very different ways. The team may fail to agree on whether the student is disturbed or what diagnostic instruments and procedures should be used in the evaluation. They may even use entirely different terms to describe the same symptoms and problems. According to Hobbs (1975b), a particular child "may be regarded as mentally ill by a psychiatrist, as emotionally disturbed by a psychologist, and as behavior disordered by a special educator" (p. 57).

Terminology. A third factor influencing personal perceptions of deviance is the terminology associated with emotional disturbance. There is little agreement among educators on the basic term that most aptly describes deviant behavior in children. Additionally, educators have asserted that the jargon used by mental health professionals has little application to the school setting (Hobbs, 1975a). An examination of psychiatric and educational terminology should prove helpful in understanding why such confusion exists.

The psychiatric terminology encountered in psychological evaluations and records of disturbed students is usually based on one of two classification systems: one developed by the Group for the Advancement of Psychiatry (1966) or one developed by the American Psychiatric Association. The latter is more often utilized, and its sourcebook—the *Diagnostic and Statistical Manual* (DSM-III) (American Psychiatric Association, 1980)—is a comprehensive classification scheme that allows assignment of a diagnostic label based on symptomatology. The DSM-III sourcebook contains ten major headings under "Disorders of Infancy, Childhood or Adolescence." Listed below are the ten headings and some examples of subclassifications:

    I. Mental Retardation
    II. Attention Deficit Disorder
       with hyperactivity
       without hyperactivity
    III. Conduct Disorder
       undersocialized, aggressive
       socialized, aggressive
    IV. Anxiety Disorders of Childhood or Adolescence
       separation anxiety
       overanxious disorder
    V. Other Disorders of Infancy, Childhood or Adolescence
       oppositional disorder
       identity disorder
       elective mutism [refusal to talk][1]
    VI. Eating Disorders
       anorexia nervosa [self-imposed semistarvation]
       bulimia [binge eating]
    VII. Stereotyped Movement Disorders
       transient tic
       chronic motor tic
       Tourette's disorder [vocal tics]
    VIII. Other Disorders with Physical Manifestations
       stuttering

> sleepwalking disorder
> enuresis
> sleep terror
> IX. Pervasive Developmental Disorders
>   infantile autism
> X. Specific Developmental Disorders
>   developmental reading disorder
>   developmental arithmetic disorder
>   developmental language disorder

This classification system was devised to facilitate communication among the medical, psychological, and psychiatric professions and to codify recommentations for medication and therapy. It has few implications for educational services, nor was it intended to do so. However, in order to foster communication between the education and mental health communities and to ensure systematic classification of behavior disorders, many states are considering adoption of the DSM-III system for identification of behavior disordered students in the schools.

The use of differing terms by educators to denote disturbance does little to clarify the concept or to promote understanding among professionals. Although the concept of emotional disturbance has undergone an evolution of labels in the past 50 years, *seriously emotionally disturbed* is the term promoted for special education services by federal regulations of Public Law 94–142. *Emotionally disturbed* is also used more frequently than the other terms in research (F. H. Wood, 1979). The majority of states have adopted this term or a similar one, such as *emotionally impaired* or *emotionally handicapped,* while a few states have adopted the term *behavior disordered* to describe this category within special education (Mack, 1980).

The term behavior disordered is often seen as less stigmatizing, less severe, more socially acceptable, and more practical than the term emotionally disturbed. The term grew out of the behavioral model which posits that teachers can see and describe disordered behavior but cannot easily describe disturbed emotions. Many educators seem to prefer behavior disordered because it seems more plausible to deal directly with disordered behavior than with disturbed emotions.

In common usage today, behavior disordered is usually applied to less severely disturbed students, whereas emotionally disturbed is reserved for the most seriously impaired. However, since the two terms are often used interchangeably, they should be viewed within the context in which they appear. In this text, the terms have been used interchangeably in keeping with the models and popular usage, but behavior disordered is the term of choice.

Sociological parameters of behavior.   Sociological parameters constitute a fourth factor that influences personal views of deviance. Behavior which causes a child to be labeled as disturbed rarely occurs in isolation; rather, it arises from interactions that are influenced by subcultural and social-role factors.

American society is comprised of a strata of subcultures: racial or ethnic groups, socioeconomic levels, religious denominations, and geographic regions are examples of various subculture boundaries. Whether explicit or implicit, each subculture has its own provisions for membership, standards of behavior, and moral codes. For example, fighting and stealing may be adaptive behaviors for streetwise, inner-city adolescents and may be condoned by their community; the same behaviors would probably be viewed as totally unacceptable by the community at large or of another subculture with different standards. Thus, subcultural expectations are one factor in setting parameters for how behavior is viewed.

Social-role expectations are another sociological parameter of behavior. Sociologists believe that a large portion of an individual's behavior can be predicted and explained on the basis of the individual's status in society and the social roles associated with this status (Brophy, 1977). Behavior that fails to conform to these expectations may be considered deviant. Age and sex roles are major factors: certain behaviors are acceptable for a certain age level or gender, but may be considered highly inappropriate for an older age or the opposite sex. For example, consider the age or gender expectations attached to the following behaviors: thumb sucking, temper tantrums, enuresis, tattling, fistfighting, and use of explicit sexual language. Each of these behaviors is generally considered normal for a certain developmental period but may alarm parents and other adults if continued in excess beyond that period. In addition, many of the behaviors are considered more acceptable for one sex than for the other.

To summarize, four factors influencing individuals' concepts of deviance are: (1) differences in personal tolerance ranges, (2) differing theoretical models, (3) terminolgy, and (4) sociological parameters of behavior. These factors influence definitions of normalcy versus deviance and, subsequently, perceptions of problem behavior.

Defining Behavior Disorders

While recognizing that numerous factors influence personal concepts of deviance, professionals still must establish a common ground for working with behavior disordered students. Defining the population to be served is the first step in reaching a workable consensus. This section explores the need for defining behavior disorders and analyzes the definition promoted by federal law.

Utility of definitions. Two major reasons for defining and labeling have been identified: for research purposes (Achenbach, 1978), and for provision of services (Hobbs, 1975b). Epstein, Cullinan, and Sabatino

(1977) outline a number of pragmatic implications of a definition: (1) the chosen definition dictates the type of intervention and program description that is used to communicate the goals to others, (2) the definition affects prevalence estimates and thus influences decisions about who will receive services, and (3) the definition influences the areas of legislation, advocacy, and personnel preparation for employment. Thus, the rationale for defining usually relates to the quality of services to be provided for the population being defined. However, a common mistaken notion is that definitions have utility in identification of specific individuals to be served by programs. Definitions may describe a general population but are not specific enough to allow individuals to be identified; instead, state and local education agencies must create regulations which outline specific criteria for identification purposes. As Hammill (1976) observes, definitions allow description of students in broad, general terms, but are much too obscure to be used as criteria for selecting individual students.

Public Law 94–142 definition. A later section of this chapter addresses the operational criteria for identification that are outlined in state regulations. Let us now turn our attention to an analysis of the federal definition for this population. The definition of emotional disturbance specified in Public Law 94–142 and its accompanying regulations was first proposed by Eli Bower in 1957. This definition has been adopted in some form by the majority of state departments of education (Mack, 1980):

> Seriously emotionally disturbed is defined as follows: (i) the term means a condition exhibiting one or more of the following characteristics over a long period of time and to a marked degree, which adversely affects educational performance: (a) an inability to learn which cannot be explained by intellectual, sensory, or health factors; (b) an inability to build or maintain satisfactory interpersonal relationships with peers and teachers; (c) inappropriate types of behavior or feelings under normal circumstances; (d) a general pervasive mood of unhappiness or depression; (e) a tendency to develop physical symptoms or fears associated with personal or school problems. (ii) The term includes children who are schizophrenic or autistic.[2] The term does not include children who are socially maladjusted, unless it is determined that they are seriously emotionally disturbed. (*Federal Register*, 1977)

Bower (1982) points out that one or more of the noted characteristics could be observed in almost all so-called normal children to some extent at some point; therefore, the crucial difference was that emotionally disturbed children exhibited such characteristics to a marked degree over a period of time. Bower made this observation about 207 students designated as emotionally disturbed:

> The emotionally disturbed children were poor learners, although potentially able to learn; they had few if any satisfactory interpersonal relationships;

they behaved oddly or inappropriately; they were depressed or unhappy and developed illnesses or phobias. It was also noted that one or more of these characteristics were true of almost all nondesignated students to some extent at different times. The crucial differentiation was based on the observation and assessment that in the emotionally disturbed child the characteristics existed to *a marked degree over a period of time.* (Bower, 1982, p. 57)

Bower believes that this definition is practical in educational settings because it avoids presumptions about the child's "intrapsychic condition" or "clinical designation"; it stays within an observable setting and within the conceptual range of school personnel; and it assumes that behavior may vary from setting to setting.

Despite Bower's attempt to stay within a practical, school-oriented framework, the definition has been the focus of considerable discussion. Bower himself (1982) takes issue with the modification of his original wording by the addition of the word *seriously* to the term *emotionally disturbed* and the exclusion of children deemed socially maladjusted. If only seriously emotionally disturbed students are to be served, the implications are that mildly or moderately emotionally disturbed students are to be excluded and, further, that educators are able to distinguish degrees of disturbance on a continuum of severity. This is only one of the many questions raised by educators who wish to make the definition operational for program planning.

F. H. Wood (1979) has outlined six questions that are answered by a good, usable definition. These criteria are applied to Bower's definition in Table 1–1. It seems that the definition distinguishes who the focus of the problem is, and how the problem behavior is described, but fails to clearly outline either the setting or the perceiver of disturbed behavior. In addition, the definition gives partial and nonspecific information on identification and planning.

Finally, it appears that the current definition falls short of the ideal expressed by Wood, and that additional research is necessary if that ideal is to be met. In a review of state policies regarding the emotionally disturbed, Mack (1980) concludes that, among others, the following questions remain worthy of research:

(1) What is the impact of the qualifier *seriously* on the identification of emotionally disturbed children?

(2) How are states operationalizing phrases such as *over a long period of time* and *to a marked degree*?

(3) How do these qualifiers affect the numbers of children served?

(4) To what extent do states without policy definitions offer programs and services for autistic and schizophrenic children?

(5) What is the impact of noncategorical definitions on identification, service delivery, and funding procedures?

Questions such as these must be answered before rendering a final judgment on the definition currently in use.

WHAT ARE THE CHARACTERISTICS OF BEHAVIOR DISORDERED STUDENTS?

This section highlights research on characteristics of students identified as disturbed. A brief case study which illustrates several characteristics also is presented.

Factors of Disordered Behavior

Research over the past 15 years has consistently yielded three factors underlying disordered behavior in children and adolescents. The classic study of Quay, Morse, and Cutler (1966) established these factors, which subsequently have been supported (Conners, 1970; Kaufman, Swan, & Wood, 1979; Quay, 1966). Quay and his colleagues analyzed teacher ratings of the behavior of 441 children in public school classes for the emotionally disturbed and found students exhibiting three major profiles:

(1) *conduct disorder*, characterized by "aggressive, hostile and contentious behavior" (Quay et al, 1966, p. 297)

(2) *personality problem*, characterized by "anxious, withdrawn, introvertive behavior" (Ibid., p. 297)

(3) *inadequacy-immaturity*, a less distinct factor involving "preoccupation, lack of interest, sluggishness, laziness, daydreaming and passivity." (Ibid., p. 298). This factor has also been linked to lack of interest in or awareness of the environment and other autisticlike behaviors.

In classrooms for the emotionally disturbed, conduct disorders and inadequacy-immaturity factors are more prevalent than personality problems (Kaufman et al., 1979; McCarthy & Paraskevopoulos, 1969; Quay et al., 1966). The finding that conduct disordered or aggressive students comprise the largest percentage is in keeping with the literature on the disturbing nature of aggressiveness. However, the prevalence of students characterized as inadequate-immature is less clear. A tentative explanation offered by Quay et al. (1966) is that teachers and school personnel may react strongly to immature children. Another plausible explanation is that the numbers of autistic or autisticlike children who are in classes for the emotionally disturbed cause this factor to be heavily loaded. The exact relationship between inadequate-immature behavior and emotional disturbance is therefore unclear, but it is clear that children whose behavior is characterized as inadequate-immature do find their way into special education classrooms alongside those characterized as aggressive.

TABLE 1–1. Usefulness of the P.L. 94–142 Definition of Emotional Disturbance

CRITERION (F.H. WOOD, 1979)	COMPONENT OF DEFINITION WHICH ADDRESSES CRITERION	CRITERION SATISFIED?
1. Who is the focus of the problem?	—student who "exhibits one or more of the following characteristics over a long period of time and to a degree which adversely affects educational performance"	yes
	—includes children who are schizophrenic	
	—excludes children who are socially maladjusted	
2. How is the problem behavior described?	—"an inability to learn which cannot be explained by intellectual, sensory, or health factors"	yes
	—"an inability to build or maintain satisfactory interpersonal relationships with peers and teachers"	
	—"inappropriate types of behavior or feelings under normal circumstances"	
	—"a general pervasive mood of unhappiness or depression"	
	—"a tendency to develop physical symptoms or fears associated with personal or school problems"	

3. In what setting does the problem behavior occur?	not explicit; school setting implied by "which adversely affects educational performance" and by one component, the "inability to learn"	unclear
4. Who regards the behavior as a problem?	not explicit; school personnel implied by "which adversely affects educational preformance" and by one component, the "inability to learn"	unclear
5. How and by whom is the definition used to differentiate disturbers from non-disturbers?	How: —must rule out "inability to learn based on intellectual, sensory or health factors" —characteristics must be exhibited "over a long period of time, to a marked degree, and must adversely affect educational performance" By whom: involvement of school personnel again implied as in #3 and #4, but involvement of additional persons is not stated	partially
6. Does the definition provide basis for planning activities, such as needs assessment, individual assessment, and program evaluation?	Insofar as one accepts the inverse of the five stated characteristics (components a–c) as global goals for an individual's program; no bases for program evaluation are provided	partially

11

Some of the specific variables comprising the factors in the study by Quay and his colleagues are presented in Table 1–2 and the variables from the Kaufman study are presented in Table 1–3. Note that the factors are almost identical and that the variables are very similar although they are based on different checklists. Despite the apparent stability of these factors, they provide few clues as to proper identification procedures and even fewer clues for intervention. At this point, the factors merely describe the populations we consistently identify as behavior disordered.

Researchers have described a fourth factor of deviant behavior which confounds the classification of behavior disorders. Quay (1972, 1975) has identified a cluster of behaviors associated with socialized delinquency or juvenile delinquency. Most of the identified behaviors relate to participation in subgroups or gangs who break rules or laws such as those against truancy, stealing, and curfew violation. Thus, students characterized as socialized delinquents have learned numerous behaviors which their peer group condones but society rejects. According to federal regulations, these students are not emotionally disturbed; the federal definition specifically

TABLE 1–2.   Variables Loading Under the Three Factors of Disturbed Behavior Identified by Quay et al. (1966)[a]

CONDUCT PROBLEM	INADEQUACY-IMMATURITY	PERSONALITY PROBLEM
defiant,* disobedient	inattentive*	shy
impertinent*	dislikes school	inferiority*
uncooperative in group	withdrawn	self-conscious*
irritable	sluggish	lacks self-confidence*
boisterous	lack of interest*	easily flustered
showoff, attention-seeking*	lazy	fearful, anxious*
bullies*	preoccupied	
temper tantrum*	daydreams	
hyperactive*	drowsy	
restless*	reticent	
negative*		
irresponsible		
swears,* profane language*		
destructive*		
jealous*		

[a]Only those variables with factor loadings of 0.40 or greater were selected for inclusion in Table 1–2.

*Indicates overlap with variables in Table 1–3.

From "Personality Patterns of Pupils in Classrooms for the Emotionally Disturbed" by Quay, Morse, and Cutler (*Exceptional Children, 32,* 1966, 297–301). Copyright 1966 by The Council for Exceptional Children. Reprinted with permission.

TABLE 1–3. Variables Loading Under the Three Factors of Behavior Identified by Kaufman et al. (1979)[a]

AGGRESSIVE, ANTISOCIAL BEHAVIOR	DISORGANIZED, NONFOCUSED BEHAVIOR	ANXIOUS, WITHDRAWN BEHAVIOR
aggressive toward children	careless, does not complete tasks	moodiness, overly sensitive,*
tries to control others* (critical, manipulative)	forgetful, does not retain	sad, irritability
aggressive toward property,* rules	does not follow directions	lacks confidence,* fears failure*
demands excessive attention	lacks comprehension of assignments	unable to express feelings
impertinent,* defiant,* negative*	short attention span*	appropriately
restless,* overactive*	distractibility	avoids participating with
jealous* (possessive, selfish)	lacks motivation,* apathetic*	children in groups
talks excessively	listening problems, difficulty	avoids difficult or new situations
temper tantrums*	comprehending	
suspicious (distrusts, blames others)	irresponsible	
untruthfulness		
obscene language,* cursing,* sex talk		

[a]Variables with loadings of 0.35 or greater in both parent *and* teacher responses are given here.

*Indicates overlap with variables in Table 1–2.

From "Dimensions of Problem Behaviors of Emotionally Disturbed Children as Seen by Their Parents and Teachers," A.S. Kaufman, W.W. Swan, & M.M. Wood, *Psychology in the Schools,*1979, *16,* 212–213. Reprinted by permission.

excludes the "socially maladjusted"—"unless it is determined that they are seriously emotionally disturbed." (*Federal Register,* 1977)

In all probability the intention of this clause was to prevent public school classrooms from becoming a dumping ground for adjudicated youth and to ensure that the legal system would continue to provide their own programs for these youth. However, there is considerable overlap among socially maladjusted, emotionally disturbed, and delinquent behavior. One estimate of incarcerated juvenile offenders who might be classified as seriously emotionally disturbed was given as 11 percent (Quay & Parsons, 1970). Haney and Gold (1973) found that of a general sample of 522 teenagers, over 80 percent admitted having committed delinquent acts, but only 10 percent had ever been arrested. Such statistics point out the overlap of normal and delinquent behaviors in adolescent populations.

Some guidelines have been developed to help differentiate between socially maladjusted and emotionally disturbed (Smith, 1979; Telford & Sawrey, 1967). Such guidelines focus on the social learning aspect; that is, socially maladjusted students have learned socially unacceptable behaviors but experience little anxiety or motivation to change because they have acceptance from a subcultural group. Although general guidelines may be helpful in ascribing differences, the actual classification of individuals remains a dilemma.

Dimensions of Disordered Behavior

The dimensions of chronicity, frequency, and severity are essential elements in determining whether behavior is normal or abnormal. Severity or extremeness of behavior is usually readily apparent because of its negative impact or shock value; an extreme behavior such as masturbation in the classroom automatically and immediately receives a great deal of negative attention. However, chronicity and frequency of behavior are not so apparent and require some record keeping on the part of school personnel.

The federal definition stipulates that the student's condition be present "over a long period of time" (chronicity) and "to a marked degree" (severity and/or frequency). The goal of such stipulation is to exclude temporary or moderate behavior problems that may be reactions to situational stress or normal developmental difficulties. Indeed, it has been established that at some point in their lives, the vast majority of children exhibit behaviors that could be classified as disturbed or pathological (Bower, 1982; Kanner, 1957; Kessler, 1966). As Kessler asserts, "There is no abnormal behavior which cannot be found in normal individuals at certain ages and under certain conditions" (p. 69).

Although no objective criteria have been established for determining what constitutes "a long period of time" or "a marked degree," there are some obvious implications. *Chronicity* refers to a pattern of behavior which has been relatively stable over time; it may even disappear for short periods of time but reappear at intervals to interfere with normal or adaptive functioning. *Frequency* and *severity* are interrelated in that the more severe the behavior, the less often it has to occur before being construed as indicative of disturbance. Consider the following examples: A junior high student verbalizes anger and hostility through profanity and threats to the teacher; if this behavior had occurred only once during the student's otherwise clean school record, it would likely be treated as an isolated incident and dismissed with a disciplinary action. If, however, it occurred two or three times a week, the student would likely be referred for some type of psychological services as well as school disciplinary measures. Another junior high student expresses anger and hostility against school authority by making a bomb threat; in this instance, the single occurrence may be considered serious enough to warrant psychological counseling or referral to other psychological services.

The classroom teacher should use an objective measure to help determine the chronicity, severity, and frequency of problem behaviors. It often proves very difficult for the teacher to distinguish disturbed from disturbing behavior, especially when the behaviors are particularly obnoxious, disruptive, or personally displeasing. In those instances, the teacher's discomfort may result in unintentional exaggeration of the severity of a problem or in overestimation of the number of times the behavior occurs. Behavior recording or the use of checklists or rating scales may be necessary to provide an objective estimate of how often the behavior actually occurs or how abnormal it is in comparison to other students' behavior. (Refer to Chapter 4 for descriptions of behavior rating scales and behavior recording techniques that may be used by teachers for screening purposes.)

Academic Functioning

In most states, a student must exhibit an academic deficiency to qualify for services as emotionally disturbed. In keeping with the provision of the federal definition that "the term means a condition . . . which adversely affects educational performance," approximately 40 states have adopted regulations mandating that academic deficiency be part of the criteria for placement (Mack, 1980). Generally, state regulations are designed either to define academic deficiency in terms of achievement test scores or to leave the decision to the judgment of assessment personnel. However academic deficiency is operationalized, the population to be served under this category should exhibit significant academic difficulty in addition to emotional or behavioral problems. Research on the population actually receiving services indicates that disturbed students do have significant academic difficulties both when compared to their normal peers (Bower, 1969) and when compared to expectancy level based on mental age (Graubard, 1964; Stone & Rowley, 1964).

Prevalence and Sex Ratio

Ranges of incidence as wide as 0.05 percent to 30 percent have been reported in the literature: the 0.5 percent (5 in 10,000) estimates usually refer only to psychotic and autistic populations. A more moderate range of 6 percent to 20 percent was reported by Graham (1979), and a range from 2.2 percent for severe problems to 12.6 percent for mild problems as perceived by teachers was reported by Kelly, Bullock, and Dykes (1974). Bower (1969), in his definitive work with disturbed pupils in California, estimated that about 10 percent of the school-aged population need intervention for behavior or emotional problems. He has taken issue with the prevalence figure of 2 percent, which was established by the U.S. Office of Education in 1975 and is considered the official prevalence figure. As Bower summarizes,

> It presents the problem as the tip of an iceberg, negating a host of consistent data that indicate that approximately 10% of children in school have moderate to severe emotional problems. (1982, p. 60)

Kauffman and Kneedler (1981) also believe that public policy makers, operating from an economic platform and without benefit of data, dictate prevalence levels for behavior disordered students. In their argument, they assert that "social policy, rather than empirical data . . . determines the extent of 'behavioral deviance' among society's children" (Kauffman & Kneedler, 1981, p. 169).

Accurate estimation of the prevalence of behavior disordered pupils is hampered by a number of difficulties, including inconsistency in definition. Some prevalence studies are based on populations actually receiving services, but the majority are based on teacher estimates in the general school population. One longitudinal study of more than 1,000 students showed that over a three-year period, 48 percent of the students were identified as having a behavior problem by at least one teacher; however, only 7.5 percent of the children were identified by teachers in all three years (Rubin & Balow, 1978). Although this study asked for designation of children with behavior problems and not for nominations for special classes, it does demonstrate the variance among individual teachers' tolerance ranges for behavior. The 7.5 percent estimate is more commensurate with other estimations of behavior disordered pupils, which suggests that a consensual nomination from a number of people over time may be more realistic than a single nomination.

While the exact sex ratio of pupils receiving services for the behavior disordered has not been established, it has been determined that boys are decidedly more "at risk" than girls (Rubin & Balow, 1971; Schultz, Salvia, & Feinn, 1974; Werry & Quay, 1971). It has also been established that the incidence of autism is four times more common in boys than in girls (Ritvo & Freeman, 1977). Estimations of the sex ratio in classes for the behavior disordered run as high as eight or nine boys to one girl (McCarthy & Paraskevopoulos, 1969; Reinert, 1976). Researchers have proposed an explanation for this disparity: behaviors that are more typical of boys are more likely to be labeled as disordered. Schlosser and Algozzine (1979) found that behavior problems typically exhibited by boys were rated by teachers as more disturbing than those typically exhibited by girls. Other researchers have found that as boys grow out of childhood and into their teens, they tend to show conduct problems and immaturity, whereas girls tend to show personality problems characterized by withdrawal or neurotic symptoms (Clarizio & McCoy, 1976; Kauffman, 1981; Schultz et al., 1974). As mentioned earlier in this chapter, conduct problems and immaturity are more prevalent in classrooms for the behavior disordered, thereby suggesting that these types of behaviors are likely to be considered disordered.

BOX 1–1. *JIM: A CASE EXAMPLE*

Jim is an 11-year-old fourth grader from a lower socioeconomic minority family. He failed second grade and is perilously close to repeating the fourth grade because he doesn't turn in assignments or complete work in class. He has been a constant source of frustration to the teachers at Willough Elementary since transferring from across town last year. His reputation as a difficult and disruptive student preceded him to his new school environment and appears to be well-earned.

Although Ms. Perkins, his current teacher, tries to handle most discipline problems herself, she has been so exasperated by Jim that she has sent him to the principal's office for disciplinary measures an average of three times a week since the beginning of school. Jim has been involved in several fights in school and on the bus; one was serious enough to get him suspended because the other student had to receive medical attention. On one occasion he pulled a knife but did not use it, and on other occasions he has told Ms. Perkins to "get off his back" and to "go to hell."

Although Ms. Perkins says these occurrences bothered her at the time, it is Jim's emotional state that upsets her most; she describes him as often "sullen and hostile," and when he gets in these moods, he talks out in class, refuses to work and becomes disruptive in any number of ingenious ways. As intervention methods, Ms. Perkins has tried reasoning, punishment by revoking privileges, and ignoring his outbursts whenever possible. She has talked to his parents, who were nice but not very supportive of the disciplinary methods suggested and, she suspects, not very capable of carrying them out. The school psychologist recommended a positive reinforcement system for nondisruptive behavior, but Ms. Perkins doesn't have the time necessary to institute it and she doesn't really feel that Jim should be rewarded for "something he should be doing anyway." She believes that Jim can best be served by someone who is trained to deal with emotional problems, such as the special education teacher. She has been keeping notes on his behavior and talking to Jim's previous teacher as well as the principal because she wants to be able to defend her reasons for making a referral.

Jim represents a typical referral to services for the behavior disordered for three reasons: (1) he is male, (2) he is from a lower socioeconomic family, and (3) he exhibits aggressive and disruptive behaviors. The fact that boys are much more likely to be identified as behavior disordered was discussed previously. Social class is a factor because more aggressive and acting-out behaviors have been found in families of lower socioeconomic status (Graubard, 1973), and these type behaviors are more likely to become classified as disturbed. A number of studies have shown that behaviors described as aggressive or socially defiant are consistently more bothersome to teachers (Algozzine, 1977; Herr, Algozzine, & Eaves, 1976; Mooney & Algozzine, 1978). Studies of actual classroom interactions between teachers and these students demonstrate that teachers tend to respond more intensely, more dominantly, and less effectively than with other types of student behavior (Rich, 1979; Rohrkemper & Brophy, 1979). Walker and Buckley (1973, 1974) summarize a number of studies of classroom interactions between teachers and aggressive or disruptive students thus: that such interactions are more likely to be negative than positive; that the teacher is much more likely to reprimand inappropriate behavior than to approve of appropriate behavior in these interactions; and that disruptive children tend to monopolize the teacher's time. Walker further states that these studies are illustrative of the frustration teachers usually encounter in dealing with acting-out children:

> It often appears that the harder a teacher tries to control an acting-out child's behavior, the less effective he/she is. This process can be physically and emotionally exhausting . . . and the child's behavior is a constant reminder that the classroom atmosphere is not what the teacher would like it to be. (Walker, 1979, p. 18)

In summary, research on disturbed behavior indicates that students who evidence conduct problems (especially aggression) or inadequate-immature behaviors over a long time and to a marked degree are likely to become labeled as behavior disordered. The majority of these students are male and manifest academic deficiencies. Although prevalence estimates vary widely, many researchers believe that approximately 2 percent of school-aged children are severely disordered, with another 7 percent to 10 percent evidencing behavior or emotional problems severe enough to warrant intervention.

HOW ARE THE BEHAVIOR DISORDERED IDENTIFIED?

It has been suggested that there are no psychological tests that measure personality, anxiety, or adjustment well enough to be useful in determining behavior disorders (Reeve & Kauffman, 1978). In addition to difficulties with measurement instruments is the problem of responsibility for identification—who has the ultimate responsibility for decision making? Before addressing these issues, let us look at the legal background of identification regulations.

Identification Procedures

Prior to the passage of P.L. 94–142, it was not uncommon for students to be evaluated with a single test and recommended for special education services by a single evaluator. In order to ensure a more comprehensive evaluation procedure involving more decision makers, a number of mandates about evaluation were laid out in P.L. 94–142:

(1) *Nondiscriminatory testing.* State and local education agencies must establish guidelines to ensure that identification procedures are not culturally or racially discriminating. The child must be evaluated in the native language or the one normally used by the child or the child's parents.

(2) *Parental involvement.* Parents have the right to participate in making decisions regarding the education of their child, including placement decisions and development of the individualized education plan.

(3) *Multiple criteria and team decisions.* No single test or criterion shall be used in making placement decisions, and a team or committee shall be charged with making the final decision.

(4) *Test validity.* Tests must be valid for the purposes for which they are used.

From these basic mandates, state agencies have adopted regulations and guidelines to assist local school districts in devising appropriate identification procedures. Although specific regulations vary from state to state, a few commonalities exist. In the case of a student to be considered for services under the category *behavior disordered,* most states require that a licensed or certified psychologist or psychiatrist be responsible for the evaluation; however, few states specify exactly what the evaluation should entail and even fewer specify the instruments to be used. Most states require that eligibility be determined by a multidisciplinary team based on information from a comprehensive assessment in a number of areas such as language, cognitive-intellectual, emotional-social, medical-physical, and behavioral. In addition, some determination of academic functioning or educational level usually is required.

Instruments Used for Identification

Selection of specific instruments and techniques is usually left up to the discretion of assessment personnel. One nationwide survey was conducted with 92 public school and residential programs to determine which tests are used to identify students as behavior disordered (Coulter, Morrow, & Gilliam, 1979); other researchers surveyed 118 mental health agencies about practices in personality assessment with youngsters through age 18 (Brown & McGuire, 1976). According to these surveys, the test batteries used in the schools are oriented toward intellectual and educational assessment, whereas the batteries used by mental health clinicians are oriented toward projective techniques.[3] The *Bender Motor Gestalt Test* (Bender, 1946) and the *Rorschach Inkblot Test* (Rorschach, 1921) are the only instruments listed as often used in both surveys. Also of note in the Brown and McGuire study is the reported use of the *Wechsler Intelligence Scale for Children—Revised* (WISC-R) (Wechsler, 1974) for personality assessment. The authors found that in all age groups, intelligence tests such as the *Wechsler* scales and the *Stanford-Binet* (Terman & Merrill, 1972) were used for personality assessment, which ". . . seems to suggest that the clinical interpretation of these tests is very popular and that more weight may be placed on this use in mental health settings than in graduate training programs" (Brown & McGuire, 1976, p. 482).

Numerous problems are inherent in the use of these instruments to identify the behavior disordered. The problem of technical adequacy looms largest. According to Ysseldyke and Algozzine (1982), technical adequacy consists of proper norms (comparison group), reliability (consistency of measurement), and validity (the extent to which the test measures what it purports to measure). When tests are used to make educational decisions about an individual, they should meet stringent standards of technical adequacy, and the question of test validity should always be phrased, "Valid for what purpose?" (Salvia & Ysseldyke, 1981).

The question of validity is particularly applicable to the use of the Wechsler scales, especially the Wechsler Intelligence Scale for Children—Revised, as a clinical personality assessment tool. At best, the Wechsler scales, like other individual intelligence tests, give information on current intellectual functioning and, to some extent, predict school success. Although the scales were not designed as personality measures they have been diverted to that purpose. Profile analysis or scrutiny of patterns of subtest scores for diagnostic purposes has become a popular abuse (Ysseldyke, 1979). The WISC-R is technically adequate when used for the purpose for which it was designed; it can be useful in establishing a basic level of functioning—but even then results should be interpreted cautiously and in the context of many other pieces of information. Its use as a personality measure violates its purpose and undermines its validity.

Projective techniques are given a critical review by Anastasi (1982), in which she cites the following points:

As a group, projectives "make a poor showing" when evaluated for technical adequacy, yet they continue to be popular clinical instruments.

The majority of projectives have "questionable theoretical rationale" and "are clearly found wanting when evaluated in accordance with test standards" (p. 589). Standardization of administration and scoring procedures, adequacy of norms, reliability, and validity are all questionable.

The validity of the Rorschach Inkblot Test and Human Figure Drawing have been found particularly suspect.

The final interpretation of a projective test may reveal more about background, training and personal orientation of the examiner than the personality of the examinee.

Anastasi concludes that projectives may best be viewed not as *tests* but as clinical tools that can provide supplemental information as an interviewing technique. She summarizes that "their value as clinical tools is proportional to the skill of the clinician and hence cannot be assessed independently of the individual clinician using them" (Anastasi, 1982, p. 590).

Thus, it appears that federal laws and regulations have had little impact on the selection of specific instruments and that projective techniques are commonly used to identify emotional disturbance. Few changes in practice have occurred since Trippe's observation in 1966 that an emotionally disturbed child is one who is so diagnosed by an appropriate mental health clinician.

Team Decision Making

Eligibility decisions for placement in special education are made by a team composed of educators and other appropriate individuals who follow the mandates of federal legislation. The multidisciplinary team must include the parents, the person responsible for assessment, an administrator, an instructional person, and whenever appropriate, the student.

Surveys of practices in eligibility decision making indicate that the teams are multidisciplinary in composition and average from five to seven members; individuals most often participating are parents, school administrators, special education teachers, school psychologists, regular education teachers, and special education administrators (Ysseldyke & Algozzine, 1982; Gilliam & Coleman, 1981; Thurlow & Ysseldyke, 1980). These surveys also identify some procedural problems in the team decision-making process.

After videotaping more than 30 actual team meetings, Ysseldyke and his colleagues at the University of Minnesota Institute for Research on Learning Disabilities evaluated these meetings thus:

> It was very difficult to find meetings that could be called placement decision-making sessions. Many team meetings were held, but most can be described as meetings to get ready for the meetings to get ready for the meeting. Often, placement decisions were made at the same meetings at which many other kinds of decisions were made. We repeatedly had difficulty attempting to specify decisions that were actually made at meetings because in most instances it was apparent that the decisions were made before the actual meetings took place. We also had difficulty in getting individuals to assume responsibility for the decisions that were made. When we asked people after the meetings, "Who actually made the decision?" nearly all claimed that someone else had been responsible for it and that they, personally, had had little power in the process. We learned to refer to this finding as the "Little Red Hen" phenomenon. (When we asked who made decisions, we were consistently told, "Not I!"). (Ysseldyke & Algozzine, 1982, pp. 148–149)

Other difficulties identified by Ysseldyke and his colleagues were minimum participation of regular education teachers and lack of congruence between assessment data presented and decisions reached by the teams.

Unequal participation of team members is a concern identified by other researchers. A study of the impact of role and perceived status of team members was reported by Gilliam and Coleman (1981). Participants at 27 decision-making meetings were surveyed to determine the status (premeeting) and influence (postmeeting) of the roles most often represented at these meetings. It was found that a hierarchy of influence among members does emerge, with special education teachers and psychologists ranking highest in both status and influence (premeeting and postmeeting). However, some roles, including parents and principals, were accorded an important status before the meetings but were ranked very low in actual contributions and influence after the meetings had occurred. Explanations offered by the authors were: (1) that those members rated as most influential after the meetings were perhaps perceived as having expertise in the specific areas being addressed, and (2) that these influential members also had assessment information such as test scores and diagnostic reports that enabled them to contribute hard data.

In summary, the identification of behavior disordered students for special class placement involves a number of procedural problems. Although state regulations attempt to make the procedure as comprehensive as possible, most state regulations are so nonspecific that decisions about instruments are left up to assessment personnel. To date, professionals have been unable to rectify a number of difficulties with instrumentation and the team decision-making process.

The Role of the Special Education Teacher in Identification

The role of the special education teacher in identification varies from school district to school district; it is usually defined by the availability of resources such as administrative and assessment personnel. In some locales, the special education teacher may be involved at all steps of the identification process and may be considered a vital part of the assessment team. In other districts, the special education teacher may be notified that he is receiving a new student—paperwork signed, sealed, and delivered— with no opportunity for any input prior to this notification. According to one survey, special education teachers are involved in screening decisions approximately 48 percent of the time, in placement decisions 85 percent of the time, and in instructional planning 89 percent of the time (Yssel-dyke & Algozzine, 1982).

Ideally, the special education teacher should be involved in all three stages of the identification process: during screening, placement, and certainly during instructional planning. Prior to or upon initial referral, the special education teacher can be a valuable resource to the regular classroom teacher in helping to obtain as much objective data as possible. Possible duties include aiding in behavior observations and behavior recording during class time, helping the teacher develop his own unobtrusive recording system, or making available some of the numerous published checklists and behavior rating scales. Participation in other data-gathering activities may be requested by the evaluator if the student is eventually referred and evaluated.

It is also important for special education teachers to participate in the placement decisions and instruction planning. Data have shown that they do participate in the vast majority of these meetings, and that they are ranked as the most important and influential members by other participants. If these data are a true reflection of practice, then the special education teacher has been assigned a leadership role in the identification process. There are a number of things one can do to prepare for this role: First, become thoroughly aware of one's own personal biases, theoretical orientations, and tolerance levels for certain types of behavior and people; second, be familiar with the specific instruments and measures used for screening and identification; third, have a working knowledge of state and local regulations governing identification procedures; fourth, believe in one's right to voice an opinion among other professionals and have confidence in one's own judgment.

SUMMARY

Little has changed in identification of behavior disorders since Trippe's assertion in 1966 that an emotionally disturbed child is one who is so diagnosed by an appropriate mental health clinician. Despite federal regulations that attempt to improve identification procedures, numerous problems continue to plague the field: confusion over terminology, definition, and classification systems; problems with technical adequacy of assessment instruments; unequal participation of team members in the decision-making process. The special education teacher is encouraged to take a leadership role both in data gathering and decision making.

KEY POINTS

(1) Personal and social concepts of deviance determine who gets labeled *behavior disordered.*

(2) The terminology and classification systems used by mental health professionals have few implications for educators.

(3) The federal definition of emotional disturbance describes a general population to be served by special education but has limited utility for identifying individuals.

(4) The dimensions of chronicity, frequency, and severity should always be considered when determining whether behavior is disordered or disturbed.

(5) The projective tests often used to diagnose emotional disturbance are best viewed as clinical interview techniques rather than tests that must meet standards for technical adequacy.

(6) Team decision making about identification and instructional planning is plagued by unequal participation of team members.

(7) Teachers can become involved in the identification process by offering observational data and information for instructional planning.

ADDITIONAL READINGS

The emotionally disturbed child: Disturbing or disturbed? by B. Algozzine. *Journal of Abnormal Child Psychology, 5,* 1977, for an article on the notion that children's behavior may be more disturbing than disturbed.

Selected readings in *Disturbing, disordered, or disturbed? Perspectives on the definition of problem behavior in educational settings,* edited by F.H. Wood & K.C. Lakin. Minneapolis: Advanced Training Institute, University of Minnesota, 1979, for discussion of the problems in defining disturbance.

Issues in assessment, Chapter 5, by J.E. Ysseldyke & B. Algozzine, *Critical issues in special and remedial education.* Boston: Houghton Mifflin, 1982, for a straightforward critique of the difficulties in special education referral and identification procedures.

Who's crazy? II, by C. Michael Nelson. In S. Braaten, R.B. Rutherford, Jr., & C.A. Kardash (Eds.), *Programming for adolescents with behavior disorders*. Reston, VA: Council for Children with Behavior Disorders, 1984, for a treatise on "craziness," which requires the reader to assess self and to question our education practices.

A practical approach to personality testing at the elementary level: The CAT Test, by R. Algozzine, G. Foster, and J. Kaufman. *Journal of Irreproducible Results*, 1979, *25*, pp. 24–25, for a spoof on measures to identify emotional disturbance.

DSM-III—Never mind the psychologist: Is it good for the children? by N. Garmezy. *Clinical Psychologist*, 1978, *31*, 4–6, for an article that questions the use of the mental health classification system with children.

The aggressive, severely behavior disordered child, by J. Murray & D. Whittenberger. *Journal of Learning Disabilities*, 1983, *16*, 76–80, for an article that discusses identification and factors related to aggression in children.

Chapter 12, Disability labeling/segregation: An alternative, by S. Stainback & W. Stainback. *Educating children with severe maladaptive behaviors*. New York: Grune & Stratton, 1980, for an alternative to our current practice of labeling for special education services.

NOTES

[1]Explanations in brackets are the author's.

[2]Subsequently amended to exclude autistic.

[3]Projective techniques, including the Rorschach Inkblot Test, are described in some detail in Chapter 3.

two

An Historical Perspective
of Deviant Behavior

Historical Views of Deviance:
  From Persecution and
  Segregation to
  Treatment of the Disturbed

Development of Educational
Services:
  Model Programs, Pioneering
  Individuals, and Political
  Trends

---

orientation

Throughout history, humans have sought to explain and to treat behavior that was considered deviant. For those of you who are preparing to teach students labeled as emotionally disturbed or behavior disordered, knowledge of the historical development of services for this population can provide perspective about your own niche—where you and your efforts fit into the overall chronology of events. However, more important than knowledge of specific people and events is the realization that deviance has always been a political and social issue, and that services for this population are a reflection of the political and social climate of the times.

OVERVIEW

Human fascination with the concept of insanity or mental disturbance can be traced to prehistoric cultures. Survival was difficult during these times, as humans were learning to cope with the natural elements. Mere physical survival was the major goal for thousands of years, and survival of the fittest was paramount to the perpetuation of the human race. Humans who were physically fit and most likely to adapt and survive were valued; the physically unfit were often shunned, left to die, or even put to death. In those early years of human existence, survival of the fittest also applied to the behaviorally deviant. A form of social Darwinism prevailed, in which survival of the group or the culture was valued above the life of the individual. Deviants, whether physically or behaviorally different, were considered a detriment to group survival and were not valued or protected.

During the era when humans were essentially helpless and exerted little control over their environment, they invented superstitious beliefs in an effort to explain and control the ills that plagued them. Supernatural causes were evoked to explain illness, disease, and the various disasters of nature such as floods, famines, earthquakes, and volcanic eruptions. Routine natural phenomena such as lightning, thunder, and fire were also attributed to supernatural causes.

Demonology, or belief in possession by demons, was common in ancient times and is prevalent in the early writings of many cultures. A logical extension of superstitious beliefs, demonology was an explanation for aberrant behavior. Both good and evil spirits were believed capable of entering the human person, and possessed individuals were accorded such varying treatments as beating, ostracism, death, or elevation to priesthood. Individuals whose demeanor suggested possession by good spirits were accorded respect and preferential treatment. If the spirits were judged to be evil, however, rites of exorcism ranging from prayer and exhortation to cruel and barbaric measures were performed to drive the evil spirits out of the body.

By creating explanations for natural phenomena and aberrant behavior, humans were able to establish some systematic attempt to manipulate the environment, thereby instilling a meager sense of control. Historians have noted that superstitious beliefs prevail in times and societies in which humans are unable to explain scientifically the environment or to exert a degree of control over the environment because of social or political restraints. Conversely, superstition is minimal in cultures in which scientific thought, political freedom, and the rights of individuals are championed. The following historical perspective demonstrates this inverse relationship, as superstitious beliefs about aberrant behavior are shown to wax and wane over the centuries. The Greeks and Romans give us the first written accounts attributing deviant behavior to purely natural causes; however, during the Middle Ages, when most scientific inquiry was effectively repressed and the church imposed tight social control, superstition again prevailed.

Historically, treatment of deviant individuals falls into three very broad phases:

(1) *segregation phase* (Early Middle Ages—1600s): The primary concern was to isolate deviants from the rest of society; hospitals and asylums were established to care for physical needs but psychological needs were essentially ignored;

(2) *transition phase* (1700s–1800s): A number of vocal advocates were successful in implementing humane treatment and establishing training schools;

(3) *service phase* (1900s–present): Attempts are made to help individuals become functional members of society.

ANCIENT VIEWS: GREEKS AND ROMANS

Although pre-Hellenic civilizations had attempted scientific thought, most historians agree that "their science was indistinguishable from theology" (Durant, 1961, p. 51). It is the ancient Greeks who are credited with enlightening their contemporaries about natural causes of mental and behavioral disorders. Chief among the early Greek contributors were the physician Hippocrates and the philosophers Plato and Aristotle. Hippocrates became a clinical observer of human behavior and was responsible for the first medical writings that systematically classified mental problems and attributed them to natural causes. He attacked the commonly accepted notion that human ailments were caused by gods and insisted that philosophical theories have no place in medicine. His most widely known theory of mental disorders concerned the four "bodily humors": Hippocrates stated that mental imbalance was the result of a disturbance in one or more of the humors—black bile, yellow bile, blood, or phlegm. Hippocrates further proposed that the cure for mental disturbance was to restore the imbalance among the humors, a precursor to modern endocrinology or the study of endocrine secretions.

Plato hypothesized three main sources of human behavior: desire (instinct), which is primarily sexual in nature and is seated in the loins; emotions, located in the heart; and knowledge (reason), located in the head. According to Plato, humans have varying degrees of these qualities, which partially account for differences in personality and styles of behavior. Plato also anticipated modern psychoanalysis by almost two thousand years in insisting that dream interpretation was a key to personality. "In all of us, even in good men, there is such a latent wild beast nature, which peers out in sleep" (cited in Durant, 1961, p. 23).

Aristotle also ventured his opinion about the causes of mental distress; he believed that very hot bile caused both amorous and suicidal impulses. Although such theories represent advanced thinking for the age in which they appeared, they hardly constituted a basis for effective treatment. As Durant summarized the scientific contributions of the Greeks:

> Greek science went as far as could be expected without instruments of observation and precision, and without experimental methods. It would have done better had it not been harassed by religion and discouraged by philosophy. (Durant, 1939, p. 348)

The Greeks did influence the thinking of several physicians who advanced naturalistic theories in later centuries. Notable among these is Aretaeus of Cappadocia, who claimed that many mental disorders were merely extreme manifestations of normal mental processes or personality dispositions. He also devoted attention to differential diagnosis of illnesses with similar clinical symptoms. Galen, another Greek physician who lived in Rome, is best known for his principle that a physical symptom could occur in a part of the body separate from the actual diseased area, which led to treatment of the illness rather than the symptom. Galen also proposed that the major causes of mental illness could be divided into either mental or physical categories.

EARLY MIDDLE AGES–1600s (SEGREGATION PHASE)

The science of mental health took a giant step backward during the Middle Ages, as demonology and other superstitious beliefs once again prevailed. Scientific explanations of the Greeks and Romans were rejected; popular thought reverted to demonology and again attributed abnormal behavior to unnatural and unscientific causes. An increase in abnormal behavior also occurred toward the latter part of the Middle Ages. One notable manifestation was group hysteria, which occurred in the form of dance manias. Historians believe that mass hysteria occurred as early as the tenth century, and descriptive accounts of dance manias were recorded in the thirteenth century. These accounts indicate that during Saint Vitus' dance, as it was commonly called, large groups of people jumped about excitedly and danced themselves into frenzies. These frenzies reached epidemic proportions in the fifteenth and sixteenth centuries but apparently faded during the seventeenth century.

In early medieval times, monasteries were havens for people afflicted with mental disorders. The clergy generally were kind to afflicted individuals, providing shelter and protection, and treating them with prayer or other rites. However, as theologians began to promote the doctrine of inherent evil and possession by demons, methods of treatment became progressively more severe. A reversion to the unpleasant methods of the ancients occurred. Coleman describes it thus: "Flogging, starving, chains, immersion in hot water, and other tortuous methods were devised in order to make the body such an unpleasant place of residence that no self-respecting devil would remain in it" (1964, p. 32).

During the latter part of the Middle Ages, most forms of mental illness were considered to be signs of consorting with the devil, and elaborate torture devices were devised to extract confessions from persons accused of practicing witchcraft. With the full support of the church and the state, hundreds of thousands of heretics and witches were beheaded or burned at the stake. Even those who dared question the existence of witches or the methods used during trials were in danger of being declared heretics and meeting the same fate. Although these trials were primarily instruments of religious and political persecution and were not aimed at the insane populace, they did provide an avenue for accusation and punishment of those exhibiting abnormal behaviors. Witch hunting peaked during the sixteenth and seventeenth centuries in Europe and spread to some American colonies. In Salem, Massachusetts, where the most notorious colonial witch trials were held, a mood of paranoia prevailed as neighbor turned against neighbor, and the slightest aberration in behavior was cause for accusation and trial.

Despite the risk of being labeled a heretic, many writers and scientists in the sixteenth century began to question openly the concepts of witchcraft and demonology. With the establishment of mental hospitals, the mentally ill were viewed as wretched creatures and victims of fate but were no longer accused of perpetrating evil through witchcraft. These early hospitals or asylums were attempts to segregate the mentally ill and were little more than penal institutions with deplorable conditions.

The first and most famous of these asylums, the Hospital of St. Mary of Bethlehem, was established in 1547 in London. Due to colloquial pronunciation it became popularly known as Bedlam, the modern meaning of which stems from the noise emanating from the London asylum. Asylums such as Bedlam were viewed by the public with great curiosity; Shakespeare even referred to the lunatics of Bedlam in one of his plays. The gradual shift in the view of mental illness that was occurring during this period is captured by Despert:

> Another questionable form of entertainment was the accepted custom of taking the children to visit the mentally ill at Bedlam and other asylums. . . . As is well known, the mentally ill were chained, starved, beaten and kept in filth and darkness. The visit was a routine holiday program akin to a visit to the zoo in our days. The difference is that strict rules apply to the teasing and tormenting of animals, whereas of the period we speak, teasing was not only legitimate but considered more or less a duty, since the insane were thought to be more or less possessed. (Despert, 1965, p. 89)

1700s–1800s (TRANSITION PHASE)

During the 1700s in Europe, a number of changes were occurring that eventually led to humanistic reforms in both child care and treatment of the mentally ill. Until the latter part of the century, children were treated more as commodities than individuals. Infant and child mortality rates were extremely high. At the age of seven, and oftentimes younger, children were expected to carry the workloads of adults; they had no rights and paternal authority was absolute (Despert, 1965).

During the middle of the eighteenth century, European writers and philosophers began to champion the rights of children and adults as individuals in society, and the French and American revolutions gave new impetus to the concepts of freedom and individual rights. Soon after the end of the French Revolution, the French physician Philippe Pinel undertook a daring experiment: he removed the chains from some of the patients at La Bicêtre, a hospital for the mentally ill in Paris. Pinel wanted to test his hypothesis that these patients would respond when treated with kindness and respect rather than cruelty and imprisonment. Fortunately for Pinel, the experiment was dramatically successful and some patients showed nearly miraculous improvement. This humane treatment was called *moral therapy* or *moral treatment* and was widely adopted both in Europe and America during the early part of the nineteenth century.

Beginning in the mid-1700s, anecdotal writings describing aberrant behavior in children began to appear. These writings were usually case studies or diaries. The most notable case study was written by Jean Itard, a student of Pinel's, who described his efforts to educate Victor, the "wild boy of Averyon." Victor had been found roaming the forests of southern France; it was believed that he had been abandoned at an early age and had managed to survive without human contact. He exhibited many bizarre behaviors and was labeled an idiot, but Itard believed that Victor was capable of learning many skills, including speech. Although Victor never learned more than a few words, Itard was successful at teaching him some social and practical skills. Itard's work was emulated by his contemporaries and is heralded today as one of the first systematic attempts to teach an individual who was mentally and behaviorally handicapped.

Another individual who furthered the cause of humanistic treatment of children was Dr. Benjamin Rush of Philadelphia. Known as the father of American psychiatry, Rush was a supporter of public education for all children and an advocate of kind and humane disciplinary methods. His writings furthered the implementation of moral therapy in American asylums in the early nineteenth century and established him as an important writer in the transition between two eras.

Despite the efforts of a few advocates of humane treatment for children, few practical advances were made prior to 1800. In fact, the state of affairs through the eighteenth century was so poor that one historian of disturbed behavior ignores this period by introducing the historical development of services for disturbed children thus: "Little attention will be given to the years prior to 1800 because there is comparatively little of value to be found in all those centuries" (Kauffman, 1977).

In the mid-1800s, reforms emerged in the treatment of the mentally ill and retarded, largely due to the efforts of a few crusaders. Chief among these reformers were Dorothea Dix and Samuel Gridley Howe. Dix, a vocal proponent of the rights of the incarcerated, waged a 40-year campaign during which she appealed not only to the general public but also to legislatures in over 20 states. Her reforms reached Canada, Scotland, and other countries. Before her career ended, Dix was responsible for the establishment of 32 mental hospitals (Coleman, 1964). Howe was renowned as a pioneer in education for deaf–blind children and served as director of Perkins Institution for the Blind before he convinced Massachusetts to establish a public school for feebleminded children. His influence was felt throughout New England, as he was instrumental in establishing other training schools that were based on a model developed in France and brought to America by Edouard Seguin around 1850.

By the mid-nineteenth century many training schools and educational programs in asylums for the insane (disturbed) and idiotic (retarded) were being established. The majority of programs were based on the concept of moral treatment, of which education was an integral part. In public schools, the passage of legislation was eventually to have an enormous impact on services for this population. Toward the end of the century, compulsory school attendance laws were enacted in a number of states. Beginning with Rhode Island in 1840, many states followed suit with compulsory attendance laws, and by the turn of the century nearly all states had enacted compulsory education legislation (Aiello, 1976). Although originally intended as a means of socializing thousands of children immigrating to the United States during this period, compulsory attendance laws had the effect of encouraging educators in public schools to deal with all categories of less able children. The subsequent planning for these children may be viewed as the beginning of the field of special education; many cities established ungraded classes for children who did not flow easily into the mainstream of public education.

Writings of this period began to focus on etiology or causes of disturbance in children. In Europe, textbooks on the concepts of childhood mental disorders offered many diverse etiologies, ranging from degeneracy and masturbation to religious preoccupation (Kanner, 1962). Although the causes proposed in such writings seem amusing today, these textbooks represent the earliest attempts to collect and solidify a body of literature focusing specifically on childhood mental disorders.

In summary, sociological changes beginning in the eighteenth century finally culminated in the late 1800s in a new awareness of children as individuals with rights and of disturbed children as deserving recipients of humane treatment and special schooling. However, the picture at the beginning of the twentieth century was still rather bleak. Although attitudes about disturbed children were beginning to change, in practice the majority of these children were receiving little more than custodial services and cursory attempts at education.

EARLY 1900s (SERVICE PHASE)

The first three decades of the twentieth century hosted a number of significant events as well as the establishment of national organizations dedicated to the welfare of disturbed individuals. One of the most significant of these was the establishment of the National Committee for Mental Hygiene, founded primarily by Clifford Beers and the psychologist William James. In 1908, Beers, a young Yale graduate, published his autobiography, *A Mind That Found Itself,* which was a personal account of his mental breakdown and subsequent poor treatment in three institutions before his eventual recovery in the home of a sympathetic attendant. Beers mounted a campaign to enlighten the general public about poor conditions and the need for improved treatment for disturbed persons. Largely as a result of his personal campaign, the National Committee for Mental Hygiene was created in 1909. Establishment of this organization is often viewed as the beginning of the mental health movement in America, which had a widespread influence on public awareness of mental health problems and led to the establishment of clinics and mental health programs for children in the public schools. By 1930 many such programs had been instituted across the country, and in 1931 the first children's psychiatric hospital was founded in Rhode Island.

During this period, other national organizations which focused on the study and education of handicapped children were founded. The Council for Exceptional Children (CEC), a lobbying organization composed primarily of educators and parents of handicapped children, was created in 1922. Members of CEC have crusaded for the rights of handicapped youth and, particularly since World War II, have been instrumental in the passage of favorable legislation. In 1924 the American Orthopsychiatric Association was formed. As the name *orthopsychiatric* implies, this organization is dedicated to research and procurement of information on childhood behavior disorders.

In 1930 an event occurred which demonstrated that both the general public and the federal government were showing increased interest in the welfare of handicapped children. This event was the White House Conference on Child Health and Protection, a milestone in the field of special education because it marked the first time that special education was nationally recognized as a legitimate part of education (Aeillo, 1976). In addition to the national publicity afforded by the conference, the participants' recommendation that the Office of Education include a department of special education was enacted in the early 1930s.

MID-1900s

Research and Emergence of Model Programs

It was also in the 1930s that systematic attempts to delineate etiology, therapy, and prognosis for severely disturbed children were set in motion. However, these attempts focused on the condition of childhood schizophrenia and were plagued by philosophical differences over the feasibility and utility of classification systems (Kanner, 1962). Notable among these early attempts at definition were Kanner's (1949) description of early infantile autism, Mahler's (1952) description of symbiotic infantile psychosis, and Bender's (1954) attempt to classify childhood schizophrenia into three distinct clinical types.

While some researchers centered on classification schemes of severely disturbed youngsters, others were turning their attention to descriptions of milder behavior disorders. A classic monograph entitled "Children's Behavior and Teachers' Attitudes" was published by Wickman in 1928. This study contrasted the attitudes of public school teachers and mental health clinicians toward 50 problem behaviors. Wickman's results suggested that whereas clinicians were more interested in withdrawing and other nonsocial forms of behavior, teachers were more concerned with classroom management and authority problems (Wickman, 1928). The Wickman report touched off a controversy that raged for the next 30 years, mainly due to his view that teachers should adopt a hierarchy of attitudes toward behavior more consonant with that of clinicians (Beilin, 1959). This controversy was fueled by widespread misinterpretation of the results; for example, many descriptions of the study failed to report that teachers and clinicians were responding to two different sets of instructions; nonetheless, the study was cited as justification for adding course work in mental health to teacher education programs across the country.

Beginning in the 1930s and continuing through the 1950s, model educational programs for severely emotionally disturbed children were established. Lauretta Bender, a distinguished psychiatrist at Bellevue Hospital in New York, was responsible for setting up classrooms for disturbed children at Bellevue in 1935. A decade later in Chicago, Bruno Bettelheim established the Orthogenic School for disturbed youth and pioneered the concept of a therapeutic milieu, a contrived environment conducive to treatment. In 1946, New York City opened the "600" schools, which were programs for disturbed youth. Around the same time, Fritz Redl and David Wineman opened Pioneer House in Detroit. This residential treatment center was for delinquent and aggressive boys, later dubbed "the children nobody wants" by Redl and Wineman (1957). Treatment at Pioneer House centered around the therapeutic milieu; Redl and Wineman chose to forego psychiatric treatment in favor of group therapy and a structured, psychologically sound environment. Pioneer House operated less than two years due to lack of financial support, but it became a model for numerous programs throughout the country, and its treatment principles continued to influence services for disturbed children.

Another model program, the League School, was founded by Carl

Fenichel in New York City in 1953. Based on his conviction that residential placement is not the ideal solution for disturbed youngsters, Fenichel opened a day school "to work exclusively with severely disturbed children who had been turned down by every school and agency except mental institutions" (Fenichel, 1974, p. 55). From a modest beginning in a Brooklyn brownstone with one teacher and two children, the League School soon expanded to capacity and by the mid-1970s was serving over 120 youngsters (Fenichel, 1974). The program at League School incorporated the basics of most current model programs: individually tailored educational plans, a multidisciplinary team approach, and an underlying philosophy aimed at the ultimate goal of teaching students self-control.

National Trends

The postwar era gave new impetus to the general special education movement, as thousands of disabled veterans returned to America to be integrated into society. As the federal government sought to provide financial aid and rehabilitation services to the veterans, parents of handicapped children became more visible and more willing to seek help. Consequently, a number of parent organizations were founded in the late forties and early fifties. The National Association for Retarded Citizens was formed in 1950, and partially due to its lobbying power, all states had passed laws pertaining to education of the mentally handicapped by 1956. However, services for disturbed students lagged behind other special populations. Among the reasons proposed for this lack of development were the reluctance of parents to become advocates because of meager economic resources and feelings of guilt (Hoffman, 1974), and a lack of direction among educators due to confusion over definition, etiology, and intervention methods. It was not until the mid-1960s that national organizations for parents and educators of children with behavior disorders were established. In 1964, the Council for Children with Behavioral Disorders, a division of CEC, was founded, and in 1965, the National Society for Autistic Children was organized as a parent advocacy group.

1960s TO PRESENT

Model Programs and Research

Beginning in the early sixties, the scattered information on educating disturbed students was molded into a cohesive body of literature. Although much of the groundwork had been laid prior to that time, it was only after 1960 that the literature began to outline specific classroom practices. The following section is an overview of model programs and works of major contributors to the field, but it is by no means an exhaustive review of the accomplishments of this era.

A highly specific description of classroom procedures for children with behavior problems was published by William M. Cruickshank and colleagues in *A Teaching Method for Brain-Injured and Hyperactive Children* (Cruickshank, Bentzen, Ratzeburg, & Tannhauser, 1961). Although the children in the experimental classroom were labeled "hyperactive" or "brain-damaged," terms that Cruickshank linked to learning disabilities, many of the youngsters experienced severe emotional problems. As Cruickshank and colleagues observed:

> If a child has a healthy body, but one that will not do what he wants it to—if he has eyes that see, but that do not see things the way other eyes see them—if he has ears that hear, but they have not learned to hear the way other ears do—he cannot tell anyone what his difficulty is: it just seems to him that he is always wrong. No one can see that he is not like everyone else, so he is expected to act like everyone else. These are the things that happen to such children. This is the kind of behavior in a learning situation which the teacher will have to understand if she is to help the child. (Cruickshank et al., 1961, p. 131)

Drawing heavily from the landmark work of Strauss and Lehtinen (1947) with brain-injured children, Cruickshank set up a pilot demonstration project housed in three elementary schools in Montgomery County, Maryland. The initial success of the program was attributed to a high degree of structure and an absence of excessive auditory and visual stimuli in the learning environment. The study specified physiologically based symptoms that interfere with learning (for example, distractibility and perseveration) and gave concomitant instructional strategies that inspired a new confidence in teaching children with such problems. However, subsequent data were not as encouraging; the overall strategy for classroom organization was questioned after the third year (Bentzen & Petersen, 1962).

In 1962, Norris Haring and Lakin Phillips published a book describing their efforts to establish successful experimental classrooms for disturbed children in the public schools of Arlington, Virginia. In *Educating Emotionally Disturbed Children*, Haring and Phillips provided explicit instructions for replication of their program. Classrooms were organized according to behavioral principles and Cruickshank's concept of a structured environment, and the total program stressed the child's interactions both at home and in school.

Pearl Berkowitz and Esther Rothman co-authored *The Disturbed Child* in 1960 and thus formed a professional liaison which produced numerous publications over the next two decades. Having received training at the Bellevue school founded by Bender, Berkowitz and Rothman initially favored a heavily psychoanalytic approach. However, their later writings reflected a more moderate approach as they moved toward a model in which both therapy and positive educational experiences were viewed as equally important to the child's developing ego and self-concept (P. H. Berkowitz, 1974). Due to their extensive research and continued involvement in several treatment settings in the New York City area, Rothman and Berkowitz are considered pioneers in the development of services for disturbed children.

One of the first instruments designed to screen children with emotional problems in the schools was published in 1962. "The In-School Screening of Children with Emotional Handicaps" (Bower & Lambert, 1962) is based upon teacher, peer, and self-ratings. The authors cautioned that it is to be used for screening only and *not* for identification or classification purposes. The instrument was based on several years' research by Bower and his colleagues in California and, for quite some time, was the only instrument available for such purposes. Ironically, the aspect of Bower's work with the most pervasive effect was not the screening instrument but the definition of emotional disturbance that accompanied the research (Bower & Lambert, 1962). This definition was adopted in the federal regulations of Public Law 94–142 in 1977 and today constitutes the basis for most state definitions.

Nicholas Hobbs is the name most often associated with the development of Project Re-ED. Funded by the National Institute of Mental Health in 1960 as a demonstration project and headed by Hobbs, pilot residential schools were established in Nashville, Tennessee, and Durham, North Carolina. The two Re-ED schools operate from an ecological philosophy,[1] which posits that all social systems of the child must be taken into account if treatment is to be effective. In accordance with this strategy, interventions in the home, school, and community are carried out by liaison teachers. Intervention in the residential program is carried out by teacher–counselors who focus on two major goals: (1) helping the child develop competence and experience success in academic areas, and (2) helping the child learn adaptive behaviors that will aid transition back into the home environment. As Hobbs states: ". . . teacher–counselors work in a coordinated effort, not to cure the child, which we believe is a meaningless concept, but to make the ecological system . . . work" (1974, pp. 155–156). Based on evaluation data, the adoption of Re-ED model by other schools, and the continuance of the original programs, Re-ED is considered a successful model for programming for disturbed children.

In the mid-sixties another model program emerged. Originally known as the Santa Monica Project, Frank Hewett's *engineered classroom* epitomizes the behavioral approach. Although a clinical psychologist by training, Hewett developed his model out of a need for pragmatism during his teaching experiences. The engineered classroom emerged from his beliefs that: (1) "you have to have structure" (avoid failure by engineering the environment); (2) "you have to have motivation" (use reinforcers); and (3) "you have to have something to say" (set up specific educational goals) (Hewett, 1974, pp. 117–127). Translated to classroom practice, "structure" involves use of activity centers and specific times for specific subjects; "motivation" involves an elaborate check system as reinforcement; and "something to say" involves establishing a hierarchy of educational tasks. (See Chapter 5 for a detailed description of the engineered [orchestrated] classroom.) Hewett's model and Project Re-ED represent two distinctly different but highly successful approaches to educating emotionally disturbed students.

In 1965 the classic *Conflict in the Classroom* was published by Nicholas Long, William Morse, and Ruth Newman. Consisting of a collection of writings from the most prominent educators of the time, this book was one of the first attempts to put together under one cover the widely divergent views of psychoanalytic, psychodynamic, and behavioral theory. Moreover, topics included identification and assessment, modes of therapy, model programs, and management techniques relevant to educational planning; consequently, *Conflict in the Classroom* was widely adopted as a textbook in teacher training institutions and retains its status as a classic and bestseller in the field.

The 1970s saw much progress in educating severely disturbed children, including autistic and psychotic. Research on etiology yielded no clear-cut answers, but research on instructional methodology became definitive. With the use of operant conditioning techniques, severely disturbed students have been taught speech and language (Hewett, 1965; Lovaas, 1966; Lovaas, 1977); eye contact and elimination of self-stimulation behaviors (Foxx, 1977, Foxx & Azrin, 1973); and attention to instruction in large groups (Koegel & Rincover, 1974). Successful classroom programs were reported by Kozloff (1975) and Donnellan-Walsh (1976). Parenting programs specifically for parents of autistic children were also established (Kozloff, 1973).

Legislation and Litigation

Another trend of the sixties and seventies was the demand for rights of the individual by most any group that perceived itself a minority: women, blacks, homosexuals, and numerous other activist groups literally stormed the streets in protest. This period of unrest and activism was unprecedented in our history and undoubtedly influenced the handicapped to press for rights sanctioned by law. Although numerous court cases were decided and several federal laws enacted that have affected the education of handicapped individuals, only the most significant of these will be reviewed.

Court cases establishing educational rights of individuals were:

(1) *Brown* v. *Board of Education of Topeka* (1954) established the educational rights of minorities and laid the foundation for further right-to-education litigation by extending to education the principles of equal protection under the law and due process under the Fifth and Fourteenth Amendments.

(2) *Pennsylvania Association for Retarded Citizens* v. *Commonwealth of Pennsylvania* (1971) established the right to education for the mentally retarded. Among other provisions, it established due-process procedures to protect the rights of parents and required accountability of school systems for periodic reevaluation of placement decisions.

(3) *Wyatt* v. *Stickney* (1971) mandated that mentally retarded in institutions be provided an educational program as part of their right to treatment.

(4) *Mills* v. *Board of Education of District of Columbia* (1971) expanded the right to education of all handicapped children and ordered that school systems develop due-process procedures for parents and comprehensive plans for identification, assessment, and placement of handicapped students.

Two significant federal laws will be reviewed in brief.

(1) Public Law 93–112 (*Rehabilitation Act of 1973*). This piece of legislation focuses on three key issues: provision of services for severely handicapped, an emphasis on research and training, and delineation of special responsibilities of the federal government. The most significant parts of this law are contained in Sections 503 and 504, which require affirmative action toward handicapped persons by employers and administrators of any programs receiving federal funds.

(2) Public Law 94–142 (Education for All Handicapped Children Act, 1975) This law has had such a powerful effect that it has guided the direction of special education since its passage in 1975. According to Turnbull (1977), the law is most easily digested by extracting six major principles:

(1) *Zero reject.* All handicapped children between the ages of 5 and 18 inclusive must be provided a free, appropriate public education.

(2) *Nondiscriminatory testing.* State and local education agencies must establish guidelines to ensure that identification procedures are not culturally or racially discriminatory.

(3) *Individual education plan (IEP).* A written statement must be prepared, with input from parents, teacher, and a representative of special education, which outlines specific educational goals and services to be provided.

(4) *Least restrictive environment.* Placement procedures must ensure that a handicapped child be removed from the regular education environment only when he or she cannot be educated satisfactorily in regular classes with use of supplementary aids and services.

(5) *Parental involvement.* Parents have the right to participate in decision making regarding the education of their child, including the development of the IEP.

(6) *Procedural due process.* Provisions are made for: the rights of parents to all records and procedures affecting placement; a surrogate parent if the child's parents are unknown or if the child is a ward of the state; and impartial hearings and appeals if the parents disagree with the placement.

In summary, the period since 1960 has been most productive for educators of disturbed children. Research became more definitive and instructional and management methods better defined. These advances

were reflected in highly successful model programs and more sophisticated literature. In the seventies, litigation and legislation designed to
procure and protect rights of handicapped individuals became commonplace and had a cumulative effect powerful enough to direct the course of
special education through the decade. A summary of the milestones in the
development of services for emotionally disturbed students during the
twentieth century is shown in Table 2–1.

CURRENT TRENDS AND FUTURE DIRECTIONS

A few current trends can be identified in research and practice. First is an
increased emphasis on services for the behavior disordered adolescent,
which traditionally have lagged behind services for children. Hampered by
difficulties at the secondary level such as the drop-out rate and distinguish-
ing the behavior disordered adolescent from the socially maladjusted or
juvenile delinquent, services for this population are now receiving unprecedented interest. A number of affective and social skills curricula have
been developed specifically for the behavior disordered adolescent, along
with numerous model programs in settings ranging from residential
schools to regular school campuses. Whereas a substantial gap in research
on characteristics and treatment for behavior disordered adolescents has
existed for decades, textbooks, monographs, and other literature focusing
exclusively on this population are becoming commonplace. Although many
issues remain unresolved and there are still youth who fall "between the
cracks" because of our labeling system (Glick, 1979), the recent proliferation of interest suggests that the decade of the eighties may well belong to
the behavior disordered adolescent.

Another definitive trend emerging in the literature on behavior disorders in the late seventies and early eighties is an increasing acceptance
and application of ecological theory. According to ecological theorists,
disturbance is not an inherent characteristic of an individual, but is the
result of the interactions of an individual with the environment. (Refer to
Chapter 4 for an overview of ecological theory.) Although first articulated
by Rhodes (1967) and Hobbs (1966) in the sixties, ecological theory has
more recently been applied to defining and identifying behavior disorders and to educational treatment in public school settings. The mental
health community has also embraced ecological theory in adopting family
systems theory and applying it to family therapy. From this and similar
research, it appears that treatment trends for the behavior disordered are
focusing more on changing the environment to be more accommodating
as opposed to changing only the individual.

A third trend is continued disenchantment with policies on defining

TABLE 2–1. 20th-Century Milestones in Development of Services for the Behavior Disordered

	EVENTS	MODEL PROGRAMS	PUBLICATIONS
Early 1900s	1909 National Committee for Mental Hygiene 1922 Council for Exceptional Children 1924 American Orthopsychiatric Association 1930 White House Conference on Child Health and Protection	1931 Children's psychiatric hospital established in Rhode Island	1908 Beers publishes *A Mind That Found Itself* 1928 Wickman surveys teachers' attitudes toward problem behaviors
Mid-1900s		1945 Bettelheim's Orthogenic School (Chicago) 1946 New York City's "600" Schools 1946 Redl and Wineman's Pioneer House (Detroit) 1953 Fenichel's League School (New York City)	1943–1954 Kanner, Mahler, and Bender attempt to define and classify severe emotional disorders
1960s to present	1964 Council for Children with Behavioral Disorders 1965 National Society for Autistic Children 1971 *Mills vs. Board of Education of D.C.* 1973 P.L. 93–112 (Rehabilitation Act of 1973) 1975 P.L. 94–142 (Education for all Handicapped Children Act)	1960 Hobbs' ReED schools (Nashville, TN, and Durham, NC) 1962 Haring and Phillips' public school ED classrooms (Arlington, VA) 1964 Hewett's Engineered Classroom (Santa Monica)	1961 Cruickshank and colleagues publish *A Teaching Method for Brain-Injured and Hyperactive Children* 1962 Bower and Lambert publish *In-School Screening of Children with Emotional Handicaps* 1965 Long, Morse, and Newman publish *Conflict in the Classroom* 1970s Successful instructional techniques reported with autistic by Foxx, Kozloff, Lovaas, and others

and identifying behavior disorders. While the efficacy of classifying and labeling for educational treatment purposes continues to be questioned from within the profession, in actuality different and presumably improved classification systems are being sought. This trend is illustrated by several state education agencies that are moving toward adopting a mental health classification system, the DSM-III, in identifying students as behavior disordered in the public schools. Issues over definition and classification are likely to be debated through the eighties and beyond.

Speaking from a broad sociological and philosophical perspective, Rhodes (1982) has made predictions related to the future education and treatment of behavior disordered students. Three of his predictions seem especially noteworthy. First, Rhodes predicts that the concept of normality will lose strength among the general population and that our efforts at classifying and labeling individuals will diminish. He further notes: "Instead of using norms to flatten out the differences between individuals, we will search out and treasure the differences" (Rhodes, 1982, p. 232). Second, Rhodes predicts that trends toward deinstitutionalization will continue in both mental health and correctional systems.

A third prediction, related to the second, is that care-giving will become debureaucratized. A primary factor in debureaucratization is the public's disillusionment with all bureaucracies in administering social services. These last two predictions are based on political and economic trends that Rhodes believes are not tied to any particular administration and thus will continue to flourish.

It should be noted that Rhodes is known for offering countertheorist views and that his predictions may be those of a visionary rather than a realist. Other public figures such as Morse (1982) and F. H. Wood (1982) believe that Rhodes is too optimistic. They propose that society is much more resistant to change than Rhodes would have us believe, mainly due to political and economic constraints. Peterson (1982) goes one step further and suggests that there are no signs of debureaucratization, and that pressures toward deinstitutionalization have in fact decreased in the past few years, due largely to economic factors. It is likely, as Morse and Wood have noted, that these particular issues will remain largely unresolved over the next few decades but will fluctuate with political and economic trends.

SUMMARY

In ancient times, mental disturbances were viewed as a sign of possession by demons, and exorcism was a popular form of treatment. Although the Greeks and Romans advanced theories of natural causes to explain such disturbances, a belief in demonology returned during the Middle Ages. The seventeenth and eighteenth centuries were periods of gradual attitudinal change toward the role of the child and the rights of the individual in society. Influenced by European writers and the French and American revolutions, reformers such as Pinel and Rush furthered the philosophy of humane treatment and moral therapy. However, prior to the 1800s few provisions for treatment were available in the United States. By the mid-1800s several training schools and educational programs in asylums had been established.

In the early 1900s the American people began to evidence an interest in the field of mental health, which led to the establishment of clinics and mental health programs in the schools. By the mid-1900s a number of pioneering programs were begun: Bettelheim's Orthogenic School in Chicago, Redl and Wineman's Pioneer House in Detroit, and Fenichel's League School in New York.

After World War II, parents of handicapped children became a powerful lobbying force, and educational legislation for the mentally retarded was enacted by all states. Services for the emotionally disturbed lagged behind other populations, but since the 1960s, research and model programs have led to a more cohesive body of knowledge. During the sixties and seventies, litigation and legislation helped secure the rights of all handicapped children to a free and appropriate public education. Trends in the eighties include an emphasis on services for adolescents, increasing acceptance and application of ecological theory, and continued disenchantment with identification and classification policies.

KEY POINTS

1. Superstitious beliefs about deviant behavior have been created by humans throughout history to give themselves a sense of control over the environment.

2. Not until the 1700s were children recognized as individuals with rights, and prior to 1800 few services for disturbed children existed.

3. The philosophy of humane treatment for the mentally ill was promoted by Pinel in Europe and by Rush in America in the early 1800s.

4. Reformers such as Dorothea Dix and Samuel Gridley Howe were instrumental in attaining rights and better treatment for the retarded and disturbed in the 1800s.

5. The enactment of compulsory attendance laws by the states forced educators to deal with all categories of less able children.

6. The autobiography of Clifford Beers and the founding of the National Committee for Mental Hygiene in 1909 had a profound influence on public awareness of mental health.

7.   Although services for the disturbed lagged behind other categories of exceptionality, by the middle of the twentieth century a number of model programs were being established.

8.   The 1970s was a decade of progress in educating severely disturbed children, as operant conditioning techniques were applied to instruction in classroom settings.

9.   Also in the seventies, legislation and litigation established the right to education for all handicapped children.

ADDITIONAL READINGS

Chapter 2, pp. 25–47, *Abnormal psychology and modern life,* by J.C. Coleman. (Fourth Edition) Glenview, IL: Scott, Foresman, 1972, for a more comprehensive record of the historical view of disturbance.

Especially for special educators: A sense of our own history, by B. Aiello. *Exceptional Children,* 1976, *42,* 244–252, for a brief overview of the history of special education.

Selected chapters in *Teaching children with behavior disorders: Personal perspectives.* Edited by J.M. Kauffman & C.D. Lewis. Columbus, OH: Ch. E. Merrill, 1974, for readings written by leaders in development of services for the emotionally disturbed (Fenichel, Hewett, Long, Hobbs, and others).

Chapter 1, pp. 1–76, of *Conflict in the classroom.* Edited by N.J. Long, W.C. Morse, & R.G. Newman (Fourth Edition). Belmont, CA: Wadsworth, 1980, for readings on how it feels to be emotionally disturbed.

A mind that found itself: An autobiography, by C.W. Beers. New York: Longmans, Green, 1908, for an autobiographical account of experiences with mental institutions in the early part of this century.

NOTES

[1]The ecological philosophy is based largely on the writings of Hobbs and William C. Rhodes, to be discussed in detail in Chapter 4.

three

Models of Disturbance: Biophysical and Psychodynamic

Biophysical Theory:
  Definition and Etiology
  Evaluation Procedures
  Applications of Biophysical
    Theory

Psychodynamic Theory:
  Definition and Etiology
  Evaluation Procedures
  Educational Applications

---

orientation

As a teacher, your personal view of disturbance partially determines how you will attempt to instruct and manage behavior disordered students. Before identifying totally with a particular theoretical model, you should be aware of the alternatives posed by other treatment models. In addition to expanding your range of information and expertise, knowledge of numerous models and techniques enables you to understand and communicate with colleagues and other professionals who are operating from different theoretical bases. The two models presented in this chapter—biophysical and psychodynamic—both view disturbed behavior primarily as an internal state of the individual which can be treated either physically or psychologically. Each model offers treatments that are often used with behavior disordered students.

OVERVIEW

Although numerous conceptual frameworks have been devised to explain disturbed behavior, the one proposed by Rhodes and Tracy (1974) has been adopted for this text. At the University of Michigan, Rhodes and Tracy carried out an extensive research project on emotional disturbance which formed the basis for five theoretical models: biophysical, psychodynamic, behavioristic, sociological, and ecological. The Rhodes and Tracy Conceptual Project was seminal in systematizing theories of child variance and in addressing disturbance from an educational perspective.

This chapter and the one that follows provide a descriptive overview of these five models. This chapter covers the biophysical and psychodynamic models, both of which view factors within the child as the primary source of disturbance. Chapter 4 covers the behavioral, sociological, and ecological models, which view the source of disturbance as the environment or the interface of child and environment (Long, Morse, & Newman, 1976). Four characteristics of each model will be addressed:

(1) definition and basic view of disturbance[1]
(2) etiology and development of disordered behavior
(3) typical evaluation procedures
(4) educational applications.

BIOPHYSICAL MODEL

Definition and Basic View

The disturbed child is one who because of organic and/or environmental influences, chronically displays: (a) inability to learn at a rate commensurate with his intellectual, sensory-motor and physical development, (b) inability to establish and maintain adequate social relationships, (c) inability to respond appropriately in day to day life situations, and (d) a variety of excessive behavior ranging from hyperactive, impulsive responses to depression and withdrawal. (Haring, 1963, p. 291)

This definition represents the biophysical view of disturbed behavior in its attribution of causality to "organic and/or environmental influences." The biophysical model is basically a disease-or medical model that presupposes that the problem or pathology lies within the individual (Sagor, 1974). Many advocates of the biophysical viewpoint are from the medical, health, or psychiatric professions who have become disenchanted with a lack of evidence supporting treatment stemming from other viewpoints. Some biophysical theorists propose purely biological causes, whereas other theorists consider the role of a stressful environment in activating dormant biological problems or genetic predispositions. In other words, some believe that biological factors rarely operate as constants but depend upon the circumstances under which an individual develops, while others believe that some combination of biological defects ultimately will be found for all mental disorders (Millon & Millon, 1974).

Etiology and Development of Disordered Behavior

The research on biological causes of disturbance is varied and complex. For this text, Sagor's (1974) original six categories of research under the biophysical model have been amended to five categories: genetic, developmental, perceptual and neurological, biochemical, and temperamental. Most of the research contained within this model was undertaken in the 1960s and 1970s with populations who were identified as autistic or schizophrenic. Children identified as autistic or schizophrenic exhibited many bizarre, repetitive behaviors and were characterized by impaired sensory perception and communication abilities. In fact, the characteristics of the syndromes were so similar that much of the literature failed to distinguish clearly between the two. It was not until 1977 that a consensual definition of autism was established.[2] Currently, autism is considered a developmental rather than an emotional disorder, and it constitutes a category of special education separate from behavior disordered. The term *schizophrenia*[3] has been dropped from popular usage as a diagnostic category for children's emotional problems, and children still identified as schizophrenic are likely to be hospitalized. However, this research is important to review for two reasons: (1) it provides insights about the cause of highly unusual and aberrant behaviors that were previously attributed to emotional causes; (2) it holds promise for treatment if definitive breakthroughs eventually can be made.

Genetic factors.   The genetic factor refers to inherited biological characteristics that may cause a predisposition toward disturbed behavior. Most of the studies in this area have focused on schizophrenia and have traced prevalence rates among sets of twins and other relatives of diagnosed schizophrenics. Although Sagor cautions that the majority of such studies dealt with adult schizophrenics and therefore may have limited applicability to childhood schizophrenia, he believes that the studies clearly show both an inherited and an environmental component in the development of schizophrenia. This conclusion is consonant with Meehl's (1969) hypothesis of an interaction between heredity (neural defects and susceptibility to stress) and environment (family and other social interactions). However, conclusions delineating the exact role of hereditary factors in the development of schizophrenia cannot be drawn.

Developmental factors.   Some researchers have noted a developmental or maturational lag that occurs in disturbed children. Bender (1968) views schizophrenia as resulting from a maturational lag at the embryonic level. In defining autism, Ritvo and Freeman (1977) have listed "a disturbance of developmental rates and/or sequences" as an essential characteristic. However, Ritvo and Freeman do not view developmental lag as the *cause* of autism. Empirical evidence of a developmental lag in schizophrenic or autistic populations is offered by Fowle (1968) and Kennard (1965), who found that certain developmental aspects of their subjects were more like those of normal infants than those of the subjects' intellectual or age peers. These studies do not offer strong support for a developmental etiology; instead, they indicate that developmental delays are often found among this population.

Perceptual and neurological factors.   Carlson (1967) offers the explanation that the autistic child is unable to make associations necessary for establishing meaning and, consequently, making appropriate responses. Thus, the autistic child is constantly encountering novel stimuli. Other researchers (Ornitz & Ritvo, 1968; Rimland, 1964) agree that the autistic child's inability to associate new stimuli with previous experience is neurologically based.

Still other investigators have described bizarre behaviors found among this population as attempts to limit sensory input. Hutt, Hutt, Lee, and Ounsted (1965) describe many behaviors associated with autism such as gaze aversion, twirling, and hand-flapping as attempts to reduce sensory input and avoid further neurological arousal. In their study of schizophrenics, McGhie and Chapman (1961) concluded that many of the bizarre behaviors exhibited in the early stages of schizophrenia may be adaptive attempts by these individuals to protect themselves from disturbing stimuli.

Rutter and Ornitz are other vocal proponents of neurological bases of disturbance. Rutter (1965) posits that childhood psychosis stems from organic damage to the brain. Based upon complex research, Ornitz suggests that the vestibular system, which modulates sensory input and motor output, "may be responsible for the strange sensorimotor behavior observed in autistic children" (1978, p. 123).

In his review of literature related to neurological causes, Sagor (1974) notes that many of the studies are marred by questionable methodology and that results should be viewed with restraint. It is evident, however, that severely disturbed children do have more neurological abnormalities than their normal peers and that further research is needed to pinpoint the causes of neurological dysfunction.

Biochemical factors.   The majority of research on biochemical factors can be divided into: (1) studies of neural transmissions (interaction between nerve cells), and (2) studies of metabolism (the body's use of chemicals to produce and use energy). Numerous neural transmission studies involving the serotonin levels of autistic children have been conducted. Serotonin is a neurotransmitter, a chemical that facilitates transmission of nerve impulses; it is found in minute quantities in the bloodstream where it is carried by platelets. Studies consistently show that autistic children have higher serotonin blood levels and higher platelet counts than nonautistic children. However, researchers are unsure that the difference is directly related to autism because of methodological problems in the studies (Ritvo, Rahm, Yuwiler, Freeman, & Geller, 1978). They insist that more carefully controlled studies are needed in which subjects are selected according to specific criteria and matched to control for age, racial, and familial factors (Ritvo et al., 1978).

Metabolic factors are proposed by some researchers who believe that schizophrenic, autistic, and other severely disturbed children and adults suffer from biochemical disturbances caused by severe vitamin deficiencies (Hoffer & Osmond, 1966; Pauling, 1968; Rimland, 1971; Vander-Kamp, 1966). Originally, many researchers claimed that large dosages of vitamin B_3 and vitamin C help metabolize adrenaline, which, in pathological cases, can be metabolized by the body into a toxic chemical causing bizarre behaviors. Other researchers reported that behavior of autistic children improved significantly as a function of the amount of vitamin B_6 in their diets (Rimland, Callaway, & Dreyfus, 1978). Although proponents are unsure of the specific mechanism through which vitamin therapy works, they remain adamant that it does work.

Whereas studies of vitamin deficiencies and serotonin levels are related to severely disordered behavior, studies of food allergies are related to less severe behaviors such as hyperactivity.[4] The concept of food allergies as a causative factor in hyperkinesis or hyperactivity has been popularized by Feingold (1975a). Feingold, a pediatric allergist, initially became interested in allergies when treating adverse reactions to aspirin; eventually he and his associates began to suspect widespread allergic reactions to salicylates, a natural compound which is contained in many fruits and which has a structure very similar to aspirin. Combining this hypothesis with known reactions to food additives such as artificial flavors and colorings, Feingold developed a strict diet that he claimed should be successful in alleviating symptoms in "about 50 percent of hyperkinetic–learning disabled children" (1975b, p. 803). Although based on biochemical research, the efficacy of both megavitamin therapy and nutrition therapy is dependent on alleviation of the symptoms. Currently, neither approach can claim unequivocal positive results.

As with studies on neurological and perceptual factors, the research on biochemical factors is promising but inconclusive in helping determine the etiology of behavior disorders. We will return to a more detailed description of efficacy studies in the applications section of biophysical research.

Temperament factors. Sagor's categories of biophysical theories are somewhat incomplete without the addition of temperament factors. Temperament refers to a behavioral style that is an inborn tendency but also highly influenced by the environment. The temperament factor emerges primarily from a longitudinal study begun in 1956 by Thomas, Chess, and Birch. Following a sample of over a hundred children from infancy to adulthood, Thomas and his colleagues (1969; 1977) identified the following nine characteristics of temperament which were stable and endured through maturity: activity level, regularity (of biological functions), adaptability, threshold of responsiveness, intensity of reaction, mood quality, distractibility, persistence, and attention span. From these characteristics, three major patterns of temperament emerged that accounted for 65 percent of the children: (1) the *easy child,* accounting for 40 percent of the sample and characterized by regularity, adaptability, and a positive approach to new stimuli; (2) the *difficult child,* accounting for 10 percent of the sample and characterized by irregularity in biological functions, poor adaptability, and negative and intense moods; and (3) the *slow-to-warm-up child,* accounting for 15 percent of the sample and characterized by a slow but eventually positive adaptability both to change and to new situations. The remaining 35 percent of the sample showed no consistent temperament patterns.

These three categories were not totally predictive of problem behavior. As might be anticipated, the *difficult child* was more likely to develop problem behaviors, but not all difficult children eventually did so. Thomas and his colleagues believed that with this type of child, interactions between the parent and child were most influential in the development of problem behavior. Parental consistency and pressure toward conformity were especially significant. Moreover, some children characterized as *easy* or *slow-to-warm-up* later manifested behavior disorders. Overall, the study showed interesting and stable styles of temperament but no clear and undisputable relationship between temperament and eventual problem behavior. Instead, environmental influences such as social pressures and interpersonal relationships were shown to interact with temperament to produce varying results.

Summary of etiology. Under the biophysical model, disturbance is variously attributed to genetic disorders, developmental lag, neurological or biochemical irregularities, or temperament. Each of these factors has its advocates backed by a body of research; however, none of the advocates can promote more than hypotheses or tentative conclusions until further research provides more definite answers. Let us now turn our attention to evaluation procedures stemming from the biophysical view.

Typical Evaluation Procedures

Identification of biophysical causes of disturbance is usually the domain of medical personnel. Although pediatricians, psychiatrists, and neurologists occupy the central role in making such diagnoses, teachers may be instrumental in detecting potential problems and initiating referrals to medical personnel. In this section, developmental histories, neurological assessment, diagnosis of hyperactivity, and biochemical laboratory tests are described. Although developmental histories and diagnosis of hyperactivity are not uniquely biophysical evaluation procedures, each has implications for treatment under the biophysical model. Both procedures yield information about individuals that may result in some form of medical or physical intervention.

Developmental histories. Extensive developmental histories should be a part of evaluations of students manifesting problem behavior because genetic problems, physical trauma, or medical conditions that affect behavior may be revealed. Information on the following conditions which may have influenced the student's physical well-being or development is typically acquired:

(1) Prenatal and perinatal conditions
problems or unusual conditions associated with pregnancy or birth

(2) Developmental milestones
ages at which the child walked, was toilet trained, talked, and so forth

(3) Physical development
severe illness, diseases, or accidents; unusual eating habits, sleep patterns or other behaviors; general activity level

(4) Social development
relationships with peers; indications of emotional tension or stress; effective discipline methods and child's reaction to discipline

(5) General health
overall physical condition; special health conditions requiring medication such as asthma, allergies, diabetes, heart condition

(6) Family history
number and age of siblings; divorce and remarriage issues; health or education problems experienced by parents or siblings; mental health problems of relatives

Experiences which may have caused neurological impairment such as malnutrition, prolonged high fever, severe poisoning, head injuries, or diseases such as meningitis and encephalitis are particularly noteworthy. Since most developmental histories depend on interviews with parents or guardians, school psychologists or other assessment personnel are usually responsible for making this information a part of the student's educational file.

An example of a comprehensive developmental history is the Diagnostic Check List for Behavior-Disturbed Children (Form E-2) compiled by Rimland (1964). This form is used in the compilation of an ongoing data bank on severely disturbed children, such as autistic or psychotic, who exhibit a "strong element of bizarreness." Selected items from the form, which are indicative of problems experienced by severely disturbed children, are given in Table 3–1.

Neurological assessment. Neurological assessment is an important aspect of biophysical evaluations of disturbance because many unusual or bizarre behaviors have neurological bases. Examples are repetitive speech and mannerisms, and overreaction to sensory stimuli such as loud noises

TABLE 3–1. Selected Items from the *Diagnostic Check List for Behavior-Disturbed Children (Form E–2)*

6. Was the child given oxygen in the *first week*?
  ___1. Yes
  ___2. No
  ___3. Don't know

14. Did the child rock in his crib as a baby?
  ___1. Yes, quite a lot
  ___2. Yes, sometimes
  ___3. No, or very little
  ___4. Don't know

22. (Age 2–4) Is child "deaf" to some sounds but hears others?
  ___1. Yes, can be "deaf" to loud sounds, but hear low ones
  ___2. No, this is not true of him

26. (Age 2–5) Does child have any unusual cravings for things to eat or chew on?
  ___1. Yes, salt or salty foods
  ___2. Yes, often chews metal objects
  ___3. Yes, other _____
  ___4. Yes, more than two above
  ___5. No, or not sure

34. (Age 3–5) Does the child like to spin things like jar lids, coins, or coasters?
  ___1. Yes, often and for rather long periods
  ___2. Very seldom, or never

56. (Age 3 and 5) Is the child extremely fearful?
  ___1. Yes, of strangers or certain people
  ___2. Yes, of certain animals, noises, or objects
  ___3. Yes, of 1 and 2 above
  ___4. Only normal fearfulness
  ___5. Seems unusually bold and free of fear
  ___6. Child ignores or is unaware of fearsome objects

69. (Before age 5) If the child talks, do you feel he understands what he is saying?
  ___1. Doesn't talk enough to tell
  ___2. No, he is just repeating what he has heard with hardly any understanding
  ___3. Not just repeating—he understands what he is saying, but not well
  ___4. No doubt that he understands what he is saying

Reprinted by permission from the Institute for Child Behavior Research, San Diego, California.

or flickering lights. However, neurological assessments are not a routine part of identifying behavior disorders in children.

Minimal brain dysfunction, brain damage, and sensorimotor problems are typically diagnosed through some form of neurological testing. Neurological screening is occasionally carried out by trained school assessment personnel, but a neurological evaluation is confined to a neurologist's office. A standard neurological evaluation assesses functioning in the areas of motor skills, coordination, reflexes, mental alertness, sensory discrimination and integrity of cranial nerves. Except for reflexes, most of these areas are assessed by asking the subject to perform verbal or motor tasks that are quite simple for unimpaired individuals. For example, to check mental alertness, the subject may be asked to demonstrate adequate memory of facts or personal information; to check coordination, the subject may be asked to touch the end of the nose with the index finger; and to check sensory discrimination, the subject may be asked to identify a number being traced in the palm of the hand. If screening measures indicate problems with these or similar tasks, the neurologist may choose to do an electroencephalogram (EEG) or other procedure which sometimes allows the site of dysfunction to be located.

The Halstead-Reitan Battery is a comprehensive neuropsychologic evaluation that assesses cognitive and adaptive ability. It is the best standardized and one of the most widely used batteries of its type. Among its subtests are measures of verbal and nonverbal intelligence, concept formation, expressive and receptive language, auditory perception, time perception, memory, perceptual motor speed, and spatial relations (Strub & Black, 1977). Administration and interpretation of the battery is time-consuming and is limited to trained clinical neuropsychologists.

Another commonly used assessment in this area is the Luria Neuropsychological Investigation (Christensen, 1975). Based upon the work of A.R. Luria, a Russian neuropsychologist, this standardized assessment contains over 260 items covering ten major areas of neuropsychological functioning, many of which overlap with those of the Reitan. In addition, responses are rated according to accuracy, speed, quality, time lapse, number of trials or number of responses. Despite its popularity, the Luria has drawbacks in that Luria himself provided no guidelines for standardized administration or interpretation, resulting in a dearth of investigations into the reliability and validity of the instrument (C.J. Golden, 1981).

Diagnosis of hyperactivity.   Hyperactivity is a syndrome characterized by short attention span, distractibility, and an increase in overall activity level. It is often accompanied by learning problems. It is not unique to the biophysical model because behavior recordings are used in its diagnosis, and behavioral interventions are sometimes employed in its treatment.

However, hyperactivity will be discussed under the biophysical model because it is often assumed to have a neurological etiology, its diagnosis ultimately depends upon the judgment of medical personnel, and it is most often treated through medication and under the supervision of physicians.

Three types of procedures are used to diagnose hyperactivity in children: (1) developmental histories including data from home and school, (2) clinical procedures, and (3) observations and recordings of behavior. It is important to obtain developmental histories because certain factors such as low birth weight, respiratory problems after delivery, and family history of learning problems have been shown to have an abnormally high occurrence among hyperactive children; however, information on behavior observed during the preschool ages of two to five is considered most important (Safer & Allen, 1976). Most hyperactive children are described by their parents as being restless and inattentive and, to a lesser extent, disruptive, destructive, or temperamental during this period. Safer and Allen consider teacher observations and school history to be more informative even than parental accounts or physicians' judgments because "hyperactivity reaches its peak in a sit-down, all-day classroom situation, an experience routinely observed only by the teacher" (1976, p. 17). In the school setting, the best predictors of hyperactivity are conduct grades, previous and current teachers' ratings of restlessness and inattentiveness, and evidence of learning problems.

Clinical procedures are used by pediatric neurologists, pediatricians, and other child specialists to diagnose hyperactivity. According to Safer and Allen (1976), these clinical procedures most often include assessments of visual-motor skills, intelligence, achievement, an electroencephalogram, and a pediatric-neurologic examination. Prescription of medication is based both on these clinical findings and information from teacher and parent reports.

Observations and recordings of classroom behavior may be obtained by a teacher or a school psychologist using a behavior checklist or some type of behavior recording. There are a number of published checklists available for teacher use, the most common of which is Conners' *Teacher Rating Scale* (Conners, 1969). On such meaures, the teacher is asked to rate the degree to which a child shows characteristics and behaviors such as impulsivity, disturbing others, fighting, inattention, failing to complete work, tenseness and crying, temper tantrums, or other signs of frustration. Under optimal conditions, more than one teacher's rating on a particular child is obtained. To obtain a behavioral record, a person trained in systematic behavior recording observes the child in both the classroom and other school settings. In this procedure, a number of behaviors such as out-of-seat or talking out are usually selected, and for short periods of time, each occurrence is recorded. Recordings of this type may be used to validate or supplement teacher ratings.

Biochemical laboratory tests.   A final area of evaluation under the biophysical model is laboratory testing of blood and urine samples. Although approximately 20 tests are routinely run, as many as 400 to 500 different laboratory tests are available at most major medical centers (Algozzine, 1981). Such lab tests may reveal malfunctioning of the body's major organs, diseases such as anemia and leukemia, and conditions such as hypoglycemia, allergies, and bacterial infections. In addition, lab tests may be routinely done on children who are on medication for conditions such as epilepsy in order to check dosage level and ensure that toxic levels are avoided. Some of these conditions, particularly hypoglycemia and allergies, have overt behavioral symptoms such as inattentiveness or lethargy which are often assumed to be problems of motivational or emotional origin. In such cases, it is especially important to diagnose and treat the symptoms as physically based problems.

Applications of Biophysical Theory

In the biophysical model, medical interventions are sought when an organic cause for disturbance is hypothesized or identified. Medical or health-related personnel are usually responsible for treatment, and the teacher's primary role is observer and monitor of the student's in-school behavior. The four major interventions employed under this model are drug, megavitamin, nutrition, and neuro-developmental therapies. These methods were not developed for exclusive use with disturbed individuals, but with the exception of neuro-developmental therapy, each has strong ramifications for behavior change. Neuro-developmental therapy focuses more on cognitive development and the learning process. Without exception, the biophysical therapies have been controversial since their introduction to the medical and educational communities. The interested reader is referred to a review article of these therapies by Sieben (1977) and the rebuttal articles by Powers (1977) and Feingold (1977). For the Feingold diet specifically, see Mattes (1983), Kavale and Forness (1983), and a rebuttal by Rimland (1983).

Psychopharmacology (drug therapy).   Psychopharmacology is the most widely used biophysical intervention. Psychotropic or mood-altering drugs are used with severely disturbed populations who may be institutionalized and with public school children characterized as hyperactive. Major tranquilizers (antipsychotics) and antidepressants are used with the more severely disturbed, and stimulants are usually prescribed for hyperactive children.

The introduction of drug therapy has drastically changed the kind of treatment that patients receive in mental hospitals and has reduced the number of patients hospitalized for long periods of time. In hospital settings, drug therapy is sometimes used in conjunction with other treatments such as psychotherapy. Major tranquilizers or antipsychotics are used to treat serious psychological illnesses such as psychoses and personality disorders. Phenothiazines are the most widely prescribed antipsychotics, with approximately 30 derivatives available. Antipsychotic drugs do not cure disorders but do help alleviate symptoms such as hallucinations and delusions. When prescribed in small doses, they also are used to relieve tension, anxiety, and agitation. Physical side effects include heart and respiratory complications. Although generally considered highly effective with adults (Hollister, 1969), the efficacy of antipsychotic drugs with children is unclear. One reason is that studies of antipsychotics with children have failed to distinguish between autistic and schizophrenic populations (Conners & Werry, 1979). Reviews of the literature suggest that the true antipsychotic effect of suppressing hallucinations and delusions is most often seen in older children with acute onset of symptoms (M. Campbell, 1973, 1975). Although helpful in controlling symptoms of hyperactivity, obstinancy, explosiveness, and aggression, antipsychotics have also been shown to depress cognitive functioning, a side effect which calls for caution in their use with school children (Conners & Werry, 1979).

Antidepressants were introduced in 1958 as a new intervention for depression (van Praag, 1977). In adults, chronic depression is characterized by extreme sadness, withdrawal, suicidal tendencies, and loss of appetite, sex drive, or energy. The tricyclic compounds such as imipramine are most commonly prescribed, but the scope of antidepressants continues to widen. Although success has been reported with use of antidepressants in treating some childhood psychopathologies (Frommer, 1967), some confusion exists over the definition of depression in children and whether it constitutes psychopathology (Lefkowitz & Burton, 1978). Efficacy studies of antidepressant medication with children remain clouded by this issue.

Use of stimulant medication for hyperactivity is a controversial issue in drug therapy. Since 1937 when Bradley reported that amphetamines fostered marked improvement in children's behavior, innumerable studies have sought to prove or disprove the efficacy of drugs in improving attention, concentration, and overall activity level. Although estimates of the number of affected children vary widely, moderate figures are provided by Sroufe (1975), who estimates that hundreds of thousands of children are on some type of drug therapy, and Krager and Safer (1974), who estimate that 2 percent of all elementary school children (about 300,000 to 400,000) are receiving medication for hyperactivity.

The two major types of drugs used to treat hyperactivity are tranquilizers (for example, Mellaril and Thorazine) and stimulants (Ritalin, Dexedrine, and Cylert, to name a few). Stimulants are most often prescribed for prepubescent hyperactive children because of their alleged paradoxical effect on activity level; approximately 30 to 50 percent show marked improvement in response to stimulant medication (Safer & Allen, 1976). In a review in 1977, Wolraich reported that there were over 60 well-controlled studies that demonstrated the effectiveness of two stimulants, Ritalin and Dexedrine, in reducing hyperactive behaviors. Side effects of stimulants, which include headaches, stomachaches, insomnia, irritability, growth inhibition, and loss of appetite, are not uncommon. After the onset of puberty, children begin to respond to stimulants much as adults do; consequently, tranquilizers may be prescribed to replace stimulant medication for adolescents.

Although stimulant medication shows remarkable results for a moderate number of children, there has been a backlash toward the nationwide trend of overprescribing. Among the most pertinent criticisms and cautions are: (1) both short-term and long-term side effects have not been sufficiently studied; (2) physicians should not be pressured to prescribe medication, and when they do, dosages should be monitored and possible side effects carefully checked; and (3) drug therapy has not been proven superior to other interventions such as behavior modification and therefore should not be considered a panacea nor used as means to avoid discharging professional responsibilities toward the needs of children (Hallahan & Kauffman, 1976; Sroufe, 1975).

A related ethical issue is the possibility of psychological dependency: some children who are on medication come to believe that they need external help to control their impulsive behavior. Especially in such cases, medication should be coupled with behavioral interventions so that the child learns to assume responsibility for her behavior and does not excuse it with pleas of helplessness. A variety of behavioral interventions have proven successful in reducing hyperactive behaviors (Schaefer & Millman, 1977), and in direct comparisons they have proven as effective as stimulant medication (Myers & Hammill, 1982). Some researchers caution that drug intervention for hyperactivity is clearly indicated only when other interventions have failed (Bower & Mercer, 1975).

Orthomolecular psychiatry (megavitamin therapy).   The basic tenet of this approach is that mental disorders result when cells in the brain are not living in the optimum chemical environment; thus, mental disorders should be treated by "provision of the optimum molecular composition of the brain" (Pauling, 1968, p. 271). Proponents believe that even with the nutrients from a recommended, well-balanced diet, some individuals fail to metabolize certain substances properly and therefore need massive dosages of vitamins to correct the deficiency. The exact deficiency has not been pinpointed, but orthomolecular theorists believe it may be genetically controlled. The B-complex vitamins and vitamin C are most commonly prescribed in large dosages for the treatment of severe disorders such as schizophrenia. Another substance often prescribed is folic acid (Pauling, 1968).

Megavitamin therapy has its skeptics as well as its advocates. The most common criticisms are that it has not provided a solid data base to support its claims (Kameya, 1974; Wyatt, Termini, & Davis, 1971), and that additional well-controlled, double-blind studies are needed. These criticisms were upheld by a task force appointed by the American Psychiatric Association (1974) and by the Committee on Nutrition of the American Academy of Pediatrics (1976). In addition, potential toxicity and ill-effects of megadoses of vitamins have not been thoroughly studied (Sieben, 1977). At present, megavitamin therapy is an imprecise method of treatment that should be carried out only under close medical supervision.

Nutrition therapy.   The concept of food allergies and the Feingold diet were alluded to in the section on etiology. The Feingold diet (Feingold, 1975b) initially eliminates all foods with the preservatives BHT and BHA, artificial colors and flavorings, and natural salicylates. Among the seemingly nutritious foods containing salicylates are apples, peaches, berries, tomatoes, oranges, grapes, and raisins. Other forbidden items are toothpaste, mouthwash, throat lozenges, cough drops, perfume, and most over-the-counter drugs such as aspirin. After a period of time, some of the foods containing salicylates are reintroduced one by one to check whether there is an adverse reaction. Many children can resume eating these foods, but the artificial additives are never reinstated in the diet. Although Feingold claimed success for only a moderate percentage of hyperactive children, the diet receives an inordinate amount of publicity because parents often report dramatic behavior changes and have established the Feingold Association, a national network of parents that in 1980 had over 50,000 members.

Research supportive of the diet is reported by Feingold (1975a), Rapp (1978), and Rose (1978), and cited by Spring and Sandoval (1976). Some skeptics suggest that reported positive changes are likely the result of placebo effects (Baker, 1980) or increased positive expectations. Others who have reviewed the research supportive of the Feingold diet caution that it is based largely on anecdotal information rather than on well-designed studies with large populations (Myers & Hammill, 1982; Sieben, 1977). An advisory committee formed by the Nutrition Foundation (1975) also found the research lacking in objective evidence and cautioned that the diet's long-term nutrient value has not been established. As with megavitamin therapy and stimulant medication, the Feingold diet, if undertaken, should be supervised by competent medical personnel.

Neuro-developmental methods.   A final type of biophysical intervention stems from developmental theories of brain damage. One extreme and highly controversial example of this type intervention is *patterning,* the Doman-Delacato treatment designed for neurologically-impaired children. Two basic tenets taken from Doman and Delacato's theory of neurological organization form the basis of treatment: (1) specific locomotor tasks affect certain levels of the brain that not only mediate motor function but also influence perception and cognition; and (2) it is important to establish hemispheric dominance in order to facilitate development of certain cognitive functions (Doman, Spitz, Zucman, Delacato, & Doman, 1960). Treatment calls for a rigid regimen of physical exercises which must be performed routinely. Specific exercises to impose hemispheric dominance and motor patterning (which is relearning and practicing the motor development sequences such as creeping and crawling) are among the activities prescribed. As with megavitamin and diet therapies, the proponents of the Doman-Delacato method claim a high degree of success but lack the hard data to substantiate such claims (American Academy of Neurology, 1967; Robbins & Glass, 1969).

Teachers' role. Without exception, the interventions employed under the biophysical model require the services of specialists: physicians, allergists, neurologists, nutritionists, and others. Therefore the role of the teacher initially appears to be restricted to making referrals and acting as a liaison among professionals. Although these functions are important, it is also essential that the teacher take an active part in monitoring the child's behavior in the classroom when the child is on medication or involved in diet or megavitamin therapy. For maximum effectiveness, the prescribing specialist needs information from both informal observation and systematic behavior recordings in the school setting over a period of time. In the case of a child involved in these interventions, fluctuations in behavior as well as symptoms of side effects should be recorded and reported to both the parents and the supervising physician. Often the teacher must take the initiative to contact and to continue communication with the physician. There is no substitute for the information that can be gleaned from observing the child on a daily basis and making interindividual and intraindividual comparisons!

The teacher can also help parents by providing information and readings on the pros and cons of some of the questionable therapies that are not standard practice in the medical community. G. Golden (1980) offers guidelines to help parents and teachers identify and critique nonstandard therapies:

(1)   They are reportedly based on biochemical or neurophysiologic theories that are incongruent with current concepts of the central nervous sytem.

(2)   They are said to be absolutely harmless.

(3)   The children with whom they are supposedly effective are a broad, ill-defined group.

(4)   The studies cited as supportive research are usually anecdotal and testimonial rather than well-controlled experimental studies.

(5)   The therapies have an emotional appeal, and their detractors are attacked defensively.

Sieben (1983) goes on to point out that nonstandard therapies may become popular through the media. For example, the author of a new book may get immediate nationwide coverage on television or the lecture circuit and therefore become an "instant expert" without subjecting her theory to peer review or rebuttal.

Parents and teachers would be wise to question any therapies designed to correct learning and behavior problems that exhibit several of these characteristics.

SUMMARY

The biophysical model assumes that there are organic causes of emotional disturbance which can be treated medically or physically. Theories of etiology, evaluation procedures, and intervention strategies are summarized in Table 3–2. The research on causative factors is promising but quite inconclusive. Such biophysical interventions as neuro-developmental methods, in addition to nutrition, megavitamin and drug therapies, are backed by very vocal proponents who generally lack the empirical data to support their claims of success.

The teacher's role is viewed as a liaison to specialists and a daily monitor of the intervention prescribed. The informed and conscientious teacher may also provide data-based information to parents regarding advantages and disadvantages of biophysical therapies.

PSYCHODYNAMIC MODEL

Definition and Basic View

The emotionally disturbed child

> . . . is so thwarted in satisfaction of his needs for safety, affection, acceptance, and self-esteem that he is unable intellectually to function efficiently, cannot adapt to reasonable requirements of social regulation and convention, or is so plagued with inner conflict, anxiety, and guilt that he is unable to perceive reality clearly or meet the ordinary demands of the environment in which he lives. (Blackham, 1967, p. 73)

The references to "thwarted . . . needs for safety, affection, acceptance, and self-esteem" and the terms "inner conflict, anxiety, and guilt"

TABLE 3–2. Summary of Biophysical Model

ETIOLOGICAL FACTORS	EVALUATION PROCEDURES
genetic	developmental histories
developmental	neurological assessment
perceptual	biochemical laboratory tests
neurological	for hyperactivity: developmental histories
biochemical	clinical procedures
temperamental	behavior recordings

APPLICATION

psychopharmacology (drug therapy)
orthomolecular psychiatry (megavitamin therapy)
nutrition therapy (Feingold diet)
neuro-developmental methods (Doman-Delacato)

61

give this definition a psychodynamic orientation. Psychodynamic theorists are concerned with the needs of the individual, and conflict, anxiety, and guilt are prime concerns of psychodynamic theorists, especially psychoanalysts who believe that any of these states may serve as catalysts for personality development. Evaluation techniques of the psychodynamic model also focus on unconscious drives, needs, anxiety, guilt, and conflict.

The psychodynamic model is a conglomerate of theories that attempts to explain motivation of human behavior. The diverse theories of psychoanalysis, ego psychology, phenomenology, Gestalt psychology, and humanistic psychology fall under its rubric. Like the psychodynamic stance which stresses the dynamics of personal growth, the field itself has been in a continual state of flux and development. Freud's theory of psychoanalytic psychology is the seminal work from which the other branches of psychodynamic thought have emerged over the past 70 years. Although arguments may be made for treatment of each of these views as separate and distinct, in this text *psychodynamic* is a broad descriptor that encompasses the other views. Psychodynamic theory will be discussed as two major schools of thought, namely, *psychoanalytic thought* as espoused by Freud and the neo-Freudians Horney and Erikson, and *humanistic thought* as espoused by Rogers and Maslow.

Psychoanalytic thought is unique among psychodynamic theories in its emphasis on unconscious drives that may conflict with conscious desires and thus cause disturbance; in contrast, other theories emphasize conscious experiences such as the individual's perceptions of the environment. In addition, psychoanalytic thought stresses a "predetermined sequence of personality growth" (Rezmierski & Kotre, 1974); that is, there are specific stages through which an individual passes in normal progress to adulthood. Psychoanalysts believe that emotional health depends upon successful resolution of the conflicts arising during these developmental stages and that disturbed emotions result when the conflicts are not resolved. Some humanistic theorists do not share this concept of the importance of sequential developmental stages; rather, they emphasize the importance of self-perception and self-understanding.

Although it is difficult to promote a singular view of psychodynamic theory, a few commonalities may be extracted. The most basic commonality is implied by the meaning of the term *psychodynamic,* which literally means "the dynamics of mental activities and processes." All theorists ascribing to the psychodynamic view are concerned about the process of development and change. As described by Cheney and Morse ". . . above all is the dynamic concern; the interrelationship within and without are seldom in a homeostatic state. There is ebb and flow, tension and resolution. Thus the inter- and intrapersonal conditions are seen in a dynamic state" (1974, p. 261).

A second commonality is that anxiety and emotional crises are important motivators of personal growth and self-development. A third commonality is that significant individuals in one's early life play important roles as catalysts or deterrents of personality growth and healthy development. The fourth common concept is the emphasis on intrapsychic reckonings of the individual. Although many psychodynamic theorists recognize the role of the environment in personality development, it is nonetheless the individual's internal perceptions and feelings about that environment—whether conscious or unconscious—that are the focus of intervention.

Etiology and Development of Disordered Behavior

Psychoanalytic theory: Freud.   Sigmund Freud (1856–1939) was a physician whose fascination with the emotional problems of his patients led him to develop a new branch of psychological theory. He was a physician by training but also a psychologist, philosopher, scientist, critic, and psychoanalyst (Reinert, 1980). Born in Freiberg in what is now Czechoslovakia, Freud moved to Vienna when he was three years old and left only when the Nazis entered the city in 1938.

According to Freud, the personality has three major systems of psychic energy, the *id,* the *ego,* and the *superego;* behavior is the result of an interaction among these three systems. The id is the original system that is present at birth and furnishes psychic energy for the other two systems. In other words, the ego is differentiated out of the id, and the superego is differentiated out of the ego. The id represents the inner world of subjective experience and has no knowledge of objective reality (Hall & Lindzey, 1970). It operates to reduce tension in the organism, that is, to avoid pain and to obtain pleasure; it is said to operate by the *pleasure principle.*

The ego develops out of a need to temper the subjective view of the id with the objective world of reality; it is the part of the id that has been modified by the external world. It obeys the *reality principle,* which is characterized by logical and rational thinking. The ego is called the executive of the personality because it controls action by mediating between the real environment and the demands of the id.

The *superego* represents the moral standards imposed upon a child by society, which are enforced by parents and other societal agents. The superego has two aspects: the positive (*ego ideal*) which rewards, and the negative (*conscience*) which punishes. The superego represents the ideal and strives towards perfection. Freud also developed the term *psychic energy* to connote mental activity. He felt that this psychic energy is fluid and is never lost or diminished, but that dynamics of personality are determined by its distribution among the three systems of the id, ego, and superego.

Defense mechanisms are a function of the ego employed to ward off threatening demands of the id and to relieve anxiety. Defense mechanisms are not inherently pathological; in fact, they are used by well-adjusted, mature adults. However, when used excessively, defense mechanisms become debilitating to the personality. They operate unconsciously and deny or distort reality so that the individual is unaware of internal conflict. The principal defense mechanisms are presented in Table 3–3.

Freud postulated five stages of psychosexual development through which a child passes from infancy through adolescence: (1) the *oral stage,* birth to two years of age; (2) the *anal stage,* two to four years; (3) the *phallic stage,* four to six years; (4) the *latency period,* six until puberty; and (5) the *genital stage,* occurring at puberty. The implications of these stages for disturbed behavior are based on two of Freud's premises. The first is that the first few years of life determine the formation of personality. The second premise is that abnormal personality development is due to *fixations* or arrests at specific stages of psychosexual development. A person may become fixated at a stage for a number of reasons, including excessive gratification, excessive deprivation, fear of transition to the next stage, and physical and psychological factors. It is possible for the personality to be arrested in only one developmental area while progressing normally through the remainder of the stages. Examples of adjustment problems resulting from pathological fixations are outlined in Table 3–4.

In summary, Freud viewed abnormal behavior or disturbed behavior as arising from the inability to resolve a conflict within a specific psychosexual stage. In his view, when an individual becomes fixated at a given stage, personal adjustment in that area becomes very difficult and the majority of the individual's interpersonal interactions become a replay of the difficulties encountered during that stage.

Neo-Freudian theory: Horney and Erikson.   Karen Horney (1885–1952) was a proponent of neo-Freudian social theory. Along with Harry Stack

TABLE 3–3. Principal Defense Mechanisms of the Ego

I.	Repression	—forcing alarming thoughts or feelings from conscious awareness
II.	Projection	—attributing causes of negative impulses or feelings to the external world rather than to oneself
III.	Reaction Formation	—adopting the behavior or attitude opposite to what one really feels
IV.	Fixation	—failing to pass into the next stage of psycho-sexual development
V.	Regression	—retreating to an earlier stage of psychosexual development *or* temporary flight from controlled and realistic thinking

Adapted from Hall (1954), and Hall and Lindzey (1970).

TABLE 3–4.   Adjustment Problems Based on Fixations at Psychosexual Stages

I.	Oral stage (birth to two years)	Sarcasm, argumentativeness, greediness, acquisitiveness, overly dependent
II.	Anal stage (two to four years)	Emotional outbursts such as rages and temper tantrums; compulsive orderliness and overcontrolled behavior
III.	Phallic stage (four to six years)	Problems with gender identification
IV.	Genital stage (puberty to adulthood)	Narcissism or extreme self-love

Adapted from Hall (1954).

Sullivan and Erich Fromm, she downplayed Freud's biological orientation and emphasized social factors in the development of abnormal behavior. Central to Horney's theory is anxiety, which stems from a child's feelings of isolation and helplessness in a world which may be perceived by the child as hostile. A child has a basic need for security which must be supplied by significant others in the child's life through warmth, support, and affection.

According to Horney, as a child struggles with anxiety and the security issue, various behavioral strategies may be tried and eventually a character pattern will be adopted. Horney postulated three such character patterns: (1) *moving toward people*, characterized by compliance, submissive behavior, and a need for love; (2) *moving against people*, characterized by arrogance, hostility, and a need for power; and (3) *moving away from people*, characterized by social avoidance, withdrawal, and a need for independence (Horney, 1937). Emotional disturbance is viewed as the adoption of one of these rigid patterns to the exclusion of the others, which results in inflexible interpersonal interactions. A *basic conflict* is experienced by individuals who have adopted a rigid character pattern; such individuals experience severe anxiety when called upon to interact in a manner contrary to the adopted pattern. For example, the person characterized by arrogance and hostility may have a difficult time in giving and receiving affection and warmth. Although healthy people occasionally experience such conflicts, the neurotic person, due to lack of a supportive environment early in life, faces such conflicts on a daily basis. Horney believed that such conflict is avoidable and resolvable if a child is reared in an atmosphere of security, warmth, love, trust, and respect.

Erik Erikson joined theorists such as Anna Freud and Heinz Hartmann in a new conceptualization of the role of the ego in personality development. These theorists view the ego not as an extension of the id, but as autonomous both in origin and function. In other words, the ego is not a passive mediator but an active force with its own energy source. The environment and societal values are central to this new view of the ego, a view that resulted in "the addition of an entire social and cultural dimension to the concept of personality growth" (Rezmierski & Kotre, 1974, p. 209).

Erikson's contribution to the understanding of disturbed behavior centers around his concepts of crisis and the importance of crisis resolution during critical periods of development. Erikson proposes eight stages of psychosocial development that roughly parallel Freud's stages of psychosexual development; as implied by the different terminology, Erikson's stages focus on character traits that arise from interpersonal interactions, whereas Freud's stages emphasize character traits arising from experience of a biological or sexual nature. According to Erikson, if the crisis in each stage is not dealt with successfully, the individual will continue to demonstrate behaviors commensurate with that stage, which may be several years below the individual's mental and physical development. Thus, Erikson stresses the developmental nature of personality growth. He further cautions that the successful resolution of a crisis is not a permanent achievement; instead, healthy adults continue to struggle with the issues on a superficial level throughout life. Table 3–5 presents the five psychosocial stages most pertinent to school ages along with adjustment problems stemming from inadequate resolution.

Humanistic theory: Rogers and Maslow.   Carl Rogers and Abraham Maslow share the basic view that human beings are inherently good and capable of actualizing their potential if they can somehow avoid the frustrating and detrimental experiences imposed by society. Rogers asserts that behavior may be understood only in terms of the individual's frame of reference, that is, one's personal experiences and perceptions of the world. In order to understand the development of conflict in an individual's world, Rogers (1959) proposes two concepts. The first is the *organismic valuing process,* which develops from infancy and refers to a regulatory system that tells the infant (organism) how well it is satisfying basic needs. This valuing process leads the infant to select, inasmuch as possible, those experiences that will be positive and enhance the organism, and to avoid experiences that will be negative and debilitating. Thus there exists an innate wisdom for preservation and actualization.

As the infant grows, experiences become differentiated between environment and self, and the young child formulates a concept of the self. As the self-concept emerges, so does a *need for positive regard,* a universal need for acceptance and respect. The need for positive regard then motivates the developing person to judge personal actions in terms of societal values. Conflict arises when the innate criteria clash with societal values so that the person is torn between the organismic valuing process and the need for positive regard. As Rogers states, disturbance or maladjustment

TABLE 3–5.   Erikson's Psychosocial Stages

DEVELOPMENTAL PHASE	PSYCHOSOCIAL STAGE	RELATED ADJUSTMENT PROBLEMS
I. Infancy	Trust vs. mistrust	Mistrust of others
II. Early Childhood (age 1–3)	Autonomy vs. shame and doubt	doubt in oneself and mistrust in environment
III. Play Age (age 3–5)	Initiative vs. guilt	Overdeveloped conscience which prevents independent action; excessive guilt
IV. School Age (age 5–10)	Industry vs. inferiority	Doubt in one's ability to perform adequately for society; feelings of inferiority and inadequacy
V. Adolescence	Identity vs. identity diffusion	Doubt about one's sexual, ethnic, or occupational identity

Adapted from E.H. Erikson (1959).

occurs when there is "an incongruence between self and experience" (1959). This incongruence is then usually dealt with either by distortion or denial of the experience. If these strategies fail, a serious breakdown of the self-concept may occur and the individual experiences *disorganization* characterized by irrational or psychotic behaviors.

Rogers proposes that incongruence can be avoided in an ideal course of development in which the infant receives only unconditional positive regard from the parents. In applying his theory to education, Rogers (1969) states that learning should be self-initiated and congruent with personal experience. The classroom should offer a climate for experiential learning, and the teacher should facilitate the learning process.

Maslow did not address emotional disturbance in depth, but his theory of human needs and motivation provides a model of health and creativity that has been widely accepted by both psychologists and educators. Maslow (1967) differentiates between basic needs, which are deficiency needs, and meta-needs, which are growth needs. The basic needs of safety, hunger, affection, security, and self-esteem are hierarchical: lower ones must be satisfied by the individual before the higher ones can be attained. Meta-needs such as justice, goodness, beauty, and unity are equally important and are not hierarchical. According to Maslow, only a very few select persons are able to realize and internalize the meta-needs; these *self-actualized* people are characterized by autonomy, spontaneity, democratic values, creativity, and a resistance to conformity. They are able to transcend rather than tolerate the environment, which is the final step in becoming fully human. Although his theory concentrates on the healthy, self-actualizing being, Maslow does eloquently address disturbed behavior:

> . . . it is now seen clearly that psychopathology in general results from the denial or the frustration or the twisting of man's essential nature. By this conception what is good? Anything that conduces to this desirable development in the direction of actualization of the inner nature of man. What is pathological? Anything that disturbs or frustrates or twists the course of self-actualization. What is psychotherapy, or for that matter any therapy of any kind? Any means of any kind that helps to restore the person to the path of self-actualization and of development along the lines that his inner nature dictates. (Maslow, 1954, p. 340–341)

The psychodynamic goal: healthy development.   Although it is difficult to distinguish a singular psychodynamic view of etiology of problem behavior, it is not difficult to perceive a singular psychodynamic goal of intervention, namely, healthy development. The process by which this goal is attained may be determined largely by variables inherent in the individual, but psychodynamic theorists agree that six basic characteristics are common in development of a healthy personality:

(1) *Attitude toward self*—a realistic view of self, including self-esteem

(2) *Resistance to stress*—an ability to cope successfully with crises and stressful situations

(3) *Autonomy and independence*—a sense of active participation in and partial control of one's life

(4) *Interpersonal relations*—awareness and acceptance of others' needs and an ability to establish meaningful relationships with other people

(5) *Curiosity, creativity, expressiveness*—the most positive aspects of human potential which find expression when individuals are nurtured rather than frustrated

(6) *Cognitive and language skills*—skills necessary for making sense of the world and for successful interaction in an educational environment (Cheney & Morse, 1974).

These characteristics form the basis for psychodynamic interventions which will be addressed after evaluation procedures are discussed.

Typical Evaluation Procedures

Psychodynamic theory is rich in evaluative instruments. Projective and self-concept measures are central to the diagnosis of emotional problems, as psychologists and psychiatrists invariably include one or more of these instruments in their test batteries.

Projectives. Projective techniques are based on the premise that, when given a neutral or ambiguous stimulus, a person will project unconscious as well as conscious feelings onto the stimulus. Projectives

> . . . tend to solicit rich material, depicting the child's perceptions and interpretations of reality. As the child imposes his own cognitive scheme on stimulus materials, he tends to reveal inner thoughts, feelings and attitudes about various aspects of his world. Such tests enable the examiner to secure material which is unobtainable through other means . . . to get at data which the child might guard against revealing, were he asked directly. (Sigel, 1960, p. 360)

The psychoanalytic premise is that information obtained from projectives comes largely from the subconscious and is therefore untappable by more direct means. As projective techniques draw upon unconscious perceptions of reality, they are less susceptible to intentional distortion or faking. However, this necessary ambiguity and lack of structure also undermines their technical adequacy in that reliability and validity data are very difficult to establish.

Projective instruments are widely used with adults in clinical settings. In their use with children, a developmental factor emerges that adds to the complexity of interpretation. A diagnostic evaluation of *abnormal* child development depends upon the concept of *normal* child development, a loosely defined concept; a child may reveal perceptions of distorted reality due to limited exposure and experience, lack of knowledge, or limited language skills. Therefore the clinician must distinguish between responses which are immature and those which are deviant. Characteristics of the child that must be considered are socioeconomic status, sex, intellectual ability, verbal facility, and fantasy skill (Sigel, 1960). Projective techniques may take the form of elicited drawings, verbal responses to inkblots and pictures, and written responses to sentence stems. Those most commonly used with children will be described.

Rorschach Inkblot Test.   The Rorschach (Rorschach, 1921) consists of ten cards, each containing a symmetrical inkblot; five are black-and-white and five contain color. The cards are presented one by one to the examinee who gives a spontaneous impression of what is seen; the examiner may then start over with the first card and ask which features were most important upon initial impression. Responses are scored according to several categories: which aspects of the blot determined the response (form, movement, color, shading); where the determinant was located; whether the response was human, animal, or inanimate; whether the response was common or original, and so forth. The number of responses in each category are analyzed to form one basis for conclusions. For example, a high number of color responses is thought to indicate emotionality, and a high number of movement responses is thought to indicate imagination. Analysis of responses for broad categories of information such as reality awareness, self-concept, emotionality, and coping mechanisms may be helpful in personality assessment of children (Halpern, 1960).

Children's Apperception Test (CAT).   The CAT (Bellak & Bellak, 1949) is a series of ten plates, each depicting animal characters. The examinee is shown the pictures one at a time and asked to relate a story about each. The CAT is designed for use with children of ages three to ten and is based on three propositions: (1) that projective techniques allow clinicians to make inferences about personality features; (2) that the animal scenes depicting activities of eating, sleeping, toileting, and punishment are especially relevant to children and thus will elicit accurate information about the way they handle such daily activities in their own lives; and (3) that children would more readily relate to and identify with animals than human figures (Bellak & Adelman, 1960). Children's responses are analyzed for thematic content or commonalities within ten categories: main theme, main hero, main needs of the hero, conception of the environment, view of other figures, significant conflicts, nature of anxieties, main defenses, severity of the superego, and integration of the ego. Interpretation is obviously psychoanalytic in nature, as needs, conflict, anxiety, and guilt are heavily weighted. Two similar measures are sometimes used with children: the *Thematic Apperception Test* (TAT, Murray, 1943), a technique using pictures of adults and designed for use with adults, and the *Education Apperception Test* (EAT, Thompson & Sones, 1973), which depicts only scenes related to school and achievement.

Sentence completions.   An expanded version of the word association technique, sentence completions consist of sentence stems which the examinee is asked to complete. They are commonly used in personality assessment because of the relative ease of administration and interpretation; they may supply the clinician with much information in a short time. Although commercially produced sentence-completion instruments are available, many psychologists develop their own informal measures. Item content is usually aimed at obtaining information about anxiety, coping skills, and attitudes toward authority figures, siblings, parents, teachers, peers, and schoolwork. Examples of instruments commercially available are *Forer's Structured Sentences Completion Test* (Forer, 1957) and the *Rotter Incomplete Sentences Blank* (Rotter & Rafferty, 1950). The *Rotter* is for use with secondary students only. The *Forer* contains 100 sentence stems within the following clusters: 35 items are designed to tap attitudes toward significant persons; 9 items allow for expression of wishes; 31 items require describing conditions conducive to guilt, anxiety, failure, inferiority, and aggression; and 25 items elicit reactions to situations typically encountered in daily living. In addition, Forer believes that omission of items or responses indicative of denial are also diagnostically significant. Sentence completion measures are generally designed to tap the same areas covered by other projectives, but the clinical interpretation is even less structured and therefore more dependent on the interpreter.

Human figure drawings.   The value of children's drawings in personality assessment lies in the assumption that spontaneous drawings may reveal information that is not distorted by difficulty with language or writing skills nor by deliberate falsification. Many psychologists believe that "drawings speak louder than words," especially in the early developmental stages (Klepsch & Logie, 1982). In addition, drawings are readily obtained, as most children enjoy drawing and do not resist the task. Klepsch and Logie (1982) outline four major projective uses for children's human figure drawings: a measure of personality, a measure of self in relation to others (group drawings), a measure of group values (of racial, cultural, or ethnic groups), and a measure of attitude toward others (drawing teachers or parents, for example). Human figure drawings have also been used to assess a child's developmental status or intellectual ability. Scoring systems for estimating intelligence from figure drawings have been developed by Harris (1963) and by Koppitz (1968).

Test administration consists of presenting the child with a white, unlined 8-by-11 sheet of paper and the general directions to "Draw a person, a whole person, not a stick figure or cartoon." No additional directions other than encouragement are given. The drawing may then be scored by a system; the Koppitz system (Koppitz, 1968) is the most widely used. The 30 emotional indicators fall into one of three types: (1) items relating to the quality of the drawing, such as size, integration, symmetry, and quality of lines; (2) unusual features such as teeth, crossed eyes, big hands, or monsterlike quality; or (3) omission of essential features such as eyes, nose, mouth, neck, arms, or legs (Klepsch & Logie, 1982). Presence of two or more indicators is considered to be suggestive of emotional problems. Koppitz also feels that the following three principles are valid and useful in clinical interpretation of human figure drawings in all children ages 5 through 12:

(1) Regardless of who is drawn, the drawing is a self-portrait, and therefore indicative of self-concept.

(2) The person who is drawn is the person of greatest importance in the child's life at that given time.

(3) Interpretation of the drawing may be twofold, for it may represent actual attitudes and conflicts *or* wishes (Koppitz, 1968).

Koppitz and other clinicians add the caveat that human figure drawings should always be used in conjunction with other measures in order to increase predictive validity.

Self-concept measures. How one views oneself in relation to others and the environment is a main concern of pscyhodynamic theorists; thus, the constructs of self-concept and self-esteem have generated much interest. Although implicit indicators of self-concept may be obtained from projective measures, some instruments have been devised explicitly for this purpose. *The Self-Esteem Inventory* (Coopersmith, 1967) and the *Piers-Harris Children's Self-Concept Scale* (Piers & Harris, 1969) were designed for use with children, and the *Tennessee Self-Concept Scale* (Fitts, 1964) for use with adolescents. *The Self-Esteem Inventory* consists of 25 items to be rated "Like me" or "Unlike me." Four factors were extracted: self-derogation, leadership–popularity, family–parents, and assertiveness–anxiety. The *Piers-Harris Scale* consists of 80 descriptive items to be answered "Yes" or "No," and six factors: behavior, school status, physical appearance and attributes, anxiety, popularity, and happiness. The total score is assigned a percentile rank to designate self-concept. The *Tennessee Self-Concept Scale* has norms for age 12 through adulthood; it is by far the most comprehensive and complex to interpret. There are 90 items to be answered on a continuum of "Completely true" to "Completely false." There are several interpretive scales, including a lie or defensiveness scale, but the items fall into five general views of self: physical self, moral–ethical self, personal self, family self, and social self. Thus, the *Tennessee* has been described as providing a thorough clinical profile of a person's self-concept (Robinson & Shaver, 1973).

Educational Application

Psychoanalytic theorists had an impact on education in the early part of the twentieth century, as forced conformity in the classroom came to be viewed by some educators as detrimental to the child's natural development. Educational practices reflecting a more permissive philosophy resulted. In addition, Freudian theorists emphasized the central role of the teacher in the crucial years of early childhood; this view was espoused by Low (1928) who believed that teachers play an important preventive role by helping the child avoid fixations by identifying repressed feelings and dealing with them in constructive ways.

By mid-century, the psychodynamic view had moderated, but the basic tenets remained unchanged. Psychodynamic theorists generally agree that the educational process should be less repressive, more facilitative of emotional expression, and more sensitive to crises experienced by children (Rezmierski & Kotre, 1974). In accordance, an educational environment should provide not only opportunities for expression and acceptance of conflicts but also active support in dealing with such conflicts as they arise.

Humanistic education. The concept of humanistic education arose largely from these psychodynamic views. Humanistic educators generally view schools as places where development of happy, well-adjusted individuals takes precedence over acquisition of academic skills. Humanistic educators are also vocal about the shortcomings of our current educational system, with the result that some of the more extreme theorists are labeled radical or countertheoretical.

A.S. Neil (1960) and his British residential school Summerhill exemplified radical humanistic education. At Summerhill, known as a "free" school, the students made their own rules about community life in the classrooms and dormitories. Attending classes was not mandatory and academic achievement was secondary to personal happiness. Neil's objective was to establish a nonrepressive atmosphere in which students freely chose what and when they would learn. Neil obviously shares the view of humanistic psychologists Rogers and Maslow that humans are fundamentally creative and, if given the opportunity, will freely choose self-enhancing courses of action.

Less radical humanistic educators are Holt and Glasser; each proposes changes aimed at reducing failure within our educational system. In *How Children Learn,* Holt (1967) takes issue with the sequential skills timetable imposed by educational curriculum; he proposes instead that children decide for themselves both the pace and the content of their learning and that the teacher become a facilitator rather than a dictator of learning. In *Schools Without Failure,* Glasser (1969) describes the atmosphere of failure propagated in our schools by such abuses as A–B–C–D grading systems, use of objective tests and the normal curve, and irrelevant homework. He further suggests that morality issues and social values should be dealt with openly in the classroom. Glasser, Holt, and Neil share the humanistic ideals that (1) children have an innate ability to learn independently and creatively; and (2) schoolwork should be relevant to students' daily lives.

Psychoeducational principles.   Long, Morse, and Newman (1980) articulate a number of principles of the *psychoeducational approach,* a term heavily steeped in psychodynamic theory. Basically, the psychoeducational approach promotes the view that emotional difficulties can best be resolved through a supportive educational environment and positive learning experiences. The following are condensed from their original list of 18 principles and beliefs:

(1)   Cognitive and affective processes are in continuous interaction.

(2)   A special environment must be created so that initially each pupil can function successfully at his level.

(3)   Teachers must be cognizant of the fact that emotionally troubled pupils have a special vulnerability to normal developmental tasks such as competition, testing, learning to share, and so forth.

(4)   Emotionally troubled pupils need to associate adult intervention with acceptance and protection, not hostility and rejection.

(5)   Teachers must listen to pupils and focus on their feelings if academic progress and behavioral change are to occur.

(6)   Crises are excellent times for teachers to teach and for pupils to learn.

(7)   Teaching social and academic skills increases the pupils' ability to deal with a stressful environment.

(8)   Pupils will identify with significant adults in their lives; therefore, the teacher's appearance, attitudes, and behavior are important factors in the teaching process.

These principles underlie psychodynamic interventions in the schools. In such interventions, educators focus on three domains of the child's life: adult–child interactions, peer group interactions, and learner interactions with curriculum (Cheney & Morse, 1974). The environment or *milieu* is also considered a valuable source of intervention for disturbed students. Each of these dimensions will be addressed.

The therapeutic milieu.   The idea of creating a supportive environment was applied to emotionally disturbed students in residential settings by Redl (1959a) and Hobbs (1966), and later extended to public school settings by Redl (1966) and Morse (Cheney & Morse, 1974). These educators sought to implement their beliefs that schools can greatly enhance a child's chance for success through careful selection of material, gradation of steps toward a goal, provision of therapeutic teaching, and by ending "demands for perfection" (Cheney & Morse, 1974, p. 341). This individualization process greatly reduces stress in the school environment, thereby providing a supportive atmosphere in which academic and behavioral gains are more easily attained. The provision of appropriate adult role models is also inherent in milieu therapy. In addition to individualizing instruction, milieu therapy may require manipulating daily schedules and activities, or involving the entire staff in an intervention plan so that consistent reactions from adults are ensured. Consideration is also given to the physical environment, including space, equipment, and props. Specific changes in the environment may be made on the basis of individual needs, with the result that the student's entire program may be tailored for maximum success.

Adult–child interactions: Crisis teacher.   The crisis or helping teacher is a concept based on Caplan's idea (cited in Morse, 1980) that during a crisis or catastrophic event, a person is more susceptible to change than when in a state of psychological equilibrium. As emotionally troubled students are likely to be routinely involved in such crises, Morse urges that teachers skilled in therapy and management techniques be available in schools to deal with these crises as they arise. He states: ". . . teachers want help, not advice, and direct assistance rather than consultation" (Morse, 1980, p. 182).

The primary role of the crisis teacher is to provide direct services to students who cannot cope in the regular classroom setting. Consequently, the crisis teacher must also be trained in remedial education techniques in order to provide support in academic subjects. A student needing such services may either be removed from the regular classroom setting for a part of the day or may remain in the classroom while the crisis teacher acts as a resource to the classroom teacher. The crisis teacher may provide small group or individually paced instruction for academics, but the overall goal for a disturbed student is the development of coping skills in both behavioral and academic arenas. In addition to providing direct services to students and acting as a resource to classroom teachers, the crisis teacher is viewed as an integral part of the therapeutic milieu. Other important functions are to work for preventative mental health through changes in the total school system, and to act as a buffer or advocate for the student when necessary (Morse, 1980).

The term *crisis teacher* has undergone an evolution; Morse preferred *helping teacher* for its less negative connotation, and special educators have adapted the term *resource teacher* from Morse's original concept. Techniques used by the resource teacher include specific crisis intervention techniques, life space interviewing, and other management techniques suggested by Redl (see Chapter 7).

Peer interactions: Group therapy and class meetings. The majority of behavior disordered students experience either occasional or chronic difficulties in relating to peers. Group therapy is one way to deal directly with problems in interpersonal skills. Groups may be highly structured and organized for a specific purpose, or goals may be loosely defined. Two types of psychotherapy groups have been described by Newman (1980). One type allows the problems of a troubled individual to become the focal point of interaction among the group members and the leader. A second type is formed by people with a common conviction or problem who band together to form a group supportive of change. In this type group, the student is often relieved and finds support in the fact that others share similar experiences and problems. Both types of groups require a leader who is skilled in therapy. Less structured but highly successful therapeutic groups are often formed around an activity such as crafts, sports, hobbies, art, or music. These activity groups also require a leader who is aware of age-appropriate needs of the group; in such groups, issues and difficulties are dealt with as they arise in the course of interpersonal interactions during activities.

Adolescents often respond positively to group sessions, probably due to strong peer allegiance and resistance to authority, which is typical of that developmental phase. Children who fear adults and authority figures also may fare better in group therapy than in individual therapy (Newman, 1980). Group therapy is occasionally used as a stepping stone from individual therapy in which the student may try out new ideas or newly acquired behaviors in a protected environment before trying them out in the real world.

Another form of peer group intervention is the regular use of class meetings. Glasser (1969) has devoted considerable effort toward implementing class meetings as a part of daily routine in schools. Glasser promotes use of three types of class meetings: (1) social-problem-solving meetings, aimed at dealing with problems and facing the group or individuals; (2) open-ended meetings, used to stimulate thought on a variety of subjects; and (3) educational–diagnostic meetings, aimed at evaluating subject content in a nonpunitive way. If implemented on a routine basis as he suggests, Glasser believes that class meetings could help to revolution-ize the repressive atmosphere often found in schools, which is counter-productive to emotional growth.

Affective curriculum. Individualizing instruction to facilitate academic success has been mentioned as an important component of a therapeutic milieu. Many psychodynamic theorists believe that affective issues should be given time and consideration equal to that given in the classroom to academics. Weinstein and Fantini (1970) were among the first to promote classroom techniques that integrate cognitive with affective concerns. Their suggested techniques include games aimed at developing sense of self and self-esteem, and activities aimed at arousing emotional involve-ment in selected issues (for example, social injustice).

Interpersonal communication skills, clarification of values, and deal-ing with emotions are seen as goals worthy of instructional time. Specific techniques in values clarification (Simon, Howe, & Kirschenbaum, 1978) and commercially available curricula are often used to promote such goals. Psychodynamic theorists also view the creative arts as legitimate therapeutic and educational experiences: play, art, music and drama may be used in the classroom as avenues for expression of feelings that may not be expressed in more conventional ways. (See Chapter 7 for a more comprehensive discussion of affective curriculum and methods.)

SUMMARY

Although the psychodynamic model encompasses varied theories, two major schools of thought—psychoanalytic and humanistic—were deline-ated in this chapter. Psychoanalytic theorists such as Freud emphasize the role of unconscious drives and conflict in determining personality. Humanistic theorists such as Rogers and Maslow stress the individual's need for accurate self-perception and self-understanding as prerequisites for healthy development. Healthy personality development is a common goal of psychodynamic theorists who are also concerned with the dynam-ics of self-growth toward that goal. Evaluation procedures arising from this model are projective techniques and self-concept measures, which are used universally by psychiatrists and psychologists in evaluating emo-tional problems. In applying psychodynamic principles to education, theorists emphasize the importance of a supportive, therapeutic school environment that encourages students to express and to deal openly with their needs and conflicts. Cognitive and affective issues are given equal status in the classroom. Views of etiology, evaluation measures, and educational applications of the psychodynamic model are summa-rized in Table 3–6.

TABLE 3–6. Summary of the Psychodynamic Model

ETIOLOGICAL FACTORS	EDUCATIONAL APPLICATION	EVALUATION MEASURES
Conflict between unconscious drives and conscious desires	Humanistic education	Projectives:
Conflict between one's view of self and societal values	The therapeutic milieu	*Rorschach Inkblot Test* (Rorschach, 1921)
Excessive use of defense mechanisms	Crisis teacher	*Children's Apperception Test* (Bellak & Bellak, 1949)
Failure to resolve normal developmental crises of a biological (psychosexual) or interpersonal nature (psychosocial)	Group therapy–class meetings	Sentence completions
	Affective curriculum	Human figure drawings
		Self-concept scales

KEY POINTS

1. An understanding of theoretical models is crucial in dealing with disturbed students because our views, evaluation procedures, and interventions are based on assumptions of these models.

2. The biophysical model assumes that organic factors cause emotional disorders that can be treated medically or physically.

3. Evaluation procedures under the biophysical model include developmental histories, neurological examinations, and biochemical laboratory tests.

4. Biophysical interventions generally have pockets of popularity nationwide but lack conclusive research to support their claims.

5. The psychodynamic model focuses upon personality and the process of emotional growth and change in individuals.

6. Healthy personality development is a common goal of psychodynamic theorists.

7. Psychodynamic evaluation procedures include projective techniques and self-concept measures that are used extensively in diagnosing emotional disturbance.

8. Psychodynamic theorists promote a humanistic and therapeutic school environment in which affective issues and personal growth are as important as academic success.

ADDITIONAL READINGS

Medical treatment of learning problems: A critique, by R.L. Sieben. In *Interdisciplinary voices in learning disabilities and remedial education.* Society for Learning Disabilities and Remedial Education. Austin, TX: Pro-Ed, 1983; A reply to Robert L. Sieben's critique, by H.W.S. Powers. *Academic Therapy,* 1977, *2,* 197–203; and a critique of "Controversial medical treatments of learning disabilities," by B.F. Feingold. *Academic Therapy,* 1977, 173–183, for review and rebuttal articles about various biophysical interventions.

The Feingold diet: A current reappraisal, by J.A. Mattes. *Journal of Learning Disabilities,* 1983, *16,* 319–323; Hyperactivity and diet treatment: A meta-analysis of the Feingold hypothesis, by K.A. Kavale & S.R. Forness. *Journal of Learning Disabilities,* 1983, *16,* 324–330; and The Feingold diet: An assessment of the reviews by Mattes, by Kavale and Forness and others, by B. Rimland. *Journal of Learning Disabilities,* 1983, *16,* 331–333, for review and rebuttal articles on the Feingold diet.

Part I, Health and pathology, pp. 3–53. In *The farther reaches of human nature,* by A.H. Maslow. New York: Viking Compass, 1971, for the views of a well-known psychodynamic theorist.

A primer of Freudian psychology, by C.S. Hall. New York: World Publishing (Mentor Books), 1954, for a condensation of Freud's theories.

The role of drugs in treating disturbed children, pp. 171–173, by L. Eisenberg. In *Conflict in the classroom.* Edited by N.J. Long, W.C. Morse, & R.G. Newman (Fourth Edition). Belmont, CA: Wadsworth 1980, for a short but useful set of principles for teachers to know about drug treatment.

The crisis or helping teacher, pp. 180–186, by W.C. Morse. In *Conflict in the classroom.* Edited by N.J. Long, W.C. Morse, & R.G. Newman (Fourth Edition). Belmont, CA: Wadsworth, 1980, for Morse's writings on his concept of a crisis teacher.

Dibs in search of self, by V.M. Axline. New York: Random House (Ballantine Books), 1964, for a popular tradebook that demonstrates how psychotherapy helped a disturbed child.

NOTES

[1]For illustrative purposes, the author has taken the liberty of selecting definitions from the literature to represent the models. Although the authors of the definitions did not create them to represent these specific models, this author believes that the selections are defensible.

[2]Autism is a behaviorally defined syndrome and a lifelong disability that appears during the first three years of life. It is characterized by disturbances in: developmental rates or sequences, responses to sensory stimuli, language and cognitive capacity, and ability to relate to people, events, and objects (Ritvo & Freeman, 1977).

[3]Schizophrenia is a chronic mental disorder characterized by inappropriate affect, delusions, and hallucinations. Many researchers believe that childhood schizophrenia can be diagnosed from physiological signs such as disturbances in patterns of eating, sleeping, language, perception, and motor and reflex activity (Kessler, 1966).

[4]Hyperactivity is a behavioral syndrome characterized by excessive motor activity and often accompanied by impulsivity and attentional deficits.

four

Models of Disturbance: Behavioral, Sociological, and Ecological

Definition and Etiology		*Behavioral Theory*
Evaluation Procedures	*according to*	*Sociological Theory*
Educational Applications		*Ecological Theory*

orientation

Each of the three models presented in this chapter views deviant behavior as arising from interactions of the individual with the environment or from the environment itself. Yet each model offers something unique to teachers. It is important for you to be familiar with behavioral theory because many classroom management and instructional techniques are based on behavioral principles. Sociological theory offers a framework from which to view schools and the roles of teachers and students in our culture's socialization process. Ecological theory offers the perspective that, in order to effect long-term change in the life of a child, we must try to change not only the child's behavior but also the systems and situations in which the child must interact.

OVERVIEW

Three theoretical models of disordered behavior are presented in this chapter: behavioral, sociological, and ecological. Although theorists associated with these models hold somewhat different views of the etiology of deviant behavior, they share the common assumption that the source of deviance is in the environment or in some interaction between the individual and the environment. Behavioral theorists focus on events in the environment that maintain an individual's deviant behavior; sociologists assert that it is social forces in the environment that cause an individual's behavior to be labeled deviant; and ecological theorists believe that both the individual and the environment actively contribute to deviance. In contrast, the previously presented models (biophysical and psychodynamic) assume that the primary source of deviance is either physically or psychologically internal to the individual. The major implication of this assumption is that treatment under the behavioral, sociological, and ecological models focuses on changing not only the individual but also the contributing factors in the environment.

BEHAVIORAL MODEL

Definition and Basic View

Emotional disturbance consists of maladaptive behavior [Ullman & Krasner, cited in Russ, 1974]. As a learned behavior, it is developed and maintained like all other behaviors. (Russ, 1974, p. 102)

These definitions indicate that behaviorists view disturbed behaviors as learned responses that are subject to laws which govern all behavior. Behaviorists assert that the only differences between most disturbed behaviors and normal behaviors are the frequency, magnitude, and social adaptiveness of the behaviors; if certain behaviors were less frequent, less extreme, and more adaptive, they would not be labeled disturbed (Millon & Millon, 1974). Therefore, behaviors are not viewed as intrinsically deviant but rather as abnormal to the extent that they deviate from societal expectations (Scheff, 1966).

Behavioral theory is based on principles of learning established primarily in laboratory studies with animal subjects. Behavioral theories are by no means unitary and may appear to have more differences than similarities. Although the differences are unreconciled and there are divisions within divisions of the major theorists, Russ (1974) has extracted the following assumptions common to most behavioral theorists:

(1) Behavior is a basic characteristic of living organisms.

(2) Behavior is modifiable through learning.

(3) Although growth and physical damage contribute to behavior, most human behavior is learning behavior.

(4) Change in behavior is a function of a change in environment; behavior adapts to environmental conditions.

(5) A lawful relationship exists between behavior and events in the environment.[1]

These five assumptions are the basis for a number of distinctive features of the behavioral model. First is the very basic proposition that most human behavior, including maladaptive behavior, is learned and therefore can be "unlearned" and new behaviors learned in its place. Second is the central role of the environment in eliciting and maintaining behaviors. Thus, behaviorists place the utmost importance on the setting in which the behavior occurs and on events immediately preceding and following the behavior. Third, behaviorism is a method that stresses observable behavior; it is not concerned with explaining intrapsychic forces or other reckonings internal to the individual. In this stance, the behavioral model is in direct opposition to the psychodynamic model which is concerned with concepts of personality growth and the subconscious forces that determine behavior.

Etiology and Development of Disordered Behavior

The simplest and perhaps the most practical way to understand behavioral theory is through its three major divisions: respondent or classical conditioning, operant conditioning, and social learning or modeling.

Respondent (classical) conditioning.　Three classic experiments are almost always cited as the bases for development of behavioral principles and the applications of those principles to treatment. In 1902, the Russian physiologist Ivan Pavlov observed that dogs in the laboratory began to salivate at cues that it was mealtime, that is, at the sight of the food dish or upon hearing the approach of the person responsible for feeding. Under experimental conditions, Pavlov established that dogs could be conditioned to salivate by pairing a neutral stimulus, a bell, with an unconditioned stimulus, meat powder. An unconditioned stimulus is an event or object that elicits an involuntary response—in this case, salivation. After several pairings, the bell alone elicited salivation in the dogs. Thus, the classical conditioning paradigm was established: an unconditioned stimulus (meat powder) could be paired with a previously neutral or conditioned stimulus (sound of a bell) to elicit a conditioned response (salivation). Learning was defined as the process of conditioning or the association of the bell with food.

The second classic experiment was undertaken by Watson and Raynor (1920) with a child known as "little Albert." At the age of 11 months, little Albert was unusually fearless and showed a fear reaction only in response to loud sounds. By presenting a white rat (neutral or conditioned stimulus) simultaneously with a loud sound (unconditioned stimulus), the experimenters soon induced fear (conditioned response) in the child by presentation of the rat alone. The fear response was demonstrated after only seven pairings and generalized to other objects such as a rabbit, a dog, fur coat, and a Santa Claus mask. The fear response was demonstrated for over a month and in a variety of settings. Learning was again defined as conditioning or association of the rat with the fear-inducing loud sound.

The third classic experiment was conducted by Jones (1924) who worked with Peter, a two-year-old who already feared essentially the same objects that Albert had been conditioned to fear: rabbits, rats, and fur objects. By utilizing a conditioning technique of pairing the presentation of a rabbit with the pleasant activity of eating, over a period of time the experimenter taught Peter to lose his fear response.

These experiments involved reflexes or involuntary responses such as salivation and the startle response, over which the individual or animal had no control. Both Pavlov and Watson believed that all learning takes place through classical conditioning, in which a new stimulus occurs simultaneously with a stimulus already eliciting a reflex response. After numerous pairings, the new stimulus alone will elicit the desired response and thus the organism is said to have learned to respond to novel stimuli or new situations (Russ, 1974).

Wolpe (1958, 1964) and Eysenck (1973) extended this notion of learned fear responses. They proposed that the classical conditioning paradigm explains phobias and other maladaptive fear responses: in non-threatening situations in which intense anxiety is experienced by an individual, conditioning occurs and the person automatically shows the fear response upon being placed in the same or similar situations in the future. Thus, learning occurs—although this time a maladaptive response—by the pairing of a previously neutral stimulus with a fear-inducing stimulus. The fear is considered maladaptive or neurotic when there is no real or objective threat inherent in the situation. Some of the most common phobias are of public speaking, visits to the dentist, and flying. Phobias are usually quite ingrained because most people avidly avoid the fear-inducing situation and therefore never have the opportunity to "unlearn" the fear. Techniques that have been proven successful by behaviorists in treating phobias will be discussed later in this chapter.

Operant conditioning.   E.L. Thorndike and B.F. Skinner have been especially instrumental in establishing and developing operant conditioning theory. Around the turn of the century, Thorndike began a series of laboratory tests with animals which established the basic principles of operant learning. Thorndike placed hungry chickens, dogs, and cats in a "puzzle box" from which they could learn to escape by manipulating levers. Once the animals escaped, they were rewarded with food. From observing and recording the animals' learning on successive trials, Thorndike formulated a "law of effect," which states that a behavior is likely to recur when followed by rewarding consequences and is unlikely to recur when followed by unrewarding consequences or punishment. Thorndike (1932) later rejected the punishment part of this law and retained only the positive part.

Skinner, a Harvard psychologist, developed Thorndike's early formulations to the extent that Skinner's name has become almost synonymous with the term *operant conditioning*. Although Skinner recognizes that respondent conditioning plays a role in learned behavior, he believes that the majority of behaviors are developed through operant conditioning, in which new responses are generated by consequences of reinforcement. Operant behavior is a voluntary response that operates on the environment to bring about certain desired consequences (the reinforcement). In operant conditioning, the *consequences* of behavior are emphasized. In contrast, respondent behaviors are involuntary and elicited by a stimulus that occurs *before* the behavior occurs.

Reinforcement and punishment are central concepts of operant conditioning theory. The most basic Skinnerian tenet is that the strength of a response increases with reinforcement and decreases without reinforcement or under punishment conditions (the same as Thorndike's original "law of effect"). According to Skinner (1953), reinforcement is the application of an event (for example, giving food) that *increases* the probability of response. Punishment is the application of a negative event (for example, electric shock) or the withdrawal of a positive event (removal of food) that *decreases* the probability of a response. Consequently, behavior change is effected through manipulation of reinforcers and punishers in the environment.

Skinner rejects the importance of hypothetical inner causes of behavior, which can neither be proven nor disproven. Although he does not deny the existence of such inner states, he believes that they are useless concepts in behavior change. He further asserts that most deviant behaviors are simply learned through operant conditioning but are deemed pathological by society. Therefore, intervention involves identifying and changing the reinforcers that are maintaining these deviant behaviors. Techniques of behavior modification based on Skinner's concept of operant conditioning are commonly used in educational settings and will be reviewed in the intervention section of this chapter.

Social learning (modeling).   Social learning or modeling is a third learning paradigm proposed by behaviorists. In this type of learning, individuals may acquire new responses by observing and subsequently imitating the behavior of other individuals, the "models." Social learning differs from operant and respondent conditioning in that individuals are not required to perform the behavior themselves and no direct reinforcement is necessary for learning to occur (Bandura, 1965a, 1965b).

After watching a model, the observer may be affected in one of three ways: new responses may be acquired, behaviors may become inhibited or disinhibited, or previously learned responses may be facilitated. For example, modeling is often used with behavior disordered students to teach a new social skill such as raising one's hand before speaking out in class. After this behavior has been learned by an individual, it may become inhibited if the teacher responds inconsistently to others in the class who raise their hands before speaking out. Or if the hand-raising behavior was previously learned but not being used by an individual, the teacher's consistent recognition of others' hand-raising may encourage the individual to use the behavior again.

The extent to which the observer is affected depends upon the extent to which identification with the model has occurred. Some of the variables influencing this identification process are age, sex, and status or prestige of the model (Bandura, 1965a). Other factors affecting social learning are whether the model is live or on film (Bandura, 1965a), whether one or more models are observed, and whether the model is punished or reinforced (Bandura, 1977).

According to social learning theorists, negative or maladaptive behaviors as well as positive ones may be learned through exposure to a model. Some theorists believe that pathological attitudes also may develop vicariously, that is, through observing the experiences of others. For example, a child who sees another child bitten by a dog feels no direct aversive consequences, but may develop a phobia or negative attitude toward dogs. In addition to vicariously learned fears, it has been demonstrated that aggressive behaviors may be imitated after exposure to aggressive models (Bandura, Ross, & Ross, 1961, 1963; Hicks, 1965). Bandura and his colleagues (1961) found that children who observed an aggressive adult model were more apt to behave aggressively than children who had observed a nonaggressive model. In a review of research on the impact of media violence on aggression in children, L. Berkowitz found consistent support for the supposition that "media violence is more likely to incite children to acts of overt aggression than to 'drain' them of their hostile energy" (L. Berkowitz, 1962, p. 236). However, he cautions that the studies show only short-term effects and do not address long-term changes in conduct.

Another pertinent area of social learning is that of self-reinforcement in which reinforcement is derived when an individual thinks about his own attitudes and behaviors in positive ways (Bandura, 1968). Thus, the individual's own judgments and personal feelings of merit become important factors in continuation of behaviors not reinforced by others or the environment. Indeed, Bandura believes that an individual's own thoughts and feelings may be powerful enough to override reinforcements readily available in the social environment. Self-reinforcement also can be systematically taught to students as a behavioral self-control technique (Workman, 1982). According to Workman, students can learn to reinforce themselves by merely imagining their involvement in a pleasant and rewarding scene or activity.

In summary, social learning theory proposes that behavior can be learned through observation and vicarious reinforcement. Thus, another dimension is added to behavioral theory by the inclusion of such concepts as vicarious learning and self-reinforcement. These concepts are based on internal mediation processes of the individual; hence, the environmental events that evoke behaviors are not as easily identified as in operant and respondent conditioning.

Typical Evaluation Procedures

In contrast to the biophysical model in which medical personnel are primarily responsible for diagnosis of disturbance, it is the teacher who often occupies a central role in the evaluation process of the behavioral model. Bower aptly describes the situation:

> The myth still exists that someone, somewhere, somehow, knows how to assess behavior and/or mental health as positive or negative, good or bad, healthy or nonhealthy, and independent of the social context wherein the individual is living and functioning. It is possible that the teacher who focuses on the child's observable behavior in school is closer to an operational reality of mental health than can be determined in an office examination. What a teacher is judging is how a specific behavior affects him as a professional person in a primary social system and how well a child can play the role of student in school. (Bower, 1980, p. 124)

Checklists and behavior rating scales. Teachers are most often involved during screening in which they are asked to judge whether a student is in need of further evaluation. Two of the primary aids to the teacher in making such a judgment are behavior checklists and behavior rating scales. In addition to providing a specific, somewhat objective structure for rating a student's behavior, these measures may help identify withdrawn or passive children who may be easily overlooked in the classroom (L.L. Brown, 1978).

Several published checklists and rating scales that provide the user with data for comparisons are available. Generally, raw scores are converted into standard scores which allow comparisons among individuals by establishing a range of normalcy. The *Behavior Problem Checklist* (Quay & Peterson, 1967, 1983) is a widely used checklist that measures four dimensions of behavior: conduct disorder (aggression), personality disorders (anxious, withdrawn), inadequacy–immaturity, and socialized delinquency. The first three dimensions are consistently found in populations who are labeled emotionally disturbed. The fourth dimension, socialized delinquency, is comparable to social maladjustment; individuals determined to be socially maladjusted are by federal definition to be excluded from services for the emotionally disturbed.

Two Devereux rating scales are commonly used in the schools: the *Devereux Adolescent Behavior Rating Scale* (Spivack, Spotts, & Haimes, 1967) for ages 13–18, and the *Devereux Elementary School Behavior Rating Scale* (Spivack & Swift, 1967) for grades 1–6. A third scale, the *Devereux Child Behavior Rating Scale* (Spivack & Spotts, 1966) is appropriate for use with children ages 8–12 in residential settings or institutions. The *Elementary Scale* is a useful screening tool and requires the rating of 46 items categorized into 11 behavioral factors (see Table 4–1).

A slightly different approach is taken by Lambert, Hartsough, and Bower (1979) in the *Pupil Behavior Rating Scale* (PBRS). In this instrument the teacher is asked to rate all the pupils in the class on 11 items or "attributes" (see Table 4–2). This procedure forces the teacher to think carefully not only about each attribute but also the relativity of its occurrence among classmates. Rather than instructing the teacher to rate a particular student in reference to normal or average students, the PBRS requires an actual rating of all students on the same items. Although more time-consuming than other scales, the PBRS forces its users to evaluate more carefully the attributes of pupils in relation to one another. It also contains peer and self-rating components.

Behavior recording. Behavior observation and recording is another method utilized by behaviorists to identify students with behavior disorders. Such recordings are often used as supplemental information to both informal and formal testing procedures. The referring teacher may be asked to keep anecdotal records, but supervisors or assessment personnel generally are responsible for observing and recording behavior of the student in question.

Recording involves direct observation of the student in the environment in which the maladaptive behavior occurs, usually the classroom setting. In the technique of time-sampling, the observer chooses several time periods to observe and then records occurrences of a specified behavior. A more difficult and generally less reliable technique is to record every behavior that occurs within very short time periods or intervals. (Refer to Chapter 7 for other systems of behavior recording.) Information derived from behavior recording may be used to supplement other information gathered during the diagnostic process and also to help plan intervention strategies.

Recording obviously involves only those behaviors that are observable and measurable. Such characteristics of behavior as frequency, duration, and type should be considered (Walker & Shea, 1976). For example, if a teacher complains about a student's behavior, it may well be that it is the type of behavior (for example, masturbation) which makes it maladaptive or deviant rather than the frequency or number of times it occurs; conversely, the important consideration may be the duration rather than the type of behavior (temper tantrums lasting 20–30 minutes versus temper tantrums lasting 4–5 minutes). In addition to frequency, duration, and type of behavior, other considerations when judging maladaptiveness are whether the behavior is developmentally or age-appropriate, and whether the behavior is situation-specific or occurs across settings.

TABLE 4–1. Devereux Elementary School Behavior Rating Scale

DEVEREUX ELEMENTARY SCHOOL
BEHAVIOR RATING SCALE *

George Spivack, Ph.D. and Marshall Swift, Ph.D.
Devereux Foundation Institute for Research and Training

DESB PROFILE

Student's Name _____   Teacher's Name _____
Student's Sex _____ Age _____   Academic Subject _____
Grade _____ School _____   Date of Rating _____

Raw Score in Standard Score Units

Behavior Factor		−1SD	0	+1SD	+2SD

Behavior Factor			
1. Classroom Disturbance	CLASS DISTURB	4 8 12 16 20	
2. Impatience	IMPAT.	4 8 12 16 20 24	
3. Disrespect-Defiance	DISRESP. DEFY	4 8 12 16 20	
4. External Blame	EXTERNAL BLAME	4 8 12 16 20	
5. Achievement Anxiety	ACHIEVE ANXIETY	4 8 12 16 20 24	
6. External Reliance	EXTERNAL RELY	5 10 15 20 25 30	
7. Comprehension	COMPRE- HENSION	3 6 9 12 16 19	
8. Inattentive - Withdrawn	INATTENT WITHDR.	4 8 12 16 20 24	
9. Irrelevant - Responsiveness	IRRELEV. RESP.	4 8 12 16 20	
10. Creative Initiative	CREAT. INITIAT.	4 8 12 16 20	
11. Need Closeness to Teacher	N. CLOSE TCHR	4 6 12 18 24	

1	2	3	4	5	6	7
1	2	3	4	5	6	7
1	2	3	4	5	6	7

Copyright, the Devereux Foundation, Devon, Pa., 1967. Used with permission.

TABLE 4–2.   Items on the *Pupil Behavior Rating Scale* (PBRS) (Lambert, Hartsough, & Bower, 1979)

1. This pupil fights or quarrels more often than the other pupils do.
2. This pupil has difficulty following directions.
3. This pupil makes immature or inappropriate responses during school activities.
4. This pupil is too dependent on the teacher and becomes uneasy without continual supervision.
5. This pupil has to be coaxed or forced to work or play with others.
6. This pupil is easily distracted.
7. This pupil behaves in ways that are dangerous.
8. This pupil has no enthusiasm for school and does not respond to or maintain interest in learning.
9. This pupil has difficulty in learning skills.
10. This pupil becomes upset or sick or may stay home from school when faced with a difficult problem or situation.
11. This pupil seems unhappy or depressed.

From *Pupil Behavior Rating Scale*. Reprinted with permission of the publisher, CTB/McGraw-Hill, Del Monte Research Park, Monterey, CA 93940. Copyright © 1979 by McGraw-Hill, Inc. All Rights Reserved. Printed in the U.S.A.

Educational Application

Behavior modification is an applied method of behavior change based on principles of operant conditioning. Success with behavior modification techniques has been claimed in a variety of settings with a myriad of behaviors. These techniques have been utilized in homes, clinics, schools, and institutions, with both groups and individuals, with both handicapped and nonhandicapped, and with behaviors as mild as off-task and as extreme as severe self-abuse. Altman and Linton (1974) outline three major reasons why the classroom is an ideal setting for behavioral techniques: (1) the classroom is a traditional place for modification of children's social and academic behavior in which the teacher is by definition a classroom manager; (2) schools have institutionalized environmental controls, and students are a "captive audience"; and (3) behavioral technology offers promise for prevention of behavior problems that have traditionally led to removal from the regular classroom and, sometimes, removal from the school system.

It is beyond the scope of this book to review the massive body of literature pertinent to the use of behavior modification in educational settings or to provide step-by-step instruction on how to implement behavioral techniques. Instead, this section will provide a descriptive overview of the techniques most commonly used in schools by outlining methods for increasing behaviors, methods for decreasing behaviors, and systematic desensitization. A number of important behavioral techniques are treated in more detail in Chapter 7. Among these techniques are cognitive behavior modification (including behavioral self-control), behavior recording, and use of reinforcers. The use of positive reinforcement undergirds most methods for increasing behaviors, including shaping and contingency contracting, which are presented in the next section.

Methods for increasing behaviors. Three common techniques for increasing a desired or appropriate behavior are shaping, modeling, and contingency contracting.

Shaping is the systematic reinforcement of a series of behaviors, each of which more closely resembles or approximates the desired behavior. In order to reinforce these approximations successfully, a teacher must analyze the final desired behavior or goal and must establish a hierarchy of responses that lead to that goal. For example, if verbal interaction is the desired goal for a particular individual, then the response hierarchy may begin with one-word responses, then build to two-word responses, complete sentences, and eventually require initiation of conversation (the final goal). Other classroom behaviors commonly modified through shaping are task completion (gradually increasing the number of problems required) and in-seat behavior (gradually increasing the number of minutes in seat).

Modeling is based on social learning theory and is most often used to teach appropriate behaviors. At its most basic level, modeling can be applied in the classroom by praising students for exhibiting the desired behaviors and ignoring undesired or inappropriate behaviors. However, as teaching social skills to behavior disordered children has become increasingly important to educators, modeling has developed into a sophisticated technique whereby desirable social behaviors are taught through demonstration and rehearsal. In *behavior rehearsing*, students are given verbal instructions and demonstrations by a model, and they are then given time to practice the behavior (Stephens, 1977).

Walker and his associates (Walker et al., 1983) have developed an entire social skills curriculum which incorporates modeling and behavior rehearsing as a part of its teaching procedure. After being given definitions and examples of the specific behavior to be learned, the student is shown videotaped examples and nonexamples of the behavior, then asked to role-play the behavior. Examples of the 28 skills taught through Walker's curriculum include: listening to the teacher, taking turns talking, using polite words, assisting others, and smiling.

Contingency contracting is a technique based on Premack's principle (1965) that a behavior with a high rate of occurrence can be used to increase a behavior with a lower rate of occurrence, or as paraphrased in Grandma's Law, "First you do X," (less probable behavior), "then you may do Y" (more probable behavior). Contingency contracting may be implemented as a simple verbal contract ("If you complete these ten math problems, then you may go to the listening center"), or it may involve a written agreement specifying duties of both teacher and student, the applicable time period, and the reinforcement. The teacher's role is that of manager or negotiator of the terms. One positive aspect of contingency contracting is that the student takes an active part in choosing the task and the reward or contingency. Contingency contracts are often used in the classroom to upgrade the quality and quantity of work.

Methods for decreasing behaviors.   Four methods commonly used in the schools to decrease inappropriate or undesirable behaviors are extinction, reinforcement of incompatible behaviors, time-out, and punishment.

Extinction is the removal of reinforcers that maintain a behavior. Applied to a classroom setting, extinction usually involves ignoring a behavior being maintained by the teacher's attention, which may be either positive or negative attention. To be effective, extinction must be planned, consistent, and applied to behavior that is not self-reinforcing (for example, tattling) or reinforced by peers (talking out in class is one example) (Walker & Shea, 1976). Extinction cannot be used with behaviors that may cause physical or psychological harm.

Reinforcement of incompatible behaviors is a technique to decrease an undesired behavior by reinforcing an opposing or incompatible response. For example, the teacher may reinforce in-seat behavior to decrease walking around the room and may reinforce hand-raising to decrease talking out without permission. Many classroom behaviors that are irritating to the teacher are amenable to this technique. Rather than punishing an undesired response, the teacher may reward the desired response which is impossible to perform simultaneously.

Time-out is removal, for a limited time period, from a setting which is reinforcing. For time-out to be effective in school, the classroom must be a reinforcing setting for the individual student with whom it is used. Additionally, time-out should only be used for behaviors that are specified with the student beforehand, and the student should understand the reason for being placed in time-out each time it occurs. The time-out area may be a designated corner of the classroom, partitioned and screened from the rest of the room, or it may be a separate room. Time-out is most effective with students who want the stimulation provided by the classroom setting; it has proven effective with students exhibiting disruptive, acting-out, or aggressive behavior.

Punishment is a technique used to decrease a behavior by presentation of an aversive stimulus or removal of a positive stimulus as a consequence of that behavior. Punishment may be psychological or physical or may consist of withholding privileges. Whichever method is chosen, the individual to whom the consequence is applied must perceive it as highly aversive. Proponents of behavior modification usually call for the use of punishment only as a last resort; they cite a number of negative side effects such as fear, tension, provision of an aggressive model, and the association of punishment with the punisher rather than the offending behavior. In addition, punishment suppresses behavior on a short-term basis but has not been proven effective for long-term behavior change. Punishment also indicates to students those behaviors which are unacceptable but it fails to indicate behaviors which are positive and acceptable as substitutes. It should not tax the reader's imagination to think of numerous punishments used by teachers in the schools; spanking, scolding, and withholding recess are some traditional examples.

Systematic desensitization. This technique was initially developed by Wolpe in the 1950s and 1960s; it is predicated on his ideas that phobias are learned fear responses and that anxiety is incompatible with relaxation. According to Wolpe (1958), the procedure of desensitization involves three basic steps: (1) establishing a hierarchy of fear-invoking stimuli, (2) learning deep-muscle relaxation techniques, and (3) pairing the relaxation state with each of the stimuli on the fear hierarchy. The last step is accomplished by asking the individual to visualize the feared stimuli while in a state of deep relaxation; in successive sessions, the client works through the hierarchy until the highest-ranking fear is faced without the accompanying anxiety or fear response.

Although desensitization was initially developed with clients in a clinical therapy setting, it has been implemented successfully in educational settings under the direction of psychologists and other behavior therapy consultants. Used successfully with a number of fears, the technique has proven especially helpful in reducing test anxiety (Beck, 1972; Deffenbacher & Kemper, 1974) and curing school phobia (Allyon, Smith, & Rogers, 1970; Garvey & Hegrenes, 1966).

Summary

Behaviorists view disturbed behavior as learned maladaptive responses. According to this model, behavior has a lawful relationship to the environment, as illustrated by the principles of operant and respondent conditioning. Whereas respondent conditioning occurs because of events preceding behavior, operant conditioning is due to events following behavior. These environmental events are manipulated by behaviorists in order to help change behavior. The impact of social learning, or observation and imitation of others' behavior, is also emphasized. Behavior modification, a system for behavior change based on these learning principles, is used widely in schools. A summary of the behavioral view of etiology, typical evaluation procedures, and educational applications are presented in Table 4–3.

TABLE 4–3. Summary of the Behavioral Model

ETIOLOGY	EDUCATIONAL APPLICATIONS	EVALUATION PROCEDURES

Respondent (classical) conditioning
Operant conditioning
Social learning (modeling)
	Methods for increasing behaviors:
	    shaping
	    modeling
	    contingency contracting
	Methods for decreasing behaviors:
	    extinction
	    reinforcement of incompatible behaviors
	    time-out
	    punishment
	Systematic desensitization
		Checklists
		Behavior rating scales
		Behavior recording

SOCIOLOGICAL MODEL

Sociology is by definition a systematic study of the structure and behavior of organized groups of people. Although sociological theory can rarely be extrapolated to fully explain individual behavior, it is important for educators to understand the role that schools play in modern society and to view student and teacher behavior from that perspective.

Definition and Basic View

The behaviorally disordered child is

> . . . the child who cannot or will not adjust to the socially acceptable norms for behavior and consequently disrupts his own academic progress, the learning efforts of his classmates, and interpersonal relations. (Woody, 1969, p. 7)

This definition illustrates the sociological point of view in its reference to social norms or expectations which the student violates, subsequently acquiring the label emotionally disturbed or behavior disordered. According to this model, disturbance is a lack of conformity to implicit or explicit social standards, rules, and norms.

As with other models, sociological theory is diverse and does not promote a singular view of the development of disordered behavior. There are, however, two common threads: (1) regardless of individual motivation, disordered behavior is deviant and nonconformist, and (2) deviance involves rule breaking and its consequences (Des Jarlais, 1974). Sociological theorists are concerned with societal forces impinging on the child, but many theorists differ in their perceptions of the role of the deviant child in society. Three major schools of thought on the child's role will be presented: the child as a rule breaker, as a victim of labels, and as a socialization failure. Subsequently, the school as a socializing agent and the child's social role as a student will be explored.

Etiology and Development of Disordered Behavior

Child as a rule breaker.   Deviance is defined by society as the breaking of social rules, generally with two results: negative evaluation by others and punishment (Des Jarlais, 1974). Social rules may be explicit, such as codified criminal laws and rules posted on elementary classroom wall charts; or they may be implicit, such as rules for eye contact and personal space which govern daily social interactions. The child labeled as deviant may break either one or both types of rules.

According to sociological theorists, societies are based on these explicit and implicit rules; if rule breaking is not viewed negatively and punished, then the social structure is undermined and in danger of collapse. Therefore, deviants or rule breakers must be negatively evaluated and punished. Many parallels have been drawn between societal treatment of criminals and disturbed individuals, such as incarceration and loss of civil and legal liberties (Goffman, 1961; Szasz, 1961). Although the official stance of society is for treatment and rehabilitation rather than punishment for deviant children, there are also a number of unofficial sanctions associated with rule breaking: negative attitudes, social stigma, and labels.

Child as a victim of labels.   Some sociologists (H. Becker, 1963; Scheff, 1966) are concerned with the impact of society's labels on individuals. The most common societal examples of this labeling process are criminal conviction, placement in a residential treatment center or institution, and placement in special education classes (Des Jarlais, 1974), with the resulting labels of "convict," "crazy," "insane," "reject," and so forth. The irreversibility of such labels and the potential detrimental effect throughout a person's life are stressed. Agents of social control such as law enforcers, educators, social workers, and psychiatrists are central to this theory because they select those individuals who will be labeled deviant. This selection process is a prime concern: everyone breaks rules but only a few are identified as deviant. Factors in the selection process are the frequency and visibility of rule breaking, tolerance level of others for rule breaking, social distance between rule breakers and agents of social control, and the power of the rule breaker within the system (Des Jarlais, 1974). In other words, the deviance of rule breaking is determined by societal perceptions and the social context in which the behavior occurs.

Special educators are concerned with labeling because special education services are predicated on the assignment of labels denoting handicap. The ethics of labeling have been questioned from within the profession. Dunn (1968) suggested that labels produce deleterious effects by reducing teaching expectations, while Blatt (1972) argued that negative effects are due to the stigma of deviancy generated by the labels. For children labeled emotionally disturbed, the stigma is especially severe. Classroom teachers consistently have been found to hold more negative attitudes toward the emotionally disturbed and the mentally retarded than toward students of other handicapping conditions (Haring, Stern, & Cruickshank, 1958; Kingsley, 1967; Parish, Dyck, & Kappes, 1979; Williams & Algozzine, 1977). Negative attitudes often translate not only to lowered expectations for behavior but also lowered expectations for academic performance (Gordon & Thomas, 1967). It seems clear that teacher expectations are a primary concern when attempting to coordinate services or mainstream these students into regular classroom environments.

Other concerns of special educators are the long-term effects of labels and the self-fulfilling prophecy phenomenon, whereby teacher expectations are communicated and the student begins to act in accordance with the perceived expectations. Although the self-fulfilling prophecy has generated a great deal of research and controversy, its relationship to special education labels has not been documented, nor have the long-term effects of these labels been clearly defined. At this point, the majority of special educators view the possible detrimental effects of labeling as a valid issue, but the administrative necessity of labeling for obtaining funds and providing services is a reality.

Child as a socialization failure. Socialization describes the process whereby one generation instills in its offspring the knowledge, attitudes, and values that it wishes to perpetuate. For the child, socialization requires the learning of these behaviors, values, and attitudes, which are necessary to play a social role.

Parents are the primary socialization agents and, according to Clausen (1968), they must discharge the following tasks:

(1) training and providing for physiological needs;
(2) providing models for language, cognition, and social skills;
(3) transmitting cultural goals and values;
(4) controlling the child's behavior within societal parameters.

Other generally less influential social agents include schools, churches, police and courts, political leaders, peers, and the mass media (Lippett, 1968). According to these theorists, there are two major sources of socialization failure. The first source is deficiency in the child or parent that results in the child's failure to acquire the desired values and behaviors. This failure produces anxiety and interpersonal conflict within the family, and the ensuing power struggle determines whether the child will be labeled deviant. A second source of socialization failure is conflicting demands from different socialization agents (for example, parents and teachers), which creates stress for the individual. In this case, the child's reaction to stress and the power distribution will determine whether the child is labeled deviant. Thus, the view of the deviant child as a socialization failure essentially presents the child as a victim of conflict that arises out of the socialization process. Power is an important concept because the distribution of power largely determines whether deviant labels will be applied.

The Nature of Schools and the Role of Students

Schools are a primary socialization agent for students of all ages. Schools not only dispense knowledge, but also values such as punctuality, patriotism, getting along with others, and subordination of the individual for the common good. By instilling such values, schools have acquired a dual role as transmitters of culture in the socialization process and as agents of social control. Consequently, schools require individual conformity to the numerous rules devised to govern individual behavior. Some rules are enforced by formal sanctions such as punishment by teachers and administrators, while other rules may be unstated formally and therefore dealt with informally. The ultimate goal of any agent of social control, including schools, is the inculcation of self-discipline or self-control. When students accept and internalize the values taught by social agents, they comply voluntarily with the rules and expectations. Therefore, the more socialized the student, the less need for control imposed by teachers, administrators, or others.

Although schools are like other formal organizations in some ways, they have two unique features that render them problematic: (1) schools require the daily interaction of adults and youngsters who are not related in a family unit, and (2) social order in schools is dependent on the compliance of students who are predominantly unsocialized; that is, the members either have not yet learned or internalized the values and skills necessary to conform (Schlechty & Paul, 1982). When viewed in this context, the problems of our education system seem normal and logical; however, they are difficult to overcome.

The child's optimal role in this system is that of a successful student. From a sociological standpoint, motivation to achieve and conformity to school rules for behavior are necessary characteristics of a successful student. However, as mentioned earlier, not all rules are posted formally and enforced consistently. In order to stay out of trouble and be successful in the student role, the student must become an astute observer of others' expectations and must learn the intricacies of rules and rule-related behavior. Many behavior disordered students are poor learners of such rule-related behavior. As Redl (1965) noted, these students are often "socially nearsighted" and their inability to read the environment accurately often gets them into trouble with the rule enforcers; consequently, they are labeled deviant.

Typical Evaluation Procedures

Large amounts of social data are generally gathered on a student during an evaluation, including social histories and behavior ratings by parents and teachers. All data are based on the perceptions of others, usually social agents, about the social interactions and behavior of the student.

Sociometric techniques represent the sociological model in exploring others' attitudes toward a given individual. More specifically, sociometrics allow peers to make judgments about who is deviant, and those who have not conformed to peer expectations are likely to be pointed out. As applied in the schools, sociometrics measure children's preferences for one another in the classroom setting. Sociometric techniques vary in specifics but usually require peer nominations for questions such as "Whom in your class would you most (least) like to work with on a project?" and "Whom in your class would you most (least) like to invite to your birthday party?" Each student in the class is then asked to name two or three classmates for all four questions. Results are commonly tallied and interpreted through a rank-order procedure or a sociogram. A sociogram is a diagram that often helps clarify results by representing visually the relationships of students with one another (see Figure 4–1).

Teachers or assessment personnel may construct their own sociometric measures. I.J. Gordon (1966) promotes the "Guess Who" technique in which students are asked to supply names to a number of descriptive items (for example, "This person is friendly. . . and nice to everybody"). One commercially available sociometric measure is the sociogram portion of the *Behavior Rating Profile* (BRP) (Brown & Hammill, 1983). This sociogram gives the teacher some flexibility in choosing from seven pairs of questions to be given the class. Each student is then asked to nominate three classmates for each of the chosen questions. After the nominations have been gathered, the students are ranked according to a difference score (acceptances − rejections = difference). This score can be converted to a scaled score for comparison purposes. The authors of the BRP recommend that the procedure be used with groups of 20 or more students.

Data from sociometric techniques may be used to provide feedback to students as to whether their choices are commensurate with the choices of others and indicative of valid social perceptions. Another use is supplementing information gained from observation and interviews, thereby providing validation of others' perceptions; however, few insights into individual behavior are gained. These techniques should always be used

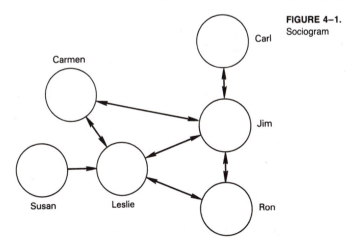

FIGURE 4–1.
Sociogram

as supplemental information rather than criteria for identification of disordered behavior, as reliability for identification purposes is questionable (Greenwood, Walker, & Hops, 1977).

Educational Applications

Interventions that are truly sociological in scope are extremely difficult to implement. The child is a much more vulnerable and accessible target for intervention than the community, family unit, educational environment, or societal norms, all of which may be contributing to the problem. Societal norms and traditional modes of interaction in the home and school are especially resistant to change. Sociological interventions are typically implemented outside of the educational setting through social work, community development programs, the welfare system, parent education, and family counseling (Long, Morse, & Newman, 1976).

One sociological intervention that has been adopted by special education is the use of advocates to deal with the emotional and financial ramifications of special education placement. With some students, an interested adult is assigned to protect the rights of the student during placement and services decisions. In such cases, the advocate's immediate aim is to act in the best interests of the individual in question. However, advocacy has larger purposes: to serve as a consumer protection agency and to "monitor and change human service agencies" (Biklen, 1976, p. 310). In order to effect such changes, thereby having an influence on policies and daily programming, advocates may utilize the following strategies: demonstrations, letter writing, fact-finding forums, demands of consumer needs and lists of grievances, use of media, boycotts, lobbying, and workshops or consciousness-raising groups (Biklen, 1976). All of these strategies are obviously intended to make changes in the social structure or the status quo; many are precursors to actual legal action in the courts.

None of these advocacy strategies attempts to change the child. If we accept the proposition that sociological theory views the environment as the primary source of deviance, then advocacy may represent the only truly sociological intervention practiced within the educational system. Examples of advocacy groups comprised of parents and other interested individuals are the various chapters of the Association for Retarded Citizens and the Society for Autistic Children. These groups actively lobby for additional funds and services.

Summary

Sociological theorists view the behavior disordered student as one who violates social norms or expectations. These theorists emphasize the role of the environment, that is, the societal forces that influence individuals and cause them to act in nonconformist or deviant ways. Nonetheless, according to this model, deviance and rule breaking must be punished in order to preserve social control, and the needs of the individual are subjected to the benefit of society. Labels and social stigma are forms of punishment often applied to deviant individuals. The deviant child is therefore considered both a misfit and an unfortunate victim of a larger social structure. There are few educational applications of sociological theory because sociological interventions depend upon changing the entire social structure. A summary of sociological theory is presented in Table 4–4.

ECOLOGICAL MODEL

Definition and Basic View

Behavioral disabilities are defined as a variety of excessive, chronic, deviant behaviors ranging from impulsive and aggressive to depressive and withdrawal acts (a) which violate the perceiver's expectations of appropriateness and (b) which the perceiver wishes to see stopped. (Graubard, 1973, p. 246)

Graubard's definition expresses the ecological view in its emphasis on both the perceiver of behavior and the behavior being perceived. The definition establishes that there are two parts to defining problem behavior: some type of behavior must exist *and* someone must be offended by such behavior. Theorists of this model espouse the view that deviance lies in the interaction of an individual with others (the perceivers) in the environment; hence the term *ecological.*

Human ecologists have drawn upon sociological and anthropological studies for support. Research which shows that certain city areas maintain steady rates of deviance has led to the initial proposal by Barker (1968) and later by Rhodes that people are "interchangeable components of an

TABLE 4–4.   Summary of the Sociological Model

ETIOLOGICAL ROLES
Child as rule breaker
Child as victim of labels
Child as socialization failure
EVALUATION PROCEDURE
Sociometrics
EDUCATIONAL APPLICATION
Advocacy

ecosystem[2] and will reflect the behaviors, traits, etc., which are character-istic of that ecosystem" (Rhodes, 1979, p. 1). Benedict (1959) and other cultural anthropologists have added the cultural relativity of deviance: behavior and traits labeled deviant or abnormal in one culture may be considered normal and even highly desirable in another.

Although sociology and human ecology are closely intertwined, there is one basic distinction: ecologists recognize the role of individual differences whereas sociologists emphasize, almost exclusively, the role of the environment in the development of problem behavior (Feagans, 1974). The importance of individual differences is supported by the Thomas, Chess, and Birch (1969) research cited earlier under the biophysical model. Thomas and colleagues found that children are born with certain temperaments or identifiable behavioral styles. However, although many children evidence temperaments that are negatively evaluated by society, there is no uniform relationship between negative temperament qualities and the development of pathology. Rather, the researchers found that environmental variables such as social pressures and the quality of interpersonal relationships interact with temperament to produce problem behavior. Such research demonstrates both the individual-differences factor of temperament and the role of the environment in the development of pathology; thus, the interactions within the child's ecosystems are the focal points of deviance.

As applied to human behavior, the ecological model implies that it is meaningless to discuss problems of behavior in isolation from the contexts in which these behaviors arise, since it is these very contexts that define the behavior as a problem. Rhodes (1967) states that the disturbance often lies in the behavioral expectations of those with whom the child must interact. A child may be judged disturbed by one person while appearing normal to another, or the child's behavior may be seen as abnormal in one setting but quite normal in another. The predictable result is that children who are judged to be the most disturbed are those who uniformly arouse negative reactions in the environments in which they interact with others. Therefore, within the ecological model, behavior is viewed as "disturbing" rather than "disturbed," and emphasis is placed not only on the child but also on other individuals and factors in the child's ecosystem.

Etiology and Development of Disordered Behavior

Theory.   Rhodes is the most vocal spokesperson for ecological theory; his arguments are persuasive but largely philosophical, as disturbances in ecosystems are difficult to define and assess operationally. According to Rhodes (1970), certain environments may be unable to accommodate the unfolding nature of children, thereby generating disturbance in the ecosystems. This view is in direct opposition to more traditional views that the child should accommodate to the environment rather than vice versa. Rhodes states that a major sign of disturbance is an increase in the amount and intensity of energy that is required by others to interact with the child, or a disturbance in the equilibrium of the ecosystem that calls attention to the child.

To operate from an ecological framework, one must accept that ecosystems rather than children are disturbed, and that ecosystems are directly influenced by the culture in which they exist. Rhodes (1967) translates these assumptions into intervention goals: the short-term goal is to intrude into the disturbed situation and help modify it, and the long-term goal is to expand the education process to develop functional yet individualistic members of society. Above all, Rhodes (1970) is adamant that we cannot hope to provide effective intervention if we "pluck" a child from a context of disturbance, attempt to fix or change him, and then place the child back into the unchanged environment from which he came.

Ecosystems.   In human ecology, the ecosystem may be defined as the various environments in which an individual routinely interacts. Components may be tangible or intangible, but they are interrelated and interdependent. People, objects, time, space, and psychological variables are all components of an ecosystem.

Students operate within a number of ecosystems; disturbed students cause "ripples of discomfort" and reverberations within these ecosystems (Rhodes, 1970). The major ecosystems of a student are shown in Figure 4–2. As depicted in the figure, the child participates simultaneously in a number of ecosystems which intersect at some points but which also retain much unshared territory. The larger, more comprehensive ecosystems (society and community) have less direct influence on the child than the smaller ecosystems (home and school). The larger ecosystems are also less amenable to change through direct intervention.

The variables in a child's ecosystem are important to analyze for two reasons: (1) to determine whether the variables are contributing to the disturbance, and (2) to determine which contributing variables are amenable to change so that appropriate intervention can be planned. For example, it might be determined that Jim's father's unemployment is causing anxiety in the home, which is having an effect on Jim's frustration tolerance and academic functioning in the classroom. Although dealing directly with parental unemployment (home ecosystem) is outside the domain of education, an analysis of the classroom situation might reveal that Jim would benefit from temporary help by adjusting the length of required assignments and/or providing some individualized tutoring (classroom ecosystem, manipulable variables).

Let us now turn our attention to some variables operating within ecosystems that directly affect student behavior. The variables listed are illustrative and not exhaustive; the majority of those listed under the

FIGURE 4–2. Ecosystems of the Child

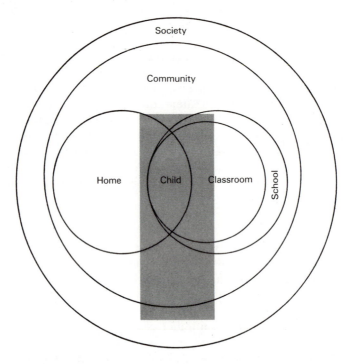

classroom and school ecosystems have a body of research relating them to student achievement or student behavior.

CLASSROOM

Teacher-student
teacher attitudes and/or expectations
teacher tolerance level for individual differences
teaching style: directed learning vs. nondirected learning
teacher interaction style: quantity and quality of interpersonal interactions
teacher–pupil ratio
Student-peers
peer attitudes: acceptance vs. rejection
number of students in class
gender, socioeconomic status (SES) and ethnic composition of group
general achievement and ability level of group
Physical environment
traditional vs. open classroom
light, colorful vs. drab
crowded vs. spacious
use of props and teaching aids

individual desks vs. tables and chairs
arrangement of desks or tables
use of centers
Curriculum
subject areas taught and subject areas stressed
placement in appropriate levels vs. placement in inappropriate level
programmed or highly structured vs. loose
objectives clearly defined or undefined
subject matter properly sequenced vs. haphazard
type of materials used
use of media
individualized vs. group-oriented
School
availability of support personnel
effectiveness of principal
number of students enrolled
general climate and/or atmosphere
school pride
urban, suburban, or rural location
philosophy of discipline
ethnic/SES mix of students
ethnic/SES mix of teachers
number of extracurricular activities
relationship with the community
Home
age, occupation, religion, and SES of parents
intact family vs. single-parent home
number and ages of siblings
education level of parents and attitude toward education
philosophy of child-rearing
methods and consistency of discipline
availability of extended family
attractiveness and comfortability of home
Community
urban, suburban, or rural setting
size of town or city
geographic location
ethnic/SES composition
major source(s) of income for workers (farming, industrial, business, etc.)
number of churches and prevailing religious denomination
economic stability
community pride
number and type of activities available: sports, family functions, theater,
    concerts, art, etc.

Society
state of economy and economic trends
general political climate
news and current events
entertainment available through media

Student contributions.   The student is an integral part of each ecosystem and, as such, contributes a number of individual characteristics that influence the workings of the ecosystem. Student characteristics pertinent to the classroom ecosystem that have been shown to influence teacher attitudes or expectations are gender (Maccoby, 1966; Palardy, 1969), race (Coates, 1972; Jackson & Cosca, 1974), socioeconomic status (Bernard, 1973; Rist, 1970), and appearance or physical attractiveness (LaVoie & Adams, 1974; Ross & Salvia, 1975). Another characteristic that may heavily influence teacher expectations is achievement (Cornbleth, 1974; Good, 1970). The literature linking achievement expectations with actual teacher interactions suggests that students who are perceived by their teachers as high achievers are afforded more positive interactions than their low-achieving counterparts (Coleman, 1981/1982).

Another influential student characteristic is behavior or behavioral style. In direct comparisons with other characteristics such as gender, ability, and attractiveness, behavior has been found to be the most potent determinant of teacher expectations (Kedar-Voivodas & Tannenbaum, 1979; LaVoie & Adams, 1974; Trevor, 1975). The behaviors that teachers find most disturbing are best described as defiant-aggressive (Algozzine, 1977; Walker, 1979). Such behaviors engender negative attitudes which are often translated into negative teacher-student interactions, thus setting in motion the rippling through the ecosystem described by Rhodes.

One of the major criticisms of the ecological theory of disturbance is that it is difficult to define, assess, and apply in schools. This section has described ecosystems and provided examples of variables within those ecosystems that influence the child as a student. The next two sections will outline how ecological assessment and intervention are carried out.

Typical Evaluation Procedures

The basic requirement of any ecological assessment is that student functioning be evaluated within a number of settings, with input from numerous individuals in those settings. Whenever possible, ecological assessment focuses on the interactions and expectations of all involved individuals. Two ecological evaluation measures will be described in brief: one an assessment technique and the other a specific instrument.

An ecological assessment technique.   Laten and Katz (1975) have out-lined a five-phase systematic procedure to be used by educators in collect-ing ecological data:

(1) *Describing the environment.* General information is gathered from set-tings in which the student is experiencing problems as well as those settings in which no problems are evident. The student's degree of success in each setting is evaluated. For example, a student might be found to be experiencing extreme difficulties during language arts period, but none in math class or during the physical education class.

(2) *Identifying expectations.* Specific expectations and demands in each set-ting are identified. Expectations for academic functioning and for social behaviors are of particular concern. For example, one teacher may lecture and require independent assignments while another teacher routinely allows class participation and plans group activities. Or one teacher may have strict discipline codes and allow no talking while another sets a freer, looser classroom atmosphere. Thus, the expectations for a student in different classes may vary widely. The primary concern is to identify those behaviors and skills that will help the student succeed in each setting.

(3) *Organizing behavioral data.* Three targets are analyzed in this phase: the background and skills of people involved in problem settings, the background and skills of people involved in successful settings, and the student's behavior and skills in each setting. Comparisons of the student's actual behavior and skills to those identified in phase two are made. Additional services and available options are identified for each setting.

(4) and (5) *Summarizing the data and establishing goals.* Information gathered in phases one through three is used to set reasonable goals for the student and for other individuals in the problem settings. Recommendations for use of specific methods, materials, or use of additional resources may be made.

This ecological technique may be used at the screening stage of evaluation to help identify problem factors in the student's environment. If interventions can be employed successfully at this point, further evalua-tion may not be necessary.

Behavior Rating Profile.   The *Behavior Rating Profile* (BRP) (Brown & Hammill, 1983) is a comprehensive behavior rating instrument. Accord-ing to its authors, the purpose of the BRP is "to provide an ecological evaluation of students' behaviors that is well standardized, highly reliable, experimentally validated, and norm-referenced. It is an ecological/behav-ioral assessment device, and, as such, it permits students' behaviors to be examined in a variety of settings and from several pertinent points of view" (Brown & Hammill, 1983, p. 2).

There are six components of the BRP: three Student Rating Scales in which the student responds to a total of 60 self-descriptive items in the areas of home, school, and peers; a Teacher Rating Scale of 30 items; a Parent Rating Scale of 30 items; and a sociogram, mentioned earlier in this chapter. Table 4–5 shows these components and respondents. After

TABLE 4–5. Respondent and Ecology Associated with the BRP Components (Brown & Hammill, 1983)

BRP COMPONENT	RESPONDENT				ECOLOGY		
	STUDENT	TEACHER(S)	PARENT(S)	PEERS	HOME	SCHOOL	INTERPERSONAL
Student Rating Scale: Home	X				X		
Student Rating Scale: School	X					X	
Student Rating Scale: Peer	X						X
Teacher Rating Scale		X				X	
Parent Rating Scale			X		X		
Sociogram				X			X

Used with permission of the publisher, PRO-ED, 5341 Industrial Oaks Blvd., Austin, TX 78735.

administration, ratings from each source are tabulated; separate norms are provided for each of the scales for students in grades 1 through 12. The summary profile allows for three independent teacher ratings and independent ratings of both parents. The BRP is very flexible in that one may either utilize input from all the scales and sources or may use any of the scales independently. The instrument can be particularly helpful in defining deviant behavior which is specific to one setting or to one individual's expectations.

Educational Applications

Ecological interventions may focus on a single ecosystem or a combination of ecosystems. As mentioned previously, the more intimate ecosystems of the child (classroom, home, and school) are more amenable to direct intervention than the larger ecosystems. However, as there is an interdependent relationship among ecosystems (refer to Figure 4–2), interventions applied in one setting may affect interactions in other settings, thus putting in motion a rippling effect.

The majority of educational interventions discussed in this section are not uniquely ecological; many are based on sociological, behavioral, or psychodynamic principles. However, each intervention is intended to make the environment more suitable for an individual student rather than attempting to force the student to fit the environment. Individual differences are taken into account. In this sense, these interventions are based in ecological theory. The targets of change are the student ecosystems of classroom, home, school, and community.

Changes in the classroom ecosystem. Physical and psychological adaptations within the classroom may be sufficient to change disturbing interactions of some students. A physical arrangement that has been used successfully in classrooms for the behavior disordered includes separate individual and group work areas, a time-out area, and a reinforcement center (Bullock, 1981; Hewett & Taylor, 1980). Use of individual study carrels and/or screens helps to eliminate distractions when independent work is required. To preserve psychological consistency, a number of clear, concise, enforceable rules are generally selected and posted on wall charts; to encourage academic success, individualized contracts, task sheets, or some clearly defined contingency may be arranged. Scheduling and routine are also important parts of the psychological environment; time limits for all daily activities are established and followed. By establishing definite limits, the teacher provides structure and helps students learn to manage time efficiently. In such classrooms, the teacher aims to create an atmosphere of acceptance and success rather than the expectation for failure that often surrounds the behavior disordered student.

Changes in the home ecosystem.   Parents have become increasingly involved with their children's educational programming since the mid-seventies. This trend was prompted by the mandates for parental involvement of P.L. 94–142 and encouraged by recognition that home–school planning results in more effective programming. The degree of parental involvement may range from monthly conferences to comprehensive behavior management systems established cooperatively by parents and teachers, then implemented by parents in the home. Parent support groups and parent training programs are often formally organized by educators.

Respite care is a potentially effective home intervention for parents of the severely handicapped. By offering additional programs for the children on Saturdays, during after-school hours, and/or through the summer months, educators can alleviate some of the stress inherent in continuous care of such youngsters. The goal is prevention of institutionalization by making the living situation more manageable and comfortable for parents and siblings. Such comprehensive programming is generally viewed as outside the domain of educational services and therefore may require cooperative planning and funding from social agencies and school systems.

Changes in school and community ecosystems.   Mainstreaming is an ecological intervention that has been occurring in our schools and communities since the passage of legislation in the mid-seventies. Arising from concern with the social ramifications of segregating handicapped students from nonhandicapped students, the legislation required educators to develop plans to ensure that handicapped children be educated with nonhandicapped to the maximum extent appropriate; that is, that handicapped children be removed from the mainstream of education only when the severity of handicap requires segregation to ensure satisfactory delivery of services.

Mainstreaming has had a profound impact on the entire educational system, as it represents a new philosophy of education backed by a mandate that handicapped children are no longer the sole responsibility of special education. Rather, special educators and regular educators are to plan and work jointly to serve these students. Unfortunately, research suggests that regular classroom teachers have generally responded negatively to these mandates and would prefer to leave exceptional children with exceptional teachers (T. Gallagher, 1974). Despite attempts to provide appropriate in-service programs for regular classroom teachers, teachers often express concern over their own perceived inadequacies to teach and manage problem children (Shotel, Iano, & McGettigan, 1972; Vaac & Kirst, 1977). Such a backlash is a common side effect of attempts to make comprehensive changes in established social institutions; it highlights the difficulties inherent in making such changes.

Deinstitutionalization is a second ecological intervention in both the school and community ecosystems. Similar to the concept of mainstreaming within the schools, deinstitutionalization is aimed at the normalization of handicapped individuals (usually retarded or disturbed) who have been institutionalized. According to Larsen (1976), in deinstitutionalization, society must strive to fulfill three goals: (1) to halt continued institutionalization, (2) to return as many institutionalized people as possible to their communities, and (3) to improve the care currently provided by institutions. Larsen (1976) has also described successful model programs and the following types of community facilities that are alternatives to institutions: residential halfway houses for 16 to 30 people; group centers similar to halfway houses but with no community involvement; small group homes for 4 to 8 persons; large group homes for 9 to 15 persons; and group foster homes, in which residential care is provided on a contractual basis.

Rhodes (1970) proposes dramatic changes in the structure and role of schools; he believes that such changes are necessary to improve the haphazard way in which we currently transmit our culture and teach children to relate to that culture. He argues that schools should have two equally important functions—instruction in academics and in daily living skills—each with its own separate curriculum and staff. Under Rhodes' model, child specialists such as counselors, social workers, and school psychologists would play an active rather than peripheral role. A massive reorganization is called for, including consolidation of community resources and creation of a curriculum aimed at adaptive living skills. According to Rhodes, such a reorganization would enable the schools to help students develop into critical consumers and functional members of society.

Changes in home, school, and community ecosystems.   Project Re-ED is a model program for behavior disordered students which is truly ecological in scope. The program was conceived by a number of theorists but headed by Nicholas Hobbs, who was motivated by a disenchantment with psychiatric programs for disturbed children and youth. Concerned with the high financial cost and lack of personnel to adequately staff such programs, Hobbs questioned the efficacy of the psychiatric approach:

> There is a real possibility that hospitals make children sick. The antiseptic atmosphere, the crepe sole and white coat, the tension, the expectancy of illness may confirm a child's worst fears about himself, firmly setting his aberrant behavior. (Hobbs, 1966, p. 1105)

Funded by the National Institute for Mental Health, Hobbs opened Cumberland House in Nashville, Tennessee, in 1962 and the Wright School in Durham, North Carolina, shortly thereafter. The short-term, residential programs are based on the supposition that the most effective treatment is one that intervenes in all ecosystems. The goal, therefore, is not to fix the child and return her to the community, but to make the child's ecosystem fit together more smoothly. The targets for intervention are not only the child but also the child's home, neighborhood, school, social agencies, and community (Hobbs, 1966).

Re-ED's treatment philosophy basically views children as capable of controlling and changing their own behavior to more adaptive ways. Trust in adults and competence in school and other life skills are viewed as the necessary bases from which changes can be made. The child's feelings are recognized and the youngster is taught to express both positive and negative feelings in socially acceptable ways.

School interventions are implemented by *teacher-counselors*. The teacher-counselor during the day functions much as a public school teacher in academics but performs the additional role of counseling and working to modify maladaptive behaviors. Education takes precedence over psychotherapy, as the ability to achieve academically is considered essential for making the child's school ecosystem work successfully. The night teacher-counselor takes over after school hours and is primarily a support person who supervises group activities and extracurricular activities. Almost all activities are undertaken in small groups (usually about eight children); the group is considered an important source of both motivation and control.

Another important role is played by the *liaison teacher-counselor* who assesses the home, school, and community and helps them prepare for the return of the student. In the school, the liaison teacher-counselor collects extensive historical information such as past academic and behavioral records, successful and unsuccessful program modifications, relationships with various school personnel, and so forth. The goal is to plan cooperatively for a smooth reentry. The liaison teacher-counselor is also available as a consultant after reentry into the school. Similar tasks are undertaken in the home and community. Parents are viewed as collaborators in effecting long-term change in their child's life. Beginning with the child's weekend visits early in the Re-ED program, the liaison teacher-counselor maintains close communication with parents and helps them plan changes that will aid the child's adaptation in the home and community. The liaison teacher-counselor also coordinates services with community agencies such as social service departments or mental health centers, which may be essential links to the child's transition. Thus, the liaison teacher-counselor seeks to establish a supportive network in the child's major ecosystems which are conducive to healthy and adaptive functioning.

SUMMARY

Ecological theorists believe that it is impossible to define disturbed behavior in isolation from the contexts in which the behavior occurs. Disordered behavior is viewed as a disturbance in the equilibrium of an ecosystem; therefore, the child is viewed as a part of the problem rather

TABLE 4–6. Summary of the Ecological Model

ETIOLOGY	EVALUATION MEASURES

Disturbances in the ecosystems of:
  classroom
  home
  school
  community
  society
	An ecological assessment technique: *Behavior Rating Profile* (Brown & Hammill, 1983)

EDUCATIONAL APPLICATIONS

classroom:	physical arrangement, rules, contracts, scheduling
home:	home behavior-management programs parent support groups parent training groups respite care programs
school/ community:	mainstreaming deinstitutionalization
home/ school/ community:	Project Re-ED

113

than the totality of the problem. In theory, all components of the disturbed ecosystem should be analyzed as possible contributors to the problem and as possible targets for intervention. In practice, analyzing and intervening in disturbed ecosystems are difficult and time-consuming. Interventions based on other models may be viewed as ecological attempts to match student needs within an ecosystem, but Project Re-ED is perhaps the only uniquely ecological model program for behavior disordered students. Re-ED is a residential program that seeks to establish changes in the student's home, school, and community before allowing the student to return to these environments. A summary of the ecological model is presented in Table 4–6.

KEY POINTS

(1) The basic tenet of behavioral theory is that all behavior, including maladaptive behavior, is learned and therefore can be "unlearned" and new behavior learned in its place.

(2) Behavioral theorists effect behavior change by manipulating environmental events which precede or follow the targeted behavior.

(3) Social learning or modeling is useful in teaching social skills to maladjusted students.

(4) Sociological theorists view emotional disturbance as a lack of conformity to the rules, standards, and norms imposed by society.

(5) Schools are a socialization agent of our culture; to play the role of student successfully, children and adolescents must conform to the rules of the system.

(6) The inability of many behavior disordered students to read the environment and to conform to it often gets them into trouble with the rule enforcers, and they consequently become labeled as deviant.

(7) Advocacy is a sociological intervention which attempts to effect change in existing social structures such as social and educational services to handicapped persons.

(8) According to ecological theorists, deviance results from the *interactions* of an individual with others in the environment; hence, ecosystems rather than individuals are viewed as disturbed.

(9) If ecosystems are disturbed, then educators must assess and intervene in the various environments in which the student routinely lives and interacts.

(10) Although ecological interventions are often difficult to implement, changes can be made in the classroom, home, and school and community ecosystems of behavior disordered students.

ADDITIONAL READINGS

Behavior modification: A practical approach for educators, by J.E. Walker & T.M. Shea (Second Edition). St. Louis: C.V. Mosby, 1980; and *Behavior modification for the classroom teacher,* by S. Axelrod, (Second Edition). New York: McGraw-Hill, 1983, for simple and practical guides to applying behavioral principles in the classroom.

How to use contingency contracting in the classroom, by L. Homme, A. Csanyi, M. Gonzales, & J. Rechs. Champaign, IL: Research Press, 1970, for more information on using contingency contracts.

The myth of mental illness, by T. Szasz. New York: Hoeber-Harber, 1966, for writings of an author who basically believes that society *creates* disturbance in individuals.

Special education for the mildly retarded—Is much of it justifiable? by L. Dunn. *Exceptional Children,* 1968, *35,* 5–22, for a classic article that represents a sociological viewpoint in questioning the effects of special education labels.

The disturbing child: A problem of ecological management, by W.C. Rhodes. *Exceptional Children,* 1967, *33,* 449–455; and A community participation analysis of emotional disturbance, by W.C. Rhodes. *Exceptional Children,* 1970, *36,* 309–314, for seminal writings on the ecological perspective.

The emotionally disturbed child: Disturbed or disturbing? by R. Algozzine. *Journal of Abnormal Child Psychology,* 1977, *5,* 205–211, for an article representing the ecological perspective in describing teacher ratings of classroom behavior.

Helping disturbed children: Psychological and ecological strategies, by N. Hobbs. *American Psychologist,* 1966, *2,* 1105–1115, for more information on Project Re-ED.

NOTES

[1]This lawful relationship is illustrated by the principles of operant and respondent conditioning which are discussed in the section on etiology.

[2]*Ecosystem* is a biological term denoting a natural community functioning as a unit.

five

Programming: The School Environment

---

orientation

The room is next to empty. It is undecorated. On the back wall above the board, posters explain the Hewett level system employed in the class. There is a shelf unit containing workbooks and references, a table with some boxes, and an old couch. There are several veteran TVs, one of which looks like it is used periodically. The room is carpeted. The classroom itself is a "portable," meaning it's a prefab unit added on when enrollment increased . . . . Chad's classroom has several titles, but it's probably best described as the district's last effort for behavior disordered students. This is where they go after "flunking" out of the other special education programs because of the way they act. Some of them do things notable enough to get there directly from regular class.*

The focus of this chapter is on taking a classroom—any classroom—and turning it into a learning environment for behavior disordered students.

OVERVIEW

Environmental planning for behavior disordered students involves not only selecting an appropriate educational placement, but also arranging the environment within that setting for optimal learning conditions. The first section of this chapter presents an overview of educational placements available for behavior disordered students, such as classes in hospitals, special schools, and regular schools. The teacher's role within these settings is also addressed.

*From Inside Special Education, by Kenneth Howell (1983, pp. 64–65).

The second section addresses environmental planning within the classroom setting. *Structure,* defined as a clear relationship between materials, instructions, room furnishings, and the student's expected response (P.A. Gallagher, 1979), is the most important aspect of environmental organization. By creating a physically and psychologically structured environment, the teacher establishes guidelines which help the student recognize a consistent relationship between expectations, behavior, and consequences. Planned use of space, equipment, and props establishes structure in the physical environment, while appropriate use of scheduling, feedback, and rules provides psychological structure. Hewett's orchestrated classroom incorporates all of these components and is featured as a model classroom.

OVERVIEW OF SPECIAL EDUCATION SERVICES FOR THE BEHAVIOR DISORDERED

> The purposes of special educators are not different from those of other educators. The focus is on the individual and his optimal development as a skillful, free, and purposeful person, able to plan and manage his own life and reach his highest potential in society. When special placements are required, the aim still remains that of maximum development and freedom of the individual; to this end, the educational program plays a crucially important role. (Willenberg, 1971, p. 424)

The preceding paragraph was written in 1971 as part of a policy statement on the purpose of special education. The statement was intended to represent the goals of special educators, but it was philosophically—and not legally—binding. Since the passage of federal legislation in 1974, both regular and special educators have been legally persuaded to take a closer look at the lofty goals of this statement and to begin cooperative programming to put them into operation.

The basis for placement of a handicapped student in the least restrictive environment originated in Public Law 93–380, the Education Amendments of 1974, which required that each state, in order to retain eligibility for federal funds for education of the handicapped, must develop a plan which contains:

> ... procedures to ensure that to a maximum extent appropriate, handicapped children ... are educated with children who are not handicapped ... and that removal of handicapped children from the regular education environment occurs only when the nature or severity of the handicap is such that the education in regular classes with the use of supplementary aids and services cannot be achieved satisfactorily. (Section 12–7)

This mandate gave rise to the idea that, whenever appropriate, the preferred placement for the handicapped child is with nonhandicapped children or in the "mainstream of society." Unfortunately, a widespread misinterpretation of this mandate occurred among educators, namely, that all handicapped children should be mainstreamed and therefore would be returned to regular classroom environments. This misinterpretation does not take into account the *appropriateness* of placement; that is, a handicapped child is to be placed in a regular education environment only if his educational needs can be met in that environment. There is little doubt that the regular classroom environment cannot meet the needs of a significant number of severely handicapped students; on the other hand, mildly handicapped students may be appropriately served in the regular classroom with support services or part-time help from special educators. Thus, in order to meet the needs of all handicapped students, a wide variety of educational settings and flexibility of services within those settings is required. The numerous alternative settings have become known as a *continuum of services*.

Continuum of Services

Alternative placements and settings in special education were conceptualized by Reynolds (1962) in the Cascade Model, which presented a continuum of services ranging from regular classroom placement (least restrictive) to residential school placement (most restrictive). Students were to be moved to more restrictive environments only as necessary and returned to less restrictive environments as soon as feasible. Deno (1968) expanded this model to include in-patient programs such as hospitals, homebound, medical, and welfare services. However, Knoblock (1983) has reconceptualized the Cascade Model into one that offers "fewer specialized programs and greater diversity in regular classrooms and settings" (p. 50). Rather than creating a greater number of outside special services in restricted settings to accommodate handicapped children, Knoblock recommends expanding the services offered within less restrictive settings. He cites individualized instructional systems and individualized behavior management systems as examples of the diversity that can be achieved in normal settings. Whether this ideal will become common practice in the schools remains to be seen.

The continuum of services that is most applicable to behavior disordered students is presented in Figure 5–1. Olson and Mercer (1981) divide the continuum of services under two headings: *integrated* and *segregated*. They describe *integrated* as placement in which the student is in the regular classroom for the major portion of the day, and the regular classroom teacher has primary responsibility for the student's instruction. Examples are the resource room and regular class placement with supportive services. *Segregated* refers to placement in which the student spends the majority of his time with a special education teacher who has the

FIGURE 5–1.   Placements for Behavior Disordered Students

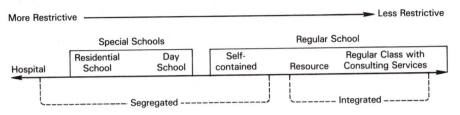

primary responsibility for instruction; examples are special classes and special schools. The next five sections of this chapter describe the most common settings for behavior disordered students and teacher roles within those settings.

Hospitals.   Students being served in hospital programs generally fall into one or more of the following categories: suicidal, drug-dependent, violent, psychotic, or those who have organic impairments accompanied by bizarre behaviors and who require medication. Chronic runaways and adjudicated youth are occasionally placed in hospital settings by the courts for security and treatment purposes. Students generally are placed in highly restrictive hospital settings because they require: (1) protection of self or others and/or (2) close medical supervision.

Day schools with low pupil-teacher ratios are often provided in hospital settings. In these day schools, programs for higher functioning students are very similar to those offered in other special schools for the behavior disordered: curriculum is individualized and the team concept is central to provision of services (see the next section on special schools). For lower functioning students, the educational program is geared toward functional skills such as communication and self-help skills. Typically, hospital day schools are heavily influenced by medical and psychological staff. Total treatment programs for individuals which include the classroom setting may be worked out by psychiatrists or psychologists; the teacher then implements the classroom segments of the treatment program. The teacher must therefore be adept at working with the medical and psychological communities and at communicating with other members of multidisciplinary teams.

The advantages of a hospital setting are that it provides not only security and protection for the individual but also medical and psychological staff who are available around-the-clock for treatment and in case of emergency. The major disadvantage is the stigma of being hospitalized for psychiatric purposes and the subsequent difficulties that may be encountered in moving the individual to a less restrictive environment. The individual may also feel a loss of personal liberties.

Special schools: Residential and day.   Students served in special schools are usually those exhibiting such severe emotional or behavioral problems that they are deemed unable to function in the public school environment but do not need the medical supervision or protective services provided by a hospital setting. Special schools may be day schools or residential schools and may be either privately or publicly funded. A major advantage of special schools is that the environment can be more tightly structured than in regular schools because the entire school program and school staff are dedicated to dealing with a population with special problems. Residential schools have the additional advantage of consistency and continuity between the "home" and school environments. The total program for an individual student is usually devised and implemented by both day staff and evening staff so that the student operates under the same regulations and expectations for 24 hours a day.

In addition to specially trained teachers, special schools are staffed with multidisciplinary personnel, usually a physician or nurse, a psychologist or psychiatrist, and counselors and social workers. The evening staff generally includes trained counselors who are available to deal with crises that may arise during the evening hours. The team concept is advocated and staffings are common, in which all team members jointly work out program objectives and assign responsibility for carrying out those objectives with individual students.

Curriculum and specific methods vary greatly from school to school, but each school generally aligns itself with a treatment philosophy that prevails within its walls. Some schools may operate primarily on behavior modification systems, whereas others provide more intensive therapy, and still others depend heavily on affective curriculum. Although most schools identify with a certain philosophy (for example, psychodynamic), they are usually eclectic in operation, which means that they have found a particular combination of behavior modification, therapy, and curriculum that suits their clientele and staff.

The teacher's role in the special school will only be partially defined by the particular treatment philosophy adopted by the school. More important is the teacher's ability to communicate and to team up with other staff. As in the hospital setting, the teacher in a special school must learn to work on a daily basis with personnel from different disciplines such as medicine and psychology. Effective programs depend upon cooperative planning and mutual support among staff members.

The major disadvantage of special schools is the difficulty involved in normalization or returning students to regular education environments. The stigma of placement in a special school is so difficult for students to overcome that some school systems are attempting to ease the reintegration through transition classes. These classes focus on independent behaviors and socialization skills, which should facilitate a student's transition from a segregated class with structure and a small teacher-pupil ratio to an integrated setting in which the student must be more or less independent. Project Re-ED is an example of residential programs that begin planning for the student's transition back into the home, school, and community as soon as the student is admitted to the program. Based on ecological theory, which emphasizes the importance of all ecosystems of an individual, Re-ED provides community liaison staff who intervene and plan cooperatively with parents, teachers, and principals for the re-entry into these environments.

Regular school: Self-contained. Students are usually placed in self-contained classrooms in regular schools because they are deemed able to function in the public schools but need more structure and/or specialized instruction than can be provided on a part-time basis. The major difference of this setting from other regular school settings is the segregated nature of the class; students usually are not mainstreamed and therefore have less contact with regular teachers and the regular education program. One advantage of self-contained classes over resource classes is that students are not exposed to environmental inconsistency or different teacher expectations because one teacher has control over the total learning environment. A second advantage is the small teacher-pupil ratio, typically about 1:5. With groups larger than five or six, the teacher is usually assigned an aide. One disadvantage is a lack of opportunity for students to model nonhandicapped peers, which may be particularly important for those with deficient social skills.

Although there is great variance in the type of interventions offered in self-contained programs, there are a few commonalities of effective programs. One set of guidelines is offered by Montgomery (1982), who believes that effective programs for the behavior disordered foster growth and change in the students that are reflected in program changes along four dimensions:

From rigid to flexible scheduling. As the student is able to handle independent learning situations, more free time is allowed and the schedule becomes more flexible.

From external to internal control. Initially, external reinforcers may be necessary; heavy supervision and planning are done for the student. Structure is lessened as the student becomes more responsible.

From short-term to long-term goals. The student initially may be able to complete only short assignments or to work for very short periods of time. Therefore, extension of work periods and delay of rewards become program objectives.

From segregation to integration. Although initially the student may need the structure and control imposed in the segregated classroom, the long-term goal is to wean the student from dependency on external controls so that she can function in integrated settings.

Regular school: Resource. Behavior disorderd students who are placed in resource settings usually exhibit milder behavior or emotional difficulties and need less academic remediation than those students placed in self-contained programs. Resource settings are one of the least restrictive settings on the continuum of services, which is an advantage to the student. While being maintained in the regular classroom for most of the day, the student can still receive individualized help in the resource room.

The ultimate goal for most behavior disordered students in resource programs is to prepare them to return and function adequately in the regular classroom. To realize this goal, the program should emphasize socialization skills and ability to function academically at a level approaching regular classroom placement. Reducing disruptive classroom behaviors and increasing independent, active learning skills are examples of program objectives that enable the student to meet this goal.

Two major types of resource room are common: categorical, which serves only one disability type of special student, in this case, behavior disordered; and cross-categorical, which serves special education students with different labels such as educable mentally retarded, learning disabled, and behavior disordered. The categorical model may be preferred by administrators and educators because it conforms to the definitions of handicapping conditions, and teachers are usually certified in one of the areas; the major advantage of the cross-categorical is that it allows grouping of children according to instructional needs and academic levels rather than handicapping condition or special education label (Wiederholt, Hammill, & Brown, 1983).

Students who are placed in a resource room spend the majority of their time in a regular classroom but are "resourced out" for periods ranging from 30 minutes to two or more hours a day. The resource teacher may have the primary responsibility for both language arts and math instruction with some students, while for others, the resource program may be limited to reading only or math only. Although the resource room ideally is supposed to supplement regular classroom instruction, it most often supplants or replaces the regular instructional program in those designated academic areas. Reasons for this replacement role are: (1) conflicts with daily scheduling between the regular class and the resource room and (2) the willingness of regular teachers to turn over their instructional responsibility to specialists. This supplanting role is one disadvantage of the resource room model. The resource teacher should promote the supplementary role whenever possible by encouraging the teacher to include the special student in regular instruction. At the very least, the resource instructional program should be coordinated with the regular classroom teacher's.

Wiederholt et al. (1983) have outlined the duties of a resource teacher and the competencies needed to accomplish such duties. According to them, the resource teacher delivers three major services to students: (1) assessment of students' educational needs, including testing and analytic teaching, (2) preparation and implementation of instructional programs, and (3) advocacy or liaison with other teachers and support personnel about the students' needs. In order to provide these services, Wiederholt et al. have identified basic competencies which include curriculum analysis, analytic teaching, organizing and managing the learning environment, and mobilizing resources within the system.

A note on accountability and credibility of resource teachers is given by Wiederholt et al. Whereas all teachers are responsible to principals, supervisors, and parents, the resource teacher is also frequently held accountable to other teachers in the school who expect information on why special education children perform and behave as they do, and what can be done about it in the regular classroom. Thus, the resource teacher is not only responsible for the resource *room* but also for a resource *program,* which encompasses a much broader role and includes acting as a resource to other teachers. To establish credibility, resource teachers must be willing to demonstrate in class the techniques or program changes they are recommending and to follow up the success or failure of such recommendations. In performing this duty, the role of the resource teacher is very similar to that of the consulting teacher.

Regular classroom with consulting services. In this setting, behavior disordered students are placed full-time in the regular classroom, and the special education teacher provides direct services to the students' teachers. As this placement represents the least restrictive environment on the continuum of services, students who are placed here have been evaluated as capable of meeting regular classroom requirements if some modifications or allowances are made. Students are often assigned to this setting under two conditions: (1) before a pullout of the regular classroom is judged to be necessary, some changes may be made in the regular classroom with the help of the consulting teacher; or (2) when a behavior disordered student already receiving services in another setting has made sufficient behavioral and academic progress, the student may be assigned to a regular class with supportive services provided by the consulting teacher. The consulting model is advantageous to the students because it is the least intrusive of all special education services and does not require the student to be pulled out of the regular classroom.

The consulting teacher is viewed as a support person and as a disseminator of information. Duties include: observation in the classroom; assessment; help with creating lesson plans, management systems, and the individual education plan; locating needed materials; in-class demonstration sessions; and suggestions for other modifications in the regular program.

Consultation focuses both on instructional and management strategies, but the latter is of more concern to teachers of many behavior disordered students. Consultation is an ongoing relationship that should be handled as a peer relationship rather than a leader-follower relationship (Montgomery, 1982), and continual follow-up with individual teachers is essential.

The role of the consulting teacher may be the most demanding because of the sensitive nature of this position within the social system of the school. As previously discussed, the school is a self-contained community with its own rules and regulations, some of which are verbalized, some of which are "understood." Montgomery (1982) offers an excellent description of some of these political realities, which include: (1) territoriality of teachers, who assume responsibility for and ownership of their assigned group of children, and (2) the view that consultants are imposed by the system rather than invited by the regular teacher and are therefore hindrances rather than helpers. Montgomery offers some suggestions for overcoming these system barriers: the consulting teacher can help overcome territoriality by consistently referring to behavior disordered students as the teacher's and by being unobtrusive when observing or visiting in the regular classroom. When observing, the consulting teacher can increase acceptance by simple courtesies such as obtaining prior permission, not taking notes, staying seated in one place rather than moving around the room, and offering the teacher positive feedback. Although the degree of involvement may vary from student to student, it is helpful to have a written job description that delineates the duties of the consulting teacher so that everyone has a clear idea of what the consulting teacher is supposed to do. The consulting teacher must be diplomatic in the truest sense of the word and must be adept at pointing out both the positive aspects of the regular program and needed modifications.

Despite support at the university level for the consulting teacher model as a viable way to integrate behavior disordered students, it has apparently not been widely adopted in the public schools (Hirshoren & Heller, 1979), and little research on its efficacy has been conducted. While some studies indicate that the consulting teacher model may be effective with mildly handicapped students (Miller & Sabatino, 1978), other research suggests that when behavior disordered students are reintegrated into regular classrooms without direct special education services, they tend to lose academic and behavioral gains (Glavin, 1973; O'Leary & Schneider, 1977). Effective consulting teacher models have been established in Minnesota (Deno & Mirkin, 1978) and in Vermont (McKenzie et al., 1970).

In summary, the placements on the continuum of services are designed to meet the needs of behavior disordered students who have different characteristics. Placement decisions are usually based on the severity of behavioral difficulties and the degree of academic deficiency exhibited by the student. However, more efficacy research on each of the models is needed. A comparison of the advantages and disadvantages of the models is presented in Table 5–1.

Teacher Expectations and Mainstreaming

In planning for an individual student, the special education teacher must address the student's potential placement or capability for movement within the continuum of services. Is it feasible to move the student from a self-contained classroom to a resource room? Or from a resource room back into the regular classroom with supportive services? If movement toward less restrictive environments is a program goal, then the special education teacher realistically must adopt an ecological stance which requires that environments be evaluated so that a match can be effected between environmental expectations and student skills.

When moving a student from one physical setting to another, the role played by significant people in those settings must be considered. The literature is replete with studies which show that behavior disordered students are consistently rated as the least accepted and the most negatively stereotyped of all exceptionalities (Haring, Stern, & Cruickshank, 1958; Kingsley, 1967; Parish, Dyck, & Kappes, 1979; Rabkin & Suchoski, 1967). One study (Vaac & Kirst, 1977) dealt specifically with the attitudes of regular classroom teachers toward mainstreaming behavior disordered students into their classrooms. With a sample of 102 respondents, Vaac and Kirst found the following beliefs: (1) that the education of behavior disordered students in special classes is superior to that provided these children in regular classes, (2) that regular classroom teachers would be unable to manage behavior disordered students in their classrooms, and (3) that these children would have a detrimental effect on the nonhandicapped children in a regular classroom setting.

Another study (Algozzine & Curran, 1979) showed that when teachers were asked to predict the school success of hypothetical behavior disordered students in a mainstream setting, their responses varied as a function of their behavioral tolerance levels. Algozzine and Curran concluded that "teachers' tolerance levels for behaviors may differentially influence their judgements about children who exhibit those behaviors" (p. 346). The authors further stated that the "goodness of fit" between teacher attitude and child behavior can "greatly influence the nature of disturbances within ecosystems" (p. 346). Algozzine and Curran believe that a careful matching between child and teacher characteristics can be a successful educational intervention.

The teacher of behavior disordered students can facilitate this matching process by identifying specific characteristics of the setting into which the student is to be mainstreamed. Which academic and social skills

TABLE 5-1. A Comparison of Settings for Behavior Disordered Students

	HOSPITALS	SPECIAL SCHOOLS (RESIDENTIAL/DAY)	SELF-CONTAINED	RESOURCE ROOM	CONSULTING SERVICES
advantages	security/protection constant availability of medical and psychological staff equipped to handle emergencies	environment tightly structured consistency between "home" and school program (residential schools only) multidisciplinary staff	small teacher-pupil ratio environment controlled by one teacher	less restrictive environment while providing indi-vidualized help	least intrusive student maintained in regular classroom
disadvantages	stigma restrictive environment total segregation loss of personal liberties	difficulty in return-ing to regular school campus segregated from non-handicapped	lack of oppor-tunity to inter-act with and model nonhandi-capped peers	sometimes supplants regular classroom curri-culum	no direct service provided

are prerequisites for successful functioning in the new setting? Is information presented primarily in lecture format or are students expected to acquire information by independent reading? Are group discussions, assignments, and projects required? Is the class grouped by ability or is everyone required to do the same level of work? How much and what kinds of individual help are available if needed? What academic-related behaviors (for example, hand-raising, on-task) are required to function smoothly? What social skills (taking turns, following rules) are required to function smoothly? These and other requirements may be determined through observation or through direct questioning of the receiving teacher(s). Most teachers are pleased to identify the crucial skills that are needed for functioning in their classrooms if the purpose for obtaining the information is to teach those skills to incoming students.

Walker and Rankin (1980) have devised an assessment instrument for the specific purpose of facilitating mainstreaming for behavior disordered students. *Assessment for Integration into Mainstream Settings* (AIMS) is designed to help identify: (1) the skills required in the receiving setting, (2) maladaptive social skills which the receiving teacher finds unacceptable, and (3) technical assistance needed by the receiving teacher in order to teach and manage the child's behavior. Walker and his associates have also developed a corresponding social skills curriculum (ACCEPTS) aimed at teaching deficient skills needed for functioning in mainstream settings. Skills taught in ACCEPTS are one of two types: those identified by teachers as critical to "successful classroom adjustment" or those which contribute to "social competence and peer acceptance." The ACCEPTS social skills curriculum is described more fully in Chapter 7.

A teacher of behavior disordered students may be employed in any one of the settings from the continuum of services. While some settings call for more specialized skills in one area, there are numerous competencies that are basic to all settings. Outside the classroom, the ability to communicate and plan cooperatively with other educators, support personnel, parents, and administrators is needed. Within the classroom, the teacher must be able to set up the appropriate physical and psychological environment, to individualize instruction through assessment and adaptation of curriculum, and to manage behavior. The next section addresses specific skills which are needed by effective educators of behavior disordered students.

Teacher Competencies for Programming

Seven major competency clusters were identified by a number of prominent teacher-educators in the field of behavior disorders:

Organization
Evaluation
Curriculum development
Instruction
Management
Reporting
Interaction

(Wood, Nelson, Gilliam, Shores, & Bullock, 1979)

For each cluster, Wood et al. brainstormed dozens of skills and then designated those considered the most critical:

I. *Organization*—ability to arrange the environment for accomplishment of given tasks
Critical Competencies: Schedule time
Design classroom—physically and psychologically
Establish a theoretical framework for instruction and management
Keep records

II. *Evaluation*—ability to secure and analyze data for decision making
Critical Competencies: Observe and record behavioral data
Use data to make instructional decisions
Choose assessment instrument appropriate to task
Design individual evaluation model in conjunction with IEP (Individual Education Plan)
Design program evaluation model

III. *Curriculum Development*—ability to secure, organize, and adapt instructional materials for instruction
Critical Competencies: Select and secure learning materials
Define appropriate curriculum
Coordinate curriculum with regular education
Sequence instruction
Write IEPs
Use evaluation data to develop and revise curricula

IV. *Instruction*—ability to interact with learners in a planned manner so that the learner accomplishes goals and objectives
Critical Competencies: Use reinforcement appropriately
Use behavioral procedures for instruction (e.g., pairing, fading, shaping)
Develop and sequence objectives

V. *Management*—ability to affect the behavior of the learner in a predetermined manner
Critical Competencies: Set rules
Clarify relationship between behavior and its consequences
Maintain consistency

Establish a continuum of positive reinforcement

Establish a hierarchy of interventions

VI. *Reporting*—ability to communicate so that the learner, parents, and other school personnel understand the content being communicated

Critical Competencies: Gather data

Summarize progress

Translate information for others

VII. *Interaction*—behaviors of receiving, responding, and valuing

Critical Competencies: Negotiate

Listen to others' points of view

Give feedback to students and parents

Establish positive interactions through mutual respect

These major competency areas are addressed at various points throughout the remainder of this text. Evaluation, curriculum development, and instruction are dealt with in Chapter 6, and management strategies are covered in Chapter 7. Reporting and interaction competencies are subsumed under communicating with parents and other community resources in Chapter 8. Organization—the ability to arrange the physical and psychological environment for optimal learning—is the focus of the remainder of this chapter.

ENVIRONMENTAL PLANNING

Need for Environmental Planning

The rationale for planning the educational environment is grounded in ecological theory, which promotes the view that ecosystems rather than individuals are disturbed. It follows that when there is disturbance in an individual's ecosystem, interventions should be applied to all facets of the ecosystem, including but not limited to the individual. As defined in Chapter 4, facets of an ecosystem include people, objects, time, space, and psychological variables. The one who intervenes is searching for changes that will increase the fit between an individual and other facets of her ecosystem.

Many early residential programs for behavior disordered children and adolescents were founded upon the principle of treatment through a well-planned, controlled environment, which made allowances for disturbing youngsters. Based on the work of English psychiatrists and of Bettelheim in this country, Redl popularized the concept of a *therapeutic milieu* in residential settings (Newcomer, 1980). As Redl (1959a) conceptualized the therapeutic milieu, the environment is carefully planned for treatment purposes, but also includes the individual's "natural" relationships and activities. If the therapeutic milieu does not approximate the natural environment of the child, then potential gains made by the child may be easily lost once she is removed from the setting.

Redl (1959a) outlined 12 variables that are important components of a therapeutic milieu in a residential setting. The components most applicable to public school programming are:

(1) *Social structure and value system.* The quality of interpersonal relationships and the values that are communicated by the teacher help set the tone for learning and behavior.

(2) *Routine.* Routine and rules can be used advantageously to promote not only security but also accommodation of child-to-environment.

(3) *Trait clusters.* Individual personality traits are considered real and valid variables in the milieu and are taken into consideration when planning activities.

(4) *Activity structure.* The type and number of activities that a student is asked to do are an important part of the therapeutic treatment plan.

(5) *Space, equipment, time, and props.* Structure and continuity are provided by efficient scheduling and by the teacher's sense of timing within the schedule: the teacher must know when to abandon an activity or postpone disciplinary action. The physical arrangement, including use of space and equipment, is also used to set expectations for behavior and learning.

(6) *System of umpiring services and traffic regulations between child and environment.* The teacher may have to interpret situations to a child either for protection reasons or to foster growth and understanding.

Although the specific components of a therapeutic milieu may vary according to setting and according to the needs of the individuals it serves, the concept is applicable to all programs for behavior disordered students. Broadly defined, a therapeutic milieu is one in which every facet of the environment is carefully planned to enhance academic and emotional growth.

In a classroom setting for behavior disordered students, the details of the environment may vary with the individual teacher's theoretical orientation and personal preference; however, the importance of *organization* and *structure* in the physical arrangement has been established. Behavior disordered students often come from chaotic environments in which they find it difficult to function; they often cannot read the environment, do not know what is expected of them, and have difficulty in predicting the consequences of their own behavior. They vary widely in their individual needs, but it has been established that the majority lack organizational skills and therefore need to have their environment highly structured and organized for them (Bullock, 1981; P.A. Gallagher, 1979; Haring & Phillips, 1962; Hewett, 1968). According to P.A. Gallagher (1979), *structure* is a clear relationship between curriculum materials, teacher instruction, room furnishings, and the student's expected response. Thus, structure has both physical and psychological connotations. The physical environment is defined by the arrangement of the classroom, including use of space, equipment, and props. The psychological environment is defined by variables such as teacher expectations, which are communicated through scheduling, feedback, and rules. It is the physical environment to which we first turn our attention.

Physical Environment

Use of space, equipment, and props. Most special educators recommend that classroom design be based on the concept of activity areas or learning centers. Bullock (1981) indicates that the ideal classroom for behavior disordered students should provide six designated areas. Each area should be physically separate and distinctly marked; expectations for the work to be done in each area are also clearly communicated. The six separate areas are: (1) for individual work, (2) for group work, (3) time-out, (4) a reinforcement area, (5) a work basket area where individual assignments are distributed and collected, and (6) a facilitative instruction area where special equipment is available for experiments and discovery learning (see Figure 5–2). Although the number and type of centers can be varied according to student needs, teacher preference, and available space, the structure provided by clearly designated areas is an important facet of programming. Another model classroom design based on the

FIGURE 5–2. Sample Floor Plan for a Resource Room

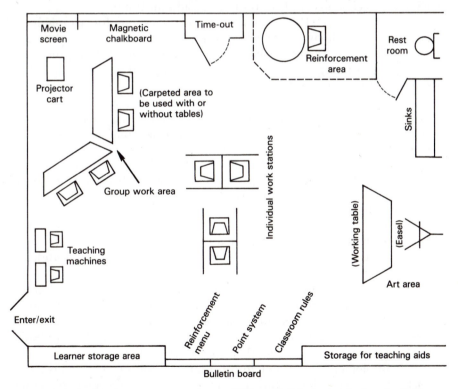

From Lyndal M. Bullock, *Educational Interventions for Children with Behavioral and/or Learning Problems.* Gainesville, FL: Florida Educational Research and Development Council, Vol. 10, Number 2, Winter, 1976. Reproduced with permission.

center concept (Hewett, 1968) is outlined in more detail at the end of this chapter.

Other professionals have offered helpful hints on the optimal organization of the classroom for behavior disordered students. Hewett and Taylor (1980) have outlined several general factors which should be considered when planning the physical arrangement:

(1) the number of students to be in the room at one time
(2) the number of adults, their schedules, and responsibilities
(3) possibilities and flexibility of furniture arrangement
(4) traffic flow
(5) acoustics inside and outside the room
(6) lighting and windows in the room
(7) number of electric outlets.

Hewett and Taylor suggest that the closer the room is to the "hub of the school" or the center of activity, the more accepted and less stigmatized it will be. If close to the principal's offices, the special class may be viewed as having the acceptance and support of the administration.

P.A. Gallagher (1979) has numerous suggestions for arranging an environment conducive to good work and study habits. In *Teaching Students with Behavior Disorders,* she gives guidelines for planning the classroom, programming, scheduling, and selecting and adapting materials. Examples of specifics are:

(1) use of U-shaped tables for group work with primary students
(2) use of attractive, artistic mobiles to designate functional areas of the classroom
(3) use of kitchen timers to structure individual work assignments
(4) use of labels on student possessions to avoid squabbling over ownership
(5) use of a large clock (with Arabic numerals) placed in a strategic place to avoid confusion over time and schedules.

The reader is referred to Gallagher for a very basic and practical text on how to set up a classroom and program for behavior disordered students.

Guidelines for maintaining physical consistency. Shores (1981) reiterates the importance of structure and consistency in the classroom for behavior disordered students. He defines physical consistency as providing students with a dependable physical environment which aids them in learning the relationship between their behavior and its consequences. In order to implement and maintain consistency, Shores recommends use of cubicles for independent study assignments and use of centers for designated group activities. Expectations for appropriate behavior in each setting are clearly defined. As with Montgomery's (1982) recommendation that the program accommodate individuals as they become more responsible, Shores indicates that the more self-control a student exhibits, the more latitude she may be allowed within the class. Rules and consequences stay the same, but the teacher may allow more individual freedom of movement and more choices within the program's limits.

Shores has identified a number of inconsistencies in the classroom that could interfere with learning (see Table 5–2). Although some of the situations may seem rather obvious, each of us can likely remember when, as learners, we were exposed to these exact situations. Such situations usually occur because of acts of omission or carelessness on the part of the teacher, but they are particularly important to avoid with behavior disordered students for two reasons: (1) the students are likely to have a low frustration tolerance and a history of frustration with academic tasks and teachers, and (2) they are seeking to establish a reliable relationship between their behavior and its consequences, which is undermined by inconsistencies and unpredictability in the learning environment. It may be helpful for the teacher to keep a checklist such as the one in Table 5–2 and to periodically review the program for inconsistencies.

Psychological Environment

The previous section on the physical environment highlighted the importance of physical structure in classrooms for the behavior disordered. Consistency or predictability was also stressed as a means for these students to establish a connection between their behavior and its consequences. In addition, the teacher should seek to maintain psychological consistency throughout the program by establishing clear expectations and guidelines for student behavior. The teacher can communicate ex-

TABLE 5–2. Possible Inconsistencies in the Classroom

Chairs and furniture arranged in a manner not conducive to learning activities
Positioning of audiovisual aids so that some students cannot see as well as necessary
Seating arrangement of students such that it is not conducive to appropriate behavior
Scheduling of difficult or frustrating activities in the afternoon
Specific areas of the room *not* designated for specific tasks
No schedule of events that remains consistent from day to day
Writing on the chalkboard when there is a glare
Reading groups placed too closely together
Cluttered activity areas
Rearranging learning materials without adequate notice given to students
Changing schedules without giving adequate notice to students
Broken equipment
Mistakes in printed material

From R.E. Shores, *Environmental consistency*. Project S.E.D., Teacher Training Module. Austin, TX: Education Service Center, Region XIII, 1981. Reprinted with permission of the author.

pectations through scheduling and providing feedback; guidelines for behavior can be established through setting and enforcing rules.

Scheduling. Behavior disordered students may easily become overwhelmed by the demands of the environment; in the classroom, they are often poor organizers of time and materials. Scheduling provides a routine that helps them to structure their time and materials more efficiently and to predict what will be required of them during the course of the day.

P.A. Gallagher (1979) views scheduling as comprehensive, systematic planning for behavior disordered students "so that their work is accomplished in an organized manner toward a final goal, which for many students is their return to the mainstream of peer group activities" (p. 229). Thus, scheduling underlies all academic planning as a means for moving the student from dependence on individualized instruction and adapted curriculum to more independent functioning in a regular curriculum. The importance of this comprehensive aspect of scheduling cannot be overemphasized; however, attention to daily scheduling helps to organize teacher and student expectations for performance in concrete terms on a short-term basis.

Hewett (Hewett & Taylor, 1980) has established a schedule for behavior disordered students which fits his personal theoretical framework. In Hewett's model classroom, periods of time each day are scheduled specifically for activities which correspond to levels in his proposed hierarchy of learning skills. For example, Hewett recommends an exploratory period immediately after lunch during which students can work cooperatively on art, science, or other projects; "exploratory" is the fourth skill level in his learning hierarchy (see page 137).

P.A. Gallagher (1979) offers several guidelines for scheduling which she thinks are especially important during the students' initial months in the special program. Some of these guidelines are:

(1)   Provide a daily schedule for each student. Daily schedules may be arranged by time periods or by subject area. Assignments should be listed on the schedule, which may then be kept by the teacher as a progress report.

(2)   Schedule work that can be completed in one day; require students to finish one task before beginning another. Adherence to these guidelines promotes a sense of accomplishment through successful completion of assigned work. This tactic is especially important for behavior disordered students who may feel overwhelmed by what they perceive as too much work or unreasonable demands.

(3)   Alternate preferred (high-probability) tasks with less-preferred (low-probability) tasks. A student should be asked to do the least-preferred activity first and then reinforced by being allowed to do the more preferred activity. This principle applies both to academics and nonacademics. Some students have no preferred academic subject; with these students, their favorite nonacademic activity should be used as the preferred task.

(4)   Provide time reminders. Many students have difficulty in organizing the alloted time for a specific assignment or activity. The teacher can use verbal cues or kitchen timers, or can require older students to monitor themselves on specific tasks.

Providing feedback.   Another factor in maintaining consistency in the classroom is teacher feedback (Bullock, 1981; P.A. Gallagher, 1979; Shores, 1981). Many behavior disordered students need almost constant reassurance that they are performing adequately. Feedback may be as general as registering approval or disapproval for a behavior, or it may be a specific, step-by-step critique of behavior or academic performance. Whenever possible, it should be presented in a positive manner. Hewett's check mark system is a systematic form of feedback that is built into the daily schedule at frequent intervals (see page 138). Whatever form it takes, teacher feedback gives the student an unmistakable cue as to the appropriateness of performance.

Feedback in the form of teacher approval or disapproval to student responses has been shown to be very powerful; in fact, some researchers believe that ability to praise appropriate student responses may be *the* most important teacher competency, and that it is the foundation for successful educational programming (Shores, 1981). It is also well known that not all students are rewarded by teacher praise or approval; with such students, positive teacher comments should be paired with other events known to reinforce the student. Whatever technique is used, the teacher of behavior disordered students should make an effort to provide continual feedback so that the student is constantly reminded of expectations and is less likely to misjudge his performance in the classroom.

Setting and enforcing rules.   Gilliam (1981b) has described rule-setting in classrooms for the behavior disordered.[1] According to Gilliam, rules are statements that regulate our conduct by specifying behaviors which will be rewarded and behaviors which will be punished. Rules are a function of society and the various agents of socialization, namely, courts, churches, schools, parents, and other sources of authority. Rules are intended to infuse some sense of order into society so that daily living is easier and more predictable. Human behavior is guided by rules that allow us to anticipate consequences and to make decisions and plans. Rules are a necessary component of psychological consistency in the classroom.

In schools, most rules are intended to establish and preserve an atmosphere of learning: behavior that interferes with a student's ability to learn, with other students' ability to learn, or the teacher's ability to teach is not allowed. The exact number of rules needed for a classroom varies with the age and intellectual abilities of the students. With students who are younger or less capable, a few highly specific rules are needed. The various settings for which rules are made should also be specified: classroom, playground, cafeteria, hall, and so forth.

Effective rules meet three standards: They are *definite, reasonable,* and *enforceable. Definite* rules are stated in clear, concise terms that leave no room for interpretation. Students must know immediately if the rule has been broken. *Reasonable* rules are attainable; that is, students have the ability to comply. If rules are not reasonable, students become frustrated in trying to comply and teachers become frustrated in trying to enforce them. In *enforceable* rules, the behaviors are explicitly defined and the behaviors are observable. In addition, the teacher must be in a position to observe and enforce all rules without depending on witnesses.

Well-stated rules are of little value if not consistently enforced. Enforcement is often very difficult with behavior disordered students who exhibit extreme behaviors and are continuously testing limits by pushing both the teacher and classroom rules. However, consistent application of consequences actually helps the student become more secure by making the environment more predictable. If a student is successful in talking the teacher out of enforcing rules just once, then the student's manipulation is rewarded and the behavior will likely occur again.

In summary, the teacher of behavior disordered students must be aware of the need for environmental planning in providing optimal learning conditions. Important variables are the physical arrangement of the classroom and psychological consistency which can be provided through schedules, feedback, and rules. Let us look at how one model classroom incorporates these variables into its design.

A Model: Hewett's Orchestrated Classroom

Hewett's (1968) classroom design[2] for behavior disordered students demonstrates how structure and organization can be built into every facet of a program and how a personal theoretical orientation can be translated into both physical and psychological components of the classroom. Developed in the mid-sixties in Santa Monica, California, Hewett's experimental classroom design has been variously called the Santa Monica Project, the engineered classroom, and, more recently, the orchestrated classroom. The design is based on behavioral principles; its major emphasis is teaching behavior disordered individuals how to become effective students by developing appropriate skills for learning and getting along with others in the classroom.

Theoretical bases. One theoretical basis for the orchestrated classroom is the learning triangle: Hewett views the learning process as a three-sided affair, with curriculum (tasks), conditions (structure), and consequences (reward) interacting to form the three sides. All aspects of the program may be traced to this concept, which, translated into daily practice, means that the teacher (1) assigns the individual a task within his capabilities, (2) specifies the amount of time and/or number of problems to be completed, and (3) specifies the reward for completion or consequences of noncompletion.

A second theoretical basis for the program is a sequence of educational goals that are both developmental and hierarchical in nature; that is, skills at each step build upon skills acquired at earlier levels. Hewett provides detailed descriptions of the behaviors required of learners at each step and a rating scale for the behaviors. Each student is evaluated and placed at the appropriate functioning level in the hierarchy. The levels are:

(1) *attention*—ability to focus on relevant cues in the environment

(2) *response*—becoming actively involved in learning by making some type of response

(3) *order*—attending and responding in a systematic fashion

(4) *exploratory*—initiating learning by exploring the environment

(5) *social*—valuing and gaining the approval of others in the school environment

(6) *mastery*—gaining competency in basic academic subjects and functional living skills.

Work centers.   The six levels of learning competence form the basis for the arrangement of the classroom into four centers. The Order Center encompasses the first three levels of the hierarchy: attention, response, and order. This center consists of a couple of tables in a corner of the room where distractions can be kept at a minimum. Skills emphasized here are participation, following directions, and task completion. The Exploratory Center (exploratory level) offers art and science activities; it is stocked with materials that encourage creativity, artistic expression, and experimentation. The Communication Center (social level) is to be used by two or more students at the same time so that social interaction occurs. A record player with headphones is provided, as are cooperative games and activities that minimize competition and maximize turn-taking. The Mastery Center (mastery level) includes the students' desks, a teaching station for small-group instruction, and two study booths that are used when a student needs a more individualized, less distracting setting in which to finish an assignment. Thus, the floor plan of the classroom is dictated by the centers and the activities to be performed at each. As advocated by Hewett and other theorists, the expectations for tasks and behaviors at each center are clearly communicated to the students. Similarities between these centers and those suggested by Bullock are apparent.

Consequences: The check mark system. Consequences are delivered through a reinforcement system of check marks that are recorded on each student's individual work record card. Checks are given for efficient student behaviors such as starting to work, observing classroom rules, respecting the work rights of others, and completing tasks. The giving of checks is very systematic: each class hour is divided into three 15-minute work periods and three 5-minute periods during which check marks are awarded. Bonus points for trying—regardless of outcome—may be given at the teacher's discretion.

Completed work record cards may be exchanged for rewards ranging from candy or other edible reinforcers to privileges and free time in the classroom. The reinforcement and exchange system need not be elaborate; the main point is that students learn that their efforts and accomplishments are systematically recognized, which leads them to establish a connection between behavior and consequences. Appropriate student behaviors are constantly reinforced.

Scheduling. Hewett plans very detailed schedules for daily activities (refer to *The Emotionally Disturbed Child in the Classroom,* Hewett & Taylor, 1980). The basics of a typical six-hour day are as follows:

first 15 minutes of day	(1)	Order task—students are assigned a short task that has a definite beginning and end; the purpose is to get them attending, focusing, and responding
until noon	(2)	Basic academic instruction periods— reading, arithmetic, language arts
after lunch	(3)	Listening—teacher reads to class for 20 minutes
50 minutes	(4)	Exploratory period—art, science, communication tasks
20 minutes	(5)	Physical education
40 minutes	(6)	Group and individual activities— music, sharing, group discussion

To summarize, Hewett's model of the orchestrated classroom is an example of how an educational philosophy can be incorporated into a total classroom design. Hewett's belief in the need for organization and structure is exemplified by the use of centers that dictates the floor plan, the check mark system that reinforces appropriate student behavior and emphasizes individual responsibility for learning, and the role of the teacher who must plan curriculum and materials, daily work assignments, and the reinforcement system. The entire program is oriented toward student accomplishment, whether it be task completion or merely exhibiting appropriate student behaviors.

SUMMARY

The teacher of behavior disordered students may be offered employment in one of a number of settings, ranging from restrictive environments such as a hospital day school to mainstream environments such as a resource room. Although the teacher's role varies somewhat from setting to setting, there are basic teacher competencies required of all teachers of behavior disordered students, regardless of setting. One of the most crucial teacher competencies is the ability to plan a learning environment which is both physically and psychologically consistent. Effective use of space, equipment, time, feedback, and rules provides a structure that clearly defines expectations for student behavior and performance. Structure and consistency are particularly important for the classroom success of behavior disordered students who, in the past, often have encountered inconsistent expectations and demands for behavior. Hewett's orchestrated classroom is offered as a model which demonstrates the essential components of a structured classroom.

KEY POINTS

(1) A continuum of special education services is designed to accommodate variation in students' academic and behavioral needs.

(2) More restrictive settings such as hospitals and special schools offer highly controlled environments that are needed by some behavior disordered students.

(3) While offering more social integration with the nonhandicapped population, less restrictive settings such as resource rooms provide less direct academic and behavioral support to students.

(4) The teacher who plans to mainstream behavior disordered students into less restrictive environments must assess and teach the skills needed to function successfully in that environment.

(5) An effective learning environment in any of these settings depends upon the teacher's ability to provide clear standards for student performance.

(6) Physical structure is provided through the well-planned use of space, equipment, and materials.

(7) Psychological structure is provided by arranging a daily schedule, providing feedback, and enforcing rules.

(8) Hewett's orchestrated classroom demonstrates both types of structure through use of scheduling, work centers, and a check mark system.

ADDITIONAL READINGS

Framework for considering some issues in special eduction, by M.C. Reynolds. *Exceptional Children*, 1962, *28*, 367–370, for Reynolds' conceptualization of a continuum of services (Cascade Model) for the handicapped.

Chapters 3, 4, 5, 11, and 12 of *Inside special education*, by K. Howell. Columbus, OH: Chas. E. Merrill, 1983, for a candid report on what it's *really* like to be involved in numerous special education settings.

Emotionally disturbed children and regular classroom teachers, by N.A. Vaac & N. Kirst. *Elementary School Journal*, 1977, *77*, 309–317, for a study of regular classroom teachers' attitudes toward mainstreaming behavior disordered students into their classrooms.

Chapter 9, Milieu therapy, by P.L. Newcomer. In *Understanding and teaching emotionally disturbed children*. Boston: Allyn & Bacon, 1980, for an overview of the therapeutic milieu and its application to school settings.

Selected chapters in *Teaching students with behavior disorders*, by P. Gallagher. Denver: Love, 1979, for specific information on arranging the physical and psychological environment of a classroom for the behavior disordered.

NOTES

[1]This section on rules and rule-setting is adapted from Gilliam (1981b) and is used with the author's permission.

[2]From Frank M. Hewett and Frank D. Taylor, *The Emotionally Disturbed Child in the Classroom: The Orchestration of Success*, Second Edition. © 1980 by Allyn & Bacon, Inc. Used with permission.

six

Assessment
and Instruction

Achievement and Behavior Disorders

Assessment:
 Informal Techniques
 Study Skills Assessment
 Observation Techniques

Instruction:
 Curriculum Planning
 Individualizing
 Adapting Materials

---

orientation

They (teachers) need to learn the *process* of education. It goes from when you first see the student, through careful assessment, careful identification of the problems the student has, all the way to presenting the lesson and monitoring its effect. The whole area of identification and assessment of student problems is essential. I'm not talking about giving labels. I'm asking "Does Johnny know his add facts, does Sally say the alphabet, does Charlie do calculus, does Ann Marie know how to spell?" Those are the kinds of questions that I think teachers should ask and be able to answer carefully.... They must select or prepare curriculum and instructional strategies from that.... After assessment comes curriculum.... Do you know how to ascertain whether that reading material you have in your classroom is really any good, or whether it's suitable for the students you have? You must know how to prepare curriculum for the school because no reading series, no math series, no spelling book is ever going to have everything a teacher will need.*

OVERVIEW

For many behavior disordered students, the classroom is a forum for failure. As Kauffman states, "Many children do not develop behavior disorders until after they enter school, and for these children one must

---

*Conversation with Marie Eaton, from *Inside Special Education*, by Kenneth Howell, Columbus, OH: Charles E. Merrill, 1983, p. 249.

consider the possibility that the school experience is a primary factor in the origin of their difficulty" (1977, p. 115). To help these students break the failure cycle, educators must recognize the frustration involved in continued academic failure and the necessity of individualizing academic programs. This chapter first addresses the relationship between achievement and behavior disorders, then offers a framework for individualizing through informal assessment, curriculum planning, and adaptation of curricular materials. In order to illustrate this assessment and planning process, a case study of a behavior disordered student is presented at the end of the chapter.

ACHIEVEMENT AND ASSESSMENT OF BEHAVIOR DISORDERED STUDENTS

Achievement and Behavior Disorders

Failure to achieve in school is one of the major characteristics of behavior disordered students (Bower, 1961; Glavin & Annesley, 1972; Kauffman, 1977). Even when compared to expected achievement based on mental age, the majority of behavior disordered students show academic retardation on measures of reading and arithmetic (Bower, 1969; Graubard, 1964; Motto & Wilkins, 1968; Stone & Rowley, 1964). Some investigators have sought to determine whether behavior disordered students experience more difficulty in one academic area than another (Cawley & Webster, 1981; Glavin & Annesley, 1972; Motto & Wilkins, 1968), but results are mixed, and at present, inconclusive. However, after reviewing the studies that assess the relationship between age and academic retardation of behavior disordered students, Cullinan, Epstein, and Lloyd (1983) concluded that "the academic deficit of a student with behavior disorders would be expected to grow larger over time, unless there is powerful intervention" (1983, p. 257).

Unfortunately, research to date has not clarified the complex relationship between learning and emotionality. However, Cullinan et al. (1983) have grouped the research linking achievement and behavior disorders into four explanatory categories: ability deficits, emotional blocks, faulty learning, and miscellaneous views.

Ability deficits. Although scores on intelligence measures among behavior disordered students have ranged from significantly below average to gifted (Morse, Cutler, & Fink, 1964; Motto & Wilkins, 1968; Stone & Rowley, 1964), a review by Kauffman (1981) suggests that the majority of behavior disordered students show average to low average scores on intelligence measures. According to Kauffman, a hypothetical frequency distribution for IQ scores of behavior disordered students (excluding severely disturbed or psychotic) would yield a mean or average score of 90 to 95. However, these statistics do not account for the level of academic retardation experienced by this population; as mentioned previously, behavior disordered students make a poor showing even when compared to expected achievement based on IQ scores.

In addition to consideration of general intellectual functioning, some researchers have assessed the relationship between learning disabilities and behavior disorders. After reviewing the literature, Cullinan et al. (1983) conclude that although learning disabled students often exhibit behavior problems, the evidence is sparse that behavior disordered students exhibit specific learning disabilities. From available studies, the conclusion may be drawn that intellectual or cognitive differences cannot wholly account for the academic difficulties experienced by behavior disordered students.

Emotional blocks to learning. It is often difficult to distinguish whether an emotional block arises because of learning problems or whether learning problems are in fact a symptom of emotional difficulties. Hawke and Lesser (1977) have differentiated between primary factors—those which initially cause learning problems, and secondary factors—those which are complicating factors in an existing learning disorder. According to Hawke and Lesser, primary emotional factors such as chronic anxiety, chronic depression, and family discord may indirectly cause underachievement because of the student's preoccupation with events unrelated to school and the resulting inability to concentrate on academics. In contrast, secondary emotional factors such as a generalized inferiority complex or negativism are learned responses to repeated failure and inability to meet standards imposed by others. Regardless of the causal relationship, most behavior disordered students do have a history of failure and a repertoire of emotional defenses against pressure to achieve.

Faulty learning. Failure to learn may be caused by student factors or by teacher factors. In order to achieve, students must play the "student" role by complying with classroom rules and teacher expectations. Students who fail to exhibit proper student behaviors usually fall far behind in academics. Teachers may contribute to faulty learning by failing to arrange the proper learning environment and failing to evaluate the effectiveness of their own teaching practices.

Miscellaneous views. A catchall category offers various other explanations of the relationship between achievement and behavior disorders. Under "miscellaneous views" are:

(1) Biological causes. Biological factors such as genetic abnormalities, brain damage, or diet deficiencies interfere with general intellectual functioning, resulting in poor achievement.

(2) Ecological causes. A misfit between child and environment causes the child to be labeled as deviant and therefore the child *becomes* both academically and behaviorally deviant.

(3) School causes. Characteristics of the school environment, including insensitivity to individual differences, inappropriate teacher expectations, and inconsistent management may contribute significantly to student underachievement.

Any of these factors—ability deficits, emotional blocks, faulty learning, biological causes, ecological factors, or school factors—could contribute to the learning problems of behavior disordered students. In the early years of educational programming for these students, the prevailing belief was that students' emotional blocks must be identified and resolved before students could be expected to benefit from academic instruction. Programs based on such beliefs provided little structure for academic learning but did provide an atmosphere of warmth and support in which damaged egos and self-concepts could be repaired. Educators soon learned that such laissez-faire classroom environments did little to help behavior disordered students overcome their difficulties, either academically or behaviorally. The philosophy of "treatment before academic instruction" has been more or less reversed, as educators have begun to view academic competence as a means for improving self-concept and fostering emotional development. Hence, educators currently consider achievement a viable avenue for improving self-esteem, and both academic and socioemotional needs are essential considerations for program planning.

Assessment: Testing for Teaching

Another essential feature of programming for behavior disordered students is individualization, which is accomplished through adoption of specialized instructional programs and/or through a clinical teaching system. Special instructional programs were initially developed for children with severe reading disabilities and were pioneered in the 1920s and 1930s by Fernald (1943) and Gillingham and Stillman (1966). Fernald developed a multisensory methodology for teaching new words to adolescents who had essentially no word recognition skills. Her work is especially noteworthy because of her interest in the emotional aspects of reading difficulties. In order to alleviate pressure to perform in reading, Fernald (1943) listed four conditions to be avoided: (1) calling attention to emotionally loaded situations by pressuring or pleading with the student to try harder, (2) using methods with which the student has already failed, (3) subjecting the student to conspicuous or embarrassing situations by singling the student out of a group or asking the student to work on age-inappropriate materials, and (4) calling attention to the student's failures rather than his successes and progress. By combining her step-by-step technique with these and other principles, Fernald was successful in teaching word-learning skills to many children and adolescents with severe reading problems.

Several decades later, in 1967, Johnson and Myklebust devised the *clinical teaching method,* an individualized approach based on observational information used to modify behavior and plan instruction. Diagnostic information offered by parents, psychologists, and other specialists is also used in planning. According to Johnson and Myklebust (1967), the clinical teaching model stresses the specialist role of the teacher as someone who is not only sophisticated in the psychology and neurology of learning but who is also able to identify strengths and weaknesses of individual students and to adjust the curriculum accordingly. The two major components of clinical teaching are the gathering of specific, objective information and the tailoring of instruction to meet the student's needs. In clinical teaching, the teacher adapts to the child's identified needs instead of expecting the child to fit time-honored teaching methods and curriculum.

Examples of other clinical or diagnostic teaching methodologies are *applied behavioral analysis* (Lovitt, 1975), *precision teaching* (Kunzelmann, Cohen, Hulten, Martin, & Mingo, 1970: Lindsley, 1971), and *prescriptive teaching* (Peters, 1965). These techniques vary in the amount of structure and precision that is required in their application; applied behavioral analysis is the most precise and clinical teaching, the least precise (Wiederholt et al., 1983). These techniques and the specific instructional systems such as those developed by Fernald also share several commonalities. According to Brown and Botel (1972), each of these systems requires: attention and active learner involvement, planned success experiences, consistent positive reinforcement and immediate feedback for the learner, overlearning of basic response units, multisensory stimuli and/or responses, interpersonal involvement, and confidence of the teacher and/or student in the methodology.

In addition, each of the clinical methodologies follows a basic sequence of steps: (1) establishment of an instructional objective or behavioral goal, (2) assessment of student skills and deficiencies pertinent to the objective, (3) prescription of a specific plan for teaching the objective, and (4) evaluation of success. The last step is especially important because of its emphasis on the success or failure of the plan rather than the success or failure of the student. The basic assumption of these techniques is that if a student fails to learn, the teacher must modify either the objective or the manner and/or sequence in which instructional steps are taught.

Informal Assessment Techniques

In order to implement an individualized program, the teacher must possess a repertoire of assessment skills. The knowledge that a student is eight years old, is in the third grade, and scored at grade level 2.3 on a standardized measure of reading achievement gives the teacher little insight on where to begin instruction or how to proceed. For proper instructional planning, the teacher must determine which skills the student has mastered and which skills the student has yet to master.

A variety of informal assessment techniques may be used in gathering this information. As explained by McLoughlin and Lewis (1981), teachers use informal assessment procedures every day when observing students at work in the classroom, when trying to find a pattern of errors in a spelling paper, or when asking a student how she solved a math problem. The term *informal assessment* is used here to denote activities for gathering information upon which to base instructional plans for individual students. In contrast to *formal assessment,* which is the use of standardized measures for comparison of an individual to his age group or some other standard, the purpose of informal assessment is to identify strengths and weaknesses within the individual. This difference may also be conceptualized as external versus internal evaluation, or as *inter*individual versus *intra*individual comparison. In informal assessment, specific skill deficits are targeted for instruction and remediation by the teacher. Among the most popular and useful informal assessment techniques are error analysis, task analysis, and criterion-referenced tests. Each of these is explored in the following section, along with study skills assessment and observation techniques.

In instructional planning for an individual, there are three basic points at which these assessment techniques are needed: (1) to ascertain initial placement in the curriculum, (2) to identify problems in moving through the curriculum, and (3) to monitor or document progress. Table 6–1 shows the primary relationship between these assessment junctures and the various informal assessment techniques. Although an assessment technique may be used for more than one purpose, the teacher should always have a specific purpose for assessing an individual and should

TABLE 6–1.   PURPOSES OF INFORMAL ASSESSMENT TECHNIQUES

INITIAL PLACEMENT	PROBLEMS IN MOVING THROUGH THE CURRICULUM	PROGRESS[a]
observation	observation	criterion-
checklists	checklists	referenced
criterion-referenced	error analysis	measures
measures	task analysis	

[a]Formal assessment measures (norm-referenced tests) also are often used to document progress.

attempt to match the technique with the type of data that is needed. For example, criterion-referenced testing is appropriate for initial placement and for monitoring progress because it yields information on mastery of specific learning objectives. The reader is referred to *Educational Assessment of Learning Problems* (Wallace & Larsen, 1978) and to *Assessing Special Students* (McLoughlin & Lewis, 1981) for excellent coverage of these and other informal assessment procedures.

Error analysis. Error analysis is an informal assessment technique that has been utilized by conscientious teachers for years. It can be applied to any subject area in which a written product or work sample is produced. The teacher simply checks the work sample for errors, categorizes the errors, then looks for a pattern among errors. Error analysis is based upon the assumption that the majority of children's errors are not haphazard; rather, they are indicative of a missing link, a particular misconception, or lack of information on the part of the child. Error analysis is an attempt to find the missing link so that the problem can be remediated. Table 6–2 shows an actual error analysis that was part of a math evaluation for a second grader. In this case, the student showed knowledge of math facts (except in problem *c*), but consistently subtracted the smaller number from the larger number, regardless of which number was the stated subtrahend in the problem. Error analysis in this case immediately leads to the hypothesis that this student does not understand regrouping in subtraction and likely does not fully grasp the concept of place value. This error analysis should be followed up with specific questions and problems involving the concept of place value and then with instruction in regrouping in subtraction.

Task analysis. Task analysis is based on the behavioral principle of specifying successive approximations (small, sequential steps) toward reaching a goal. According to McLoughlin and Lewis (1981), task analysis is a tool for assessment and instructional planning. It serves an assessment function when it is used with a specific task with which a student experiences difficulty; the task is broken down into a series of subtasks, and the

TABLE 6–2. Error Analysis of Subtraction Problems for a Second Grader

(A) ✓ 6 −2 = 4   (B) ✓ 9 −4 = 5   (C) 46 −13 = 34   (D) ✓ 16 −4 = 12

(E) 22 −18 = 16   (F) 380 −96 = 316   (G) 500 −402 = 102

subtask that poses difficulty for the student is specified. Task analysis serves an instructional planning function when the teacher breaks down an objective or a learning task into smaller, teachable units. With lower functioning students who are either young or severely handicapped, task analysis is likely to be used routinely for instructional planning as a method of sequencing and implementing curriculum. With higher functioning students, it is likely to be used for assessment of specific skill deficits in problem areas.

The general steps to task analysis are:

(1)   State the task or objective in behavioral terms.

(2)   Break down the task into a hierarchy of prerequisite skills; include entry-level skills.

(3)   Determine the order or sequence of the skills.

(4)   Teach each step in the skills hierarchy.

(5)   Provide feedback to the student.

The steps of task analysis should always be discrete and sequential: each step should differ in at least one definable or observable element, and each step should be appropriately placed in the hierarchy of skills that build upon one another until the final objective is attained (Myers & Hammill, 1982). According to McLoughlin and Lewis (1981), subskills may be sequenced either according to *time* (for example, putting shoe on foot before lacing) or according to *difficulty* (for example, learning to recall facts from reading passages before learning to make inferences). An example of task analysis is presented in Table 6–3.

Task analysis can be applied to most learning objectives, tasks, and curricula. If done properly, it is time-consuming but can be quite helpful in specifying steps to be taught next. It has been used very successfully in teaching self-help skills, prevocational, and vocational skills to the severely handicapped. It has also been applied successfully to mathematics instruction because of the discrete and sequential nature of math skills.

Criterion-referenced testing.   In criterion-referenced testing, a child's performance is measured against an absolute or a specific predetermined criterion (Wallace & Larsen, 1978). In contrast to norm-referenced testing, in which students are compared to a norm or a standard based on others' performances (such as grade level), criterion-referenced testing does not yield comparisons among students. Rather, an instructional objective is set, a criterion for mastery is decided, and a student is evaluated against the criterion: the student has either mastered the criterion or has yet to master it. In criterion-referenced testing, each item serves as an instructional objective and therefore each item has direct applicability to instruction.

TABLE 6–3.   Task Analysis

OBJECTIVE: Upon request and without a model, Jon will legibly
               print his first name.
PREREQUISITE SKILLS: Ability to hold a pencil and to execute straight,
               circular, and semicircular lines
SEQUENCE OF SKILLS:

1. Given a printed model with boldface letters, traces over
   each letter. Example:

   Jon

2. Given a printed model with the letter "J" in dotted lines
   and "on" in boldface, traces over each letter.

   ⸚Jon

3. Given a printed model with the letter "J" omitted, prints
   "J" and traces "on."

   —on

4. Given a model with "J" omitted and "o" in dotted lines, prints
   "J" and traces "on."

   — ⸚n

5. Given a model with "Jo" omitted and "n" in dotted lines,
   prints "Jo" and traces "n."

   ——⸚

6. Given three blanks, prints "Jon" legibly.

   — — —

7. Given no model, prints "Jon" legibly.

Criterion-referenced tests are commercially available from publishers, but many teachers choose to construct their own measures based on a favored curriculum or a particular skills sequence. Howell, Kaplan, and O'Connell (1979) suggest these simple steps: choose a specific skill or ability, then write a performance objective describing the skill and how it would be evaluated. Howell et al. (1979) further propose that the performance objective include:

1. what the student must do
2. under what conditions the student will perform
3. how well the student must do to pass (mastery).
Example: When given a list of ten sight words from the Scott Foresman
           primer, the student will correctly pronounce at least eight of ten.

The teacher is cautioned to exercise flexibility in setting criteria. If a child fails to meet an established criterion, then the teacher must decide whether: (1) the student needs more work to master it or (2) the criterion is too difficult or inappropriate (Hallahan & Kauffman, 1976).

Following are brief descriptions of two commercially available criterion-referenced tests which are applicable to nonhandicapped as well as special populations:

Basic School Skills Inventory-Diagnostic (BSSI-D) (Hammill & Leigh, 1982). This instrument focuses on readiness skills of four- to seven-year-olds in six areas of school performance:

(1) daily living skills
(2) spoken language
(3) reading readiness
(4) writing readiness
(5) math readiness
(6) classroom behavior

Although a criterion-referenced test, the BSSI-D also provides norms for comparison to peers. The accompanying manual offers suggestions for teaching unmastered items.

Multilevel Academic Skills Inventory (MASI) (Howell, Zucker, & Morehead, 1982). The MASI is a comprehensive criterion-referenced measure of basic academic skills taught in grades one through eight. It provides 200 objectives in math and 110 in reading and language arts; these areas are further divided into math computation, math application, decoding, comprehension, handwriting, spelling, and vocabulary. Objectives from the money subtest under "math application" are listed in Table 6–4.

In summary, criterion-referenced testing is an assessment method

TABLE 6–4. Objectives from Money Subtest of the MASI (Howell, Zucker, & Morehead, 1982)

Know money vocabulary.
Know banking vocabulary.
Know budget vocabulary.
Use four-operation calculator to solve knowledge problems.
Know names of coins and currency.
Know values of coins and currency.
Identify symbols for money.
Know symbols for money.
Determine the change due, using the fewest possible coins, for purchases costing less than $1.00.
Determine the change due for purchases costing more than $1.00 and less than $20.00.
Write checks for bills.
Enter credit and debit in checkbook record and balance.

© 1982 by Bell & Howell. The *Multilevel Academic Skills Inventory* is published by Charles E. Merrill Publishing Company, a Bell & Howell Division. Reprinted with permission of the publisher.

that yields results directly applicable to instruction. Teachers who choose to develop their own measures should be careful to set appropriate criteria for individual students and to adjust the criteria if necessary. Likewise, if using one of the commercially available criterion-referenced instruments, the teacher should not rely entirely on the instrument for instructional planning. Rather, the teacher should critically evaluate the scope and sequence of objectives; the discriminating teacher may find gaps in criterion-referenced tests that he will want to fill in with supplemental lessons. If these cautions are regarded, criterion-referenced testing can be a valuable aid to instructional planning.

Study Skills Assessment

Skills for studying and learning are often neglected areas of assessment and instruction. When a student fails to learn, school personnel invariably look for intellectual, emotional, or personality factors rather than concentrating on how the student learns. Assessment of learning skills and study habits is a productive tactic because the variables are amenable to change, whereas changes in personality or other personal factors are much more difficult to effect. Educators often erroneously assume that students know how to prepare themselves and organize material for efficient learning; thus, study skills are rarely taught as part of the curriculum. As one researcher states, "study may not be possible until the student learns how-to-learn" (V. Brown, 1978, p. 79).

Assessment of study skills is particularly important with behavior disordered students, who often have an impulsive approach to academic tasks, a trait related to errors in reading and inductive reasoning (Kagan, 1965; Kagan, Pearson, & Welch, 1966), and failure in the early grades (Messer, 1970). Many programs for behavior disordered students have begun to incorporate self-control techniques, which help overcome impulsivity. Although this addition is much needed, self-control is only one of the many skills required in becoming a successful student.

Successful students also must possess sound study skills and work habits. The term *study skills* in this text refers to a broad complement of skills used by students to organize their learning environments for maximum efficiency. The learning environment encompasses time and place of study as well as learning materials. A degree of independence and self-discipline is also implied; V. Brown (1978) uses the term *independent study behaviors* to denote the same concept. According to Bragstad & Stumpf (1982), the following skills are among those mastered by successful students: time management, facilitating memory, note-taking, test-taking, and streamlining, which is an organized approach for comprehending new material. These skills are obviously for older or higher functioning students who need to know how to become independent learners. With this type student, self-assessment is an appropriate way to identify poor study habits that require intervention. Such assessments are available in *A Guidebook for Teaching Study Skills and Motivation* (Bragstad & Stumpf, 1982) and the *American Study Habits Survey* (American Guidance Service, 1964) for junior high and secondary students.

With younger or lower functioning students, the task of assessing study skills lies primarily with the teacher. V. Brown (1978) outlines four techniques for teacher assessment of independent study behaviors:

(1) *Observation of work habits*—recording in-class observations

(2) *Discussion with the student*—discussing work habits, possibly using report cards as the stimulus

(3) *Scrutiny of class requirements*—evaluating how well the student matches a particular teacher's requirements and expectations

(4) *Separation of "Can-Do and Doesn't" from "Can't Do"*—using contingency management to assess the former and task analysis for the latter.

Arrangement of the learning environment is an important part of efficient studying and learning. The previous chapter dealt with strategies for arranging physical and psychological environments conducive to learning; however, even specially designed classrooms and programs that meet the needs of the majority of behavior disordered students may be inappropriate for any given individual. Learning styles are highly idiosyncratic and therefore should be an integral part of assessment for instructional planning. A comprehensive inventory for assessing the learning style of an individual is presented in Table 6–5.

Observation Techniques

Observation has been defined as the "process of systematically looking at and recording behavior for the purpose of making instructional decisions" (Cartwright & Cartwright, 1974, p. 3). "Instructional decisions" refer both to academic skills and to behavioral or social skills which are needed to function effectively in the classroom. In programs for the behavior disordered, social skills often must take priority because many students have developed behaviors that interfere with the acquisition of academic skills. Failure to comply with teacher requests and off-task behavior which results in failure to complete assignments are examples of behaviors that must be changed before optimal learning can occur.

All effective teachers evolve their own informal observation strategies; however, observation is a skill which can be developed through practice and through use of a number of techniques. Before using observational strategies, teachers should be aware of a few general but important guidelines. First, identify the purpose of the observation. For example, is it to collect data on a student for a specific behavior to be targeted for change, or is it to gain more comprehensive information about a given area

TABLE 6–5.   Learning Style Diagnosis

1. Time	When is the student most alert? In the early morning, in the afternoon, in the evening, at night?
2. Schedule	What is the student's attention span? Continuous, irregular, short bursts of concentrated effort, forgetting periods, etc.?
3. Amount of Sound	What level of noise can the student tolerate? Absolute quiet, a murmur, distant sound, high level of conversation?
4. Type of Sound	What type of sound produces a positive reaction? Music, conversation, laughter, working groups?
5. Type of Work Group	How does the student work best? Alone, with one person, with a small task group, in a large team, a combination?
6. Amount of Pressure	What kind of pressure (if any) does the student need? Relaxed, slight, moderate, extreme?
7. Type of Pressure and Motivation	What helps to motivate this student? Self, teacher expectation, deadline, rewards, recognition of achievement, internalized interest, etc.?
8. Place	Where does the student work best? Home, school, learning centers, library media corner?
9. Physical Environment and Conditions	Floor, carpet, reclining, sitting, desk, temperature, table lighting, type of clothing, food?
10. Type of Assignments	On which type of assignments does the student thrive? Contracts, totally self-directed projects, teacher-selected tasks, etc.?
11. Perceptual Strengths and Styles	How does the student learn most easily? Visual materials, sound recording, printed media, tactile experiences, kinesthetic activities, multimedia packages, combinations of these?
12. Type of Structure and Evaluation	What type of structure suits this student most of the time? Strict, flexible, self-determined, jointly arranged, periodic, self-starting, continuous, occasional, time-line expectations, terminal assessment, etc.?

From the book, *Practical Approaches to Individualizing Instruction,* by Rita Dunn and Kenneth Dunn. © 1972 by Parker Publishing Company, Inc. Published by Parker Publishing Company, Inc., West Nyack, NY.

(social behavior or reading skills)? Second, be specific. If a behavior is to be changed, it must be defined in observable and measurable terms. Third, be systematic; that is, choose an observation technique and system of recording suited to the purpose. Fourth, use observation as an ongoing component of assessment. A single observation or even several observations during the span of a week or more may not yield information that is typical of the student.

Two observational measures often employed are checklists and behavior rating scales. These techniques require a minimum expenditure of time and can be helpful in focusing the teacher's attention on specific criteria. A number of published behavioral checklists and behavior rating scales were described in Chapter 4. Published measures are advantageous because they offer normative data so that individuals can be compared to peers.

There are two types of checklists for assessing academic skills. Skills checklists are composed of a hierarchy of skills in a selected subject. Problem-oriented checklists are composed of a listing of potential problems in a subject area. The resourceful teacher will find a variety of both types of checklists in the areas of readiness skills, self-help skills, written and oral language, handwriting, reading, spelling, and arithmetic, all readily available from textbooks, curriculum guides, journals, and publishers of tests. Checklists for observation of oral and silent reading problems are very common; most standardized reading tests and reading inventories include checklists of reading difficulties.

One disadvantage of checklists and rating scales is that behaviors to be assessed are preselected. When targeting behaviors are to be changed, the teacher needs more specific information and will want to use other behavior recording methods. (Four types of behavior recording are explained in Chapter 7.) Because it is either the frequency or the duration of many behaviors that concerns teachers, two of the most useful types of behavior recording are *event recording* and *duration recording.* In event recording, the frequency of the behavior is tallied: for selected time periods, every occurrence is recorded. Hitting is an example of a behavior that is often monitored through event recording. Duration recording is used when it is the duration rather than the frequency which is of concern (examples are noncompliance and long, drawn-out tantrums). In duration recording, the beginning and end of the behaviors are carefully timed and recorded.

Behavior recording can be used not only in collecting data to plan interventions but also in evaluating the effectiveness of interventions and in monitoring progress. Some researchers believe that behavioral assessment also should be used to monitor positive behaviors such as creativity (Goetz & Baer, 1973) and prosocial behaviors such as sharing because they are usually incompatible with disruptive behaviors (O'Leary, 1975). Refer to Chapter 7 for more complete information on observation techniques.

INDIVIDUALIZING INSTRUCTION

Individualizing instruction is the logical extension of individualized assessment; the two are grounded in the same basic philosophy of education: that students are a heterogeneous group of individuals with differing needs who require differing methods and levels of instruction. Many teachers have difficulty in making this philosophy operational, as evidenced by the inevitable questions such as, "But why should I reinforce Mark for getting only eight out of ten problems correct when the rest of the class is assigned twenty problems?" The willingness to individualize instruction represents a personal philosophy toward education that is as important to the instructional process as the choice of specific techniques. In fact, educators have come to realize that the quality of the teacher-student relationship may be the single most important factor in successful teaching (Epanchin & Dickens, 1982).

Individualization is an attempt to fit the curriculum and program to the child rather than vice versa. Newcomer (1980) defines individualizing instruction as "gearing instructional activities to the child's level of competence" (p. 255). This gearing is accomplished by assessing a student's educational level, deciding what the student needs to know, then choosing appropriate methods and materials. Or as Stephens (1977) explains, the *what* is the curriculum or content, and the *how* is the method or instructional approach to delivering content.

A Framework for Curriculum Planning

A comprehensive curriculum for behavior disordered students should incorporate three major components: academics, socioemotional development, and vocational or career planning (see Figure 6–1). As indicated by the diagram in Figure 6–1, these three components overlap and share many subcomponents. For example, self-concept is viewed as central to successful functioning in all three spheres.

Academic needs are obviously a prime concern in planning programs for behavior disordered students. A student must exhibit an achievement deficiency in order to qualify for services and, conversely, must demonstrate ability to achieve satisfactorily in the regular classroom with little or no support before being returned to that environment. Therefore, one of the first and most important decisions a teacher must make about an individual student is whether the ultimate goal is mainstreaming or functional competence for daily living. In the case of the former, emphasis on study skills and achievement in the basic areas of reading, language arts, and mathematics are warranted. In the latter case, competence in daily living skills and career planning should take precedence over academics.

A second curriculum component is socioemotional development. Behavior disordered students typically experience problems with interpersonal relationships, self-concept, and self-control. Conflict and inability to cope with stressful situations pose daily problems for these students. Teachers must respond to these needs by establishing individual goals for behavior change and for development of social skills that foster success

FIGURE 6–1.
Components of Curriculum Planning

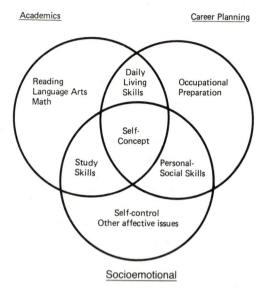

Academics   Career Planning

Reading
Language Arts
Math

Daily
Living
Skills

Occupational
Preparation

Self-
Concept

Study
Skills

Personal-
Social Skills

Self-control
Other affective issues

Socioemotional

experiences in school. A number of affective curricula are available to help students learn to deal with these and other issues. Affective curricula and curricula designed specifically for teaching social skills and self-control are described in Chapter 7.

Vocational or career planning is the third major component of comprehensive curriculum planning. Whereas *vocational training* usually refers specifically to acquisition of job-related skills, *career education* encompasses daily living skills, personal-social skills, and occupational and academic competence (Brolin & D'Alonzo, 1979). Proponents of career education suggest that academic and personal-social skills training should be planned with the individual's life goal in mind. For handicapped persons, two major questions should be addressed:

(1) Where will this student live after leaving the public schools: Independently in the community? At home? In an institution?

(2) Where will this student work after leaving school: A competitive job market? In a sheltered workshop? Or will he remain jobless?

Brolin & Kokaska (1979) outline 22 major career competencies in three curricular areas: daily living skills, personal-social skills, and occupational preparation. Under *daily living skills,* Brolin and Kokaska list abilities such as managing family finances and utilizing leisure time. Under *personal-social skills,* the authors include self-confidence, problem solving, and communicating adequately with others. Under *occupational preparation,* they discuss exhibiting appropriate work habits and behaviors, and the ability to seek, secure, and maintain employment. Planning and instruction in these competencies should begin early in the student's educational career and should continue through graduation from public education. All curriculum goals should be periodically evaluated for relevance to the student's life outside the classroom and to long-term goals.

General Guidelines for Individualizing

In order to plan successful programs for individual students, the teacher must bear in mind two basic tenets of specialized education: the uniqueness of the individual, and the need for planning in vocational, social, and academic areas. These three areas are not necessarily distinct and separate areas for programming. In practice, vocational, social, and academic skills may be combined in the same activity or lesson plan. For example, a single lesson plan for junior high students on money management might require three or four students cooperatively to work out a weekly household budget; such a lesson includes academic skills (math), social skills (interacting cooperatively for a common goal), and career and/or vocational skills (developing a household budget).

It is in instructional programming that assessment data become useful. After utilizing observations and records of previous performance to determine an individual's general functioning level, the teacher should employ selected informal assessment techniques to refine knowledge of the student's skills. Only after obtaining more specific assessment data can the teacher identify the needs of the individual; consequently, each learning task selected by the teacher should be tied to one of these identified needs. P.A. Gallagher provides detailed programming guidelines which are applicable to social, vocational and academic skills. The major steps are:

(1)   Establish a long-range goal:
Example: George will be able to tell time. (academic skill)

(2)   Specify a target behavior or performance objective:
When presented with a clock or worksheets with clock faces, George will tell time to the hour.

(3)   Specify prerequisite skills for the task:
Counts to 12.
Can read the numbers to 12.
Can write the numbers to 12.
Can read at the second-grade level.
Can follow two-step verbal directions.

(4)   Make a list of teacher activities necessary to teach the task:
Read about the sequence of concepts for learning to tell time.
Obtain materials: a clock face rubber stamp, an old clock with movable hands, and a working clock with Arabic numerals 1–12.
List steps on guide sheet.
Design worksheets.

(5)   Task-analyze or break down the task into small, incremental steps:
. . . Identifies the number to which the short hand is pointing.
Identifies the number to which the long hand is pointing.
etc. . . .

(P.A. Gallagher, 1979, pp. 154–155. Used with permission of Love Publishing)

Gallagher notes that the last step is by far the most time-consuming and therefore may be approximated for some goals. For example, the teacher may collapse several related steps of a task analysis into a single, larger step. However, if the student fails at the task, the teacher should scrutinize the task analysis to see whether the steps are small enough or essential information has been omitted.

In addition to these five steps, the teacher must plan for *type of student response, immediate feedback,* and *reinforcement of correct responses* (P.A. Gallagher, 1979). In *student response,* does the teacher want the student to write, circle a word, point, match, or verbalize? The response mode should be varied in order to increase interest and motivation. Many published curricula incorporate unusual response modes such as rubbing answer blanks with treated materials to reveal the correct answer. This method of response has the added value of *immediate feedback,* another facet of successful programming. Immediate feedback is especially important with behavior disordered students who are likely to be impulsive, easily frustrated, or unable to delay gratification. Ways to ensure prompt feedback are one-to-one interaction with the teacher or an aide, use of commercially prepared programmed materials or computer software, and preparation of answer keys which are readily available for self-check on independent assignments. A final planning component is *reinforcement of correct responses,* another necessity for behavior disordered students who are accustomed to failure. Most classroom programs for behavior disordered students incorporate some type of reinforcement system. Nonetheless, it is important for the teacher to stress correct answers and responses rather than incorrect ones on each assignment. Giving of tokens, points, tangibles, or other extrinsic reinforcers should be coordinated with the overall program goals for the individual; teacher praise or checks may be sufficient.

P.A. Gallagher (1979) also emphasizes the importance of programs that are self-paced and require active responses. Active responding ensures that students cannot withdraw or react passively to lessons; self-pacing ensures that students will be evaluated only according to their own performance, which helps eliminate some anxiety and frustration associated with competition with other students in the classroom.

Students also have responsibilities in the individualized classroom. The student role is that of an independent learner who has both instructional and social responsibilities (Dell, 1972). Dell outlines a number of specific duties under these headings. Under instructional responsibilities, the student is expected to take an active part by:

making some choices of objectives
selecting activities from a teacher-designed list
making independent use of instructional materials, including media
asking for help when necessary
sticking to the schedule and finishing assignments.

The major social responsibility is helping to maintain an environment conducive to learning by modeling good learning and social behaviors. Whenever appropriate, students should participate in plans for modifying their own behavior by helping to select intervention goals and reinforcers that are mutually acceptable to teacher and student. Teacher expectations for these and other student responsibilities in the classroom should always be explicit and, whenever possible, incorporated into class rules.

The Individualized Education Plan (IEP)

Requirement of a written individual education plan (IEP) for each student receiving special education services is an outgrowth of Public Law 94–142. The intent of the law is to ensure cooperative planning and documentation of educational services, educational goals, and the annual progress of each student. Although procedures for writing the IEP vary from school system to school system, P.L. 94–142 requires that the following people be present when the IEP is written: a representative of the local school system who is knowledgeable about special education, the teacher, parents or guardians,[1] and, when appropriate, the student. Regulations also mandate that each IEP contain the following elements:

a statement of the student's present level of functioning
a statement of annual goals, including short-term objectives
a statement of specific educational services to be provided and extent to which the student will participate in regular education
a time line for initiation and duration of services, and criteria for evaluation.

The format for the IEP is generally determined by the local school system, which provides its own standard form. In addition to the required components, many IEPs also specify those responsible for delivering services, methods and materials to be used, and information on motivation. For behavior disordered students, educators should include behavioral techniques and possible disciplinary actions; by obtaining parental consent prior to beginning the program, potential problems may be averted. For example, use of a time-out procedure for specified acts of aggression or noncompliance may be agreed upon by parents, teachers, and administrators, and subsequently written into the IEP.

Ideally, the IEP is the culmination of data-gathering and instructional planning for the individual student; it should be a helpful instrument for summarizing plans and monitoring student progress. In reality, many special educators view the IEP as burdensome paperwork that has little relevance to the student's actual program but is completed to satisfy regulations. Further, procedural problems in IEP team meetings have been identified: namely, unequal participation among participants and little congruence between data presented and decisions reached (Ysseldyke & Algozzine, 1982). However, despite variation from system to system and problems in the IEP procedures, special education teachers are generally present at IEP meetings (Ysseldyke & Algozzine, 1982) and are expected to contribute to instructional planning decisions (Gilliam & Coleman, 1981). The special education teacher can provide direction to the team if allowed the time for a thorough assessment of the student's strengths, weaknesses, and interests, which can then be translated into long-term and short-term goals. A sample IEP is presented in the case study at the end of this chapter.

Adapting Materials

Selecting curricular materials is the final step in individualizing a student's program. Previous steps were: (1) assessment of the student's functioning level, (2) consideration of academic, social, and career goals, and (3) completion of an IEP with long-term educational goals and short-term instructional objectives. Next, the teacher must plan curriculum to meet those educational goals. Curriculum may be loosely defined as the *content* and the *organization of the content* to be taught.

Epanchin and Dickens (1982) acknowledge that there is no generally accepted curriculum for behavior disordered students but that special educators do agree on the importance of long-range curriculum planning, the necessity of individualizing, and the need for a curriculum that is therapeutic. In order to minimize failure and adapt existing materials so that a therapeutic function is served, the teacher may find it helpful to pose several questions about an individual:

> Does the student require more than the usual amount of repetition before grasping new concepts?
> After new concepts are learned, are frequent reviews necessary?
> Does the student respond better to oral or written instructions?
> How many sequential steps can the student remember and execute at one time?
> Is the student easily overwhelmed by presentation of

A large number of problems per page,
more than one type of problem per page, or
too many words on a page?
Is the student distracted by colors and pictures?
Does the student need a consistent format for the same type problem or a varied format to stimulate interest?
Does the student work better alone or in small groups? Is the student's preferred response mode oral or written?

Curricular lessons and materials may then be adapted to meet individual needs by strategies such as providing more repetition, filling in information gaps, doubling the number of review sessions, providing more and smaller incremental steps, changing the presentation format, and skipping some rote work to increase motivation.

A few guidelines for selecting or adapting materials may be helpful. The appearance and difficulty level of selected materials is important, as strong emotions may be elicited by educational materials. Materials should be different from those used in the past in other classrooms. (The very sight of a basal reader has been known to send a student into tantrums.) Precautions should be taken to ensure that selected materials appear neither too difficult ("Why try?") nor too easy ("That's kid-stuff!"). As a rule, it is better to begin at a level where success is easily obtained and to build rapidly once confidence has been established. Materials should also be scrutinized according to the following variables:

(1) *Emotionally-laden content*—personal experiences to which a particular student is sensitive or information that may be provocative to the group

(2) *Cultural appropriateness and transferability to the real world*—relevance to the students' world as students perceive it

(3) *General appeal*—popularity of the materials among students

(4) *Clear format*—format is varied to avoid boredom but is not so variable that confusion results (P.A. Gallagher, 1979).

Epanchin and Dickens (1982) offer the following criteria for choosing appropriate materials for teaching in the content areas:

(1) *Readability.* Are vocabulary, sentence structure, and sentence length commensurate with the reading level of the student?

(2) *Content load.* Is material overloaded with too many concepts or are the concepts vague and abstract?

(3) *Organization.* Are main ideas clearly emphasized and are sufficient examples given?

(4) *Interest and motivational appeal.* Do students respond positively to the material?

A final consideration is the effect of an individual's emotional state on learning and academics. Although special educators no longer consider emotional health to be a strict prerequisite for learning, the interaction between emotions and learning must be taken into consideration. Whenever possible, the teacher should form hypotheses linking emotional state to learning progress in the individual. For example, Julian, a highly anxious student who has experienced repeated failure in math, refuses to attempt any work that seems to even approximate math. If sensitive to this rather normal reaction to failure, the teacher can make several adjustments. While allowing Julian to openly express his dislike for math, the teacher may require him to complete only one math problem per math period; expectations for completion of that problem are clearly established and completion is rewarded. In this case, the teacher hypothesizes that Julian's frustration and anxiety about math will fade when the requirement is minimal and the teacher is willing to accept a very limited product in order to get Julian to complete any math assignment at all. Although extremeness of behavior is a characteristic of behavior disordered students, daily manifestations of extreme frustration, withdrawal, anxiety, anger, or other emotions must be dealt with in curriculum planning as well as in behavior management plans.

SUMMARY

Individualized programming is indicative of an educational philosophy that recognizes the unique needs of individual students. Individualization involves assessment of student needs and the translation of needs into educational goals and lesson plans. Teachers may accomplish individualization by adopting a diagnostic or clinical teaching model and by developing a repertoire of informal assessment skills, including use of observation, error analysis, task analysis, and criterion-referenced testing.

Comprehensive instructional planning involves three major components: academic, social, and vocational-career. Selected curricular goals should relate to the individual's total life plan and should be continually evaluated for relevance to that plan and to the individual's life outside the classroom. The interaction of emotional state and learning progress is a prime consideration in planning curriculum for behavior disordered students.

An IEP is required for any student receiving special education services; it may serve as a vehicle for cooperative planning and as a summary of educational goals and services to be provided. In order to help the student achieve stated goals, the teacher will find it necessary to choose curricular materials carefully and to adapt them to the student's special learning needs. Although no curriculum has universal approval for behavior disordered students, special educators unanimously agree that individualization is the key to breaking the failure cycle.

BOX 6–1.   *BRIAN: A CASE STUDY*

Description and Background Information

Brian was recently identified as behavior disordered and recommended for placement in the resource room for three hours daily; he is eight years old and in the second grade after having repeated first grade. His second-grade teacher reports that Brian is below average in math and is failing reading and language arts; she further describes him as "sullen, uncooperative, and given to alternate bouts of withdrawal and aggressive outbursts." She said that he generally reacts to failure by completely withdrawing and refusing to talk. He has severe astigmatism and has been prescribed glasses, which he refuses to wear because they are uncomfortable and make him "nervous." He has broken or lost his glasses so frequently that his mother no longer tries to get him to wear them. He was seen by the speech pathologist for both language development and articulation problems last year but was dismissed due to lack of cooperation.

Brian lives with his mother and an older sister, aged ten. His parents have been divorced for four years; after the divorce, the father moved to another state and has not contacted the family since then. The mother is working on her college degree and supports the family on her part-time wages as a waitress. According to the mother, Brian was very close to his maternal grandmother, who lived next door to them until she moved to another state last year. He formerly spent many evenings and weekends with the grandmother, who gave him a lot of personal attention and helped him with his schoolwork. His mother describes Brian as very dependent on her and his sister; his two or three friends are much younger than he is. She also says that Brian "doesn't mind very well" and that she "doesn't know what to do with him."

According to testing by the school psychologist, Brian is functioning in the low average-to-borderline range of intelligence. His visual-motor skills are quite deficient and when asked to copy a printed passage of three sentences, his product was primarily illegible. All achievement measures placed him at the beginning first-grade level, with math being a few months higher. Although the psychologist stated that test results were considered valid overall, she also stated that Brian's uncooperativeness could have affected test results. Despite frequent breaks and use of food reinforcers, Brian sometimes refused to do a task or finish one he had started. Because of Brian's erratic behavior and visual-motor problems, the psychologist referred him to a neurologist who found distinct abnormalities of left hemispheric functioning and subsequently placed him on an anticonvulsant medication. Brian is currently being monitored by the neurologist.

The school psychologist also observed Brian during reading class. On several days during the observation period, Brian sat with arms folded and head down when he was supposed to be working on independent workbook assignments. He was recorded to be on-task 10 percent of the total time observed.

Informal Assessment

The resource teacher, Ms. Reese, begins her data-gathering the first day Brian arrives in the resource room. She observes what he chooses to do with free time as well as his interaction with the other students. She notes that when given a worksheet that she is sure Brian can do, he only stares at it. The second, third, and fourth days Ms. Reese begins an informal assessment in 20- to 30-minute periods. In reading, she finds that Brian can read the primer stories from his basal reader only because he seems to have memorized them. When given an unfamiliar passage at the same level, he cannot read it. When given word lists at the primer level, he demonstrates a sight vocabulary of fewer than ten words. When asked to write some words from a dictated list, he spells correctly only the word "go." On the *KeyMath Diagnostic Arithmetic Test,* a criterion-referenced measure, Brian showed strengths on subtests of numeration (sets, number recognition, and number sequences) and concept of fractions (relationships of the part to the whole). He showed a complete inability to deal with word problems or money. In computation, he knew number facts under ten but could not work addition or subtraction problems requiring knowledge of place value. During these assignments, Ms. Reese observed Brian's approach to tasks, his attention span, his preference for certain tasks over others, and his response to praise from her. She now has some idea of how and where to begin instructional planning.

Behaviorally, Brian has shown no aggressive outbursts in the four days he has been in the resource room. During assessment, he became very frustrated and refused to talk or attempt tasks when they became difficult for him. Ms. Reese responded by reassuring him and changing tasks. He initiated no conversation with other students in the room but responded when they approached him. He indicated an interest in the reinforcement system and the fact that other students were receiving tokens for completing assignments.

The IEP

Based on information from the school psychologist's report, observations, and the resource teacher's informal assessment, the following individual education plan was designed for Brian:

SUMMARY OF PRESENT LEVELS OF FUNCTIONING

Reading: preprimer level, sight word vocabulary of fewer than ten words
Spelling: does not spell
Math: knows number facts under 10
          counts meaningfully to 20
          understands sets and concept of fractions

Handwriting:prints name legibly
can copy single words but not sentences legibly

ANNUAL GOALS

To read and comprehend stories at
first-grade level

As sight vocabulary improves, to
copy short sentences legibly

To work addition and subtraction
problems with two- and three-digit
numbers

To show knowledge of time and
money appropriate to his developmental level

To improve speech articulation and
language skills

To interact socially with classmates

To complete independent work
assignments

EVALUATION CRITERIA

Scores an instructional level of
1.5 or higher on the *Diagnostic
Reading Scales*

Given several short sentences,
copies them legibly according to
teacher judgment

Given ten addition and subtraction
problems with two- and three-digit
numbers, works with 80 percent accuracy

Scores at a commensurate level on
KeyMath time and money subtests

Pronounces with 100 percent accuracy the
sounds targeted for articulation
therapy; shows improvement in
language skills on the *Peabody
Picture Vocabulary Test-Revised*
and a teacher-made assessment of
abstract reasoning skills

According to teacher records,
participates in daily P.E. activities and talks to classmates
while doing so; otherwise initiates
conversation with peers on a daily
basis

According to teacher records,
routinely completes 80 percent of
independent work assigned

SHORT-TERM OBJECTIVES

Develop a sight vocabulary of 50 words

Develop a sight vocabulary of 100 words

Read and comprehend a short passage
composed of familiar sight words

Legibly copy single words from sight
vocabulary

Legibly copy three- to five-word
sentences

Demonstrate knowledge of place value

Compute two-digit addition problems

Compute two-digit subtraction problems

Tell time to the hour

Identify coins and currency up to $1.00

PERSONS RESPONSIBLE

Resource teacher

Resource teacher

Resource teacher

Resource teacher

Resource teacher

Resource teacher

Resource teacher

Resource teacher

Resource teacher

Resource teacher

Pronounce "th" and "s" sounds correctly	Speech pathologist
Improve oral vocabulary	Speech pathologist
Improve abstract thinking skills through antonyms and synonyms	Speech pathologist
Participate in P.E. activities with classmates	Regular classroom teacher
Initiate at least one conversation daily with classmates	Regular classroom teacher and resource teacher
Complete at least one independent work assignment daily in the resource room	Resource teacher

Educational Services to be Provided:

Resource services in reading, language arts, and math, three hours daily. Speech and language development therapy, twice weekly, 30-minute sessions.

Percent of Time in Regular Classroom:

50 percent.

Initiation and Duration of Services:

Both resource and speech services begin immediately and continue until a committee review is held in six months.

Individualizing Curriculum

Ms. Reese realizes that a number of curriculum adaptations will have to be made in order to get Brian off the failure track. Heretofore it was difficult to separate "can't do" from "won't do," but after consideration of all assessment information, it appears that much of Brian's "uncooperativeness" was based on his inability to do the tasks required.

Because Brian is very frustrated with trying to read and shows little knowledge of phonics despite two years of instruction, Ms. Reese decides to use the *Peabody Rebus Reading Program* (Woodcock, 1967). The *Peabody* initially requires reading only rebuses, or picture words. It has the additional advantages of being programmed and self-paced; after completion of the program, the reader should have a sight vocabulary of 120 words. Spelling will be delayed until Brian has developed such a sight vocabulary.

In handwriting activities, Ms. Reese will give Brian special primary paper, which has texturally raised lines to help guide the writer. Assignments initially will be very short and will require copying from a model at the desk rather than from the board. Ms. Reese hopes that toward the end of the year, Brian will have improved enough to write short language experience stories with his reading vocabulary words.

In math, Brian needs a slow pace, repetition, and frequent reviews of new information. He seems to understand much better if given concrete examples or materials, so Ms. Reese will use cuisenaire rods (colored wooden rods), the abacus, and other manipulable materials whenever possible.

Behaviorally, the goals are to help Brian develop conversational skills with peers and to finish his assigned classroom work. The teacher feels that Brian is less likely to withdraw if these goals can be attained. As Brian evidenced interest in the token system used in the resource room, he will be allowed to earn tokens on a daily basis for attaining specific behavioral goals.

A final consideration is that of career-vocational goals. As Brian is dependent on others and far behind his age peers academically, Ms. Reese believes that the curriculum should be aimed at equipping Brian with functional academic skills and other self-help skills that will allow him to develop some independence. As much of the curriculum as possible will be geared to real-life experiences and to helping Brian cope with his everyday environment.

KEY POINTS

(1) Primary reasons for failure to achieve among behavior disordered students include ability deficits, emotional blocks, and faulty learning and/or faulty teaching.

(2) Prior to effective instruction, teachers must identify the specific skills to be mastered by an individual student.

(3) Skills can be identified through a variety of informal assessment techniques.

(4) Study skills are an often neglected part of the curriculum: many students need to learn how to learn.

(5) Observation techniques can be used to specify functioning both in academic and social-behavioral domains.

(6) Individualization requires: (a) assessing a student's educational level, (b) deciding what the student needs to know, and (c) choosing suitable methods and materials.

(7) In curriculum planning for behavior disordered students, a balance among academic, socioemotional, and career goals should be sought.

(8) Breaking the failure cycle through attaining success in school is an important step in improving students' self-concepts.

ADDITIONAL READINGS

Selected chapters in *Assessment in special and remedial education,* by J. Salvia & J.E. Ysseldyke. Boston: Houghton Mifflin, 1981; and selected chapters in *Educational assessment of learning problems: Testing for teaching,* by G. Wallace & S.C. Larsen. Boston: Allyn & Bacon, 1978, for more comprehensive information on the basics of assessment, plus assessment of specific areas (reading, math, language, perceptual, intelligence, etc.).

Developing observation skills, by C.A. Cartwright & G.P. Cartwright. New York: McGraw-Hill, 1974, for practical, step-by-step instructions on acquiring skills in observation.

Chapter 6, Issues in intervention, by J.E. Ysseldyke & B. Algozzine. In *Critical issues in special and remedial education*. Boston: Houghton Mifflin, 1982, for a discussion of important issues in choosing and evaluating educational interventions.

Chapter 11, Curriculum design and educational programming, by B.C. Epanchin & V.J. Dickens. In J.L. Paul & B.C. Epanchin (Eds.), *Emotional disturbance in children*. Columbus, OH: Chas. E. Merrill, 1982, for a chapter on special considerations in adapting curriculum for the behavior disordered.

Chapter 3, The mildly handicapped class, by K. Howell. In *Inside special education*. Columbus, OH: Chas. E. Merrill, 1983, for a short but informative reading on curriculum planning in a resource setting.

Goal analysis for behavior problem learners, by E.L. Hill. *Academic Therapy*, 1978, *13*, 289–299, for an article that not only discusses how problems in learning and behavior are intertwined but also offers examples of how to set attainable goals.

NOTE

[1]Parents may waive their right to be present by signing an informed-consent form.

seven

Methods
for Management

---

orientation

As a teacher of behavior disordered students, you can expect to deal with the whole gamut of misbehavior, from mild forms of noncompliance to full-blown aggressive outbursts. Managing problem behavior while providing emotional support will be a major challenge in your work. Regardless of your best efforts at environmental planning and individualizing instruction, your students will need special interventions to help them learn to cope with frustration, to deal with emotional issues, and eventually to manage their own behavior.

OVERVIEW

This chapter addresses techniques and curricula that can be used with behavior disordered students. Various management methods and materials are described under four major headings: direct intervention techniques, cognitive techniques, behavioral techniques, and curriculum. A theoretical rationale and description of each technique or curriculum are offered. This chapter is intended only as an overview of methods; within each section the reader is referred to additional sources that provide more comprehensive information. Techniques actually selected for use by an individual teacher depend on a number of factors, including the teacher's training, personality and interaction style, the philosophy of the school and the special education program, the resources available to the teacher, and the characteristics of students. No one technique or curriculum will enable the teacher to deal effectively with all of the difficulties that arise in the classroom, but careful consideration of these factors enables the teacher to choose from a repertoire of intervention methods that are both personally satisfying and effective.

Many of the methods described in this chapter require special training for effective implementation. Teachers should fully understand the rationale and goals of these methods, and they should receive supervision and feedback when first trying the methods with students. Methods falling into this category are life space interviewing, crisis intervention, reality therapy, and rational-emotive therapy. A notable exception is Redl's management techniques, which can easily be adopted by regular and special education teachers. Also, the teacher who is well-schooled in behavior modification should be able to apply behavioral techniques and to extend these skills to cognitive behavior modification and behavioral self-control without additional special training. The affective and social skills curricula described at the end of this chapter do not require special training. Most published curricula are packaged with adequate instructions for use by teachers and counselors.

These methods are used primarily in special education programs on regular campuses and in special schools. Although most of the techniques would be applicable to all students in regular settings, they are rarely used in these settings because of time constraints or requirements for one-to-one attention. In public schools, it is usually the special education teacher or counselor who utilizes these methods, and in special schools or residential settings, the entire staff, including teachers, psychologists, and administrators, may have expertise in using them. Some school systems employ a consulting teacher or a crisis teacher; the individual filling either of these roles should be able to use several of these intervention strategies effectively.

DIRECT INTERVENTION TECHNIQUES

The management techniques described in this section are an out-growth of ecological theory. As described in Chapter 4, ecological theorists believe that disturbance lies in the interaction or reciprocal relationship of children with their environment. These techniques are aimed at helping children cope with their environment and the people and events therein. In contrast to traditional counseling or psychotherapy in which an adult interviews the child "in considerable detachment" from the actual problem events, the adult using these techniques intervenes directly in the problem situation as it is happening (Redl, 1959b). Such techniques may be labeled as ecological because the aim is not so much to change the child but to help the child adapt to the immediate environment. From this perspective, the teacher of behavior disordered students is in the best position to help the student make positive adaptations to the classroom environment. Among the most widely used of these techniques are Redl's management techniques (Redl & Wineman, 1957), life-space interviewing (Redl, 1959b), and crisis intervention. The latter are applied most often in volatile, threatening situations.

Redl's Management Techniques

Redl (1966) developed a four-notched scale of behavior management that has proven helpful to teachers of behavior disordered students. The scale includes permitting, tolerating, intervening, and preventive planning. .

Permitting.   Although teachers often emphasize what students are *not* permitted to do, they do not often emphasize what students *are* permitted to do. It is important for students to have freedom of movement and freedom of expression within a range that is sanctioned by the teacher. In addition to creating a more pleasant atmosphere by making students more comfortable, permission reduces their need to test limits. For example, students should be told that it is permissible to be boisterous and to run on the playground or that it is acceptable to express an opposing opinion in class. Sometimes permission may be given in a contract form, which means that for a specific time period the student is permitted to behave in a certain way that is not usually acceptable. However, limits are firmly established and it is understood that the contract is temporary.

Tolerating.   A second alternative is to tolerate behavior, which means that although the teacher does not approve of the behavior (as in permitting), no penalties or punishment are levied. When using this technique, the teacher should clearly communicate that the behavior is being tolerated, that is, that the teacher does not approve but will not make an issue of it at this particular time. Tolerating demonstrates that the teacher can be flexible yet still retain control. Some reasons for tolerating behavior are:

1. *the developmental phase of students*—third graders who tattle and sixth graders who giggle and whisper;
2. *situational behavior*—unusual behavior which may be precipitated by illness, divorce of parents, or a death in the family;
3. *relationship building*—with students who are distrustful of adults or have a history of problems with adult authority figures;
4. *wrong place or time*—inappropriate setting, such as in public or two minutes before the final dismissal bell.

Intervening.   The teacher will not be able to permit or tolerate some behaviors that surface in the classroom. Intervention is necessary when rules are broken or when physical or psychological danger is imminent.

when to use this

The teacher may also choose to intervene to prevent trouble or when the teacher's own tolerance limits have been exceeded. After a decision to intervene has been made, there are a number of techniques specified by Redl (Redl & Wineman, 1957) that may be used at different times to effect different outcomes.[1] These techniques are for management of mild negative behaviors; they are not a substitute for a well-planned behavior management system nor for more intensive aid for seriously disordered students.

Planned ignoring. Much behavior is performed for its goading value and will disappear if left unchallenged. The difficult part of this technique is acquiring the ability to determine which behaviors are so superficial that they will disappear without teacher attention. For example, the teacher may choose to ignore pencil-tapping or other noise-making which is obviously intended to get a response from the teacher.

Signal interference. Often children do not think of consequences before they act. If a teacher catches the child's eye or waves a finger, it may be enough to curb the behavior. This technique is also known as "cueing." A significant look, a gesture, or calling the student's name are cues that may be used, for example, *before* a student passes around an objectionable picture to classmates.

Proximity control. The teacher moves near a misbehaving student to indicate control or puts a hand on the shoulder to indicate interest and support. For example, the teacher who is walking around the classroom while explaining an upcoming project can easily move toward two students who are engrossed in a private conversation. The teacher need not break stride nor stop talking in order to make his presence felt.

Interest boosting. When coping with a new experience that might be difficult to handle, the student may need the interest of an enthusiastic adult in order to get started or to continue. One way to boost interest is simply to ask questions about a pet project or a current classroom assignment.

Hypodermic affection. An affectionate word or gesture from the teacher may diffuse frustration or hostility. A smile, a wink, or a pat on the back can convey much-needed empathy to the student.

Tension decontamination through humor. This technique is a well-timed attempt at kidding the student out of being upset, or using humor to relieve tension. For example, making a joke, a wisecrack, or laughing at oneself is especially effective when the class has set the teacher up to be the butt of a prank.

Hurdle help. Students may avoid starting an activity or assignment because it is too difficult. Hurdle help involves guiding the student through the intermediate hard spot on the way to a goal. Teacher prompts include: "Do you need some help getting started?" "Do you understand what you're supposed to be doing?"

Restructuring. Abandon an activity or scheduled event when it is not working. Substitute an alternative activity. For example, when the class is unusually restless, give a short break or shift from an individual seatwork assignment to a group discussion.

Direct appeal to value areas. Rather than taking an authoritative stance to demonstrate control, the teacher can choose to appeal to students' values. This technique helps the students understand the reasons for standards and rules and it involves them in making decisions rather than receiving ultimatums. For example, the teacher can appeal to a student's sense of peer approval: "The other students aren't going to be very happy with you if you continue to argue and cause us to miss the art activity."

Removing seductive objects. Certain objects have such inherent appeal to youngsters that the teacher soon learns that it is impossible to compete with such objects and that it is best simply to remove them from the scene. As Long and Newman (1965) state:

> Certain objects have a magnetic appeal and elicit a certain kind of behavior from children. For example, if a child has a flashlight, it says "Turn me on"; if he has a ball, it says "Throw me"; if he has a magnifying glass, it says, "Reflect the sunlight"; if he has a whistle, it says "Toot me"; if he has a pea shooter, it says "Shoot me"; and so on. (p. 360)

Antiseptic bouncing. If a child has reached a state where he is inaccessible to other techniques, removing him from the group for a few minutes may help him regain control. This is not a time-out procedure for punishment purposes. For example, sending a giggling child out of the classroom for a drink of water or on an errand allows the child a chance to regain control before reentering the classroom.

Preventive planning. Redl's fourth management alternative is preventive planning. If students consistently misbehave during certain time periods or in certain places, then changes in class schedules or school procedures may be necessary. Another example of preventive planning is refusal to hold a meeting with a small group of students in a large area such as the gym or cafeteria; such open spaces often invite misbehavior which is contagious and can easily spread. The ability to set up and maintain an environment that is both orderly and predictable is a very important competency in dealing with behavior disordered students.

Effective teachers will find that they already employ some of these common-sense techniques for surface misbehavior in the classroom. However, these techniques will not be sufficient for more serious difficulties which arise in classrooms for the behavior disordered. The life space interview has been found to be helpful in exploring the feelings and actions of emotionally troubled youngsters. For dealing with volatile or potentially violent behavior, teachers should receive training in crisis intervention methods. Each of these methods is explored in the remainder of this section.

The Life Space Interview

Although the life space interview was pioneered in residential settings as part of a therapeutic milieu for behavior disordered students, it may be used in the classroom and in the home (Redl, 1966). To be effective, the interview should be conducted by an adult "who is perceived by the child to be part of his 'natural habitat or life space,' with some pretty clear role and power-influence in his daily living" (Redl, 1965, p. 364). The adult's role is not to exercise authority but to gain an idea of the child's perceptions of a given event.

Redl (1959b) differentiates between two types of life space interviews: emotional first aid on the spot and clinical exploitation of life events. The primary difference between these two is the goal for the interview, a decision that is made in the initial stages but which, if necessary, may be changed in the middle of the interview. As its title implies, *emotional first aid on the spot* is a temporary support in which the teacher seeks to help the student overcome an immediate obstacle or work through a difficult situation. There is no long-range plan or treatment strategy other than provision of temporary relief and support. In contrast, the intention of *clinical exploitation* of life events is to exploit a momentary experience in order to facilitate long-range goals for a particular student. Consider the following example:

> The teacher realizes that Sue Ellen is having a particularly bad day, which began with an argument with her mother before she left home this morning. Sue Ellen has a long-standing habit of rationalizing or making elaborate excuses for her obnoxious behavior. When she begins to taunt a classmate, the classmate blows up and a near-scuffle ensues. Arriving at the scene, the teacher may choose simply to break up the argument and talk to Sue Ellen about her difficult day (emotional first aid) or may decide to use the event to illustrate to Sue Ellen her habit of taking out her frustration on others and then excusing it (clinical exploitation).

In reality, the decision would be affected by several factors, such as the severity of the offense, the degree to which both parties are upset, and the time and setting of the incident. Regardless of its specific goal, the life space interview is intended to intrude into the student's life space and enable the teacher to obtain the student's view of a given situation. It may be used to intervene when a student is involved in a difficult or potentially troublesome situation, or it may be used soon after such a situation has occurred. A cooling down period is discouraged, as the life space interview should occur as soon as possible and as close in physical proximity as possible to the troublesome event. Selected subcategories of both types of interviews are briefly described in Table 7–1.

Redl (1959b) outlines a number of criteria for conducting the life space interview. Three are especially important in the classroom setting:

(1) *Central theme relevance.* The interview should be used with appropriate frequency and for appropriate reasons with an individual; overuse undermines its effectiveness. In other words, the teacher must evaluate both the severity of an incident and its relevance to overall goals for the individual.

(2) *Mood manageability.* If the student or the teacher is in the wrong mood—too excited, too tired, or too grouchy—it may be best to wait for another occasion.

(3) *Issues around timing.* Although the strength of the life space interview is its focus on the *here and now,* clinical exploitation interviews may occasionally have to be postponed because of scheduling (lunch or a break), or until enough emotional first aid has been administered.

Other practical guidelines for conducting the interview are offered by Brenner (1963). The teacher should conduct the interview in a polite, conversational manner, without moralizing or asking the student to explain or defend behavior. It is best to focus on *what* actually happened rather than *why* it happened. The student should be aided in finding acceptable alternatives or devising a plan to avoid repeating the troublesome situation. Use of the life space interviewing school settings is promoted by Brenner (1963), and by Morse (1969b), who recommends it as a problem-solving technique in less serious situations or with students who are experiencing adjustment problems.

Although the life space interview has met with widespread accep-

TABLE 7–1   Categories and Selected Subcategories of the Life Space Interview (Redl, 1959b)

EMOTIONAL FIRST AID ON THE SPOT
    DRAIN-OFF OF FRUSTRATION ACIDITY—sympathizing with a student
        who is upset at an interruption in scheduling or during a
        pleasant activity
    SUPPORT FOR MANAGEMENT OF PANIC, FURY, AND GUILT—providing support
        during a tantrum or emotional outburst, and afterward, helping
        the student gain perspective
    UMPIRE SERVICES—helping a student make a decision or mediating
        in conflicts such as quarrels and fights
CLINICAL EXPLOITATION OF LIFE EVENTS
    Reality Rub-in—helping a student to interpret situations clearly
        and to see the relationship between behavior and its consequences
    MASSAGING NUMB VALUE AREAS—appealing to a student's personal
        value system (e.g., fairness, peer approval)

---

tance as an intervention technique, little systematic research on its effectiveness has been conducted. Reilly, Imber, and Cremins (1978) studied its use with adolescent special-needs students in a resource room setting, and DeMagistris and Imber (1980) carried out an efficacy study with eight behavior disordered adolescent males in a residential setting. Both studies were supportive of the effectiveness of the life space interview in reducing individuals' inappropriate behaviors, which were targeted before intervention occurred. DeMagistris and Imber (1980) reported decreases in maladaptive behaviors ranging from 31 percent to 72 percent and a concomitant improvement in subjects' academic performance.

In their study, DeMagistris and Imber clearly differentiated between the life space interview and "having a discussion with the student about his inappropriate behavior" (1980, p. 24). First, life space interviews occurred in a private setting rather than in the classroom where further confrontations were likely to develop. Second, in life space interviews, students were allowed to state their perceptions of an incident rather than being immediately criticized by the teacher, which often happened in discussions. Third, in the life space interview, the teacher consistently attempted to show the student how his behavior was affected by the group's behavior; reference to group dynamics was not a part of typical discussions. Fourth, whereas discussions often resulted in punishment or standoff between teacher and student, in life space interviews the teacher required the student to identify alternative ways of coping. DeMagistris and Imber concluded their study by calling for additional research on the effectiveness of the life space interview in numerous educational settings.

Crisis Intervention

The role of the crisis teacher as envisioned by Morse (1965) was described in Chapter 3. According to Morse, the crisis teacher should be specially trained and available on the spot to deal directly with crises as they arise. However appealing, this model of services has not been widely adopted; rather, most school systems deal with students who precipitate crises by placing them in a classroom for the behavior disordered either on a part-time or full-time basis. Teachers of behavior disordered students are generally expected to deal with crisis situations in the school setting.

Gilliam (1981a)[2] has developed a training module for crisis intervention techniques that stresses three equally important phases of a crisis situation: precrisis, during crisis, and postcrisis.

Precrisis.   There are three major steps in the precrisis phase. The first step is knowing whether a crisis situation exists. According to Gilliam (1981a), a crisis is an "occasion when a child's behavior requires immediate attention to protect the physical and/or psychological safety of the child, teacher, and others" (p. 13). The defining characteristic of a crisis is behavior that is out of control and potentially harmful; *it is not the type or frequency of behavior that determines a crisis, but the predicted effect that the behavior will have on others.*

Preventive planning is the next step in the precrisis phase. Preventive planning includes establishing physically and psychologically consistent environments that enable students to predict what is expected of them. Redl conceptualizes preventive planning as the teacher's ability to anticipate potential problems and arrange the environment accordingly. The teacher can avoid many problem situations by careful planning. In addition, Gilliam offers these suggestions:

(1)   Rules are clearly established, consistently enforced, and rule infractions are dealt with as unemotionally as possible.

(2)   The teacher does not threaten, moralize, argue, or provoke the student.

(3)   Whenever possible, opportunities are provided to allow the student to save face and preserve self-respect.

(4)   Whenever possible, the teacher intervenes before a rule is broken.

A third step in the precrisis phase is the ability to predict when a crisis will occur. The teacher may develop this ability by becoming familiar with a student's crisis behavior history and by being alert to precrisis behaviors such as frustration or anger signs. From the student's behavioral history, the teacher should try to determine exactly when and where crisis episodes have occurred, what the student's specific behaviors were, what event precipitated the episode, who was involved, and what happened as a consequence of the episode. By obtaining such information, the teacher is often able to see patterns of behavior or to identify behaviors that signal that a student is in danger of losing control. Some examples of precrisis behavior are refusal to comply with teacher requests, oppositional responses, verbal challenges, arguing, complaining, swearing, disruptive or attention-seeking behavior, restlessness, confusion, and a significant increase or decrease in voice volume.

During crisis.   During a crisis, the single most important factor is the teacher's composure and self-control. Composure during a crisis can only be maintained if the teacher is prepared and has a plan of action. The teacher must first determine the immediate objective for the student, which is usually to stop the behavior being exhibited. If the student is out of control, the teacher should remain calm and talk to the student in a firm but unemotional manner. Force should only be used as a last resort.

Gilliam differentiates between two types of crisis management strategies. The first is used when the crisis is of a nonviolent nature and the student is not physically aggressive. The second management strategy is used when the student poses a physical threat by such acts as hitting, choking, or using or threatening to use a weapon. Verbal assaults and self-injurious behaviors are also considered as violent acts and are treated as aggressive crises.

In case of nonviolent crises, Gilliam suggests using a technique called "One-Two-Three-Bounce." In this technique, two warnings are given the student (steps "One" and "Two"). The third step is the application of the stated consequence if the behavior does not stop, and the "Bounce" step is the removal of the student to a time-out or exclusion area.

In managing aggressive crises, the teacher should answer three questions before taking action:

(1)   What is the situation?
      Where is the student. . .the other students?
      What is the danger in the situation?
(2)   What options are available?
      Can the behavior be safely ignored or can the student be redirected into another area of activity?
      What technique will work best in this situation—humor, authoritative request, etc.?
(3)   Where do you want the student to go?
      Will the student go there without force?

In aggressive crisis situations, the teacher should always send for another adult and should never attempt physical intervention until help arrives. Teachers should also remember that aggression begets aggression and should only make defensive moves to protect themselves. Teachers of behavior disordered students should receive specific training in crisis intervention and in self-defense techniques.

Postcrisis.   Immediately after a crisis subsides, the involved student is usually susceptible to adult intervention. When both the student and teacher are calm enough to hold a conversation, the episode should be discussed. Life space interviewing is very useful in postcrisis situations, as the teacher's role is to help the student realistically review the sequence of events. Together, the student and teacher should identify events that preceded the crisis and identify alternative responses or other courses of action the student could have taken to avoid losing control. The goal of the interview is to develop a plan to prevent the problem from reoccurring.

The development of schoolwide or districtwide policies for crisis management is vital. Specific policies for use of time-out, physical restraint, and other punishment procedures should be approved by administrators prior to implementation. Parents and students should be informed of all such policies. After a crisis event has occurred, the teacher should document the sequence of events in writing and make the information available to the principal and parents.

COGNITIVE TECHNIQUES

Cognitive approaches to working with behavior disordered students are best exemplified by Glasser's reality therapy (1965) and Ellis' rational-emotive therapy (1973). Both are considered cognitive techniques because they are based on the underlying premise that individuals can learn to control, change, and redirect their behavior by changing their thoughts and attitudes. In contrast to traditional psychotherapy, which indirectly focuses on cognitive processes (including thoughts buried in the subconscious), these techniques directly address cognitive processes by attacking illogical and irresponsible thinking. Moreover, in contrast to traditional therapies, cognitive therapists consider the past irrelevant; their intent is to help individuals understand present and future behavior by restructuring their thinking about it.

Cognitive techniques may be implemented in the school setting by therapists, counselors, or teachers who have been trained in their use. Reality therapy and rational-emotive therapy are both cognitive problem-solving techniques that readily lend themselves to application in the schools.

Reality Therapy

In reality therapy, Glasser (1965) emphasizes only present and overt behaviors as the targets for therapy and change; in this respect, it is similar to behavioral therapy. Reality therapy is best understood in terms of the three R's—*responsibility, reality,* and *right-and-wrong. Responsibility* is the keystone of reality therapy; Glasser holds the nontraditional view that people become disturbed because they are irresponsible and therefore they can become undisturbed by learning to become responsible. Responsible behavior is defined as the ability to meet one's needs without infringing upon the rights of others to meet their needs. *Reality* is an important concept because disturbed individuals deny the reality of the world around them; they do not understand or accept the rules and regulations of society, they deny connections between their behavior and its consequences, and they become adept at blaming other people or external events for their difficulties. Reality therapists do not accept rationalizations or excuses as valid justifications for behavior. The third *R, right-and-wrong,* sets reality therapy apart from most other therapies that avoid attaching value judgments to behavior. According to Glasser, disturbed or deviant behavior is wrong because it is harmful to the individual or to others. Therefore, the individual must learn to view his maladaptive behavior as wrong and must learn to behave in more adaptive ways.

Reality therapy consists of three general stages: establishing an involvement, forcing a value judgment, and finding alternative ways of behaving or coping. Specific steps for implementing reality therapy are:

(1) *Get involved.* Establish a mutually trusting and caring relationship with the student.

(2) *Ask the student to describe his behavior.* Ask the student, "What are you doing?" Or in the case of a specific incident, "What did you do?"

(3) *Force the student to make a value judgment.* The teacher forces the student to judge his own behavior as adaptive or maladaptive by asking, "Is it helping you?"

(4) *Develop a plan.* Teacher and student jointly develop a plan to help the student make positive changes.

(5) *Require a commitment.* Get a commitment from the student, preferably in the form of a written contract.

(6) *Allow no excuses.* The contract must be honored; no excuses are accepted.

(7) *No punishment is administered for failing to honor the contract.* The student is allowed to suffer the natural consequences of violating established rules and regulations, but no specific punitive action is taken by the teacher.

Love and discipline are integral components of reality therapy. The adult stance shows love through involvement, and discipline through demands for responsible behavior. It is also important to note that the adult never makes value judgments for the student; if the student does not accurately appraise her behavior, then she is left to experience the natural consequences but is asked repeatedly to make value judgments about the behavior.

Reality therapy obviously requires certain cognitive and language capabilities. Glasser (1965) and Towns (1981) have reported successful applications of reality therapy with adolescent populations. Newcomer (1980) recommends its use in settings where the adult has substantial control over the consequences of irresponsible behavior, such as residential settings.

Rational-Emotive Therapy

Rational-emotive therapy (RET) was developed by Albert Ellis (1962, 1973) who believes that individuals maintain many maladaptive behaviors through irrational thinking. Although Ellis recognizes the role of environmental and biological factors in the development of behaviors and emotions, his position is that irrational thinking leads to negative emotions and behavior. Rational-emotive therapy is based on the premise that humans are capable of rational thinking and can divest themselves of irrational thought. The "rational" part of RET refers to restructuring one's thinking, and the "emotive" part refers to the resultant changes in emotions. It is difficult to align RET with any other major theory, but it is similar to cognitive behavior modification in its emphasis on positive self-talk to effect behavior change (see page 183.).

Ellis (1980) distinguishes between rational and irrational beliefs: a rational belief is congruent with an individual's long-term goals, and an irrational belief interferes with the achievement of these long-term goals. Whereas rational beliefs are characterized by responsibility to oneself and society, irrational beliefs lead to conflict with other individuals and with society. Ellis contends that people are socialized to adhere to irrational beliefs through messages in the media and from significant people in their lives. Ellis (1977) identified over 250 irrational beliefs, most of which center around a few basic themes. Examples of irrational beliefs are:

(1)   I must have sincere love and approval almost all of the time from all of the people I find significant.

(2)   I must prove myself thoroughly competent, adequate, and achieving or I must at least have real competence or talent at something important.

(3)   Life is awful, terrible, horrible, or catastrophic when things do not go the way I would like them to go.

(4)   Emotional misery comes from external pressures, and I have little ability to control my feelings or rid myself of depression or hostility. (Ellis, 1977)

Ellis promotes the ABC model for disputing irrational beliefs. The "A" represents an *activating event,* which is unpleasant or bothersome; the "C" represents *consequences,* which are negative emotions, behaviors, or actions. Most people believe that consequences or emotions ("C") are a direct result of an event ("A"). Ellis insists that there is a "B," an intermediate step that represents the *beliefs* one holds about the event, and that it is these beliefs that actually cause the consequences. These "B" statements may be rational statements about the event, which lead to positive or neutral consequences, or may be irrational statements about the event, which generate negative consequences. In RET, the individual learns to recognize and dispute irrational beliefs and to replace them with more adaptive rational beliefs. The following example illustrates the relationship of A, B, and C.

A(EVENT)	B(BELIEF)	C(CONSEQUENCE)
upcoming final exam	irrational: "I'll die if I don't make an 'A' on this exam; nothing is more important!"	extreme anxiety
upcoming final exam	rational: "I'd like to do well on this exam and it would be nice to get an 'A,' but my personal worth doesn't depend on it."	slight anxiety, confidence

It has been found that RET is an effective counseling technique (Smith & Glass, 1977), but Ellis claims success only with populations who have mild emotional difficulties and who are motivated to change their behavior. Towns (1981) suggests that RET is useful with adolescents in coping with cycles of emotional upheaval.

Zionts (1985) advocates the use of RET in schools in three ways: (1) as a personal mental health program for educators, (2) as a counseling or intervention technique for students with emotional problems, or (3) as an affective curriculum. In the first case, teachers may be taught to use RET to examine their own belief systems about students and the educational process, which can lead to more realistic thinking and fewer self-imposed demands in their professional roles. The use of RET can be especially effective in helping teachers to become more assertive and to cope with stress and burnout.

When RET is used as a counseling technique, students must make a commitment to try to restructure their thinking, and students and teachers must work together to attack long-held, irrational beliefs. Zionts (1985) outlines both student and teacher roles in RET. In group sessions, the teacher's role is to monitor interactions and to ensure that it is the students' irrational beliefs being attacked and not the students themselves. In addition to being well-schooled in disputing irrational beliefs, the teacher should exhibit empathy and warmth while helping students to solve problems. The primary task for students is to make a commitment and to be honest about their beliefs; they must avoid dishonesty for the sake of approval. After student and teacher roles are established, group discussions center around the ABC technique. Initially, a student identifies a troublesome *A* (event) or an unpleasant *C* (feeling or behavior), which is the target for change. The group process then focuses on identifying the other components of the ABC model and disputing the irrational beliefs that are maintaining the negative emotions. Some areas that commonly surface in group RET sessions in the schools are test anxiety, the need for approval, the need to be competent and achieving, and dealing with anger.

The third application of RET in the schools is an affective curriculum for all grade levels. As a curriculum, RET exercises follow a developmental sequence with three goals: (1) the ability to identify and understand feelings, (2) awareness that feelings result from beliefs, not events, and (3) recognition of the overall RET process (Zionts, 1985). Zionts devotes a chapter to RET activities and reference materials, which include topics such as "Feelings Charades," "Sifting Facts from Opinions," "Who Causes Your Feelings," "The Shoulds of Society," and a variety of RET songs that are sung to popular tunes. As a curriculum, RET can be used alone or in conjunction with RET counseling strategies and group sessions.

Cognitive Behavior Modification

Bridging both cognitive and behavioral theories are a number of procedures that collectively have become known as *cognitive behavior modification*. Very basically defined, cognitive behavior modification (CBM) refers to the effect that self-talk or inner speech has on an individual's behavior. Lloyd (1980) has extracted five common attributes of CBM procedures:

(1) A self-imposed treatment is taught—for example, self-instruction, self-control, self-assessment, self-monitoring, or self-reinforcement.

(2) Verbalization is usually a part of the technique.

(3) A problem-solving strategy is identified.

(4) Modeling is used to teach the technique.

(5) The technique is usually aimed at helping students to become more reflective and to evaluate alternatives before responding.

The goal of most CBM techniques is to train students, through self-talk, to develop strategies or to problem-solve for themselves. Such techniques have shown promise for both social and academic improvement in studies with hyperactive boys (Douglas, Parry, Marton, & Garson, 1976) and with aggressive boys (Camp, Blom, Hebert, & van Doorninck, 1977). Although the focus of such studies generally is on academic-related behaviors (for example, on-task) rather than on academic skills per se, improvements in academic skills have been reported (Hallahan, Lloyd, Kosiewicz, Kauffman, & Graves, 1979; Robin, Armel, & O'Leary, 1975). The following section highlights several CBM techniques, including "Think Aloud" and self-control methods.

The "Think Aloud" technique.[3] Cognitive behavior modification techniques have been used successfully with impulsive students who lack the internal controls that enable them to think before they act (Meichenbaum & Cameron, 1974; Meichenbaum & Goodman, 1971). Researchers have directed efforts toward teaching these students to pause and evaluate a situation before responding. The "Think Aloud" program was developed by Camp and her colleagues (Camp et al., 1977; Camp & Bash, 1978) as a problem-solving strategy for young aggressive boys. In "Think Aloud," students are taught to ask themselves four basic questions:

(1) What is my problem? or
      What do I have to do now?

(2) What is my plan? or
      How can I figure a way to do it?

(3) Am I using my plan? or
      Am I doing what I said I'd do?

(4) How did I do? or
      Did I do it?

The "Think Aloud" technique offers a framework for organizing information, brainstorming alternatives, evaluating the selected plan or solution, and either reinforcing oneself for success or coping with failure. When teaching these techniques, the teacher should model ways to cope with errors, as many of these students are trying to break out of a failure cycle. "Think Aloud" is obviously a general problem-solving technique; other CBM products that are task-specific have been developed (Robin et al., 1975).

Self-control is a related issue that is very important in dealing with behavior disordered students. Self-control has been defined as "one's capacity to flexibly and realistically. . . regulate personal action or behavior in a given situation" (cited in Fagen & Long, 1979, p. 68). Techniques for teaching behavioral self-control have been systematized by Workman (1982). A self-control curriculum developed by Fagen, Long, and Stevens (1975) is highlighted in the curriculum section of this chapter.

Behavioral self-control. The teaching of behavioral self-control (BSC) to students is in keeping with the basic behavioral tenet that an individual's dependence on external controls must gradually be shifted to dependence on internal controls. Workman (1982)[4] outlines three reasons for teaching BSC and indicates three behavioral areas in which it has proven successful. One reason for teaching BSC is that the teacher will not always be around to guide students' behavior by providing feedback and administering reinforcement; therefore, students should learn to monitor and evaluate their own behavior. Second, BSC is a method for teaching students to take responsibility for their actions. Third, BSC may be more effective than traditional behavior modification techniques in helping students maintain positive changes over time and in different settings. As Workman (1982) asserts, "BSC provides students with a means of functioning at their best in the 'real' world" (p. 11).

Three areas in which BSC has proven most successful are: on-task behaviors (for example, complying with teacher directions, working on assignments); academic product behaviors (number of correct math problems on homework or tests, number of correct spelling words on spelling list, etc.); and disruptive behaviors (out-of-seat, talking out, verbal threats) (Workman & Hector, 1978).

Three basic components of BSC were identified by Glynn, Thomas, and Shee (1973) and adopted by Workman: self-assessment, self-monitoring, and self-reinforcement (see Table 7–2).

Self-assessment. Students learn to assess their own behavior by self-examination and determination of whether a specific behavior was performed. Various methods of self-assessment may be used. In *self-rating*, an objective standards such as a rating scale is given the student. For example, a student may be asked to rate, on a scale of 1 to 5, the amount of time he was on-task during a math assignment. In *self-instruction*, students

TABLE 7–2. Components of Behavioral Self-Control (Workman, 1982)

SELF-ASSESSMENT	SELF-MONITORING	SELF-REINFORCEMENT
self-rating	frequency self-monitoring	overt self-reinforcement
self-instruction	interval self-monitoring	covert positive reinforcement
verbal mediation training		

use self-talk to cue themselves about a specific task and then to give themselves feedback. Self-instruction is a step-by-step verbal guidance technique that is used specifically to reduce impulsive behavior and to increase on-task behavior with elementary-age students (Workman, 1982). *Verbal mediation training* (Blackwood, 1970) is very similar to self-instruction but is more useful with older students. The teacher prepares an essay for each targeted inappropriate behavior; when a student manifests the behavior, he is required to copy the essay. Each essay poses four questions and then offers answers. The questions are: "What did I do wrong?" "What is wrong with that behavior?" "What should I have been doing instead?" and "Why should I have been doing. . .?" (the behavior named in answer to the third question).

Self-monitoring. Students learn to monitor and record their performance on a specified behavior. In *frequency self-monitoring*, the student records every occurrence of the target behavior. This technique has been used to increase academic performance and to decrease inappropriate behaviors such as out-of-seat. In *interval self-monitoring*, the student records whether a behavior occurs during a given period of time. Workman, Helton, and Watson (1982) found that this technique was successful in increasing the on-task behaviors of a preschooler. Self-monitoring was also found to be successful in decreasing disruptive behaviors of elementary and adolescent students (Bolstad & Johnson, 1972; Gottman & McFall, 1972).

Self-reinforcement. Students learn to reinforce theselves for appropriate classroom behaviors. In comparison studies, this approach was more effective than external reinforcement only (Bolstad & Johnson, 1972) or teacher-controlled reinforcement (Fredericksen & Fredericksen, 1975). *Overt self-reinforcement* involves rewarding oneself at appropriate times with a tangible reinforcer such as a token or check mark. In *covert positive reinforcement*, students do not receive tangible rewards; rather, they are taught to imagine themselves performing the behavior and then to imagine receiving the valued reward. This technique has been shown to strengthen the imagined target behavior (Workman & Dickinson, 1979, 1980).

In summary, Workman (1982) offers step-by-step guidelines for teaching behavioral self-control in the classroom through the basic methods of self-assessment, self-monitoring, and self-reinforcement. The interested reader is referred to Workman's book, *Teaching Behavioral Self-Control to Students.*

Although much of the research on cognitive behavior modification and self-control is encouraging, researchers have voiced concerns over generalization and maintenance of behaviors acquired through these methods (McLaughlin, 1976; Stokes & Baer, 1977). Whether students will exhibit these acquired behaviors across settings (generalization) and over time (maintenance) is a question that should be addressed in further research.

BEHAVIORAL TECHNIQUES

Behavior modification techniques are based on the principles of operant and respondent conditioning and social learning. These principles were described in detail in Chapter 4 along with methods for increasing behaviors, and methods for decreasing behaviors (see Table 7–3). At its most basic level, application of behavioral principles involves identification of events or objects in the environment that can be manipulated in order to effect behavior change. In applying behavioral principles to the classroom, the teacher must be able to target behaviors for intervention and to manipulate consequences in order to increase, decrease, or maintain those behaviors. To do so, the teacher needs three basic skills:

(1) the ability to identify target behaviors
(2) the ability to collect behavioral data
(3) the ability to apply and manipulate reinforcers effectively.

Target Behaviors

The first step in a behavior intervention plan is identification of the target behavior, that is, the behavior to be changed. Target behaviors are usually chosen because: (1) they are positively evaluated and should be increased, such as emerging social skills; (2) they are negatively evaluated and should be decreased, such as disruptive behaviors; or (3) they are positively

TABLE 7–3. Behavior Management Techniques and Skills

METHODS FOR INCREASING BEHAVIORS	METHODS FOR DECREASING BEHAVIORS
shaping	extinction
modeling	reinforcing incompatible behaviors
contingency contracting	time-out
	punishment

GENERAL BEHAVIOR MANAGEMENT SKILLS
identify target behaviors
collect behavioral data
use reinforcers

evaluated, are being exhibited at appropriate rates, and should be maintained, such as academic skills. Existing positive skills and behaviors should be recognized by the teacher so that individuals will be motivated to continue exhibiting them and so that other students can model them.

A target behavior must be defined in terms that are observable and measurable. In other words, the teacher and others must be able to see or hear it, to count or time it. Observability and measurability are necessary characteristics if data are to be collected and if people are to communicate clearly about the target behavior. In addition, the target behavior should be as specific as possible. Under what conditions is the behavior manifested? Consider the following descriptions of behavior:

Lara talks too much.
Chris doesn't pay attention.
Adrian is out of her seat all of the time.

These descriptions of behavior are so vague that they impart only a general idea of what the problem actually is. For the first example, "Lara talks too much," more specific information might center around the following: Does she talk too much to peers or to the teacher? Does she talk too much on the playground, in the cafeteria, in line, or during independent work assignments? Does the talking usually occur during a particular subject or class period? Does she talk out in class without permission? Is her talking interfering with her ability to do her work, her classmates' ability to do theirs, or the teacher's ability to teach? By describing the behavior more specifically, the teacher may find that the target behavior is actually Lara's talking to peers during independent math assignments. Further exploration might lead to the discovery that Lara's talking is motivated by her insecurity about math and her reluctance to begin working on math assignments. The original target behavior of decreasing Lara's talking would then change to increasing her confidence with math problems.

The teacher should select a single behavior to be targeted for intervention at one time. If there are several behaviors the teacher would like to change, the behaviors should be ranked according to priority, and the teacher should begin with the most important one. Working on several target behaviors at a time has proven both confusing and ineffective.

Once a target behavior has been selected, data should be collected so that its frequency or duration can be quantified and an intervention plan begun.

Data Collection

Although teachers invariably wince at the suggestion that they collect data in their classrooms, there are two excellent reasons for data collection: precise measurement of a specific behavior may give the teacher an idea of the best way to change it, and precise measurement allows the teacher to accurately judge the effectiveness of an intervention (Alberto & Troutman, 1982). Four observational recording methods are easily utilized in the classroom: event recording, interval recording, time sampling, and duration recording. Choice of method is usually dictated by the type of behavior targeted for change.

(1) *Event recording* is used when the rate of occurrence or frequency of a behavior is the primary concern. In event recording, the teacher chooses a specific observation period and makes a tally mark or other notation every time the behavior occurs. The chosen behaviors must be *discrete;* that is, they must have an observable beginning and an observable end. Examples of behaviors often recorded by this method are hitting, sharpening pencils, completing an academic task, and talking out in class without permission.

(2) *Interval recording* is used primarily with behaviors that have such a high rate of occurrence that event recording is not feasible. The teacher chooses a short time period, which is then divided into equal intervals of seconds; within each interval, the teacher records whether the behavior occurred at any time during the interval. Interval recording offers an estimate rather than an exact count of behaviors. Its chief disadvantage is that it often requires an additional person to observe and record because it is difficult to do while maintaining class. Examples of behaviors often recorded by the interval method are on-task behaviors such as writing or attending to a worksheet, off-task behaviors such as talking to a classmate or being out-of-seat, and self-stimulation behaviors such as hand-flapping.

(3) *Time sampling* is similar to interval recording, but with two differences: the observation period is divided into longer intervals of time, and the observer records whether the behavior is occurring the moment when the interval ends. It is helpful to use a kitchen timer to indicate the end of a time interval. For example, the teacher may choose 5-minute intervals within a 30-minute observation period; when the timer goes off, the teacher looks to see whether the behavior is occurring, then records and resets the timer. A major disadvantage is that many occurrences of a behavior may be missed because recording occurs only as the time interval is ending. Thus, behaviors occurring immediately before or immediately after would not be counted. Time sampling is most appropriate for behaviors of high frequency or long duration such as out-of-seat or thumb sucking.

(4) *Duration recording* is used when the length or duration of a behavior rather than its frequency is of concern. For example, the teacher may find that a certain child does not go into a tantrum often, but when she does, it seems to disrupt the class for an interminable time. Duration recording is used with discrete behaviors: the beginning and end of the behavior are carefully timed and recorded. The teacher may choose duration recording for behaviors such as out-of-seat or off-task if the amount of time rather than the number of times is of concern. Other behaviors appropriate for duration recording are on-task behaviors and questionably long trips to the water fountain, the bathroom, or the pencil sharpener.

The teacher most likely will want to use behavioral data to design interventions for individual students. After selecting an appropriate recording method that fits the behavior(s) to be changed, the teacher should collect *baseline* data, which is the level of occurrence of the behavior prior to intervention. Baseline data provide the foundation for planning intervention and behavior change.

According to Alberto and Troutman (1982), the observer collecting baseline data should be aware of both the stability and directionality of behavior. Stability refers to consistency in the level of the recorded behavior; if recorded levels are fairly consistent, then the observer can be confident that a representative sampling of behavior has been obtained. In addition, the recorded behavior should show a definite trend or directionality: it should show an increase, decrease, no change, or inconsistency. If recorded data show both stability and directionality, then the data can be used to plan interventions.

The most basic intervention design is the *AB,* in which *A* represents data collected during the baseline phase, and *B* represents data collected during the intervention phase. A comparison is made between *B* data and *A* data to determine the effectiveness of intervention. The *AB* design is a quick and simple way to evaluate an instructional or behavioral intervention. For more complete information on methods of behavior recording and intervention designs, the reader is referred to Alberto and Troutman's *Applied Behavior Analysis for Teachers* (1982).

Reinforcement

After becoming proficient at data collection, the teacher must learn to use *reinforcement* effectively. In this section, basic principles and schedules of reinforcement will be briefly presented, along with suggestions for identifying effective reinforcers. A reinforcer is defined as a consequence of behavior that may increase or maintain that behavior, and reinforcement is the application of a reinforcer. The relationship among behaviors, reinforcers, and reinforcement is depicted in the following general examples:

BEHAVIOR	REINFORCER	REINFORCEMENT
studying	good grades	professor gives an 'A'
attendance at work	money	boss signs and hands out paycheck
finishing seatwork assignment	free time	teacher allows 10-minute break

The success of a behavioral intervention program depends upon effective use of reinforcers. The two major classes of reinforcers are *primary* and *secondary*. Primary reinforcers are those biologically satisfying to an individual, such as food and liquids. Ice cream, raisins, cookies, crackers, popcorn, fruit, sodas, and the ever-popular M & Ms are examples of primary reinforcers often dispersed in classrooms.

Whereas primary reinforcers may be necessary with younger or more severely handicapped students, secondary reinforcers usually work with older or mildly handicapped students. Secondary reinforcers have a value that is learned rather than biological or innate; examples are activities, social rewards, and tokens which may be exchanged for something desirable. Use of secondary reinforcers is always preferable to use of primary reinforcers because the goal is eventually to remove any external reinforcement for appropriate behavior. Many students will work for secondary reinforcers and do not need primary reinforcers. The teacher should therefore attempt to use naturally occurring events or social rewards before using primary reinforcers. Or as Alberto and Troutman (1982) succinctly state, "Don't kill flies with an elephant gun" (p. 175).

The most basic—but sometimes overlooked—aspect of a reinforcer is that it must be valued by the student who is receiving it. Preferences for rewards are highly individualistic and the teacher should never assume that a particular reinforcer will be effective with every student. It is a good idea for the teacher to prepare a list of acceptable reinforcers (a *reinforcement menu*) and to let the students choose from the list. However, the ultimate evaluation of whether a reinforcer works is the effect it has on the target behavior. Only after a reinforcer has been applied and has the desired effect can it be evaluated as truly successful or reinforcing.

In some cases, such as with a student who is severely handicapped or unwilling to identify reinforcers, the teacher may have to identify reinforcers for the student. One way to identify reinforcers is to find out about the student's reinforcement history, or things for which the student has worked in previous programs. Another way is to simply observe what the student does during unstructured or free time. A third method for use with severely handicapped students is a reinforcement sampling, in which the teacher brings several possible reinforcers to a work session with the student and then proceeds by trial and error. When presented with an array of reinforcers that are within reach, the student may respond to certain ones. The teacher can then test the student's preference in successive work sessions with very simple tasks. It may take several such sessions to identify numerous reinforcers. Examples of primary and secondary reinforcers are listed in Table 7–4.

Walker and Shea (1976) outline a number of basic guidelines that the teacher should follow when using reinforcement:

(1) *The reinforcer is given only when the appropriate behavior is manifested.* A selected reinforcer must not be freely available to the student, but must be earned by engaging in the specified behavior. Also, the teacher must be careful not to reinforce inappropriate behavior inadvertently. A common example is teacher attention to misbehavior; although the teacher may call a student down or make a disapproving statement, the student may perceive any teacher attention as positive and thus be reinforced by it.

TABLE 7–4.   Reinforcers

PRIMARY		SECONDARY
	TOKENS	MATERIALS
cereal	poker chips	balloons
peanuts	other colored plastic chips	ink stamp pad
chips	stars	pennies
ice cream	checks	stars
Coke	happy faces	bubbles liquid
raisins	points	badges
fruit	ink stamps	books
popcorn	play money	magazines
crackers	hole punch	play dough
candy	paper clips	bookmarks
M & Ms		calendars
juice		puzzles
other food and drink		stationery or writing pads
		toy jewelry
		records
		flash cards
		bean bags
		art supplies

ACTIVITIES/PRIVILEGES

grade or staple papers	typing
teacher's helper for the day	listening to music with headphones
tutor others	using tape recorder
janitorial tasks in class	painting or drawing
sit with teacher	drawing on chalkboard
sit in special spot	skipping nap time
pass out snacks	writing a letter
read to the class	taking photographs
choose story for teacher to read	skipping an assignment or test
class librarian	playing with board games
distribute and collect materials	playing with puppets
being first in line	class Coke break
run errands	
leading an activity	
free time	

(2) *Reinforcement should be initiated at a level of performance below the baseline.* Initially the student must be able to attain reinforcement without undue effort; otherwise, the student may never buy into the reinforcement system at all. If the required performance level is too high, the student is likely to become discouraged and to stop trying before experiencing success.

(3) *Appropriate behavior must be reinforced immediately.* This guideline is especially important in the initial stages of intervention; immediate reinforcement helps ensure that the student makes the association between behavior and its consequence and that intervening inappropriate behaviors are not reinforced.

(4) *During the initial stages of intervention, the appropriate behavior must be reinforced each time it is exhibited.* If the behavior is not reinforced consistently in

the beginning stages, the student may fail to adopt it as part of her behavioral repertoire.

(5) *Once the behavior has been established at a satisfactory level, it should be reinforced intermittently.* This guideline is based on the principle that a student is more likely to maintain a newly acquired behavior if the reinforcement is intermittent rather than constant; under such conditions, the student knows that reinforcement will occur but does not know when to expect it. Thus, the behavior is maintained at high rates.

Depending upon the type of behavior to be reinforced, the teacher may select from several patterns or schedules of reinforcement. According to Walker and Shea (1976), the most common are:

Fixed ratio. Reinforcement is presented after a specific number of responses are given by the student.

Variable ratio. After an acceptable level of response has been established through fixed ratio, the behavior should be maintained by varying the number of responses that are required before the student is reinforced.

Fixed interval. Reinforcement is presented after a specified period of time has elapsed.

Variable interval. The periods of time before reinforcement is presented are varied so that the student cannot predict when the reinforcement will occur.

See Table 7–5 for examples of these four schedules of reinforcement.

(6) *Social reinforcement should always be given along with tangible reinforcement.* Tangible reinforcers (such as food, drink, and tokens) should always be accompanied by social reinforcers (such as praise or a smile) because the ultimate goal of behavioral intervention is to develop the student's internal motivation to behave appropriately. The teacher should initially use tangible reinforcers only if necessary and should gradually replace tangible reinforcement totally with social reinforcement.

Skills necessary for application of behavioral principles to the classroom setting have been discussed in this section. The ability to identify

TABLE 7–5. Examples of Four Reinforcement Schedules

	RATIO	INTERVAL
Fixed	Student completes 20 problems to receive 10 minutes of free time.	Student is rewarded for remaining in seat for 5 minutes.
Variable	Teacher rewards student, on an average, every third time student raises hand.	Teacher gives individual attention, on an average, every 15 minutes in response to acceptable behavior during the time period.

From Walker, James E., and Shea, Thomas M.: *Behavior modification,* ed. 2, St. Louis, 1980, The C.V. Mosby Co.

target behaviors, collect behavioral data, and manipulate reinforcers form the basis for setting up any behavior management plan. Other important applications of behavioral theory are contingency contracting and token economies. Contingency contracting is a form of instructional or behavior management in which an "if . . . then" contract is made; if the student performs a specific responsibility, then a specific reinforcer is given. (See *How to Use Contingency Contracting in the Classroom*, Lloyd Homme, 1969, for more comprehensive information.) Token economies are often used successfully in the classroom to improve both social and academic skills (Kazdin & Bootsin, 1972; O'Leary & Drabman, 1971).

In a token economy, the teacher sets up a token system in which accumulated tokens earned for good behavior can be traded in for selected reinforcers. Tokens may be poker chips, play money, check marks, stars, or points. For more information on setting up a token economy, the reader is referred to Hewett and Taylor's *The Emotionally Disturbed Child in the Classroom* (1980) and to Alberto and Troutman's *Applied Behavior Analysis for Teachers* (1982).

Research on the efficacy of behavior management techniques in the school setting is too voluminous to review here. Behavioral techniques have been demonstrated to be effective with individuals and groups, and with students with all types of handicaps, low functioning as well as high functioning. Behavioral techniques have been effective in increasing appropriate target behaviors and in decreasing inappropriate target behaviors. Teachers of behavior disordered students should become particularly familiar with the classroom applications of token economies, contingency contracting, and time-out, as these techniques are often used in programs for the behavior disordered.

CURRICULUM

Teachers of behavior disordered students face a difficult question: should academic skills or affective concerns take precedence in the educational curriculum? Most special educators agree that neither area should be neglected in favor of the other; however, striking a balance between the two on a daily basis in the classroom poses a challenge. Knoblock (1983) proposes that teachers adopt a "caring curriculum," an outgrowth of humanistic education which emphasizes both academic and emotional development. According to Knoblock:

> In short, a caring curriculum involves more than teaching. It conveys to students that they are worthy of great consideration; that they can and will become more competent; and that the world of ideas, concepts, and information may be of interest and value to them. It also acknowledges that students may face difficult life circumstances, but it creates a learning envi-

ronment that responds to the human desire for growth. Teachers are often dismayed by the pressures under which many children live: broken homes, poverty, community rejection. Although a caring curriculum cannot solve such problems, it can help structure a student's school experience to foster feelings of self-worth and competence . . . in the context of developing positive relationships with teachers and peers.

(Knoblock, 1983, pp. 153–154)

Curricula developed for exploring affective concerns and for teaching self-control and social skills are reviewed in the remainder of this chapter. Also described is a curriculum which combines affective and academic concerns into a developmental framework.

Affective Curricula

A number of commercially available affective materials can be incorporated into the school program on a regular basis. None of these affective curricula were developed specifically for use with the behavior disordered population; instead, the materials were developed for use with all students in order to serve a preventative function. The majority focus on areas such as self-concept or communication with others. A few of the most widely used materials will be briefly reviewed.

The principles of transactional analysis (Berne, 1965) have been simplified for children in *T.A. for Tots* (Freed, 1973) and *T.A. for Kids* (Freed & Freed, 1977). According to Dr. Freed, the purpose of the series is to help young children realize that they are "OK" and to help them relate better to parents and to other adults. Specifically, children are helped to deal with their emotions of anger, fear, joy, love, friendship, and responsibility. The major instructional materials are books that chronicle numerous childhood difficulties, but optional materials include filmstrips, cassette tapes, records, posters, and games. A third book in the series, *T.A. for Teens* (Freed, 1976) is for use with students in grades 7 through 12; it focuses on the topics of drugs, sex, authority, rebellion, and independence.

Magic Circle or the *Human Development Program* (Besell & Palomares, 1970) is a curriculum for developing interpersonal communication skills through small groups. Booklets are provided for preschoolers through sixth graders, but the Magic Circle is the main feature of the curriculum. On a daily basis, a number of children (8 to 13) gather in a circle on the floor to discuss a selected topic on human relations. Six weeks each semester are devoted to one of three topic areas: (1) understanding similarities and differences between self and others, (2) identifying and using one's own abilities, and (3) understanding social relationships. A supportive atmosphere is established within the group, in which sharing of personal ideas and experiences is encouraged by the teacher. Ground rules for Magic Circle discussions forbid interrupting, confronting, or belittling others. The teacher's role is to present curriculum lessons and to lead the Magic Circle discussions.

Toward Affective Development (TAD) (Dupont, Gardner & Brody, 1974) was developed as an affective curriculum for students in grades 3 through 6. The 191 sequenced lessons are categorized into five units entitled, "Reaching In and Reaching Out," "Your Feelings and Mine," "Working Together," "Me: Today and Tomorrow," and "Feeling, Thinking, and Doing." Two primary emphases are peer interactions and career choices. Included in the curriculum package are a manual of activities, discussion pictures, duplicating masters, filmstrip and audio-cassette, and career folders that illustrate 37 different jobs. The teacher has three basic roles: modeling the discussed behaviors, giving verbal reinforcement to students, and monitoring student activities.

Another popular affective curriculum is *Developing Understanding of Self and Others-Revised* (DUSO-R) (Dinkmeyer & Dinkmeyer, 1982). Developed around a central character—DUSO the Dolphin—the program provides stories and activities aimed at developing self-concept, responsibility, and decision-making skills. In addition to providing manuals, storybooks, records, cassettes, and activity cards, DUSO-R offers the unique feature of hand puppets and puppet activity cards. Two levels of the kit are available, one for use with grades K–2, and the other for use with grades 3–4. Both levels are organized into three units: developing understanding of self, developing understanding of others, and developing understanding of choices.

The authors outline three specific objectives: (1) to help children learn more words for feelings, (2) to teach that feelings, goals, and behavior are related, and (3) to help children learn to express feelings and goals and to talk openly about behavior. In DUSO-R, the teacher facilitates group lessons and projects, but also takes an active role in helping children to clarify and process their experiences.

The teaching of values and moral judgment in the schools is advocated by Simon (Simon, Howe, & Kirschenbaum, 1978) and by Kohlberg (Kohlberg & Turiel, 1971). Both have developed approaches for incorporating the study of values into school curriculum; both approaches are based on the premise that educators are undeniably socialization agents and therefore should teach values development in a systematic and responsible manner. Simon's approach is popularly known as *values clarification*. In values clarification, teachers are to avoid moralizing or attempting to instill a set of values; rather, students are helped to develop their own value systems. A handbook of activities is provided in which three themes are prevalent: prizing one's beliefs and behaviors, choosing one's beliefs and behaviors, and acting on one's beliefs (Simon, et al., 1978). These activities stress the process of valuing rather than imposing a set of values. Kohlberg's approach, namely moral development, also stresses the process of decision making about personal problems and values. Moral development is a cognitive-developmental approach based on Kohlberg's idea that values curricula should be matched to the developmental level of the child. Discussions of moral dilemmas are the basis for this program.

Although numerous studies have supported the effectiveness of Simon's values clarification techniques, Lockwood (1978) analyzed the methodology of 13 of these and found them lacking in merit. One study supportive of Kohlberg's moral development (Blatt & Kohlberg, 1975) was assigned a high merit rating by Lockwood. The majority of these studies were marked by the difficulties that undermine many attempts to evaluate affective programs.

The efficacy of affective programs is difficult to evaluate for a number of reasons. First and foremost is the difficulty in measuring affective concepts or constructs, such as "communication skills," "self-concept," and "understanding oneself." The majority of research studies utilize some measure of self-concept, which may be an established, commercially produced instrument or one developed by the authors of the affective program being evaluated. As Medway and Smith (1978) point out, the use of differing definitions and instruments to measure the same concept is not likely to produce consistent or comparable results. A second difficulty is that most of these measures are a form of self-report or self-evaluation. Wylie (1974) has distinguished several difficulties inherent in self-evaluation, primarily that subjects tend to give socially acceptable responses and that great differences exist across situations and across subjects in their willingness to self-disclose.

In a review of research on four popular elementary-level affective programs, Medway and Smith (1978) concluded that mixed results occur mainly because of differences in choices of outcome measures, length of program treatment, and the training or qualifications of the program administrator (for example, teacher or counselor). Elardo and Elardo (1976) offer the criticism that most affective curricula are developed and field-tested without provision for any ongoing research that would evaluate long-term program effectiveness.

In summary, although special educators recognize the importance of integrating cognitive with affective concerns in the classroom, the effectiveness of commercial affective curricula remains unproven. However, this state of affairs may be a reflection of inconsistencies in research methodology and program implementation rather than ineffectiveness of the curricula per se. Another concern is the lack of research on the efficacy of affective programs with behavior disordered students; as Epanchin and Monson (1982) summarize, "Affective education for exceptional children has not yet been systematically studied" (p. 418).

A Self-Control Curriculum

Special educators have long recognized a need not only for remedial methods but also for methods aimed at the prevention of learning and behavior problems. The psychoeducational curriculum for teaching self-control was developed by Fagen, Long, and Stevens (1975) to help meet this need. According to its authors, the curriculum can easily be adopted as part of a schoolwide preventive program.

Fagen and colleagues developed the self-control curriculum over a period of five years. According to Fagen and Long (1979),

> . . . during the period from 1968–1973 we developed a curriculum to promote direct classroom instruction in basic enabling skills for self-control. . . . Through a process of classroom observation and analysis of disruptive behavior in both special and regular school settings, a core set of eight skill clusters were identified. Four of these skill clusters rely heavily on intellectual or cognitive development, while the other four are more related to emotional or affective development. These eight skill clusters are summarized as follows:
>
> *Selection*—Ability to perceive incoming information accurately.
>
> *Storage*—Ability to retain the information received.
>
> *Sequencing and Ordering*—Ability to organize actions on the basis of a planned order.
>
> *Anticipating Consequences*—Ability to relate actions to expected outcomes.
>
> *Appreciating Feelings*—Ability to identify and constructively use affective experiences.
>
> *Managing Frustration*—Ability to cope with external obstacles that produce stress.
>
> *Inhibition and Delay*—Ability to postpone or restrain action tendencies.
>
> *Relaxation*—Ability to reduce internal tension.
>
> (Fagen & Long, 1979, p. 70).

The curriculum is composed of eight areas that correspond to the eight skill clusters. Each area is broken down into units, each with its own goals and learning tasks. Teacher instructions and materials are provided for each learning task. For example, under the skill area *Managing Frustration* are three units: "Accepting Feelings of Frustration," with two learning tasks; "Building Coping Resources," with nine learning tasks; and "Tolerating Frustration," with 22 learning tasks. The authors suggest that the curriculum be taught in one of three ways: (1) over the course of one school year, with one area taught per month; (2) in one semester, with one area taught per two weeks, and selected problem areas retaught or recycled during the second semester; or (3) depending on the needs of the class, selected parts of the curriculum may be taught for any period of time at the teacher's discretion.

Minimal research on the effectiveness of the psychoeducational self-control curriculum has been conducted, but preliminary investigations indicate that subjects showed significant improvement on measures of general school adjustment (Stevens, 1973; Vaden, 1972), but not on school achievement (Vaden, 1972).

Social Skills Curricula

The importance of social skills in the classroom setting becomes increasingly evident as mainstreaming becomes common policy in the schools. Students who do not make it in the regular classroom are often deficient in the skills that enable them to function as independent learners and to get along with teachers and their classmates. Students who have been in special education programs and are entering mainstream settings have two major adjustments to make: (1) they must meet the teacher's expectations for appropriate social behavior and academic standards, and (2) they must learn to interact with a new peer group (Walker et al., 1983).

The majority of behavior disordered students are deficient in social skills and do not fit either teacher or peer expectations for classroom behavior. (In fact, they are often placed in special education because of this deficiency.) In addition, the label of "behavior disorders" has a stigma which often generates negative expectations; thus the mainstreamed behavior disordered student faces an especially difficult adjustment period in which he must strive to overcome negative expectations and fit smoothly into the regular classroom environment.

The teaching of social skills is important not only to facilitate mainstreaming but also to foster social adjustment and competencies outside the classroom setting (Stephens, 1977). Most social skills curricula offer a variety of communication and courtesy skills which can be applied to interpersonal interactions in any setting. Two social skills curricula will be described: one that was developed for the elementary populations (*ACCEPTS*), and one that is applicable to all age levels (*Social Skills*). References to two curricula for adolescent populations will be made. All four of the curricula are based on behavioral principles and are implemented through behavioral techniques.

Social Skills Curriculum (Stephens, 1978). *Social Skills* is a basic skills curriculum for individualizing instruction with learning disordered and behavior disordered students. Included are reading and arithmetic curricula for kindergarten through third-grade levels, and a social skills curriculum applicable to any age and grade level. According to Stephens (1977), the *Social Skills* curriculum is "not intended to include every behavior students need to acquire while in school. It is, however, an attempt to assist teachers to consciously and systematically instruct students in social behavior" (p. 120). For each social skill in the curriculum, there is a corresponding behavioral objective, assessment task, and instructional strategy. Stephens offers 136 social skills that are grouped under the following categories and subcategories:[5]

ENVIRONMENTALLY-RELATED BEHAVIORS

Care for Environment   Dealing with Emergency
Lunchroom   Movement around Environment

SELF-RELATED BEHAVIORS

Accepting Consequences   Ethical Behavior
Expressing Feelings   Positive Attitudes toward Self
Responsible Behavior   Self-care

INTERPERSONAL BEHAVIORS

Accepting Authority   Coping with Conflict
Gaining Attention   Greeting Others
Helping Others   Making Conversation

TASK-RELATED BEHAVIORS

Asking and Answering Questions   Attending Behavior
Classroom Discussion   Completing Tasks
Following Directions   Group Activities
Independent Work   On-Task Behaviors
Performing before Others   Quality of Work

As a specific example, under *Task-Related Behaviors,* four skills are taught under "Quality of Work":

(1) to turn in neat papers
(2) to accept correction of school work
(3) to use teacher's corrections for improving work
(4) to review work to correct errors

To implement the curriculum with an individual, teachers follow four basic guidelines in the manual:

(1) Define the skill to be taught.

(2) Assess performance of the skill according to personally acceptable criteria and select a teaching strategy.

(3) Implement one of the recommended teaching strategies: modeling, role playing, behavior rehearsing, contingency contracting, or social reinforcement.

(4) Evaluate effectiveness of the strategy.

If the student fails to perform the skill at acceptable level after instruction, Stephens (1977) recommends four possible options. First, the instructional strategy may be changed to a different one. Second, the reinforcement may be changed to a more powerful one and care taken to ensure that the reinforcement immediately follows the behavior. Third, the task may be broken down into smaller steps. Fourth, the student may lack prerequisite skills that require further instruction.

In one study with two elementary and two junior high students, targeted social behaviors showed significant improvement after application of Stephen's principles for teaching social skills (La Nunziata, Hill, & Krause, 1981). Modeling, contracting, and social reinforcement, singly or in combination, were found to be effective instructional strategies.

A Curriculum for Children's Effective Peer and Teacher Skills (ACCEPTS)- (Walker et al., 1983).   The ACCEPTS program was developed specifically to help mildly and moderately handicapped youngsters acquire the social skills necessary for functioning in a mainstream environment. Two types of skills are emphasized: those that enable the students to function as independent learners in the classroom, and those that contribute to social competence and peer acceptance. A direct instructional approach is used to teach a total of 28 skills appropriate for elementary-age students. The skills related to classroom functioning in ACCEPTS were selected according to data gathered from a national sample of teachers who were asked "to rate the importance of 56 adaptive behaviors in facilitating a successful classroom adjustment" (Walker et al., 1983, p. 1). Those behaviors that consistently received the highest ratings were then included in the curriculum; thus, ACCEPTS has the advantage of a data-based rationale for its selection of specific skills. The following components are offered in ACCEPTS:

> a placement rating scale and procedures to be used for selecting students who need the training
> a nine-step direct instruction procedure to be used with each skill
> scripts for teaching each skill
> videotapes with positive examples and negative examples for 23 skills
> activities for one-to-one, small group, large group, or class instruction
> role-play activities to determine skill mastery
> behavior management procedures to help teach and maintain the skills

The authors strongly promote the position that social skills can be most effectively taught through direct instructional techniques coupled with behavior management techniques to strengthen and maintain the skill. They also provide step-by-step guidelines for implementation; the teacher is advised what to do when a student gives an incorrect response or fails to perform a skill to criterion.

The 28 skills are grouped under five major categories:

CLASSROOM SKILLS
Listening to the Teacher
When the Teacher Asks You to
    Do Something

BASIC INTERACTION SKILLS
Eye Contact
Using the Right Voice
Starting

Doing Your Best Work
Following Classroom Rules

GETTING ALONG SKILLS

Using Polite Words
Sharing
Following Rules
Assisting Others
Touching the Right Way

MAKING FRIENDS SKILLS

Good Grooming
Smiling
Complimenting
Friendship Making

Listening
Answering
Making Sense
Taking Turns Talking
A Question
Continuing

COPING SKILLS

When Someone Says "No"
When You Express Anger
When Someone Teases You
When Someone Tries to Hurt You
When Someone Asks You to Do
   Something You Can't Do
When Things Don't Go Right

Other commercially available curricula have been developed for teaching social skills to adolescents. *Skillstreaming the Adolescent* (Goldstein, Sprafkin, Gershaw, & Klein, 1980) offers a manual and a set of training audio-cassettes for the teaching of 50 social skills. Goldstein et al. (1980) use a four-step behavioral format to teach the skills that were developed for use with aggressive, withdrawn, immature, and developmentally delayed adolescents. The *Asset* program (Hazel, Schumaker, Sherman, & Sheldon-Wildgen, 1981) is a multimedia package focusing on eight social skills areas, such as problem solving, resisting peer pressure, and giving and receiving feedback. The authors promote its use with a wide range of adolescents, from those experiencing typical adolescent problems to those labeled delinquent.

The effectiveness of social skills training has been established in reviews of literature (Van Hasselt, Hersen, Whitehill, & Bellack, 1979; Gresham, 1981, 1982). Positive outcomes of systematic social skills training include improved coping skills, social competence, and increased peer acceptance. The efficacy of social skills training is somewhat easier to establish than the efficacy of affective development because social skills trainers usually identify specific skills in behavioral terms and set objective criteria for success. Therefore, the goals and objectives of these programs are easier to evaluate. However, the effectiveness of specific social skills curricula remains to be established. As with affective curricula, long-term systematic evaluation of each social skills curriculum is needed. Walker et al. (1983) identify four additional areas for future research on social skills training and handicapped children: (1) validation of different models of training, (2) effectiveness of the training within mainstream settings, (3) the impact of training on classroom adjustment and peer interaction competency, and (4) transfer of learning across settings.

A Developmental Curriculum

Mary M. Wood and her colleagues at Rutland Center in Atlanta have developed a curriculum that addresses both affective and academic needs of severely disturbed and autistic children ages 2 to 12 (M. M. Wood, 1975; Wood & Swan, 1978). Developmental therapy curriculum is based on the assumption that these children need special help in progressing through five normal developmental stages in four basic areas: behavior, communication, socialization, and academics. These four categories constitute the curriculum areas. The five developmental stages describe the individual's degree of involvement with the environment: the stages begin with *responding to the environment* and move through *working with others in groups* to *taking initiative in new situations*.

Each child is individually assessed and placed at the appropriate developmental level within each of the curriculum areas. Activities and materials are selected accordingly. Approximately 150 emotional-developmental milestones are identified and taught through the developmental therapy curriculum. A very positive aspect of this curriculum is that it integrates the primary needs of the behavior disordered child into a single curriculum. It also is one of the few curricula that specifically addresses the needs of preschool disturbed children. The interested reader is referred to *Developmental Therapy*, by Mary M. Wood (1975).

SUMMARY

A variety of management techniques are used by educators of behavior disordered students. Selection of specific interventions depends on a number of factors, including the teacher's training and interaction style, the goals of the program, and the needs of the students. All of the techniques are based on certain theoretical assumptions. *Direct intervention techniques* such as life space interviewing and crisis intervention focus on working with students while problem events are occurring. The *cognitive techniques* of reality therapy and rational-emotive therapy share the basic premise that an individual can learn to change behavior by first changing thoughts and attitudes. Cognitive behavior modification bridges cognitive and behavioral theories in its application of self-talk and self-monitoring to effect behavior change. *Behavioral techniques* require identification of events or objects in the environment that can be manipulated in order to change behavior.

Teachers should also be familiar with nonacademic curriculum. Curriculum for exploring affective issues and for teaching self-control and social skills can be incorporated into classes on a regular basis. Various curricular materials that focus on affective development are commercially available, as are curricula for teaching social skills.

KEY POINTS

(1) Redl's management techniques offer common-sense, preventative guidelines for managing surface behavior.

(2) In life space interviewing and crisis intervention, the teacher takes an active role in exploring (1) the student's feelings which precipitated the problem event, and (2) alternative ways of coping with those feelings.

(3) Reality therapy emphasizes responsibility and helps the individual identify irresponsible thoughts and actions that are maladaptive.

(4) Rational-emotive therapy emphasizes rationality and helps the individual identify irrational beliefs that maintain detrimental behavior and emotions.

(5) Cognitive behavior modification offers techniques for problem solving and for teaching behavioral self-control.

(6) To use behavioral techniques in the classroom, teachers must be able to identify target behaviors, to collect behavioral data, and to apply reinforcement effectively.

(7) Most published affective curricula focus on development of self-concept and/or communication skills.

(8) Social skills curricula teach skills that are needed by students to get along with peers and to function effectively in the classroom setting.

ADDITIONAL READINGS

The concept of the life space interview, by F. Redl. *Conflict in the classroom.* Edited by N.J. Long, W.C. Morse, & R.G. Newman (Fourth Edition). Belmont, CA: Wadsworth, 1980; and Life space interview in the school setting, by M.B. Brenner. *American Journal of Orthopsychiatry,* 1963, *33,* 717–719, for further information on the life space interview.

Adaptive frustration management, by S. A. Fagen. In *Conflict in the classroom.* Edited by N.J. Long, W.C. Morse, & R.G. Newman (Fourth Edition). Belmont, CA: Wadsworth, 1980, for guidelines on helping students deal with frustration.

Schools without failure, by W. Glasser. New York: Harper & Row, 1969, for application of Glasser's reality therapy to school settings.

Chapters 9–11 of *Teaching disturbed and disturbing students,* by P. Zionts. Austin, TX: Pro-Ed, 1985, for application of Ellis' rational-emotive therapy to school settings.

Teaching behavioral self-control to students, by E.A. Workman. Austin, TX: Pro-Ed, 1982, for a handbook that outlines the basics of behavioral self-control.

The concept of punishment, by F. Redl. In *Conflict in the Classroom.* Edited by N.J. Long, W.C. Morse, & R.G. Newman (Fourth Edition). Belmont, CA: Wadsworth, 1980; Behavior modification? Caution! by P. Gallagher. *Academic Therapy,* Spring, 1976, 357–363 (also in *Conflict in the classroom;* The effective use of punishment to modify behavior in the classroom, by R.V. Hall, S. Axelrod, M. Foundopoulos, J. Shellman,

R.A. Campbell, & S.S. Cranston. *Educational Technology*, April, 1971, 24–26; and Legal and ethical considerations for the use of timeout in special education settings, by D.L. Gast & C.M. Nelson. *The Journal of Special Education, 11*, 1977, 457–467, for readings that offer cautions in using punishment and other behavior modification techniques.

Intervention strategies for promoting self-concept development, by H. Leviton & J. Kiraly, Jr. *Academic Therapy, 14*, 1979, 535–546, for general but practical suggestions for teachers to use in enhancing self-concept.

NOTES

[1]Reprinted with permission of Macmillan, Inc. from *The Aggressive Child* by Fritz Redl and David Wineman. Copyright © 1957 by The Free Press, a Corporation.

[2]This section on crisis intervention is adapted from Gilliam (1981a) and is used with the author's permission.

[3]From B.W. Camp, and M.A.S. Bash. Think Aloud. Increasing Social and Cognitive Skills. A Problem-Solving Program for Children. Primary Level. Research Press, 1981. Reprinted with permission.

[4]Adapted from Edward A. Workman, *Teaching Behavioral Self-Control to Students* Copyright 1982. Used with permission of the publisher, Pro-Ed, 5341 Industrial Oaks Boulevard, Austin, TX.

[5]From *Social Skills in the Classroom* by Thomas M. Stephens. © 1978 All Rights Reserved. Reprinted by permission of the author and publisher.

eight

Ecological Programming: Home and Community

Home:
  Parent-child Dynamics
  Parent Roles in Education
  Working with Parents

Community:
  Social Systems: Social, Legal,
    Mental Health
  The Educational System
  The Teacher as Liaison

---

orientation

As Rhodes (1970) asserts, we can no longer take a child from a system which is disturbed, attempt to fix the child, place the child back into the unchanged system, and call it satisfactory treatment. Instead, we must attempt to increase the fit between the child and the expectations of others in the systems in which the child lives and interacts. As a teacher, you can help increase the fit by working closely with parents and with involved social systems within the community.

OVERVIEW

Every child is an inseparable part of a complex web of interrelated systems. For "normal" children, these mini-social-systems function appropriately and may be defined as congruent or balanced. When the systems break down, we term them incongruent or unbalanced. We also tend to place the blame for such incongruence on the child, rationalize our action by labeling the child as emotionally disturbed, and plan our interventions to focus on remediating the identified child's emotional disturbance while neglecting the other aspects of the system. (Apter, 1982, p. 139)

Educators, psychologists, and other child-care specialists are beginning to recognize the futility of treating the child while ignoring the systems in which he functions (Apter & Conoley, 1984; Hobbs, 1982; Minuchin, 1970; Rhodes, 1970). Instead, professionals are beginning to advocate an ecological approach to treatment, which focuses on imbalances or disturbances in systems. The child is seen as a part of the disturbance, and interventions are aimed at promoting changes not only in the child but also in other people and factors in the environment. The goal of ecological intervention is to reduce the discrepancy between environmental expectations for a child and the capabilities of that child to fulfill those expectations. According to Apter (1982), ecological programs are based upon the following assumptions:

(1)   Each child is an inseparable part of a small social system.

(2)   Disturbance is not viewed as a disease located within the child, but rather as discordance (a lack of balance) in the system.

(3)   Discordance may be viewed as a disparity between an individual's abilities and the demands or expectations of the environment—"failure to match" between child and system.

(4)   The goal of any intervention is to make the system work, and to make it work ultimately without the intervention.

(5)   Improvement in any part of the system can benefit the system.

(6)   This broader view of disturbance gives rise to three major areas for intervention:
a.   Changing the child
b.   Changing the environment
c.   Changing attitudes and expectations. (Apter, 1982, p. 69)

This chapter promotes an ecological orientation to programming for behavior disordered students. The focus of the first section is the home, which is the most influential ecosystem of a child. The focus of the second section is the community ecosystem, which is composed of three subsystems that impact the lives of behavior disordered students: social-welfare, legal-correctional, and mental health. The teacher's role in working with parents and these community systems is emphasized throughout the chapter.

HOME-SCHOOL INTERFACE

Perhaps with no other handicapping condition does successful intervention depend so heavily upon parent involvement. Many educators have discovered the futility of trying to change behaviors exhibited at school that are being maintained in the home environment. In contrast, if inappropriate behaviors are consistently discouraged in both the home and in school, the student is more likely to choose more appropriate ways of behaving. Cooperative parents and teachers make a formidable team that provides consistency across ecosystems and prevents pitting home against school. For elementary and middle-school students, the home is still a significant source of influence and control. Changes are most easily made in these formative years before loyalties shift from parents and teachers to peers. Parental involvement also enhances counseling efforts with youngsters. Many theorists are beginning to view parental involvement in counseling sessions with disturbed children as a necessity (Abrams & Kaslow, 1977).

While recognizing the need to provide consistency between the home and school ecosystems, teachers must also realize that barriers to communicating with parents may exist. As illustrated by mid-twentieth century writing on "refrigerator mothers" in which cold, rejecting parenting was cited as a causal factor in autism, psychologists and educators historically have been willing to blame disordered behavior on disordered homes and poor parenting. Although much has been written to dispute the idea that parental rejection can cause autism (Creak & Ini, 1960; Peck, Rabinovich, & Cramer, 1969; Rutter, Bartak, & Newman, 1971; Wing, 1967), the belief persists that parents of autistic children are responsible for their child's disorder (Gilliam & Coleman, 1982). Interactions between parents and educators often have been undermined by issues of guilt and blame. Parents of students with emotional problems often feel responsible or guilty, and educators may unwittingly exacerbate such feelings by pointing out inadequate discipline or management practices in the home. Thus a guilt-blame cycle may be easily instituted but not easily erased. The role of parenting in the development of behavior problems in children has been studied in research on parent-child dynamics.

Parent-Child Dynamics

Considerable effort has been devoted to specifying the characteristics and child-rearing practices of parents of behavior disordered children. A number of emotional difficulties in children—aggression, withdrawal, and neurotic and psychosomatic problems—have been related to parental rejection, punitiveness, and permissiveness (Anderson, 1981a; Becker, 1964; Martin, 1975). Friedman (1973), in studying family roots of school behavior disorders, outlines the following crucial factors: (1) the manner in which the family deals with authority issues, rewards, and punishments, (2) the psychological and interpersonal climate of the home, and (3) non-contradictory standards and consistent discipline by both parents. However, no parental personality characteristics or specific child-rearing techniques have been shown to cause behavioral pathology (Kauffman, 1977). Instead, an emerging body of literature suggests that child characteristics such as temperament may be causal factors in the development of undesirable *parent* behaviors and interaction styles.

Many theorists are adopting the position that parent-child relationships are bidirectional in nature (Bell, 1968; Bell & Harper, 1977), or reciprocal in influence (Anderson, 1981a, 1981b, Bronfenbrenner, 1979; Martin, 1975; Patterson, 1975). As Anderson states, "The child is seen as an elicitor of parent behaviors and as responding in ways which may serve to positively or negatively reinforce parent behavior, or to extinguish or punish it" (1982b, p. 83).

Bidirectional theory is particularly applicable to students exhibiting hyperactivity or behavioral excesses. Researchers have found that hyperactive or overactive children tend to elicit more severe disciplinary or controlling behaviors from their parents than do their normal peers (S.B. Campbell, 1973, 1975; Stevens-Long, 1973). In studying parent-child interactions of aggressive children, Patterson (1975; Patterson & Cobb, 1973) observed that an aversive behavior from either party elicits an aversive response and results in a gradual escalation of aversive exchanges. Anderson (1981b) summarizes the literature in this area by stating that parents are likely to respond to high frequency or intense behaviors by increasing their efforts at control; in turn, increasing parental control often elicits the child's control behaviors, and a negative pattern becomes established over time.

Conversely, Anderson (1981a) lists several parental variables that have been shown to promote positive social behaviors in children: warmth and responsiveness, consistent discipline, demands for responsible behavior, and purposeful modeling, teaching, and reinforcement of desired behaviors. Anderson stresses that what parents do with their children is more important than global personality or attitudinal variables.

Many researchers advocate a systems approach, in which the functioning of the family as a unit is the object of study. From a six-year research project on families and family systems factors, Beavers (1977) has identified eight variables that he believes are operating in optimal or healthy families but are absent in dysfunctional families. Beavers considers these variables to be important in environments that "attempt to develop human competence." Such environments include families and clinical and educational settings. These eight variables are:

A systems orientation. This complex philosophy can be illustrated by three basic assumptions:

1. Individuals need a group, a human system, in order to function optimally. The primary human system, the family, is left behind for other systems as the individual matures and acquires independence.

2. Human behavior results from many variables rather than a single cause. Dysfunctional families often have rigid expectations and explanations for one another's behavior; in contrast, healthy families realize that motivation for human behavior is complex and may have numerous causes.

3. Humans are limited in the power they have over others. The extreme positions of absolute power or helplessness are unhealthy in interpersonal relationships.

Boundary issues. An optimal family operates much like a living cell: while possessing internal strength and integrity as a unit, the family facilitates interchange with the outside world. The optimal family recognizes that the whole system must prosper in order for the individual to prosper; the family also views negotiation and compromise as situations in which the integrity of all individuals is preserved.

Contextual clarity. The context of family interactions are well established in optimal families. For example, there is clear definition of generational boundaries (who is parent, who is child) and a strong parental coalition.

Power issues. Power is shared among members of healthy families, who recognize that coercive or authoritarian control occasionally may be necessary to enforce family rules. However, these families also acknowledge that another legitimate form of power is based on strong, positive interpersonal relationships.

Encouragement of autonomy. Optimal families realize that an individual must become autonomous by establishing a separate identity and taking responsibility for his behavior. Open communication and respect for the uniqueness of individuals are characteristics of this variable.

Affective issues. People in optimal families are involved with one another in warm, empathetic ways. Conflicts are dealt with openly and without punishment for expression of negative feelings.

Negotiation and task performance. When given tasks requiring cooperation from all members, optimal families are able to organize themselves, use input from one another, negotiate differences, and produce an effective response.

Transcendent values. Healthy families are able to accept and adapt to changes brought about by the passing of time and the subsequent changes in family structure. Changes such as children growing into adulthood and the death of grandparents are accepted as an inevitable part of the growth cycle.

According to Beavers (1977), children who grow up in families marked by these eight characteristics develop into healthy individuals who are unusually competent.

Other researchers have attempted to identify variables in the parent-child relationship that influence the child's performance in school. I.J. Gordon (1969) has identified three sets of family factors that influence both intellectual functioning and personality development in children. *Demographic factors,* which include income, social class, ethnicity, and quality of housing, are not very amenable to change. Numerous *cognitive factors* include educational aspirations parents have for their children, degree of academic guidance, language level and style, use of community resources, quality and quantity of verbal interactions among all family members, and availability and parental use of educational material in the home. *Emotional factors* include consistency of discipline, parental self-esteem, expectations that are communicated to the child, and amount of time parents are willing to devote to their children. Given that these influential variables operate in the home, I.J. Gordon (1969) states that the primary goal of parent involvement is to improve the family's capacity to provide a nurturing learning environment. Parents can be encouraged to take numerous roles in accomplishing this task.

Parental Roles in Education

Ehrlich (1981) has identified four roles that parents may adopt in educating their children: parents as supporters of their child's classroom efforts, parents as motivators and teachers, parents as advocates of educational competence, and parents as providers of independence training.

Supporters.   Parents may show interest in their children's academic efforts by verbally praising achievements, attending parent-teacher conferences, and taking time to discuss homework or school-related problems at home. Parental support has been linked not only to children's high academic achievement but also to high self-esteem and positive attitudes toward school (Fox, 1964; Mize, 1977). Ehrlich (1980) found a relationship between the anxiety level of children in class and their perceptions of their parents' involvement in school matters. He suggests that the child may learn that if difficulties in school arise, the home may be a source of support and that the child's knowledge of parental support "may serve as a buffer against classroom anxiety" (Ehrlich, 1980, p. 53).

Motivators and teachers.   Parents may provide academic assistance in the home by tutoring and by reading with their children. Both forms of assistance have been successful in improving academic performance (McKinney, 1975; M.B. Smith, 1970). Provision of study time and space for the child in the home also may be motivating by taking the pressure off the child to find a quiet time and place to study. The strength of parent involvement as a motivator is demonstrated in studies that have shown that students' in-class behavior improves when classroom rewards for appropriate behavior are coupled with rewards dispensed by parents in the home (refer to home-based reinforcement systems, p. 214).

Advocates.   Parents who value education communicate this value to their children in many ways: by providing and using books and educational materials in the home, by setting high expectations and standards for achievement, and by encouraging and directing their children toward intellectual pursuits (Ehrlich, 1981). Positive parental attitudes toward schooling often are adopted by the offspring.

In studying differences in parental behavior of high-achieving versus low-achieving elementary-age students, Rankin (1967) found the following variables to be significant: helping the child correct inadequate schoolwork, requiring high grades, desiring a college education for the child, and communicating with school personnel. Thus, positive attitudes and active involvement with schools appear to be important parental correlates of children's achievement.

Providers of independence. This parental role is related more to child-rearing practices and the general home atmosphere than to home-school relationships. Parents who provide independence training are warm and supportive in their dealings with their child, yet they make demands for self-reliant behaviors. Other variables contributing to growth as independent learners are consistent management practices and the child's participation in family activities. Roles of parent involvement are summarized in Table 8–1.

Working with Parents: Strategies

If special educators are to establish viable teacher-parent relationships, they must accept and abide by two basic tenets: (1) that their role with parents is a consultative one, and (2) that parents should be viewed as individuals, not as a homogeneous group.

The first tenet was articulated by Hobbs (1975a) in his statement that parents must be recognized as special educators and experts on their children, while educators and psychologists must learn to be consultants to parents. Regardless of educational level or parenting skills, all parents can offer valuable insights about their child's development and level of functioning. Information on early development, stressful family relationships, and unusual environmental influences may prove crucial in helping the teacher understand the child's current functioning. When information is solicited from parents and their opinions are treated with respect, a bond of trust can be established that lays the groundwork for cooperative planning.

TABLE 8–1.   Roles of Parent Involvement (Ehrlich, 1981)

A SUPPORTER:	A MOTIVATOR/TEACHER:	AN ADVOCATE:
praises	reads with child	values education
attends teacher conferences	tutors if necessary	models use of books
discusses homework or school problems	provides time and place for study	sets standards for success
	AN INDEPENDENCE PROVIDER:	
	is warm and supportive	
	is consistent in discipline	
	demands self-reliance	

The second tenet is that parents of handicapped children are not a homogeneous group. Parents differ greatly in the degree to which they participate in educational programming for their children. All parents of handicapped students have a legal right to participate in decision making regarding their child's placement in special education services and in developing an individualized education program. While some parents communicate regularly with school personnel and are heavily involved throughout special education procedures, others may waive their rights to be actively involved. Similarly, some parents may know very little about alternative special education programs and placements, due process procedures under P. L. 94–142, and other legal issues; other parents may be well-informed about the law and have definite ideas about what their child's educational program should entail. Some parents are knowledgeable about their children's difficulties and very skilled at managing their child's behavior, while others may need training to develop management skills. The point is that parents have differing levels of awareness and skills that teachers must accommodate when involving parents in education. As Webber and Gilliam (1981) state, "Parents, like children, are individual in their needs. . .teachers must individualize their expectations for parents, just as they do for children" (p. 7).

Teachers can encourage parent involvement in education in a number of ways. The next section offers general suggestions for working with parents and more specific information on parent groups and home-based reinforcement systems. Just as intervention techniques should be tailored to the students with whom they are used, so should parent involvement strategies match parental capabilities and needs. For parents who are interested in learning more about management techniques, teachers can be instrumental in setting up parent education groups. Parents who are experiencing high levels of stress may improve their coping skills by participation in a support group or in counseling. Another alternative for parent involvement is a home-based reinforcement system, which can be especially helpful under two circumstances: (1) when the teacher is unable to find sufficiently motivating reinforcers in the school environment, and (2) when the teacher wants to get parents involved with their child in a positive reward system.

General suggestions.   Once teachers recognize and accept parents as partners in the educational process, they can be creative in finding ways to involve parents. Rich, Van Dien, and Mattox (1979) suggest the following general strategies:

Give home learning tips and activities to supplement classroom work.
Use the resources of the home for materials and ideas for different subject areas.

Capitalize on special skills or talents of parents by asking them to participate in classroom, school, or community projects.

Arrange events and meetings with a teaching purpose.

Set up father-oriented events and make a special effort to reach single parents and working parents.

Inform parents on a regular basis about what's happening at school.

Encourage parents to visit the school and to confer on a regular basis.

Other ways to involve parents which have been instituted by school districts include:

regularly scheduled parent-teacher conferences
newsletters mailed to parents
series of child- and education-related workshops
parent training to support school programs at home. (Ehrlich, 1981).

Parent groups. Organized parent groups are usually one of two types: (1) support groups, established to provide a support system among parents who have similar concerns, or (2) educational groups, established for the purpose of giving information or teaching specific skills. Support groups serve the function of getting parents together, often on an informal basis, to discuss concerns and frustrations relating to parenting and the education and management of their children. The impetus of support groups may come either from teachers or parents, but can be successful only if parents take an active role in sharing their needs and concerns. It is often a good idea for teachers to take very passive roles in parent support groups so that parents feel free to provide their own leadership. Many parent support groups are organized around social gatherings or fund-raising activities.

In contrast, educational parent groups are usually conducted much like classes or workshops, with a specific agenda and a set number of meetings at a regular time and place. Educators or psychologists are generally responsible for organizing and conducting these groups. Topics such as behavior management in the home and improving parent-child communication are offered. Groups aimed at teaching parents to tutor their children also fall into the category of educational groups.

Several packaged programs including materials and guidelines for conducting parent groups are available (Dinkmeyer & McKay, 1976; T. Gordon, 1970; Simpson & Combs, 1978). For example, *Parenting the Exceptional Child: A Workshop Manual* (Simpson & Combs, 1978) was developed for educators to use in teaching behavior management procedures to parents of autistic children and youth. The program was designed to operate for a minimum of four weeks. In addition to learning an overview of general behavior principles, parents learn to identify target behaviors, measure and graph behaviors, and apply intervention techniques.

Parent Effectiveness Training (T. Gordon, 1970) is an example of a popular parent education program. Parent Effectiveness Training (PET) focuses on improving communication skills between parent and child. A group of 10 to 12 parents meets for a series of workshops over an eight-week period. Communication skills such as active listening and problem solving are taught through discussion, demonstration, and role-playing. Teachers, counselors, and psychologists have used PET satisfactorily.

Many parents need more support than can be provided by empathetic teachers or by parent groups. Individual or family counseling may be particularly indicated for parents of behavior disordered students, who usually face stressful situations on a daily basis. Parents may become so overwhelmed by financial problems, marital stress, or the day-to-day responsibilities of managing a family that the additional stress of their child's behavior problems becomes too much to handle.

Although teachers should lend a sympathetic ear to parents, it is beyond the scope of teacher responsibility—and training—to provide counseling services. However, the teacher is often in a position to be the first to recognize a plea for help and can be instrumental in making a referral. Some signals that may indicate a need for professional counseling are:

Parents are experiencing a period of unusual financial difficulty, marital discord, or other emotional upheaval.

Parent(s) routinely expresses feelings of helplessness or depression.

Parent(s) feels out of control of the child.

Child is habitually in trouble with the juvenile authorities.

Parent(s) chronically appears to be under a high level of stress.

Parent(s) is beginning to impose upon the teacher's time (at home or at school) with personal problems.

In order to make appropriate referrals, teachers should become familiar with community resources that offer counseling and other psychological services. It is a good idea to know the background and training, credentials, and theoretical orientation of counselors and therapists to whom referrals are made. Many counselors and therapists specialize in school-related problems, child psychology, or family therapy; it is best to match parental needs to the specialty area of professionals. Teachers can be of benefit to parents by helping them gain a realistic picture of their child's capabilities and behavior relative to school functioning. Teachers can also help parents set up behavior management systems in the home, which is the focus of the next section.

Home-based reinforcement systems.   Over the past decade, special educators have come to realize that home-based reinforcement systems can have a powerful impact on students' classroom behavior. In a review of 24 studies, Barth (1979) found that home-based reinforcement systems have been successfully applied with students in kindergarten through high school and in a variety of settings such as group homes, special classes, and mainstream classes.

The rationale for home-based reinforcement systems is that the traditional report card system has merit, but is not sufficiently motivating to all students. Home-based reinforcement programs utilize the concept of report cards, but differ in that the reported behaviors are more specifically delineated, and reports are sent home much more frequently. All home-based systems employ some type of home-school communication, specify certain desirable or undesirable behaviors, and enlist parental aid in applying consequences.

In the studies reviewed by Barth (1979), successful programs varied somewhat on these major factors:

(1)   Report period. In most cases, home-school reports initially were sent home on a daily basis and then faded to a weekly or biweekly basis.

(2)   Type of behavior. Some programs merely reported target behaviors as "occurrence-nonoccurrence," while others reported a variety of behaviors across settings. Typical target behaviors included task completion, improved accuracy on academic tasks, and reduction of disruptive or aggressive behaviors.

(3)   Parental response. Although all studies specified the desired parental response, some programs merely required praise for good behavior, while others set up sanctions or response-cost systems for parents to implement. Numerous methods of contacting and involving parents were used successfully: contact was made in groups, individually, in person, by telephone, and through letters. The teacher is more likely to get parents involved in home-based systems if there is a payoff for them. One way to provide reinforcement for parents is to target obnoxious behaviors exhibited both in the home and in the classroom. Parents should also be given support and recognition for their efforts.

In many of the programs, weekly allowance or sums of money were used as back-up reinforcers; in others, only verbal parental praise was used as a reinforcer. Other systems used home privileges as reinforcement. Barth (1979) concludes that for some students, feedback and social reinforcement are sufficient to motivate positive change. For others, social reinforcement motivates change but does not sustain it, while for a third subgroup, feedback and praise are sufficient to cause and maintain improved behavior. As in setting up consequences and reinforcers for any behavior management program, teachers must tailor the home-based reinforcement system to the individuals for whom it is designed. In one study, six different contracts were tried with aggressive adolescents and their parents before a successful contract was found (Cohen, Keyworth, Kleiner, & Libert, 1971). Before the program succeeded, the researchers had to find strong incentives and had to eliminate competing reinforcers.

One example of a successful home-based reinforcement system was reported by Budd and Leibowitz (1976). The system was set up with six four- and five-year-olds who had manifested chronic and severe behavior problems throughout their preschool and kindergarten years. The children's school day was divided into 12 periods, each lasting a few minutes, and the children were awarded a token sticker for each period during which they met the criteria for appropriate behavior. Three behaviors were eventually targeted: (1) off-area (out-of-seat, out of the designated activity area), (2) a motor attack on another person, and (3) negative statements about another person. On each day during which a child earned eight or more stickers, the youngster was allowed to take the token card home to exchange for prearranged privileges. The target behaviors decreased significantly after implementation of the program, and follow-up indicated that all six children were being maintained in regular classrooms.

In summary, studies on home-based reinforcement programs have shown that a variety of systems can be successfully implemented. Home-based programs have been effective with students of all ages and in numerous settings, and with students who are emotionally disturbed, mentally retarded, or from different cultural or ethnic groups (Barth, 1979). The success of these cooperative home-school programs underscores the power of parent involvement in their children's education.

Working with Parents: Conferencing Skills

To communicate effectively with parents in conferences, teachers should be skilled in building relationships, setting goals for each conference, and dealing with conflict.

Relationship building. The quality of parent-teacher conferences largely depends upon the teacher's ability to develop a relationship based upon mutual trust. Kroth and Simpson (1977) have listed four factors that aid teachers in building trust with parents. First is the teacher's willingness to take risks: when teachers feel capable and confident in dealing with others, they are more inclined to become involved and to share some responsibility with parents. Second is the joint establishment of clear expectations for parents: when parental responsibilities are clearly defined and agreed upon, the probability of follow-through is much increased. A third way to develop trust is to know the capabilities and constraints of the parents so that unrealistic expectations do not arise. For example, Kroth and Simpson note that parents may fail to attend meetings because they do not have transportation, or may fail to respond to a written memo because it is not written in their language or at their reading level. The teacher should not assume that failure to respond is indicative of lack of caring. A fourth way to develop trust is to provide feedback and reinforcement, especially if parents are involved in behavior management programs with their children.

Teachers will find it easier to communicate effectively with parents if they are good active listeners. Kroth (1975) defines an active listener as one who knows how to encourage the conversant to talk. The active listener reflects and clarifies the other's message and evidences a body posture that indicates interest (eye contact, nodding, and so forth). Teachers should try to balance speaking time—neither parent nor teacher should monopolize the conversation. Teachers should also try to avoid using jargon and "talking at" parents without heeding their reactions.

Setting Goals.   Parent conferences are usually called for three reasons: to get information, to give information, or to problem-solve. Although any given conference may cover all three categories, the teacher should have a specific goal in mind for every conference.

The initial interview with parents of a student is often primarily for gathering information about family and home factors that affect the student's functioning. Kroth and Simpson (1977) suggest the following interview format:

Statement of the problem. Elicit parents' assessment of and feelings about their child's difficulties; if the parental assessment differs drastically from the professional assessment, try to ascertain why the discrepancy exists and, if necessary, give the parent more information.

Developmental history. If unavailable in the student's records, get a complete developmental history including conditions around birth, developmental milestones, illnesses and injuries, and any unusual conditions that may have affected the child's development. If a developmental history is available, it is good to explore the parents' perceptions of the effect of some of the past difficulties on the child's current behavioral and cognitive functioning.

Personality history. Encourage parents to discuss their child's personality factors such as extreme likes and dislikes, and attitudes toward peers, school, family, and home. Behavior patterns relative to tantrums, accidents, activity level, sleep patterns, reaction to parental discipline, or emotional difficulties should be explored. Ask parents to note some of the child's strengths.

Sociological information. Tactfully ascertain information about the home that will help in understanding and planning for the child. Such information may include cultural, ethnic, and religious background of the family, other languages spoken in the home, ages and gender of siblings, parental attitudes and child-rearing practices, and the hours that parents are available for child supervision and for participation in conferences or other school activities.

School history. Ask parents to share information about relationships with previous teachers and programs; find out what interventions were successful in the past.

Parental goals and expectations. Explore the parents' expectations for you as the teacher and for the current educational program. Compare their responses to your own plans. Discuss long-term goals for the child's future and compare parental goals to the child's capabilities.

A second type of interview focuses upon giving information to parents. Such information may be general program information, an explanation of special education policies, or a special intervention for which the teacher wants to enlist parental permission or help. In other information-giving interviews, teachers may set up a home-school report system or give a progress report. Teachers should carefully prepare factual information and should solicit the backing of their principal when policies are being explained or unusual interventions are being suggested.

To report progress, most teachers of behavior disordered students institute some form of parent-school communication other than the routine report card. Daily, weekly, or biweekly notes have been used successfully in home-based reinforcement systems. Teachers may also phone parents to give them progress reports; parents of behavior disordered students are often shocked to receive positive reports about their child over the telephone, as they are much more accustomed to receiving negative reports. Regardless of which reporting system is used, teachers should schedule periodic parent conferences in order to give information about academic and behavioral progress.

A third type of interview involves problem solving. It is not unusual for teachers and parents to find themselves in disagreement over various facets of the student's program. Some of the most common causes of conflict are: different opinions or values, thwarted needs, resentment of authority, and feelings of inadequacy or jealousy (Institute for Parent Involvement, 1980). Regardless of the cause, conflicts are best resolved by obtaining as much information as possible, analyzing the information, and then generating possible solutions.

Dealing with conflict.   When parents become frustrated or angry, the teacher may become the outlet for their aggression. Upon being verbally attacked, one's initial reaction is to counterattack or to defend oneself vehemently; both reactions are counterproductive to further communication. The Institute for Parent Involvement (1980) offers some very specific guidelines for handling aggressive parents:

(1)   Use active listening to convey interest; write down the parents' complaints.

(2)   Exhaust parents' list of complaints; ask if they have any to add to the list. Ask them to clarify any complaints that are too general or vague.

(3)   Ask parents for suggestions for solving the problems they have brought up; write these down also.

(4)   Respond to loud talking by speaking softly.

(5)   Avoid arguing, explaining, or defending yourself, as this often feeds aggression.

Adhering to these guidelines will often diffuse the parents' frustration or anger; it is difficult for them to remain angry at someone who is earnestly and quietly attending to their complaints. Often the initial complaint is not the real problem, which may never surface unless the lines of communication are kept open.

Do's and don'ts.   The development of trust and the enlistment of parents as partners in the educational process are keys to successful teacher-parent relationships. Setting a goal, organizing information, and preparing ahead of time for parent conferences are ways to enhance communication during the conference. In addition, Simpson (1982) offers the following tips:

DO'S

Maintain a sense of humor.
Be accepting of yourself and the parents with whom you work.
Be positive and sincere.
Demonstrate respect for the parents.
Listen.
Use language that the parents can understand.

DON'TS

Attempt to have all the answers.
Argue with parents.
Make agreements or promises that you may not be able to keep.
Patronize parents.
Make moralistic judgments.
Minimize what the parents have to say about their child.

A summary checklist.   Table 8–2 contains a conference checklist that can be used for planning and evaluating parent conferences. The preconference section gives reminders for preparing the interview—including a reminder for arranging a pleasant physical environment. During the conference, the teacher is reminded to state the purpose of the interview, to encourage information sharing, to summarize, and to end the conference on a positive note. The postconference section offers suggestions for follow-up with parents, students, and other involved school personnel.

In summary, teachers who view parents as partners in the educational process are likely to effect changes in a student's home environ-

TABLE 8–2. Conference Checklist

PRECONFERENCE

_____ 1. NOTIFY
  PURPOSE, PLACE, TIME, LENGTH OF TIME ALLOTTED
_____ 2. PREPARE
  REVIEW CHILD'S FOLDER
  GATHER EXAMPLES OF WORK
  PREPARE MATERIALS
_____ 3. PLAN AGENDA
_____ 4. ARRANGE ENVIRONMENT
  COMFORTABLE SEATING
  ELIMINATE DISTRACTIONS

CONFERENCE

_____ 1. WELCOME
  ESTABLISH RAPPORT
_____ 2. STATE
  PURPOSE
  TIME LIMITATIONS
  NOTE TAKING
  OPTIONS FOR FOLLOW-UP
_____ 3. ENCOURAGE
  INFORMATION SHARING
  COMMENTS
  QUESTIONS
_____ 4. LISTEN
  PAUSE ONCE IN A WHILE!
  LOOK FOR VERBAL AND NONVERBAL CUES
  QUESTIONS
_____ 5. SUMMARIZE
_____ 6. END ON A POSITIVE NOTE

POSTCONFERENCE

_____ 1. REVIEW CONFERENCE WITH CHILD, IF APPROPRIATE
_____ 2. SHARE INFORMATION WITH OTHER SCHOOL PERSONNEL, IF NEEDED
_____ 3. MARK CALENDAR FOR PLANNED FOLLOW-UP

Reprinted with permission from the University of New Mexico Institute for Parent Involvement, Albuquerque, New Mexico.

ment that carry over to classroom functioning. All educators should be skilled at communicating with parents in parent conferences. Other strategies for parent involvement in education should be individualized to match the capabilities and interests of parents. In keeping with ecological theory, the goal of parent involvement is to make adjustments in the home ecosystem which will accommodate the child and make the system work more smoothly. Parents and teachers together should decide whether participation in activities such as parent groups or home-based reinforcement systems will be beneficial to the child.

COMMUNITY-SCHOOL INTERFACE

The community constitutes another major ecosystem in the life of a child. In this chapter, the term *community* refers to the various social systems and other agencies, organizations, and services that may affect the behavior disordered child. The community ecosystem can include social workers, psychologists, ministers, Scoutmasters, coaches, neighborhood friends, police or probation officers, and other acquaintances or societal agents. Each of these people potentially can help increase the fit between the child and the child's community. Interventions in the child's ecosystem can either be aimed at helping the child adapt to the expectations of others in the environment or at changing systems to accommodate the child. In the former case, the child causes less of a disturbance in the ecosystem; in the latter case, the ecosystem becomes flexible enough to absorb the disturbance. The remainder of this chapter addresses changes in education and other major social systems of the behavior disordered student.

Social Systems

Apter (1982) discusses three major systems other than education that may impact the lives of behavior disordered students: social-welfare, legal-correctional, and mental health (see Figure 8–1).

Social-welfare. A variety of social services are provided to eligible families, including health services, family planning, housing services, emergency aid, and protective services for minors. Services are delivered primarily through the efforts of caseworkers who decide eligibility and devise service plans for families. Families of behavior disordered children may become clients of the social-welfare system for reasons unrelated to the child, or they may become clients as a result of reported abuse, neglect, or exploitation of that child. Children are rarely direct recipients of social services unless it is protective services that may result in legal removal from the home.

Social caseworkers are more likely to be interested in a child's school functioning if abuse or neglect is suspected or if parental custody is in question. Because the teacher is in the position to observe on a daily basis, the teacher may be asked to make judgments about the child's general emotional state or physical welfare. By sharing information about home and school functioning, teachers and caseworkers gain a clearer picture of the child's total environment and are better equipped to plan interven-

FIGURE 8–1.   Systems Impacting on Behavior Disordered Students

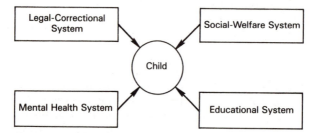

Reprinted with permission from *Troubled Children/Troubled Systems* by Stephen J. Apter. Copyright 1982, Pergamon Press.

tions. Although their duties vary, many caseworkers coordinate all social services received by a family; therefore the caseworker generally has a network among other agencies which can be valuable when attempting to discover potential resources or to provide additional services to a child. Teachers should not be reluctant to contact caseworkers to investigate suspected abuse or to help find pertinent community resources.

Legal-correctional system.   Many behavior disordered youth have histories of arrests or other incidences of lawbreaking. The police and the courts have discretionary powers that allow great latitude in dealing with juvenile offenders. Before making a court referral, police can use a number of alternatives, such as verbal warnings with release to parent custody, referral to a social agency, or temporary custody at the police station. According to one report, about half of all juvenile arrests are dealt with by police and never reach the courts (Atwater, 1983).When a youngster is taken to court for an offense, the judge may let him off with a warning, give him probation, or assign him to a restricted setting such as a group home, halfway house, detention center or training school.

Although the number of halfway houses and group homes has increased in recent years, the majority of juvenile offenders are still placed in detention centers (short-term) or training schools (long-term). As in adult correctional facilities, the stated goal of these juvenile treatment centers is rehabilitation of the individual for a productive life in the mainstream of society. Unfortunately, institutionalized youth often become more antisocial during their incarceration, resulting in low rates of rehabilitation. Community-based interventions such as providing group homes and increasing the number of juvenile offenders placed on probation are examples of systems changes aimed at improving the rehabilitation process.

The legal system is responsible for the education of juveniles placed in an institutional setting. However, the public education system is usually responsible for youth placed in community-based programs. The teacher may need to work with houseparents or probation officers on matters of school attendance and other conditions of probation. The teacher should also try to arrange as positive a learning experience as possible for the student.

Mental health system.   It is a certainty that teachers of behavior disordered students will at some time come in contact with members of the mental health system. Psychologists or psychiatrists are usually responsible for diagnosing behavior disorders and emotional disturbance; they may subsequently see students in individual or group therapy. Some school systems contract with psychologists and psychiatrists in private practice for such services, but many school systems depend upon the personnel in their local mental health centers for these services. The centers are usually staffed by psychologists, psychiatrists, and social workers who may very widely in background, training, and theoretical orientation. Outpatient services also vary but usually include diagnostic services, psychotherapy or counseling, chemotherapy, and consultation to local school systems. Many centers have outreach programs aimed at promoting mental health and preventing alcohol and drug abuse. Depending on local resources, inpatient services may be provided in hospitals, halfway houses, or other residential settings.

Two mental health interventions for behavior disordered children and youth that warrant attention are institutionalization and use of medication. Based upon the recommendation of psychologists, psychiatrists, or multidisciplinary mental health teams, disturbed youngsters may be placed in institutional settings or prescribed psychotropic medication. As Hobbs (1982) points out, these practices are contrary to an ecological orientation because each isolates the child as the sole focal point of intervention:

> Often wisdom lies simply in *not* doing something that may impede the restoration of the ecosystem, such as institutionalizing the child or prescribing tranquilizing drugs. Both of these acts create abnormal situations; they cut off or distort feedback of information needed to modify or redirect behavior, and thereby impair an essential component of the regulatory process in all living systems. From an ecological perspective, the widespread practice of sending disturbed children out of a state for treatment elsewhere makes no sense at all. This convenient but expensive practice makes it impossible to build a sustaining ecosystem for the child and thus impedes a return to normal patterns of development. (Hobbs, 1982, p. 186).

Ecological theorists advocate numerous interventions within the home and community ecosystems before interventions aimed at changing the child are considered.

Systems changes.   According to Apter (1982), there are a number of obstacles inherent in the social, legal, and mental health systems that impede ecological services delivery:

services not tailored to the needs of individual clients
poor working relationships among agencies
decision makers who do not perceive the need for services
lack of appropriate planning for services
prohibitive cost of mental health services
inability to reach potential clients
political and social resistance to change
medical model that focuses on pathology rather than preventative services
lack of clear definition of mental health
services that dehumanize and frustrate clients.

In order to combat some of these difficulties, Apter proposes several major areas for change across the three systems. First is a more effective use of resources. One-to-one treatment programs reach only a small segment of the population and are not cost-effective: there will never be enough trained specialists in any of the systems to deal on an individual basis with the social, legal, and mental health problems existing in our society. Hobbs (1982) estimates that if all the psychiatrists and clinical psychologists and one-third of the social workers and psychiatric nurses in this country were available to work with emotionally disturbed children, their individual caseloads would be approximately 360 children at any given time. Some school systems and mental health systems are attempting to combat this problem by shifting to a consultation model in which trained personnel give direct services to a mediating person (such as a teacher or counselor) who can then use the acquired skills with a number of others. The purpose of the consultation model is to build a broader base of expertise within the system.

A second needed change is systems reorganization, in which adjustments are made in the structure or policies of existing programs. The mainstreaming movement resulting from P.L. 94–142 is an example of systems reorganization in education. The trend toward deinstitutionalization or maintaining disturbed or retarded individuals in the community with support services is an example of systems change in mental health. Both of these changes are attempts to adjust the environment to accommodate individuals with special needs.

Other needed systems changes are an improved communication network and an increased sense of professionalism. Rather than requiring massive reorganization, these changes are dependent upon the attitudes of individuals within the systems. Essentials for developing professionalism are respect for the goals of other systems, a nonterritorial view of services, and a willingness to share both the responsibility and rewards for providing services. Educators, social workers, and representatives from the legal and mental health systems have many opportunities to demonstrate professionalism when planning programs and placements for behavior disordered students.

The Educational System

In keeping with the ecological view which asserts that the environment is a legitimate target for intervention, Apter (1982) proposes two major changes in our educational services delivery system: the total school and the systems-oriented resource teacher.

The *total school* is based partially on Hobbs' (1975b) idea that schools should coordinate all services received by special-needs children. The total school philosophy recognizes the reciprocal relationship of students with peers, parents, and others in the community. A primary goal of the total school is coordination of all services needed by students through "a careful matching of individual children's needs and available human and material resources" (Apter, 1982, p. 88). A secondary goal of the total school is prevention of emotional disturbance by promoting acceptance and accommodation of individual differences. The academic agenda is expanded to include affective curriculum aimed at helping the students gain self-understanding and self-control.

Role descriptions of personnel in the total school model also would be different from most existing roles. The *systems-oriented resource teacher* (SORT) model is a prime example of role redefinition. Rather than focusing exclusively on direct services such as teaching, the SORT model encourages resource teachers to take on indirect, preventative, and linking services (see Figure 8–2). These indirect services include consulting with other teachers, working with parents, providing in-service programs, serving as liaisons with other community resources, initiating preventative programs, and coordinating services to individual children (Apter, 1982). The reader who is interested in systems changes in education is referred to Apter's excellent treatise, *Troubled Children, Troubled Systems* (1982).

The Teacher as School and Community Liaison

The teacher's role as liaison within the school and community is a natural extension of the ecological view of troubled systems. The concept of liaison teacher-counselors was incorporated in the original Re-ED Project in the 1960s, and it has evolved into a general liaison specialist position. According to Hobbs (1982):

> . . . any person concerned with facilitating human development can perform the liaison function, provided he appreciates the richness of the ecological perspective and acquires the new skills required by the role. . . . The function of the liaison person is to help members of an ecosystem conceptualize what keeps the system from working, identify sources of discord, modify behaviors, mobilize resources required to achieve shared goals, and acquire the capacity to deal with excessive discord in the future. As a tool for accomplishing these goals, the liaison teacher-counselor helps devise an "ecological assessment and enablement plan." (p. 214, 215)

FIGURE 8–2.
Roles of the Systems-Oriented
Resource Teacher

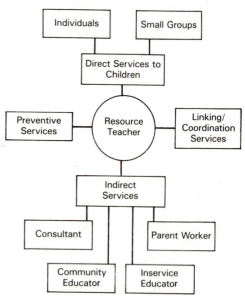

Reprinted with permission from *Troubled Children/Troubled Systems* by Stephen J. Apter. Copyright 1982, Pergamon Press.

Perhaps most importantly, the liaison teacher

> ... is interested in what it is that keeps ecosystems from working; she is not interested in what is wrong with people—not the child, or the parents, or teachers, or others. The question is: What needs to be changed in order for the system to work reasonably well? (p. 217)

The liaison teacher must be alert not only to sources of weakness or ecosystem pathology but also to sources of strength, the pivotal people who can help effect change (Hobbs, 1982). The liaison teacher must take the role of a facilitator rather than a manager because the primary responsibility for changes must remain with the people who are internal to the ecosystem.

Apter (1982) offers some general suggestions for teachers who wish to fulfill a liaison role:

WORK WITH THE CHILD

Build new competencies.
Change priorities.
Obtain necessary resources.
Find more appropriate environments.

WORK WITH THE ADULTS

Alter perceptions.
Raise or lower expectations.
Increase understanding or knowledge.
Restructure activities.

WORK WITH THE COMMUNITY

Bring more resources into the school.
Allow more entry into community.
Develop coordinating ties.

DEVELOP NEW ROLES

Resource teacher.
Diagnostic-prescriptive teacher.
"Linking" person.

DEVELOP NEW PROGRAM MODELS

Community education/schools.
Outdoor education.
Alternative public schools.
Focus on prevention.
Teach "mental health."
Preventive mainstreaming. (Apter, 1982, pp. 70–71)

Teachers may also develop indirect service roles as consultants and coordinators. The role of consultant was addressed in Chapter 5 under the consulting teacher model. The effective consultant views himself not as an expert who gives advice, but as a peer who is available to collaborate and problem-solve. In addition to providing more cost-effective services, consulting has the potential for changing the skills, attitudes, and expectations of the consultee, thereby making changes in the ecosystems of students. Persons who may benefit from consultant services from special educators are regular class teachers, parents, principals, and other administrators.

In the role of coordinator, the teacher would have the primary responsibility for overseeing all community services received by a particular student. Coordinators generally devise a comprehensive treatment plan, secure and monitor services, and conduct follow-up after termination of services. An effective coordinator is familiar with community resources, knows how to get services for an individual child, and maintains a working relationship with cooperating agencies and organizations. The coordinator role is similar to the liaison position outlined by Hobbs, but differs in that the coordinator is more concerned with securing, monitoring, and

TABLE 8–3. Community Resources for Behavior Disordered Students

RESOURCE	FUNCTION/SERVICES
social services	health services, family planning, housing, emergency financial aid, protective services for minors
mental health agencies	counseling, preventative programs, treatment for drug and alcohol abuse
legal system	rehabilitation programs for offenders
vocational rehabilitation agencies	job-securing services
associations for handicapped children	advocacy, lobbying, parent support
day and residential camps	short-term therapeutic environments
telephone hotlines	emergency counseling, suicide prevention, prevention of child abuse
civic, fraternal, and charitable organizations	funding for special projects or special needs
Big Brother, Big Sister	volunteers to spend leisure time with disadvantaged children
YMCA, YWCA, city/county recreation department	special recreation programs
Scout troups, other youth organizations	involvement with other youth and with community

coordinating services than in making extensive changes in ecosystems. Available services vary greatly from community to community; a sampling of services and organizations found in many locales are listed in Table 8–3.

SUMMARY

Ecological interventions require changes in students' home and community ecosystems. Many ecological theorists view the teacher as the ideal person to coordinate these changes. To effect changes in the home ecosystem, teachers must first recognize parents as partners in the educational process and must be able to communicate with them in conferences. Parents and teachers together should choose strategies through which parents can become involved in their child's education. Teachers of behavior disordered students also are often required to share information or coordinate services with representatives of various community systems, including social-welfare, legal-correctional, and mental health.

Within the educational system, two models for change are proposed by Apter (1982): (1) the total school, which would be the site for coordinating all services received by all children, and (2) the systems-oriented resource teacher, which would offer fewer direct services and more indirect services such as consulting, providing inservice, working with parents, and coordinating other community services. These models exemplify a truly ecological approach to educating behavior disordered students.

KEY POINTS

(1)   To intervene effectively in the lives of behavior disordered students, educators must coordinate their efforts with those of parents and other social agents in the community.

(2)   Parents can become involved in their child's education in a number of ways: tutoring, participating in parent groups, and instituting home-based reinforcement systems.

(3)   Conferencing with parents should be a valued and routine part of working with behavior disordered students.

(4)   Conferencing skills include building relationships, setting goals for each conference, and dealing with conflict.

(5)   Community ecosystems of many behavior disordered students involve the social-welfare, legal-correctional, and mental health systems.

(6)   Needed changes within the systems include reorganization, more effective use of resources, and an improved sense of professionalism and communication among agency personnel.

(7)   The teacher who wishes to be a liaison among ecosystems can provide indirect services such as consulting and coordinating.

ADDITIONAL READINGS

Communicating with parents of exceptional children, by R.L. Kroth. Denver, CO: Love, 1975; *Conferencing parents of exceptional children*, by R.L. Simpson. Rockville, MD: Aspen, 1982; and *Parent conferences as a teaching strategy*, by R.L. Kroth & R.L. Simpson. Denver, CO: Love, 1977, for additional readings on conferencing and working with parents.

Parents are teachers: A child management program, by W.C. Becker. Champaign, IL: Research Press, 1971; and *Families: Applications of social learning to family life*, by G.R. Patterson. Champaign, IL: Research Press, 1971, for practical handbooks on basic behavior management for parents.

Chapter 5, Related systems and roles, by S.J. Apter & J.C. Conoley. *Childhood behavior disorders and emotional disturbance*. Englewood Cliffs, NJ: Prentice-Hall, 1984, for further information on the social systems that usually affect behavior disordered students.

Selected chapters in *Troubled children/troubled systems*, by S.J. Apter. Elmsford, NY: Pergamon Press, 1982, for a thorough treatment of the ecological approach and its application to education.

Applications of ecological theory: Toward a community special education model for troubled children, by S.J. Apter. *Exceptional Children*, 1977, *43*, 366–373, for an article describing an ecological model for special education.

nine

Adolescents

orientation

The fine line between deviant and nondeviant behavior during adolescence is implied by Morse's observation that "All secondary teachers are teachers of disturbed adolescents" (1969a, p. 442). It is common for today's adolescent to experiment with drugs and sex and to evidence many other forms of behavior that can be characterized as "borderline deviant." In addition to experimenting, which is a normal part of adolescence, behavior disordered adolescents evidence extremeness of behavior and maladaptive coping patterns which result in their being labeled. If you plan to teach this population, you should be prepared to deal with numerous problems that are not often found in younger behavior disordered children.

OVERVIEW

The mere use of the term *adolescence* generally evokes images of awkwardness, self-consciousness, and conflict. Adolescents typically experience a period of rapid changes in physical, cognitive, and social development which they enter into as children and emerge from as adults. The first section of this chapter explores some of the major issues plaguing adolescents during these years and causing friction between them and the adults in their lives. The primary adolescent issues that educators must deal with in the schools are related to antisocial behavior, nonattendance, drug abuse, sex, and self-destructive behavior.

Experimentation is a natural part of adolescent development. The majority of adolescents experiment and eventually adopt ways of behaving that allow them to function as young adults in society. In contrast, behavior disordered adolescents fail to learn coping strategies that allow them to adapt. For these students, behavioral and counseling interventions are often necessary to help them learn more acceptable ways of coping with their environment. Although development of educational services for behavior disordered adolescents has lagged behind services for behavior disordered children, many school systems have established successful model programs for this population. Two public school model programs for behavior disordered adolescents are reviewed at the end of the chapter.

DEFINING ADOLESCENCE AND BEHAVIOR DISORDERS IN ADOLESCENCE

Adults sometimes cynically regard adolescence as a "disease" that only time can cure, suggesting that parents would do well to bury their offspring at age 12 and dig them up again at age 20. At the same time, some critics contend that adolescence has become artificially prolonged as a "tribal subculture," so that there is little assurance of adulthood even at 20. (Atwater, 1983, p. 1)

Adolescence is a developmental period of the human growth cycle occurring between the ages of approximately 12 and 20. For most adolescents, it is an awkward period in which they are no longer considered children but have not yet attained adult status. The onset of adolescence is generally considered to be marked by the rapid physiological changes occurring during puberty. The demise of adolescence is less well-defined by markers such as legal independence and the acquisition of adult responsibilities. There is no clearly defined upper limit of adolescence, or age at which individuals officially pass over from adolescence into adulthood. Unlike many primitive cultures which clearly separate childhood from adulthood by ceremonial rites of passage, our modern culture allows the individual nearly a decade of preparation for the responsibilities of adulthood.

Adolescence is best defined as the period of transition from childhood to adulthood, a period of flux in which the adolescent may act as mature and responsible as any adult on one day and then revert to childish behavior the next. Adolescence is a time in which individuals redefine their identities based on rapidly changing potential in many areas of their lives.

Developmental Changes

Studies of the modern adolescent reveal a period of upheaval in three developmental areas: physical, cognitive, and personal-social.

Physical.   Rapid changes in physical development mark the onset of puberty and the adolescent period. Hormonal secretions from the hypo- thalamus and pituitary gland are responsible for physiological changes manifested in growth spurts of height and weight, and in sexual matura- tion. Girls generally become sexually mature and capable of reproduction at age 12 or 13 and reach their approximate adult height and weight at about age 15 or 16. Boys mature sexually at age 13 or 14 and reach their approximate adult stature at age 17 or 18. Commensurate changes in skeletal and muscular structure also occur during this period.

Such drastic physiological changes in the adolescent require an ad- justment in body image which may be reflected in self-concept. As they attempt to adjust mentally to their rapidly developing physiques, adoles- cents can become preoccupied with physical characteristics and attractive- ness. They are sensitive to societal standards of beauty and are often highly self-critical. Girls tend to be more concerned about their physical appearance than boys, who tend to be more concerned about physical competence or prowess (Conger, 1973). Another issue is the age at which an individual matures; while early maturers may be thrust into social situations which they are not yet prepared to handle, late maturers often experience undue anxiety about their development.

Cognitive changes.   In addition to physiological changes, the onset of puberty generally is accompanied by an increasing capacity for complex and abstract thought. In Piaget's theory of cognitive development, adoles- cence corresponds with the stage of *formal operational thought.* Formal thought is marked by the ability to think abstractly and to hypothesize. In contrast to the previous childhood stage of concrete thought, which is limited to perceived reality, formal thought encompasses hypothetical possibilities (Inhelder & Piaget, 1958). This shift from the real to the possible enables an individual to generate and discard hypotheses (hypo- thetico-deductive reasoning), much like the scientist does. For example, younger children usually generate a single explanation for an event based on their perception, and they are unable to discard this explanation even when subsequent experience proves them wrong; the child's perception *is* her reality. Adolescents in the formal operations stage are able to discard an explanation when it fails to fit the facts and are able to generate other possible explanations. Hypotheses are secondary to their reality (Inhelder & Piaget, 1958). Other characteristics of formal thought include increased flexibility and imagination, and capacity for logic and propositional thought ("if-then" hypotheses).

Some implications of formal thought in adolescents are summarized by Atwater (1983):

> The emergence of abstract thought at this age helps to explain much char- acteristic adolescent behavior. For one thing, it helps to explain why adoles-

cents become so idealistic and romantic on the one hand, yet more critical and cynical on the other. It also explains why adolescents are so busy clarifying their own identity, yet suffer from the accompanying conflicts and confusion. The newly discovered capacity for abstract thought may also explain the characteristic self-centeredness of this stage of life. (p. 72)

Although formal thought generally is acquired between the ages of 12 and 16, there is much variation among individuals in capability for formal thought. Some adolescents and adults never attain it. An alarming percentage of high school seniors (66 percent) and college freshmen (50 percent) have been found to be operating at the concrete stage (McKinnon, 1976; Renner & Stafford, 1976). Most researchers, including Piaget (1972), recognize that formal thought is not automatically attained, but can be facilitated through appropriate educational experiences. Effects of social class and intelligence on the acquisition of formal thought have been found to be negligible (Kuhn & Angelev, 1976; Neimark, 1975).

Personal-social changes.   Along with physical and cognitive changes, adolescents experience tremendous upheaval in personal ideology and social relationships. The old rules of childhood suddenly don't work any more. The adolescent is thrust into a period of experimentation with new rules, new roles, and an emerging concept of a new self. Three major personal-social changes that occur during this period are noteworthy: the search for identity, independence, and peer approval.

The *search for identity* involves the individual's attempt to integrate the old childhood self with potential for a new adult self. Erikson (1968) dubbed this phenomenon "identity versus role confusion" and included it as the fifth stage of the eight stages of psychosocial development (see Chapter 3). According to Erikson, the search for self is a normal developmental process that may reach crisis proportions but must be resolved if optimal personal growth is to be attained. Conflict, anxiety, self-doubt, and experimentation are all part of the process as adolescents try to find out who they are and what distinguishes them as individuals from their peers. This period is also marked by egocentrism or extreme self-centeredness, during which individuals may become painfully self-conscious. This acute self-consciousness is illustrated by Elkind's (1974) concept of the *imaginary audience,* in which adolescents feel as though they are constantly being watched and evaluated by everyone as if on stage and performing for an audience. A preoccupation with others' perceptions is the major outcome of this stage of egocentrism.

A certain degree of role confusion is unavoidable as the individual tries out various points of view and periodically adopts new styles of interacting, but role confusion is detrimental when it becomes so extreme that the individual loses the boundaries of self. Extreme role confusion and loss of sense of self are frequently found among severely disturbed (psychotic) adolescents. Another difficulty is the adoption of a negative identity, which often happens when adolescents have no positive role models to emulate (Hauser, 1972). Many youth from impoverished communities or unhappy homes turn to delinquency or street gangs as ways to establish an identity, albeit an unacceptable one by society's standards.

A second major issue for adolescents is the *development of independence* or autonomy. While not wanting to jeopardize the emotional security provided by the home, the adolescent constantly struggles to establish an identity separate from parents yet recognized as legitimate. Increased self-sufficiency and decision making are a large part of independence, yet adolescents do not consistently manifest these skills even when acquired; rather, an individual may be unusually mature and self-sufficient in one moment and quite dependent the next. Such fluctuations make teenagers' behavior difficult to predict and sometimes exasperating for adults to deal with.

Open rejection of parental values and questioning of authority are classic symptoms of developing independence. The home is typically the focal point of conflict over independence issues, as the adolescent wants to have more decision-making power, to be afforded some privileges, and generally to take more control of her life. Issues that cause conflict in most families of adolescents are dress, use of the family car, dating, daily chores, school performance, and use of drugs (Atwater, 1983). The parents' sense of authority and the adolescent's sense of increasing autonomy are challenged by the almost daily conflicts that arise over these issues. Various influences on parent-child conflicts are summarized in Table 9–1.

A third and extremely important change that occurs in the lives of adolescents is the *shift in allegiance from family to peers*. Peer approval supersedes most other social aspirations at this point in the individual's development. An inordinate amount of time is spent in cultivating friendships and dating relationships, and for many teenagers the telephone becomes an essential instrument for gathering information about the rapidly changing social scene at school.

The adolescent's emerging identity is closely allied with peer approval and acceptance. Social acceptance is generally based on social conformity; to be "in," one must speak, dress, look, and act like everyone else. Although the styles change over the years, each generation creates a "fringe" element, which is the ultimate adolescent statement of identity through conformity. (Consider the beatniks of the fifties, the hippies of the sixties, preppies of the seventies, and punks of the eighties.) The generation gap is often purposefully widened by use of lingo and slang.

In addition to seeking acceptance from the larger peer group, many adolescents seek further support from cliques, which are small, informal

TABLE 9–1.   Some Influences on Parent-Adolescent Conflicts

AGE: Although the number of conflicts tends to decrease with age, older adolescents pose more serious conflicts involving the use of the car, sex, or drugs.

SEX: The frequency and type of conflict tends to vary by sex. According to one study, family problems made up 22 percent of the difficulties reported by adolescent girls, but only 10 percent of those reported by boys. Parents are more likely to have conflicts with their daughters over dating and sex, and conflicts with their sons over taking care of property or use of cars.

SOCIAL CLASS: The type of conflict often reflects social-class values. Working-class families tend to worry more about their teenagers' being obedient, polite, and staying out of trouble in school. Middle-class families tend to be more concerned about their teenagers' taking the initiative, being competitive, and doing well in school.

FAMILY SIZE: The larger the size of the family, the more parent-adolescent conflicts occur, and the more often parents use force in settling such conflicts. However, this is true mostly for middle-class families; the efforts to control conflicts do not vary with the size of working-class families.

PARENTAL AUTHORITY AND FAMILY ATMOSPHERE: An unhappy marriage or home life tends to increase parent-adolescent conflicts; unhappily married, authoritarian parents evoke the most conflicts.

TOPICS: Common sources of conflict are dress, daily chores, use of the car, dating, and use of cigarettes or alcohol. Other conflicts of special concern to both generations are staying out late and school performance, especially failure at school. Some of the most heated conflicts occur over sex and drugs.

From E. Atwater, *Adolescence.* © 1983, page 117. Reprinted by permission of Prentice-Hall, Inc., Englewood Cliffs, N.J.

groups of friends who do things together. These cliques are loosely structured but usually identifiable within a school or neighborhood setting. While some cliques are based on common interests such as music or sports, others are based on popularity or status within the system. The street gangs alluded to earlier also represent the adolescent need for peer acceptance.

Although all adolescents experience some degree of pressure from peers, the amount of needed peer approval varies widely. The ultimate resolution of the need for peer acceptance depends in part on the quality of the parent-adolescent relationship. With parents who are perceived as nonsupportive, rejecting, or punitive in other ways, the individual may respond with a total shift of allegiance from family to the peer group. For adolescents whose parents are perceived as understanding and supportive, a gradual transition can be made from total reliance on the family to a more balanced sense of self-acceptance, which includes but is not limited to peer approval. This transition may not be complete until the individual is well into adulthood. The need for peer approval has a strong impact on motivation and therefore has many implications for the classroom setting, which will be addressed later in this chapter.

In summary, the entire adolescent experience is best viewed as a normal developmental process of identity redefinition. As Schmid and Slade note, all adolescent behavior is an "experimentation to successfully adapt to the demands of life," and is meaningful when viewed in this context (1981, p. 369). The struggles between parent and teenager, and between teacher and teenager over issues such as school attendance, grades, and social behavior are all part of adolescent experimentation. While most adolescents experience stress and exhibit some deviant behavior, they eventually learn the skills that will enable them to cope in an adult world. In contrast, adolescents who fail to develop adaptive patterns of coping with demands for appropriate social behavior are often labeled behavior disordered.

The Behavior Disordered Adolescent

What distinguishes behavior disordered adolescents from their peers? During adolescence, which is a normal developmental period noted for upheavals and rapid changes in all areas of life, it is often difficult to determine exactly what constitutes maladaptive, disordered, or deviant behavior. McDowell and Brown (1978) note that two well-accepted definitions of behavior disorders (Bower, 1960; Kauffman, 1977) evolve from work with children and have two commonalities: inability to establish appropriate relationships with others, and demonstration of behaviors that fail to meet the expectations of others. Since these characteristics are often found in normal adolescents, deviance in adolescents is more appropriately defined by the frequency or severity of the offending behavior (McDowell, 1981). As in childhood psychopathology, the extremeness of behavior can be considered an underlying characteristic of adolescent psychopathology.

Other researchers have attempted to define behavior disorders in adolescents more clearly by identifying specific dimensions of problem behavior. In two studies, researchers asked parents of adolescents referred for mental health services to rate their children on behavior checklists. Results indicated two dimensions of problem behavior, internalizing (keeping feelings of distress inside, resulting in depression or psychosomatic symptoms) and externalizing (striking out at others or the environment), which have also been identified with younger children (Achenbach & Edelbrock, 1979; Miller, 1980). In another study, Epstein, Cullinan, and Rosemier (1983) asked teachers to rate the behaviors of behavior disordered and normal adolescents on the *Behavior Problem Checklist* (BPC) (Quay & Peterson, 1967). The BPC is composed of four dimensions: Conduct Disorder, Personality Problem, Inadequacy-Immaturity, and Socialized Delinquency; it has been used extensively with behavior disordered children. Epstein et al. (1983) found that behavior disordered adolescents were rated as significantly more maladjusted on the Conduct Disorder and Personality Problem dimensions only; there were no significant differences in ratings on Inadequacy-Immaturity and Socialized Delinquency. Conduct Disorder is characterized by aggressive, hostile, and contentious behavior, and Personality Problem is characterized by anxious, withdrawn, and introvertive behavior. Cullinan et al. (1983) conclude that these results are similar to previous investigations with adolescents because Conduct Disorder resembles the dimension of externalizing, and Personality Problem resembles the dimension of internalizing.

In a review of long-term follow-up studies, Safer and Heaton (1982) found that children with moderate-to-serious behavior problems were likely to manifest the same difficulties in adolescence and sometimes in adulthood. It appears that research to date has failed to document significant characteristics of behavior disordered adolescents that distinguish them from behavior disordered children.

Research on issues related to identification and educational interventions with this population is lacking, possibly due to the fact that educational services for behavior disordered adolescents have lagged far behind services for younger pupils (Nelson & Kauffman, 1977). We will return to educational intervention and model programs later in this chapter. The next section addresses a number of problems that are experienced by both behavior disordered adolescents and their normal peers. While not unique to behavior disordered adolescents, these issues are significant considerations for all secondary students, and the teacher of behavior disordered adolescents can expect to deal with many of these problems on a regular basis.

DEALING WITH ADOLESCENT ISSUES IN THE SCHOOLS

Taking into account the extremeness of behavior that is typical of behavior disordered students, educators should expect routinely to be confronted with nonattendance, antisocial behavior, sex-related problems, drug use, and self-destructive behavior. Each of these issues and educational interventions for each are discussed in this section.

Nonattendance and Antisocial Behavior

Although compulsory attendance laws have been in effect in most states for several decades, many adolescents do not attend school on a regular basis. Educators traditionally have been unable, through coercion or other means, to motivate a certain proportion of adolescents to attend classes regularly. Estimates of chronic nonattendance or truancy at the junior high level range from 1 percent to 2 percent in middle-class neighborhoods to 15 percent in inner-city schools (Safer & Heaton, 1982).

High rates of absenteeism are accompanied by school failure and, eventually, high drop-out rates. Despite an increasing percentage of youth who finish high school, as many as 25 percent of all 18-year-olds will not finish high school or attempt to take the high school equivalency exam (Dearman & Plisko, 1979). Although the exact relationship between students labeled as behavior disordered and school failure and drop-out rates is unknown, it is known that a significant percentage of dropouts have experienced severe learning and adjustment problems. In studies of dropouts, 40 percent were shown to have serious learning problems (Block, Covill-Servo, & Rosen, 1978), and 50 percent were shown to have serious maladjustment problems (Ahlstrom & Havighurst, 1971). The majority of dropouts are from disadvantaged homes, with a disproportionate number from the lower socioeconomic strata. In addition to a decreased potential earning power, dropouts are more likely to engage in antisocial or delinquent behavior (Schreiber, 1963).

The term *antisocial* is used here to refer to any act, aggressive or nonaggressive, which is against the law or which is seriously disruptive in the school setting. Law-enforcement agents and judges have substantial leeway in dealing with law-breaking youth. As a result, only a fraction of juvenile offenders are ever brought into court; instead, they are often lectured and warned or given probation. The majority of juvenile offenses are considered crimes only because they are committed by people who are not legally adults. The most common of these so-called *status offenses* are truancy, running away from home, drinking in public, and incorrigibility (Gibbons, 1981).

Also of concern to educators are crime and vandalism in the schools, which have dramatically increased during the seventies and eighties. One study showed that between 1970 and 1973, assaults on teachers increased by 77 percent, assaults on other students increased by 85 percent, homicides increased by 18 percent, and the incidence of confiscating weapons rose by 54 percent (U.S. Senate Subcommittee to Investigate Juvenile Delinquency, 1975). The same investigation found that in 1973, the cost of school vandalism was approximately $500 million, an amount equal to the total expenditure for textbooks in the previous year. More recently, New York City School officials reported confiscating 130 handguns from students during a single year (Rosenblatt, 1980). McDowell (1981) cautions that adolescent antisocial behavior should be viewed within a sociological context. Today's adolescent may be more prone to stress, subjected to more peer pressure, and provided with fewer incentives for orderly behavior than adolescents of other eras. Nonetheless, the potential for violence in the classroom is a reality.

Suspension-Expulsion

The most common interventions in public schools for nonattendance and antisocial behavior are suspension and expulsion. Suspension of a student by the principal is effective for periods of up to ten days and, as established by litigation, it must be accompanied by a parent conference and a hearing. Expulsion is the exclusion of a student for a longer period of time, generally a term, semester, or a year. Expulsions also must be accompanied by a hearing. In several studies attempting to ascertain major reasons for school suspensions, nonattendance and antisocial behaviors consistently were ranked in the top three (Safer, 1982). However, neither the logic of suspending students for not coming to school nor the effectiveness of suspension as a disciplinary tool has been proven. Expulsions generally are given for more serious infractions such as violent behavior, or illegal acts such as possession of drugs or weapons.

The use of suspension and expulsion as disciplinary measures for behavior disordered students has been questioned ethically and legally. Litigation has established a few basic points: (1) Schools cannot expel students whose handicap causes them to be disruptive without providing an alternative educational placement (Doe v. Koger, 1979); (2) The burden is upon local and state education officials to determine whether the student's behavior is a manifestation of the handicap (S-1 v. Turlington, 1981); and (3) Expulsion constitutes a "change in educational placement," which invokes the due process procedures of P.L. 94–142 (S-1 v. Turlington, 1981). In addition, if the student has been properly identified as behavior disordered or emotionally disturbed, the individual education plan (IEP) committee must make provisions for appropriate disciplinary action in the future (Phillip Pratt v. Board of Education of Frederick County, 1980). Although the court decisions appear well-intentioned in protecting the right to education for the behavior disordered, many issues remain unresolved (for example, Exactly how does one determine whether a specific act is directly related to an emotional handicap?).

State education agencies vary widely in their provision of regulations to help resolve these issues. In a review of state regulations, Barnette and Parker (1982) found that of 26 states responding to a questionnaire, only nine had specific policies for suspension and expulsion of the behavior disordered. Many other states have suspension and expulsion policies for handicapped students but do not single out the category of behavior disordered. Barnette and Parker conclude that within local school systems, the IEP committee can play a key role not only in outlining strategies for academic progress and disciplinary measures but also for ensuring that acts of suspension or expulsion are in accordance with state and federal regulations.

Sex-related Problems

An increasing number of adolescents are becoming sexually active at younger ages, a fact easily explained from a sociological perspective. More permissive attitudes toward sex and trends toward accepting a greater number of options for sexual expression have permeated American culture since the mid-twentieth century. Improved forms of contraception, including the birth-control pill, have made sexual experimentation less hazardous and more appealing for many adolescents. However, despite easier access to information and increasing availability of contraceptives to today's youth, the problems accompanying sexual activity such as premarital pregnancy and venereal disease have continued to increase. It is obvious that a large percentage of adolescents either remain ignorant about contraceptive information or do not seek out contraceptive devices for a number of reasons, including embarrassment, trusting to luck, and fear of adult reprisal.

For thousands of young women each year, the failure to use contraceptives results in pregnancy. Adolescents under the age of 15 have the largest percentage of premarital pregnancies than any other age group (Furstenberg, 1976). This group is also obviously the least prepared emotionally or financially to provide for the needs of an infant or to provide a stable home environment for a growing child. However, the younger the woman, the more likely she is to choose marriage over the other options of abortion, adoption, or rearing the child alone (Condry & Siman, 1974). Although marriage has traditionally been the most socially acceptable option, abortions are becoming more frequent. About one-third of the legal abortions performed in the United States each year are for young women, mostly unmarried, under the age of 19. According to census information, twice as many white women as black women seek abortions; black women tend to carry their pregnancies to term and keep their babies (U.S. Bureau of the Census, 1980).

Another problem associated with sexual activity is venereal disease. Sexually active, older adolescents are at risk of contracting one of the three most common forms of venereal disease: gonorrhea, syphilis, or herpes. The incidence of gonorrhea has reached almost epidemic proportions; although one government source found that a million cases were reported in the United States for a single year, the true incidence level was estimated to be about two million (NIAID, 1981). Gonorrhea is especially insidious because its symptoms may go unnoticed, resulting in infertility in women and sterility in men. Herpes is a viral infection that is also reaching epidemic proportions and also can affect fertility and newborn infants. Syphilis is much less common, but if untreated it can have extremely debilitating effects such as neurological damage. Although many adolescents are knowledgeable about symptoms and effects of venereal disease, a sizeable percentage do not know how to prevent its transmission or what treatment is available in most states without parental permission.

Delinquent sexual behavior among adolescents has not been sufficiently researched to draw many conclusions. Sexual misbehavior by females consists primarily of nonviolent contact with willing male partners, and the only distinctive form of sexual delinquency for female adolescents is prostitution (Erickson, 1984). On the other hand, delinquent sexual behavior by males may either be violent, as in rape, or nonviolent, as in exhibitionism. Child molestation is another sexual offense almost exclusively instigated by males. Although there are few empirical studies solely with adolescent sex offenders, there is some evidence that sexual assaults, including rape, are more linked to aggression and to antisocial tendencies than to sexuality (Erickson, 1984; Lewis, Shanok, & Pincus, 1979). This finding also holds true with adult offenders. Erickson (1984) argues that "there is little that is unique about sexual delinquency, male or female. Arguments in favor of specialized programs must be based on the inadequacy of regular programs (for juvenile offenders) in dealing with sexual matters" (p. 31). Erickson then goes on to outline some guidelines for sex education, which is the focus of the next section.

Sex Education

Many sex-related problems could be minimized if adolescents were better informed about sex-related issues. Although it is argued by some that the home is the proper place for such information to be dispensed, the majority of adolescent students report that their parents do not give them the information they need; further, students report a desire to be given more sex education in school (Sorenson, 1973). Minimal information needed by adolescents includes facts on sexual anatomy and functioning, venereal disease, birth control, abortion, and informative discussions on such anxiety-provoking issues as masturbation and homosexuality. Most experts agree that in addition to providing factual information, sex education programs should also explore sexual values and attitudes. The view that sexuality is a part of basic human relationships can be promoted by all educators.

It may be argued that because schools are socialization agents, sex education should be a part of regular junior high and senior high curricula. According to one nationwide survey, over three-fourths of parents agree; however, due to a vocal minority of parents who disagree, the majority of states have laws that either prohibit or restrict sex education in the schools (Atwater, 1983). For example, many states that allow sex education also prohibit the subject of birth control to be taught. Thus a wide discrepancy exists between the information that states allow to be taught in the schools and the information that both students and experts believe is helpful during the adolescent years.

Sex education should be a part of all adolescent treatment programs. In many locales, Planned Parenthood organizations have sex education materials appropriate for use with adolescents. Sex education programs should encourage self-expression while teaching responsibility for one's sexual behavior (Knopp, 1982). For male adolescent sex offenders, Erickson (1984) suggests that a well-trained male staff member take a detailed sexual history in order to demystify sexual issues and to establish a relationship in which the adolescent can begin to express sexual concerns. Erickson warns that with adolescent offenders, premature attempts to explore sexual issues in coeducational groups may increase resistance rather than promote growth. With groups of nonoffenders, however, coeducational discussion may facilitate more comprehensive understanding of sexuality issues.

Despite its controversial nature, sex education in the public schools should be addressed. A common argument against sex education—that increased knowledge leads to increased sexual experimentation—has not been validated. What has been validated are alarming numbers of premarital pregnancies and incidences of venereal disease among the adolescent population. It should be clear to educators and parents alike that the ostrich approach—of pretending that if we don't talk about sex the problems will go away—is untenable.

Drug Use

Experimentation with mood-altering drugs is a hallmark of adolescence. Availability of many drugs on the street, a lowered drinking age in many states, and misuse of prescription drugs may account for some of the increased drug use among today's adolescents. The drugs most widely used by high school students are alcohol, tobacco, and marijuana. Amphetamines, barbiturates, inhalants and miscellaneous other drugs are used to a much lesser extent by this age group. Prevalence studies have shown that by the time adolescents reach their senior year in high school, the vast majority (87 percent of the females, 93 percent of the males) have tried alcohol, two-thirds have used marijuana, and about one-sixth have experimented with barbiturates, inhalants, or amphetamines, including cocaine (Johnston, Bachman, & O'Malley, 1980; Social Research Group, 1975). Refer to Table 9–2 for a summary of reported drug use by high school seniors. Note that these percentages include students who reported using the drug even once; a much smaller percentage reported continued or habitual use. Many of the students reported using a drug only once or twice because of curiosity or using a drug sporadically for recreational or social purposes.

Nonetheless, drug use among adolescents is a cause for concern. Alcohol, which is legal after a certain age and socially acceptable by many

TABLE 9–2. Percentage of High School Seniors Who Report Having Used Drugs

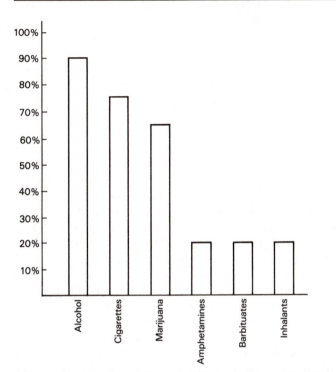

Adapted from Johnston, Bachman & O'Malley, 1980; and Social Research Group, 1975.

standards, is the most widely used and misused drug by teenagers. According to one estimate, approximately 10 percent of all youngsters between the ages of 12 and 17 are now or will become alcoholics, and approximately 30 percent will exhibit continued use of alcohol (Schmid & Slade, 1981). In addition to physical and psychological dependency caused by alcohol are the dangers of driving while intoxicated. Studies have shown that alcohol use has been a factor in almost half of all fatal car accidents, and the majority of these involve drivers under the age of 21. Such statistics have encouraged some states to raise the legal drinking age to 21; currently, about half the states require a person to be 21 before he can legally purchase alcohol.

Another legal and socially acceptable drug is tobacco, or more specifically, nicotine. Since the adverse publicity surrounding the Surgeon General's Report in 1965 linking cigarette smoking to lung cancer, the incidence of smoking among youth has declined. However, tobacco use still has a sizeable following. In 1980, 21 percent of the high school seniors in one study reported that they smoked on a daily basis (Johnston et al., 1980). Cigarettes are known to be physically addicting and to be highly carcinogenic, causing lung ailments and several forms of oral cancer. Individuals who both drink and smoke are at high risk because alcohol increases the carcinogenic effect of nicotine (Whelan, 1978).

Another drug favored by adolescents is marijuana. Popularized by hippies and the college crowd of the 1960s, marijuana has become a common part of the American drug scene. Although still illegal, it has become more and more socially acceptable and is touted by many as less harmful than cigarettes or alcohol. However, marijuana use does have drawbacks. Habitual use often results in lowered academic performance because of its effects on concentration and memory. High levels of marijuana ingestion also impair motor performance and ability to maneuver a car in traffic. However, the most detrimental effect of marijuana is the psychological dependency it fosters, and for this reason many experts discourage its use by adolescents (National Institute on Drug Abuse, 1980). It has been shown that nonusers do better academically in high school than moderate users of marijuana, but these differences tend to fade during the college years (Lawrence & Velleman, 1974).

Numerous other drugs are used by adolescents with less frequency than alcohol, tobacco, or marijuana, but with great potential for damage. "Hard" drugs such as cocaine and heroin are not likely to be used frequently by this age group because of the expense. Amphetamines and sedatives are more likely to be misused by adolescents because of availability through prescriptions. Amphetamines ("speed," "uppers") are commonly prescribed for weight loss, and sedatives ("downers," barbiturates, and tranquilizers) may be prescribed to alleviate anxiety or to promote sleep. The prescribed use of sleeping pills and tranquilizers has become so widespread among middle- and upper-class families that many adolescents need only to shake down their mother's purse or to raid the family medicine cabinet for a ready supply. In addition, mild amphetamines are available over the counter in the form of diet pills. The major dangers resulting from misuse of amphetamines and sedatives are physical and psychological addiction, overdosing, and potentially lethal effects of mixing the drugs with alcohol. Amphetamine use, although not physically addicting, can be psychologically addicting and can cause depression, aggressiveness, and other undesirable psychological states.

There are many reasons for adolescent drug use. One is that during this period of experimentation with many life options, adolescents try out many new experiences that were unavailable to them as children. Experimenting with mood-altering drugs is one of these experiences. A surprising number of adolescents report that their parents either modeled the use of drugs or introduced them to alcohol, tobacco, or marijuana (Atwater, 1983). Conversely, many adolescents experiment with these and other drugs out of defiance or rebellion against parents and other authority figures. Students from homes with a high degree of family stress are also prone to begin using drugs. And as with other areas of adolescent life, peer pressure to experiment with drugs is a powerful motivator.

The damaging effects of drug misuse are not limited to physiological side effects. For adolescents who are trying to learn to cope with life and who are struggling to become adults, the psychological side effects can be especially deleterious. Chronic or heavy use of drugs can postpone these struggles, which are an essential part of the transition from childhood to adulthood. Drug-dependent adolescents make little progress toward becoming responsible, functioning members of society. Students who are occasional users may suffer only temporary difficulties, but they are more likely than nonusers to have problems in school or on the job. Educators can play an important role in detecting and helping ameliorate drug misuse.

Drug Abuse Education

The majority of the population reacts emotionally or moralistically to the topic of drug abuse among adolescents. The drug abuse programs of the early sixties reflected this moralistic tone. Many of these school- and community-based programs utilized scare tactics such as having ex-addicts or police vehemently condemn the use of drugs. Often, misinformation or biased information was given in hopes of discouraging drug use. Unfortunately, the effect of most of these efforts was to undermine the credibility of drug education programs and to further entrench adolescents against "the establishment." Due to the shortcomings of early programs, subsequent programs began to avoid moralizing and to focus upon providing accurate, unbiased information. Many programs also began to incorporate activities in values clarification in order to help students make their own decisions and take responsibility for them.

Currently, research on the effectiveness of drug education yields few consistent results. According to Wong (1979), there is some support in the literature that programs which combine unbiased information and values-processing may affect attitudes and behavior toward drug use. However, many of the studies are marked by methodological problems, and researchers caution that little is really known about the long-term effects of drug education programs.

From research and work in drug abuse programs, Wong (1979) has developed a model for drug education. Wong outlines activities in three separate areas that he believes are the bases for prevention of drug abuse. Inclusion of the first one, *human skills,* is based on the assumption that drug abuse results from an individual's unmet needs or deficiencies in coping with life. Activities in this area emphasize development of interpersonal skills such as communication, and intrapersonal skills such as self-confidence and self-identity. The second area of the model, *alternatives*, is based on the assumption that altered consciousness, the usual result of drug use, can be a positive and desirable experience for human beings. Recommendations to attain an altered state of mind through means other than drugs are given; for example, physical highs can be attained through dance or exercise, and spiritual highs can be achieved through meditation or yoga. The third area of the model, *information provision*, is based on the assumption that accurate, reliable information from credible sources will help youth make better choices. Complete and accurate information should include facts about long- and short-term use, and the pleasures as well as the hazards of drug use. Randall and Wong (1976) also suggest that when a preventative drug education program is being developed, certain tenets should be kept in mind: (1) that drugs are readily available to youth, (2) that drugs produce a high that is desired by many people, (3) that drug use does not inevitably result in physical or emotional harm, and (4) that the desired highs produced by drugs can be achieved by other means.

Lewis (1975) has offered guidelines for the development of effective drug education programs:

Evaluate the level of student sophistication about drugs.
Involve students in the planning process.
Differentiate between drug use and abuse.
Avoid sensationalizing.
Emphasize decision making.
Discuss the factors promoting abstinence.
Include research data and the comments of drug-experienced people.
Include drug education as a part of classroom experience.

Lewis further notes that drug education programs might be more effective if the goal were responsible decision making rather than complete abstinence. When adults do not moralize or advocate total abstinence, students may make more realistic appraisals and feel less of a need to rebel against adult values or authority.

Most drug education programs have a preventative focus and may not be suitable for students who are already into heavy or chronic drug use. In such cases, other intervention measures may be necessary. Jardin and Ziebell (1981) offer guidelines for teachers to follow when they suspect a student of having a drug problem. Before action is taken, however, Jardin and Ziebell warn that two things must be clearly understood by all involved parties. First is a clear statement of school policy about legal issues regarding drug possession and *observed* use of drugs on the school grounds. Second, when the student is only *suspected* of drub abuse, the issue is one of treatment and not of discipline or control. Once these issues are clearly articulated, teachers may take action in the following sequence:

Identification. The most accurate clue to drug use is a drastic and sustained change in a student's attitude, temperament, work habits, work quality, or grades. The teacher should solicit information from other school personnel before a suspicion is voiced. The teacher should also describe the resulting unacceptable behaviors to the student and obtain the backing of an administrator before further action is taken.

Parent conference. The purpose of meeting with the student's parents is to define the problem, to obtain parental input about what steps they intend to take, to get the parents' opinion about the role the school should take, and to get a commitment to try a plan of action.

Family conference. A family conference that includes the student and a school representative should be held as soon as the parents come up with a plan of action. The proposed plan should be parent-initiated and school-supported.

Follow-up. If outside help for the student is part of the plan, the teacher should check on whether it has been obtained. Continued contact with parents is essential, and if representatives from the mental health or legal-correctional systems have become involved, the teacher should maintain periodic contact with them.

Self-Destructive Behavior

Emotionally troubled youngsters may be prone toward self-destructive behaviors such as suicide and severe eating disorders.

Suicide. The most extreme form of self-destructive behavior is suicide. Adolescent suicide has increased dramatically over the past 20 years; it is the third leading cause of death among adolescents ages 15–19 (Holinger, 1979). While females in the general population attempt suicide more often than males (Weiner, 1980), males actually commit suicide three or four times more often (U.S. Bureau of the Census, 1980).

Researchers have attempted to identify factors contributing to adolescent suicide. The acute onset of so many developmental changes during the adolescent years, which leads to increased suggestibility and hypersensitivity, has been posed as one underlying factor (Miller, 1975). Chronic or extreme depression has also been linked with suicidal behavior, although depression is likely a correlate rather than a cause of suicide. In other words, the events and emotions that cause an individual to be depressed may eventually lead to suicide.

Another factor is alienation, or a feeling of irreparable aloneness, which may be manifested through broken romances, little contact with peers, poor communication and conflict with parents, and divorce of parents (Wenz, 1979). Other recurrent themes in suicide victims are feelings of being helpless and powerless (Seligman, 1975), and unresolved feelings over loss of a parent or other close relative at an early age (Atwater, 1983). Psychotic adolescents also may be at high risk of attempting suicide: in one study of hospitalized adolescents, 40 percent reported that they have experienced auditory hallucinations (voices) telling them to kill themselves (Winn, 1969).

Other researchers seeking clues to motivation have studied those who unsuccessfully attempt suicide. Farberow and Litman (1970) categorize the suicidal population into three types: (1) those who really do not want to die but want to make a dramatic statement to others, constituting almost two-thirds of the population; (2) those who are ambivalent about dying and therefore use slow-acting methods which allow for intervention, constituting about one-third of the population; and (3) those who are intent on dying and use immediate or violent means so that intervention is impossible, constituting about 3 to 5 percent of the population. Weiner (1980) estimates that the ratio of attempted suicides to actual suicides among adolescents is at least five times higher than the ratio in the general population. These statistics suggest that suicide attempts, especially among adolescents, are a plea for help from unhappy individuals who do not necessarily see death as the most desirable alternative.

Teachers and other significant adults in the lives of teenagers can play key roles in suicide prevention. Signals for high risk individuals have been identified by Jacobs (1971): a long history of problems that escalate during adolescence, social isolation that becomes progressively more pronounced, and loss of hope due to the breakup of a meaningful relationship. Although there are no simple solutions to adolescent suicide, Konopka (1983) offers some general preventative guidelines for adults to follow:

> maintaining open and honest communication
> setting an atmosphere of loving respect
> providing creative outlets
> accepting strong emotions, both positive and negative.

Both Konopka (1983) and Atwater (1983) stress that lines of communication must be kept open, especially if suicide threats or attempts have been made. The vulnerable adolescent is likely to be extremely sensitive to others' opinions and reactions, and the single best predictor of subsequent attempts is whether the adolescent is able to maintain communication with others.

Eating disorders. Two self-destructive eating disorders, *anorexia nervosa* and *bulimia,* are more prevalent among adolescent girls than among other populations. Anorexia nervosa is a self-imposed restriction of eating that results in severe, sometimes life-threatening, weight loss. It is ten times more common in girls than in boys, and is most likely to occur in adolescent girls around age 14 or 15. If untreated, less extreme cases of the disorder are likely to continue into adulthood.

The cause of anorexia is currently unknown. Anorexics have been characterized as over-controlled and meticulous and as coming from over-controlled homes, which engendered emotional conflict (Ushakov, 1971). Although psychoanalytic theories (for example, fear of becoming sexually mature) have been proposed, it is most practical to view anorexia as a phobia of being overweight or fat. Anorexia usually begins with dieting, which becomes an obsession; consequently, the individual loses all perspective of appropriate body weight. Even when abnormally thin, the individual cannot lose the fear of becoming fat and therefore does not resume normal eating habits. It has not been determined whether most anorexics are overweight before they begin dieting. One study of anorexics over a 50-year period found that only 30 percent had been overweight and that 37 percent reported that they began dieting for reasons of their own, without external suggestions or provocation.

Previously, 10 percent to 20 percent of anorexic girls died of starvation. However, the mortality rate has sharply decreased in the past few years, since anorexia has been more readily diagnosed and treated. Behavioral interventions have proven successful in treating anorexia (Azerad & Stafford, 1969; Brady & Rieger, 1975). Positive reinforcement for weight gain has induced anorexics to begin eating and to eventually lose their fear of becoming fat.

Bulimia is an eating disorder in which the individual eats an abnormally large amount of food and then induces vomiting or uses laxatives to remove the food before it can be digested. For this reason, it is often called the "binge-and-purge" syndrome. Bulimia differs from anorexia in that bulimics are often of normal weight; thus their abnormal eating habits may not be known to others. Bulimia may be characterized as a form of obsessive-compulsive behavior: bulimics cannot rid themselves of the idea of going on a food binge (obsessive), and once the food has been ingested, cannot resist the urge to get it out of their system (compulsive). Currently, less is known about bulimia than about anorexia, but treatment generally consists of psychotherapy and participation in support groups with other bulimics. If teachers suspect that a student is experiencing either of these eating disorders, referral to a local mental health support system should be made.

INTERVENTIONS WITH BEHAVIOR DISORDERED ADOLESCENTS

Over the years, program development of behavior disordered adolescents has received much less attention than program development for younger children for several reasons. The difficulty of identifying behavior disorders is compounded during adolescence, a time in which the vast majority of students test the limits of normality in their search for self-identity. A second confounding factor in both identification and services delivery is the distinction between behavior disordered adolescents (who are to be served in public school programs) and juvenile delinquents (who are to be served by the juvenile correctional system). Although these two populations are theoretically considered to be separate, in reality the two often overlap. Another factor impeding program development for behavior disordered adolescents is the lack of clear-cut research on the effectiveness of specific approaches to dealing with important issues such as career preparation, sex-related problems, and drug abuse. Despite these factors, a growing interest in developing model programs and researching the efficacy of specific interventions for this population has become evident. The remainder of this chapter explores career education alternatives, behavioral and counseling interventions, and model programs that hold promise for dealing with the behavior disordered adolescent.

Career Education and Prevocational Training

Career education is often viewed as a comprehensive curriculum area, and prevocational training is viewed as instruction in specific job-related skills. In this section, the reader is introduced to a working knowledge of each of the concepts. First, a general career education model is discussed, followed by a model prevocational program for severely behavior disordered adolescents.

Career education.   It is a common belief that effective career education programs help to make the school day more relevant to adolescents, thereby increasing their motivation to stay in school. Ideally, career education is a valuable component of education for all students, handicapped and nonhandicapped. In reality, however, career education suffers from a confusing history and from a lack of unity in program development and implementation. Despite the fact that career education for the handicapped is backed by federal legislation (P.L. 94–142; The Rehabilitation Act of 1973; 1976 Amendments to the Vocational Education Act of 1963), services to this population are, at best, sporadic. Kolstoe (1981) reported that in 1981, only about one in 30 handicapped students in special education was being served by career education programs.

Brolin and Kokaska (1979) conceptualize three major competency areas within a career education curriculum: (1) daily living skills, (2) personal-social skills, and (3) occupational guidance and preparation. Twenty-two competencies in these three skill areas are outlined in Table 9–3. According to these authors, career education encompasses more than prevocational or occupational training; it also includes skills for functioning independently and for sustaining interpersonal relationships on the job and in the community.

Career education is viewed as a body of knowledge that is best taught on a developmental basis from kindergarten through graduation. Note that the competencies listed in Table 9–3 under occupational preparation range from a low-level skill of exploring occupational possibilities to a high-level skill of seeking and securing employment. Most career specialists recommend that career education begin in kindergarten and continue through the elementary years with an emphasis on awareness and exploration of career possibilities. In the junior and senior high years, students should receive more specific instruction in developing work habits, acquiring specific occupational skills, and seeking employment.

The role of the special education teacher in career education varies according to the roles assumed by other personnel in the system. Few special education teachers have the background or training to carry out comprehensive career development programs. However, special education teachers are taught to individualize instruction and to identify meaningful instructional units for students. They are also required to devise

TABLE 9–3. Career Education Curriculum Competencies

DAILY LIVING SKILLS

1. Managing family finances
2. Selecting, managing, and maintaining a home
3. Caring for personal needs
4. Raising children, family living
5. Buying and preparing food
6. Buying and caring for clothes
7. Engaging in civic activities
8. Utilizing recreation and leisure
9. Getting around the community (mobility)

PERSONAL-SOCIAL SKILLS

10. Achieving self-awareness
11. Acquiring self-confidence
12. Achieving socially responsible behavior
13. Maintaining good interpersonal skills
14. Achieving independence
15. Achieving problem-solving skills
16. Communicating adequately with others

OCCUPATIONAL GUIDANCE AND PREPARATION

17. Knowing and exploring occupational possibilities
18. Selecting and planning occupational choices
19. Exhibiting appropriate work habits and behaviors
20. Exhibiting sufficient physical-manual skills
21. Obtaining a specific occupational skill
22. Seeking, securing, and maintaining employment

individual education plans (IEPs), which can easily include career education objectives.

If a suitable career development curriculum is not readily available to the special education teacher, the infusion method can be adopted. In the infusion method, the basic academic curriculum is maintained while supplementing academic units with lessons and activities related to career development. The teacher who decides to infuse or incorporate career education skills into academic curriculum should follow a conceptual model such as the one presented in Table 9–3. Broad skill areas can then be selected as annual goals for the IEP and task-analyzed to identify short-term objectives. Two examples of how career education goals can be written into IEPs are given in Table 9–4.

A model prevocational program.   One model for a successful prevocational program for severely behavior disordered adolescents was reported by Gable (1984). Participants were youths ages 15 to 17 in a psychiatric residential setting in Virginia. Problems leading to residential placement were reported as "aggressive acting-out behavior, immature withdrawn behavior, self-injurious behavior, theft, chronic disruption or school avoidance, sexual acting-out, runaway, and other delinquency status offenses" (Gable, 1984, pp. 59–61). The youths were also reported to evidence severe academic retardation in relation to their intellectual ability.

The prevocational program consists of three major components: (1) an academic-remedial curriculum, (2) a social skills curriculum, and (3) prevocational training/work experience. The academic curriculum is based on functional, life-related skills. Within the academic framework, participants are rated daily on amount of participation, work accuracy and attitude, and independence or self-maintenance. The social skills curriculum is composed of interpersonal skills needed to function in a work setting. Students are rated daily on five competencies: following directions, using appropriate language, interacting with peers, interacting with adults, and exhibiting self-control. The prevocational component includes activities ranging from seeking employment to actual work experiences. The program offers instructional units developed for specific jobs, and the students are given ample time to master basic job-related skills in these units before being placed in a work setting. Some work settings are on-campus, while others are community-based.

After only one year of operation, program evaluation results were encouraging: participants showed appreciable academic gains and maintained an acceptable level of work performance and behavior in 94 percent (31 of 33) of the placements. Anecdotal reports also suggested that participants evidenced more age-appropriate behaviors and more responsibility than they did prior to their participation in the program.

To summarize, it is important that teachers of behavior disordered adolescents make provisions for systematic instruction in skills related to securing and maintaining employment. Career education is usually conceptualized as a broad curriculum area that should begin in kindergarten and continue until graduation from high school. Teachers can easily infuse or incorporate career education objectives into IEPs. Another option is to gear the total curriculum, including academic objectives, toward prevocational training as illustrated in the model program.

Behavioral Interventions

Utilization of behavioral techniques with adolescents warrants some special considerations. It is generally not too difficult to find reinforcers for a child, and, between parents and teachers, the child's environment may be fairly easily arranged to control reinforcement. In contrast, adolescents have much more control over their environment, and many of the reinforcers that worked in childhood no longer work in adolescence. It may be difficult for teacher and student to mutually agree upon suitable reinforcers, as adolescents will often name reinforcers that are either illegal or unethical (alcohol or pornography, for example). Another factor is the emergence of peer group influence as a major motivator for adolescents, which may diminish the adolescent's need for adult approval (social reinforcement). Behavior disordered adolescents in particular often do not place a premium on the usual social incentives, which may further limit the range of possible reinforcers.

Despite these potential difficulties, token economy and contingency management systems appear to be useful with behavior disordered adolescent populations. (See pages 189–193 for a brief review of these concepts.) Towns (1981) reviewed research in this area and found that token economies that were successful with adolescents fall into three categories: those utilizing home-based reinforcement systems, those using group contingencies, and those using self-determined reinforcement. As discussed in Chapter 8, home-based reinforcement systems can have a powerful effect on in-school behavior if parents and teachers work out a cooperative plan. Typical targeted behaviors in home-based systems include completing homework and other study behaviors, and typical reinforcers include watching television and other social privileges in the home and community.

Due to the influence of peer pressure among adolescents, group contingencies may be more successful than individual contingencies. In group contingencies, reinforcement is dependent upon the cooperation of every member of the group: if any member fails to exhibit the agreed-upon behavior, then no one receives the reinforcement. Group contingencies have been applied with behavior disordered adolescents to increase task-related behaviors in the classroom (Graubard, 1969), and to

TABLE 9–4. Examples of Career Education Goals in IEPs

CURRICULUM AREA: ANNUAL GOAL:	MATHEMATICS Rita will increase her skills in the basic mathematical processes of addition, multiplication, subtraction, and division.	CURRICULUM AREA: ANNUAL GOAL:	LANGUAGE ARTS Beth will increase her written language skills.
SHORT-TERM OBJECTIVE:	Given a series of 10 one-digit multiplication problems, Rita will compute correct answers with 90% accuracy.	SHORT-TERM OBJECTIVE:	Given a specific subject, Beth will demonstrate the ability to organize ideas in written paragraph form, beginning with a topic sentence.
CAREER EDUCATION ACTIVITY:	Cut out newspaper advertisements and coupons for grocery store items. Use them as the basis for math problems and such related activities as budgeting and	CAREER EDUCATION ACTIVITY:	Have students take turns assuming responsibility for a Weekly Career Report. Using a simple interview form as a guide, interview a parent,

planning a simple meal. Place related coupons and teacher- or student-made worksheets in separate manila envelopes. Students may assist in the collection of materials and in writing problems. Examples: (1) Select and list items totaling no more than $5 to take on a picnic. (2) Find the cost of two loaves of bread. (3) Find the coupon that tells the cost of a can of pork and beans. Multiply to find the cost of five cans.

neighbor, or community acquaintance regarding her or his occupation, work location, type of activities performed during the work day, and any other interesting information desired. Use the information gathered to write short reports in paragraph form. One report is presented in class each week, then posted on a class or school bulletin board. Students will benefit from role-playing interviews in class before trying it on their own.

From J.S. Lamkin, *Getting Started: Career education activities for exceptional students (K-9)*. Reston, VA: The Council for Exceptional Children, 1980.

increase school attendance (Alexander, Corbett, & Smigel, 1976). In these studies, tangible rewards such as money and intangible rewards such as free time were used successfully.

At the secondary level, it is especially important to involve students in planning behavioral interventions. Thus it is not surprising that many successful token systems utilize self-determined reinforcement. However, self-determined reinforcement was found to be enhanced by teacher evaluation (Santogrossi, O'Leary, Romanczyk, & Kaufman, 1973) and by teacher attention to appropriate behavior and inattention to inappropriate behavior (Main & Munro, 1977).

Token systems are based upon contingency management, which is in turn based upon the Premack Principle: that high probability behaviors can be used to increase low probability behaviors (Premack, 1965). High probability behaviors of adolescents include listening to music, talking to one another, playing pinball or video games, and participating in sports or other recreational activities. Low probability behaviors include studying, completing classwork, and finishing homework. Although token economies have been successful with behavior disordered adolescents, teachers may choose to forego tokens and to implement a simplified contingency management system whereby the student is presented with an "If-then" proposition. ("If you finish your class assignment, [low probability behavior] then you may listen to music through the headphones" [high probability behavior]). Successful use of contingency management with these types of activities has been reported by Main and Munro (1977) and Cohen, Filipczak, and Bis (1970).

Despite the apparent success of token economies and contingency management in helping to change student behavior, many educators and researchers are concerned about the *generalization* of behavior change: does the student manifest the acquired behaviors in settings other than the one in which contrived reinforcement is presented? In hopes of partially offsetting generalization difficulties, researchers are turning to self-control and self-management techniques. One such study was conducted by Marshall and Heward (1979) with eight institutionalized juvenile delinquent males. In a 13-session course, each student was taught to self-select a target behavior, to record baseline data on that behavior, to design and implement an intervention, and to evaluate the success of the project. Results indicated that: (1) the students correctly implemented the self-management techniques, (2) the target behaviors showed improvement (although exact percentages were interpreted cautiously due to reliability problems), and (3) by self-report, the students felt that they were successful in modifying their target behaviors.

Behavioral self-control and social skills training were discussed in Chapter 7 but bear mentioning again because of their special applicability to the adolescent population. Behavioral self-control and other forms of cognitive behavior modification are especially important with adolescents because these techniques emphasize the shift from external to internal controls. The shift to internal controls becomes important as the behavior disordered individual matures and experiences more choices and options, while at the same time fewer restrictions are imposed by adults in the environment. Although some environmental controls are evidenced in the highly structured classrooms of many adolescent programs, the individual must learn to cope with increasing demands for independence and responsibility, which can be enhanced through self-control techniques. An emphasis on student self-control and student responsibility for outcomes also helps eliminate the power struggles between teacher and student so often found in adolescent classrooms.

Social skills training is also an important consideration in programming for behavior disordered adolescents. In addition to the benefit of increasing the probability of successful mainstreaming, social skills training can foster the development of social competence outside the classroom setting (Stephens, 1977). Development of social competencies is especially important for behavior disordered adolescents who have been characterized as "socially nearsighted" and as lacking in social judgment. Moreover, interacting with peers in an acceptable manner is important competency for all adolescents to whom peer acceptance is one crucial determinant of self-worth. The concept of social skills training and two social skills curricula appropriate for adolescents were outlined in Chapter 7.

Counseling Techniques

A variety of counseling techniques are available to behavior disordered adolescents. Techniques employed in individual therapy sessions vary according to the preference and training of the therapist, but most focus upon some combination of self-understanding and the changing of behaviors that are maladaptive to the individual. Although family therapy has been available for years, only recently have researchers begun to view it as necessary for effecting long-term change in the life of a child. Because friction between parent and child is a normal part of the adolescent developmental phase, parent involvement in therapy is especially important for this age group. In fact, one study found a moderately high success rate for adolescents in therapy whose parents were involved in some part of the treatment plan, and a 100 percent failure rate for adolescents whose parents were not involved at all (Rosenstock & Vincent, 1979).

Another form of counseling especially effective with adolescents is group therapy. Group therapy may yield more satisfactory results than individual therapy for adolescents for several reasons. A strong allegiance to peers and need for peer approval is one factor. This strong identification with peers can be both a source of support and a source of pressure to conform to the group's ideas and mores. With some adolescents, there is the additional factor of rebellion against adults or authority figures. Such an attitude, when coupled with an exaggerated need for privacy, often leaves an adult therapist with a sullen, noncommunicative client.

Teachers who are trained to work with behavior disordered students can implement group sessions in the classroom on a routine basis. Towns (1981) offers some guidelines for the teacher who wishes to set up and lead adolescent groups. Initially, the teacher must expect students to be highly anxious; such tasks as sharing feelings and learning to confront one another openly are very anxiety-provoking to adolescents. As a way to relieve the anxiety, students will resort to teasing or picking on one another. The first requirement for the teacher as group leader is therefore to maintain order, which may be partially accomplished by setting rules for the group (no interrupting, no name-calling, and so forth). However, according to Towns, the most essential element is to have a specific task for each group meeting; if left unstructured, the group may easily disintegrate into acting-out and testing limits. The task may be something external to the group, such as a particularly cogent news item, or it may be internal to the group, such as an argument that has been brewing for some time among several group members. Presenting a task and maintaining structure are the key elements to leading adolescent groups.

Glasser (1969) promotes the use of group discussions or class meetings as a tool that helps students increase their involvement with school and decrease their likelihood of failing. Other purposes of the meetings are (1) to improve thinking skills and increase confidence in verbal ability, (2) to solve class problems and increase class cohesiveness, and (3) to help make the classroom more relevant to the students' everyday lives. Meetings are to be of short duration (10 to 20 minutes) and held on a daily basis or a minimum of three times per week at a regularly scheduled time. To facilitate communication, students should be seated in a circle. Glasser advocates three types of meetings. The first type, the *educational-diagnostic meeting*, is directly related to the current curriculum and is designed to give the teacher a quick evaluation of teaching-learning effectiveness on a specific concept or subject. Students are never graded or evaluated on their participation in these groups. The second type, the *open-ended meeting*, is designed to help students develop thinking skills related to a particular topic. Chosen topics may be related to the curriculum or may be for sheer fun (for example, "What fictional character would you most like to be? Why?"). Third type of group, the *problem-solving meeting*, is designed to help students cooperatively brainstorm and solve problems related to living in the real world. This type of meeting has the most therapeutic value because it helps students to overcome obstacles by generating their own solutions, thereby instilling some sense of control over their environments. Prior to each meeting, the teacher should determine its type based on pressing needs of the class or the teacher's immediate goals for the class.

As group leader, the teacher should avoid moralizing or making judgmental statements. Students should feel that the meetings are a forum during which they may speak freely and honestly. The teacher should also take an active part and provide direction to the group and support to those who may feel threatened. Ground rules should always be established and maintained.

Model Programs

Two well-established model public school programs for behavior disordered adolescents will be reviewed in this section: the Mark Twain School in Montgomery County, Maryland, and the Harrison Secondary Program in Minneapolis, Minnesota. Although these programs espouse the same major goal and share common characteristics, they operate from different treatment philosophies. A review of these model programs demonstrates how the needs of adolescents can be met by utilizing principles from several theoretical models.

The Mark Twain School has been serving severely emotionally handicapped pupils in Montgomery County since 1972. Students who are enrolled are characterized as having such complex emotional and behavioral difficulties that success in a regular classroom is unattainable (Laneve, 1979). The major goal of the school is to provide students with educational and social skills that will enable them to return to a regular school placement. To achieve this end, a highly individualized program is provided to each student for a maximum of two years, at which time the student is expected to return to the regular school environment. Students in grades 5 through 12 are served in three smaller schools within the larger school.

The core of the Mark Twain program is the teacher-advisor (TA). Each TA is assigned 9 to 12 advisees who meet together daily to discuss problems and issues at home or at school. The TA is also responsible for each advisee's individual education plan and for involving the advisee's parents in at least four conferences each year. Other duties include:

orientation of the student to the school
creating and monitoring the IEP
counseling on an individual basis and in groups
coordinating with parents and other staff members
setting up the environment for student's eventual return to the community, including follow-up (Laneve, 1979).

Alternative placements are offered within the program so that a student may be placed in a highly structured, self-contained class with a low teacher-pupil ratio, or in a less structured class that more closely approximates the regular classroom format. This feature is obviously designed to facilitate the long-range goal of returning students to the regular classroom environment.

The treatment philosophy at Mark Twain is based on Glasser's reality therapy (see pages 179–180), which is characterized by becoming personally involved and teaching students to take responsibility for their behavior. The staff's role is to become involved with students, to help provide alternatives to irresponsible behavior, and to obtain commitments for behavior change from the students. Punishment is not a part of the treatment plan, but time-out may be used for disruptive or threatening incidents, and physical restraint may be used if the student is out of control.

Other features of the school are a parent program and a support system for the staff. Together, TAs and a social worker plan and implement parent programs that (1) establish on-going communication between parents and school, and (2) offer educational seminars on topics such as reality therapy, parent effectiveness training, and assertiveness. The support system for the staff is designed to help prevent burnout by providing times and avenues for catharsis, and occasional social activities such as luncheons.

Another model program, the Harrison Secondary Program, opened its doors to behavior disordered junior high students in the Minneapolis area in 1975. The population typically served is low functioning academically and is comprised of approximately one-half minorities and a male-female ratio of 6:1 (Braaten, 1979). The students typically have not responded to a variety of other treatment programs; many have court records or were previously treated in residential centers. The primary goal of the program is to provide students with services that will allow them to remain in public schools while developing appropriate academic and social skills. Like the Mark Twain School, the Harrison program has three levels of possible placements that vary in degree of structure and pupil-teacher ratio. Individualized educational and treatment plans are based on the Behavioral Objective Sequence, a set of specific objectives divided into six areas: Adaptive, Personal, Communication, Interpersonal, Academic Task Behaviors, and Counseling.

Treatment at Harrison is based primarily on the social-learning tenet that normal and disturbed behaviors are learned in the same ways and therefore students can learn more adaptive ways of behaving. This philosophy is implemented through behavioral technology. A point system is used to reinforce behavior and provide feedback. A maximum of five points per period are awarded, and students may trade these in for tangible rewards or for free time in the student lounge where music and a variety of games are available. Behavioral contracts are also used in which students outline behaviors that can be expected of them in return for privileges such as taking an elective class or participating in extracurricular activities. Feedback is an important component of the program, as students are formally evaluated every six weeks, and progress reports are sent both to the home and to the home school on a regular basis. Another behavioral feature is use of time-out for unmanageable behavior; students may also elect to go to time-out if they feel too stressed to function in the classroom.

A series of elective courses are offered during the school year. Specially designed courses on drug education and sex education are available. In addition, topics such as music, crafts, black culture, and team sports are covered. As mentioned earlier, elective courses are considered a privilege to be earned through adherence to a behavioral contract.

The Harrison staff attempts to establish a network with others in the student's home and community ecosystems. Parents are routinely contacted about their child's program, and counseling or educational services are available to them. Members from the mental health, legal-correctional, and social-welfare systems are also often involved in the student's total treatment plan.

The similarities between these two successful programs are noteworthy. First, both programs attempt to provide students with the academic and social skills they need to function in as normal an environment as possible. Second, the programs offer alternative classroom placements so that an individual student initially can be placed in a highly structured environment and can move to a less structured environment if warranted. Third, each program has provisions for a time-out procedure for disruptive or unmanageable behavior. Fourth, both the Mark Twain and the Harrison programs value coordination with parents and other significant persons in the students' home communities. Regardless of theoretical orientation, these four points appear to be essential elements of successful programming for behavior disordered adolescents.

SUMMARY

Adolescence is a transitional period between childhood and adulthood that is marked by rapid changes in physical maturation, cognitive development, and personal-social relationships. Intertwined with physical and cognitive changes are the adolescent's struggles for identity, independence, and peer approval. These struggles often cause the adolescent to clash with parents and teachers on a daily basis. In the schools, such clashes generally occur over issues of school nonattendance, antisocial behavior, and sex- and drug-related behavior. Self-destructive behavior such as suicide and severe eating disorders are also manifested among this population. Educators need to be prepared to deal with these issues on an individual basis and with well-planned programs in career education, drug abuse education, and sex education.

Behavior disordered adolescents need special interventions in the schools to help them learn more adaptive coping patterns. Behavioral self-control and social skills training are especially appropriate for adolescents. In addition, behavioral interventions such as token economies and contingency management have proven effective in many programs for behavior disordered adolescents. Due to a strong peer group influence among these youngsters, group counseling has been used successfully in helping them learn to communicate and to problem-solve. A review of two model programs for behavior disordered adolescents revealed two strong philosophical commitments: (1) helping students acquire the academic and social skills that will enable them to function in normal environments, and (2) helping parents and other community personnel to understand and accommodate the adolescent in the home and community ecosystems.

BOX 9–1.   *BEHAVIOR DISORDERED ADOLESCENTS: A TEACHER'S VIEW*

It was bound to be an interesting year for me because it was the first year I'd taught in a public school since my college days. For three and one-half years I'd taught in a psychiatric setting with doctors, social workers, psychologists, nurses, nutritionists, child-care workers, and what would later seem like a cast of thousands for support services. That year I was teaching in one of the largest and poorest school districts in the state, in an area of town where people were highly transient. I was assigned to a self-contained classroom for seriously behavior disordered junior high school students.

From the information in my students' folders I learned that I would have one of the most ethnically diverse groups imaginable, including a Polynesian American and an American Eskimo. As it turned out, ethnicity was not a problem in developing cooperative work groups. The problem in group interaction seemed to arise from the fact that my students were evenly divided between those with a very tenuous contact with reality, and those who had a firm grasp on reality but chose to walk on the fine edge with the local police. The other little twist was that of my ten students, only one was female.

Early on, my aide and I knew that we would have to watch our delinquent group very carefully because they began to manipulate and "borrow" from the less discerning students. We addressed the problem through careful seating arrangement, giving each student a single desk with some sort of barrier to limit visual contact with other students where academic work was to be completed. We structured group activities so that the more vulnerable of our students never worked with our more cunning students unless they were under the direct supervision of the aide or the teacher. We also worked very hard to foster friendships between the students, and eventually some of our delinquent students became very protective of the others.

Our group activities had to be carefully designed so that competition did not become a destructive dynamic. Team members were chosen by the aide or the teacher. Most of the activities were cooperative, but those that were competitive had rules about such things as "seeing how long we can keep the ball in bounds" or giving points for assists. Some days the electricity in the air was just too tense to try to involve the group in a game; on such days, science lessons might be adjusted to include a nature walk. The key element in all our planning was flexibility. There were a lot of beautiful lesson plans that were put on hold because the students' needs shifted so quickly.

The most difficult adjustment for me was dealing with the isolation and lack of support personnel. I was accustomed to working in a setting where everyone was dealing with handicapped children and trying to promote each child's potential. In the public school setting, not only were there no psychologists, no social workers, no child-care workers, but there were no other special education teachers on my side of the building! I was the only faculty member who ate lunch with her students, and frequently the only adult to be seen in the cafeteria at noon. When I talked with the principal about mainstreaming my students, she painfully admitted that there were only three teachers in the building who would give my students a chance—and two of them taught the same subject.

There may be a dozen solutions to the problem of not having support personnel, but I only found one that worked—looking for help outside the school system. By the end of the fall semester, I knew most of the juvenile probation officers in that section of town. I met with or called the students' parents at least once a week, even if it was a chat at the curb or a five-minute phone call. I checked with the local United Fund office to locate as many social service agencies as I could, and then I developed friendships with some of the staff members. Within my building, I used any excuse I could find to bring other teachers into my room so that they could see for themselves that we were just another class. When a student was having a good day, he might earn the privilege of running errands, not only for me but also for the other teachers in our area. Before too long, teachers on our hall were asking why such a nice child was in my class.

There weren't any miracle cures in our class, but there were some significant changes. All of the students managed to stay out of the juvenile detention facilities for the year. None of the furniture was damaged. One student gave up being a mountain lion during free time. One young man learned to eat with a knife and fork and to stop talking with the plastic alligator he kept in his pocket. Three of our students did go to mainstream class, but only one progressed to the point of not needing the support of a self-contained class the next year. Although we would have liked to have seen more progress, I know how hard all of us had to work to achieve these goals.

Contributed by Dona Stallworth

KEY POINTS

1. Adolescence is an awkward developmental period in which individuals are no longer children, yet not quite adults.

2. Rapid physical and sexual changes in adolescents are accompanied by adjustments in body image and self-concept.

3. Struggles for identity, independence, and peer approval are hallmarks of the normally developing adolescent.

4. Research with behavior disordered adolescents has failed to differentiate characteristics of adolescent psychopathology from characteristics of childhood psychopathology.

5. Behavioral deviancy in adolescence is best viewed in terms of the severity and/or frequency of the offending behavior.

6. The teacher of behavior disordered adolescents should expect to deal routinely with problems related to sex, antisocial behavior, use of drugs, and self-destructive behavior such as suicide.

7. Some special interventions in schools that foster more adaptive coping patterns are behavioral self-control, social skills training, prevocational training, token economies, contingency management, and group counseling.

ADDITIONAL READINGS

Adolescence, by E. Atwater. Englewood Cliffs, NJ: Prentice-Hall, 1983, for an excellent overview of adolescent psychology and related issues (for example, sexuality, juvenile delinquency, moral development, and vocational choices).

Adolescent drug and alcohol abuse, by R.A. Jardin & P.W. Ziebell. In G. Brown, R.L. McDowell, & J. Smith (Eds.), *Educating adolescents with behavior disorders.* Columbus, OH: Chas. E. Merrill, 1981, for a practical chapter on dealing with drug abuse in the schools.

Supportive therapies, by E.L. Phillips. In G. Brown, R.L. McDowell, & J. Smith (Eds.), *Educating adolescents with behavior disorders.* Columbus, OH: Chas. E. Merrill, 1981, for an overview of supportive therapies (bibliotherapy, writing therapy, and music and art therapy) and their use with adolescents.

A personal adjustment curriculum for secondary behaviorally disordered students, by C.J. Houchens. In S. Braaten, R.B. Rutherford, Jr., & C.A. Kardash (Eds.), *Programming for adolescents with behavioral disorders.* Reston, VA: Council for Children with Behavior Disorders, 1984, for a description of an affective curriculum developed for use with behavior disordered adolescents.

Adolescent suicide, by G. Konopka. *Exceptional Children,* 1983, *49,* 390–394, for a thought-provoking article on suicide.

Selected chapters in *School programs for disruptive adolescents,* edited by D.J. Safer. Baltimore: University Park Press, 1982, for information on interventions and school programs for delinquent and disruptive youth.

How to motivate adolescents: A guide for parents, teachers, and counselors, by L. Nielsen. Englewood Cliffs, NJ: Prentice-Hall, 1982, for a handy paperback tradebook on motivation for parents and teachers of adolescents.

ten

Severe Behavior Disorders

orientation

Jordi is diagnosed "childhood schizophrenic."
"He drank his milk slowly, watching her as she did the dishes.
Then she asked, 'How was it, Jordi?'
'The man was the same on the train.'
'What man?'
'The man who sat.'
'Who sat, Jordi?'
'The big stranger.'
'But how was school, Jordi?'
'School, pool, fool, tool. So jiggle, jiggle.'
He took the jiggler out of his pocket and left the house. The sun was going down, and he felt cold. He went back to the house and put on his sweater. Then he dangled the jiggler and waited.
The jiggler took him all over the neighborhood. He checked all the places—the tower, the busy street, the subway station. All of it was like before.
Then it was dark, and he felt the jiggler lead him home.
After supper he was very tired. He went to his room and fell asleep."

(From *Lisa & David/Jordi*, T. I. Rubin, 1962, p. 22)

OVERVIEW

Psychotic, schizophrenic, autistic . . . professionals disagree over what constitutes a severe behavior disorder and even whether use of the term is justifiable. However, few professionals deny that a group of children and adolescents exists for whom the more traditional methods of special education and therapy are unsuccessful: these children exhibit severely maladaptive behaviors and are very low functioning in cognitive and social domains. Many of these children are nonverbal, deficient in basic self-help skills, and engage in self-stimulatory or self-injurious behavior.

The premise of this chapter is that children with these characteristics require modifications in their educational programs that are quite different from those required by less severely disordered children. Such modifications include developing a curriculum oriented toward functional activities and selecting specialized instructional techniques that meet the unique needs of these youngsters. The first section of this chapter defines the behavioral and cognitive characteristics of this population; the second section delineates the needed modifications in curriculum and instruction; the third section addresses four major issues of concern to teachers of severely behavior disordered students: eliminating self-stimulatory and self-injurious behavior, developing language-communication skills, planning vocational programs, and dealing with parents of the severely disordered.

DEFINING SEVERE DISORDERS

The label *psychotic* generally has been accepted as a generic or umbrella term for children with severely debilitating disturbances in affect or behavior. However, controversy has arisen over whether subclassifications of psychotic behavior are helpful. Many researchers believe that autism and schizophrenia constitute two separate syndromes worthy of diagnostic labels (Freeman & Ritvo, 1981; Kanner, 1943; Neel, 1979), whereas others believe that research has not delineated characteristics definitively enough for subclassification (Blau, 1962; Kauffman, 1977).

Such controversy has plagued research in this area since the two syndromes were first identified: the group of children whom Bender (1942) studied and labeled as "childhood schizophrenics" were clinically similar to those identified as "autistic" by Kanner (1943). Bender used medically oriented diagnostic criteria such as difficulties with central nervous system integration and functioning. Although Kanner used behavioral criteria in describing autism, the symptoms he described could be manifestations of central nervous system dysfunction (inappropriate responses to objects, stereotypical or repetitive actions, disinterest in relating to people, insistence on "sameness" in the environment). Adding to the confusion, Bleuler (1911/1950) used the term *autistic* to refer to the with-drawn state of schizophrenics, and Goldfarb (1961, 1964) outlined nine diagnostic criteria for childhood schizophrenia, seven of which are also characteristic of autism.

Autism

Despite the confusion, schizophrenia and autism are currently considered by most researchers to be separate and distinct syndromes. Autism origi-nally was included in the P.L. 94–142 definition of emotional disturbance but was removed in 1981 and placed under the category of "Other Health Impaired." The Diagnostic and Statistical Manual of Mental Disorders (DSM–III) of the American Psychiatric Association, which was revised in 1980, includes autism under "Pervasive Developmental Disorders." These changes in diagnostic classification systems were a result of two trends: (1) updated research which suggests that autism is a developmental disorder rather than an emotional disorder, and (2) a political move backed by parents and other advocacy groups to remove autism from the category of emotional disorders.

Beginning in the early seventies, a proliferation of research on au-tism emerged, due largely to advances in medical research technology and the successful application of behavior modification principles to severely maladaptive behaviors. In 1977, as a result of coalescing the recent re-search on autism, the Professional Advisory Board of the National Society for Autistic Children (NSAC) adopted the following definition of autism:

> Autism is a severely incapacitating life-long developmental disability which appears during the first 3 years of life. It occurs in approximately 5 out of every 10,000 births and is 4 times more common in boys than girls. It has been found throughout the world in families of all racial, ethnic, and social backgrounds. No known factors in the psychological environment of a child have been shown to cause autism. . . . Autism is a behaviorally defined syn-drome. The essential characteristics are typically manifested prior to 30 months of age and include disturbances of: (a) developmental rates and/or sequences (in motor, social-adaptive, or cognitive pathways); (b) responses to sensory stimuli; (c) speech, language and cognitive capacities; and (d) capaci-ties to relate to people, events and objects. (Ritvo & Freeman, 1977)

Specific behavioral characteristics under each of these four categories are listed in Table 10–1.

Statements that autism is found in families of different cultures with varying backgrounds and that there are no known causal factors in the psychological environment of a child are direct repudiations of the psy-chogenic theory. Touted by several of the early researchers in this area (Bettelheim, 1959; Goldfarb, 1961; Kanner, 1943; Szurek, 1956), the psy-chogenic theory suggests that negative personality characteristics of par-

TABLE 10–1. Behavioral Symptoms of Autism (Gilliam, Webber, & Twombly, 1980)

A. DISTURBANCES OF DEVELOPMENTAL RATES AND/OR SEQUENCES
BEHAVIORAL SYMPTOMS
Gross motor milestones normal but fine motor milestones are delayed
Delay in speech
Not toilet trained
Regressions in motoric skills, e.g., stops walking, talking
Delay in social adaptive and cognitive milestones
B. DISTURBANCES OF RESPONSES TO SENSORY STIMULI
BEHAVIORAL SYMPTOMS: VISUAL
Close scrutiny of visual details
Nonuse of eye contact
Prolonged staring
Prolonged regarding of hands or objects
Flicking hand in front of eyes
Attention to changing levels of illumination
Over-/underresponse to visual cues
Ritualistic arrangement of objects
AUDITORY
Close attention to self-induced sounds
Nonresponse to varying sound levels
Overresponse to varying sounds
Seems not to hear
TACTILE
Hypo-/hyperresponse to touch
Hypo-/hyperresponse to temperature
Prolonged rubbing of surfaces
Sensitivity to food textures and bizarre food preferences
No response to painful stimuli
Licking inedibles
Self-injurious behaviors
OLFACTORY
Smells objects/repetitive sniffing
Very specific food preferences
Licking inedibles
Bizarre food preferences
VESTIBULAR
Over-/underresponse to gravity stimuli
Whirling without dizziness
Preoccupation with spinning objects
PROPRIOCEPTIVE
Whirls self for long periods of time
Rocks self for long periods of time
Lunging/darting about
Toe walking/prancing gait
Hand-flapping
C. DISTURBANCES OF SPEECH, LANGUAGE, AND COGNITIVE CAPACITIES
BEHAVIORAL SYMPTOMS
Mutism
Echolalia
Inappropriate timing and content

Flat affect, atonal, arhythmic speech
No speech initiation
Lack of conversational speech
Hyperactive speech
Immature syntax
Absence of gestures
Noncommunicative speech
Delayed onset
Perseverative speech
Pronoun reversals

D.   DISTURBANCES OF THE CAPACITY TO RELATE TO PEOPLE, EVENTS, AND OBJECTS
BEHAVIORAL SYMPTOMS
Absence of social smile
Withdrawn from people
Limpness or stiffness when held
Avoids eye contact
No friendships
Does not attend to social stimuli
Not responsive to others' expression or feelings
Resists being touched
Does not imitate other children at play
Often frightened or anxious
"Looks through people"
Inappropriate attachment to objects

---

ents are causal factors in the development of autism. Terms such as *cold, unresponsive, rejecting,* and *personality disordered* were cited as parental characteristics that caused children to become totally withdrawn from social interaction. However, subsequent research has not borne out the psychogenic theory. Research that refutes this stance can be divided into two categories: (1) that which found no significant differences between parents of psychotic or autistic children and parents of normal children (Creak & Ini, 1960; Peck et al., 1969; Rutter et al., 1971), and (2) that which supports a physiological or biochemical causation of autism (Des-Lauriers & Carlson, 1969; Hutt, Hutt, Lee, & Ounsted, 1964; Ornitz, 1978; Rimland, 1964, 1971; Ritvo et al., 1978). Although the specific etiology of autism remains unclear, researchers have found sufficient evidence of biochemical and/or neurological abnormalities in autistic children to rule out parental pathology as a causal factor.

The most marked characteristics of autistic children are their inattention to people and their seemingly obsessive attention to sensory stimuli and objects. For example, while many autistic children do not willingly attend to another person's voice or give eye contact, they may spend unusually long periods of time staring at flicking lights or spinning objects. They are often overresponsive or underresponsive to pain, touch, or changes in temperature or lighting. The insistence on sameness in the environment identified by Kanner (1943) in his original study means that any change in routine, however slight, is potentially upsetting. For example, the dinner table must be set with exactly the same utensils or the same route to school must always be taken, or the child may become very upset, throw tantrums, and insist on having it done "the right way."

Although some autistic children are highly verbal, speech is usually nonexistent or severely delayed and appears to have little communicative value for the majority of this population. The symbolic use of language is lacking, as evidenced by the absence of imaginative play in younger children and failure to understand the use of symbols in older children. Echolalia, which is parrotlike repetition of words and sentences, and pronoun reversal (for example, use of "I" for "he" or use of "he" to mean "everyone") are common. Receptive language is also usually very poor, resulting in an inability to understand others at a basic level. Thus, comprehensive language difficulties at both functional and symbolic levels are a central characteristic of autism.

The intelligence of autistic children has been misinterpreted in the past, largely due to the existence of splinter skills among some autistic children. While functionally retarded, some autistic youngsters have displayed remarkable rote memory for television commercials, poems, speeches, songs, or other long passages requiring high levels of memorization. Such skills led Kanner (1943) and others to hypothesize that autistic children actually have normal-to-superior cognitive abilities that are masked by emotional and communication problems. However, subsequent research has shown: (1) the majority of autistic children score in the moderately retarded range on intelligence tests (Bartak & Rutter, 1973; DeMyer, 1975), (2) that such scores are reliable over time and are valid estimates of the child's functioning (Baker, 1979; Rutter, 1978), and (3) that IQ and language level are the best predictors of potential functioning for an autistic individual (DeMyer, 1975; Lovaas, Koegel, Simmons, & Stevens, 1972; Rutter, 1978).

Schizophrenia

As mentioned previously, the terms *autism* and *childhood schizophrenia* were first used in the early forties and were often used interchangeably in research. It is therefore difficult to trace the development of the concept of childhood schizophrenia as a syndrome separate from autism, and the terms are still sometimes used interchangeably. In the late seventies and early eighties, a trend emerged toward subsuming the old concept of childhood schizophrenia under the label of autistic; the psychiatric and psychological communities endorsed this trend in their classification system—the DSM-III—by deleting childhood schizophrenia as a category and by classifying autism as a developmental disorder.

However, many professionals believe that schizophrenia can also be found in children. Although the onset of schizophrenia generally occurs in adolescence or young adulthood, some children do exhibit symptoms of schizophrenia. Despite the fact that schizophrenia is a label for adults in the DSM-III, children may be so classified if they fit the diagnostic criteria. In addition, the federal definition of emotional disturbance outlined in P.L. 94–142 allows for the inclusion of schizophrenic children. The following characteristics are typical of schizophrenic children:

(1) *Inappropriate affect.* Affect and emotions are inappropriate for given situations and may change rapidly with no apparent reason. May exhibit little or no affect, or be highly anxious or explosive.

(2) *Disinterest in surroundings and deterioration from previous levels of functioning.* Loses interest in self-care and in interacting with others. May stop eating, bathing, or taking any care in dressing. Parents, friends, and teachers may get only a minimal response. Usually a deterioration of functioning, that is, skills and behaviors previously attained are no longer evident.

(3) *Variable behavior.* Inappropriate behaviors or symptoms may come and go; periods of normalcy are interspersed with periods of bizarre behavior, during which strange language and inappropriate affect are evident.

(4) *Inappropriate speech.* May be highly verbal and have experienced normal language development, but speech becomes disjointed or bizarre. Voice tone or pitch may change drastically or child may exhibit echolalia. May talk to self. May use nonsense words or put words together in a sentence that doesn't make sense. In extreme cases, child may create his own language of nonsense words. Such language deterioration usually reflects disorganized thought processes.

(5) *Delusions or hallucinations.* A hallmark of adult schizophrenia, which may or may not be present in child schizophrenia. Delusions are totally irrational, false beliefs. Examples of rather common delusions are the beliefs that one is actually a famous personality (Jesus Christ and Napoleon are popular choices for adults) or feelings of persecution (for example, "Others can steal my thoughts and use them to harm me"). Hallucinations may be either visual or auditory; some schizophrenic children report having conversations with voices that sometimes tell them to do things.

Some schizophrenic children experience distorted perceptions of sensory stimuli such as light and touch, and some exhibit repetitive motor activity such as body rocking or hand movement. These symptoms are also typical of autistic children, which has added to the confusion in making differential diagnoses. However, there are a few differences that help distinguish between autism and schizophrenia. First is the age of onset. By definition, autism occurs in the first 30 months of life, and symptoms such as highly irregular sleep patterns, aversiveness to being touched, held, or cuddled, and abnormal patterns of development in speech and motor skills during the first three years are usually noted by parents. In contrast, schizophrenia is rarely diagnosed until age six or older, after much normal physical, cognitive, and social development has already occurred. A second point of differential diagnosis is the occasional presence of delusions and hallucinations in schizophrenic children and the absence of these symptoms in autistic children.

A third point of differential diagnosis is in language usage. Although schizophrenic children may use language inappropriately or in a bizarre manner, they generally have a grasp of the syntax and the function of language. Autistic children are often mute, echolalic, or characterized by a severe language delay. Even after careful language programming, many autistic children fail to understand the functional use of language.

A fourth point is that most schizophrenic children naturally relate to people and the environment, although on a sporadic basis and sometimes in a bizarre manner. In contrast, autistic children are more attentive to objects and sensory stimuli in the environment than they are to other people; they must often be taught to attend to human voices and to make eye contact. Bettelheim (1967) described this difference by remarking that the schizophrenic child withdraws from his world but the autistic child never enters it.

Although teachers may be asked to describe a child's functioning level or to keep behavioral data, the differential diagnosis of psychotic behaviors is primarily the domain of psychologists and psychiatrists. Whether a child is labeled as autistic or schizophrenic will have little bearing on the educational program that is designed and implemented by the special education teacher. Instead, the teacher should focus on educationally relevant characteristics, which are described in the next section.

Mildly Disordered versus Severely Disordered Behavior

Although there is some disagreement over whether disturbed behavior can be subdivided into mildly/moderately disordered and severely disordered, Kauffman (1977) suggests that such a differentiation should be made on the basis of intervention need. This stance seems defensible, as educators realize that the programmatic needs of these two groups vary widely. Teachers find that schizophrenic or autistic children require a more restricted environment, a lower-level curriculum, more individual attention, and more structure in acquiring behavioral and academic skills than higher functioning behavior disordered students.

Stainback and Stainback (1980) differentiate between mildly disturbed and severely disturbed by comparing the two groups on a number of educationally relevant characteristics: intelligence, achievement, attention to task, hyperactivity, withdrawal, aggression, and helplessness.

Intelligence and achievement. Mildly disturbed students most often have IQ scores in the low-normal range but are significantly behind their peers in both grade placement and achievement. The majority of psychotic students score in the retarded range on IQ tests and perform either at very basic academic levels or at preacademic levels.

Attention to task. Mildly disturbed students often have trouble focusing their attention on *relevant aspects* of tasks, or for long enough periods to finish a given task. They may have difficulty in screening out distracting stimuli. On the other hand, severely disturbed students tend to be overselective, that is, to focus on one specific aspect of a task and be unable to shift to another aspect or to see the total context of the task.

Hyperactivity. Hyperactivity and its correlate, impulsivity, are often found among both mildly and severely disturbed students. Students in both categories vary widely on these characteristics: some mildly disordered students are very hyperactive and impulsive, whereas some severely disturbed may have normal or even lowered activity levels.

Withdrawal. This characteristic ranges in degree from shyness to total oblivion to the environment. Mildly disturbed students may be anxious about making friends or fearful of becoming involved in any social interaction, including initiating conversation with peers or the teacher. Psychotic children may show very little interest in the environment; if left to their own preferences, autistic children would probably choose not to interact at all with other people.

Aggressive behavior. If a child displays sustained verbal or physical aggression, the chances are good that he will eventually be labeled behavior disordered. Mildly disordered students generally use abusive language or threats, are oppositional, and may have occasional aggressive outbursts of a verbal and physical nature. Severely disturbed students may be chronically violent; autistic and schizophrenic students tend to be more self-abusive than abusive of others.

Helplessness. Mildly disturbed students may appear disinterested or feel unable to take control of their daily lives, resulting in an inability to set personal goals or to respond to goals set by others. Severely disturbed students may be extremely depressed, suicidal, or highly dependent on others for even basic self-care.

These characteristics and their relationship to severity of disturbance are examined in Table 10–2.

In summary, differentiating between mild-moderate behavior disorders and severe behavior disorders is most helpful when planning interventions. More specific labels for the severely disturbed such as schizophrenic or autistic are important primarily for administrative purposes;

TABLE 10–2. A Comparison of Mildly Disordered and Severely Disordered Students

CHARACTERISTIC	MILDLY DISORDERED	SEVERELY DISORDERED
intellectual or cognitive ability	average IQ in low normal or dull normal range	average IQ in mentally retarded range
achievement	generally achieve at a lower level than their IQ level would infer	markedly deficient in academic areas; function at rudimentary levels in self-help skills, reading and math
attention to task	tendency toward under-selectivity, which is difficulty in screening out distracting stimuli	tendency toward overselectivity, which is focusing on limited aspect of a task
hyperactivity	frequently are hyperactive and impulsive	frequently are hyperactive and impulsive
withdrawal	may consistently refrain from initiating contact with others; may exhibit shyness or immaturity	may lack contact with reality and be oblivious to surroundings
aggression	may be negative and oppositional but generally not violent	may be chronically violent or self-abusive
helplessness	no interest and unwilling to try; applies to specific tasks and life in general	may be depressed, suicidal, or unable to care for self

Adapted from S. Stainback & W. Stainback, *Educating Children with Severe Maladaptive Behaviors.* New York: Grune & Stratton, 1980. Reprinted by permission of the publisher and the authors.

rarely do such labels provide the classroom teacher with information for instructional planning. Instead, for this population, the teacher must evaluate functioning in a number of areas and plan instructional methodology using refined behavioral techniques. Classroom planning for the severely behavior disordered is the focus of the next section, and it is here that the special needs of the severely disordered become most evident.

PROGRAMMING FOR SEVERELY DISORDERED STUDENTS

Working with the severely behavior disordered poses a challenge for educators not only in the hetereogeneity among individuals but also in the variability of functioning within individuals. Skill development in autistic children is particularly varied. For example, an autistic child may possess excellent rote memory or read at a basic level yet be unable to go to the bathroom without help. Other special problems with this population are unusual difficulties with language-communication skills and with socialization. Receptive and/or expressive language may be severely impaired;

when coupled with disinterest in the environment, such deficits can impede even basic social development. As a result, these students are often functionally retarded in most situations inside and outside the classroom.

Deciding What to Teach

Curriculum areas.   A program for severely behavior disordered students should include five basic curriculum areas: language-communication, self-help, social, academics, and vocational.

Language-communication. Communication skills of this group can be very baffling, as some students have well-developed language abilities, while others are totally nonverbal; some have fairly high receptive language but minimal expressive language, and others are echolalic or have well-developed speech but attach no meaning whatsoever to the words. The primary goal of this curriculum area is to provide the individual with a means of communicating with others, whether it be through speech and language development, sign language, or with a communication board. A minimum level of communication is obviously a prerequisite for establishing a teacher-student relationship and moving to other curricular areas. If a student is language disordered, the services of speech therapists or language therapists are usually included in the student's individualized program; however, if a specialized language program is to be effective, it must be incorporated into the child's daily classroom experiences by the special education teacher. The issue of teaching communication skills to this population is dealt with later in this chapter under "Special Issues."

Self-help. The major goal of teaching self-help skills is to enable a child to function independently in everyday life. Areas in self-help include toileting, dressing, eating, and safety. Student mastery of objectives within the self-help area usually requires the teacher to task-analyze and/or to model the desired skill.[1] Many published curricula for the severely handicapped include task analyses or specific behavioral programs for teaching self-help tasks such as tying shoelaces, zipping jackets, brushing teeth, and toileting. Along with communication development, this curricular area should take precedence with lower functioning students.

Social. The teaching of social skills to psychotic children is predicated upon minimal communication skills and the absence of interfering negative behaviors. In addition to their disinterest in the environment mentioned previously, many psychotic children engage in self-stimulating behavior, self-injurious behavior, or repetitive motor activity. Examples are rocking or whirling the body, hand-flapping, head-banging, and arm-biting. Such extreme behaviors obviously interfere with socialization and should be controlled or eliminated. The elimination of negative behaviors should be followed by the direct teaching of positive social skills such as responding to another's statements, introducing oneself by name, and initiating conversation. Any conversational and behavioral skills that enable the child to fit more easily into the peer group or the larger community are appropriate teaching objectives.

BOX 10–1. *A GLIMPSE INTO A CLASSROOM FOR AUTISTIC CHILDREN*

He sat gleefully spinning the saucer on the tiled floor. As the saucer vibrated to a stop, his eyes danced with excitement and he sang his nonsensical tune, "ee-ah, ee-ah, ee-ah." As he sang, he rocked back and forth, seemingly oblivious to the others in the room. When the saucer stopped, he picked it up and with almost artistic skill flipped it into another rapid rotation. Infrequently his eyes would dart to other children in the room, but only as if to confirm their position about him, never to establish contact. As if it were a magnet, the spinning saucer compelled his attention. Again the song, "ee-ah, ee-ah, ee-ah."

In a corner the teacher was saying, "Joey, touch red," indicating a red block on the desk top. With almost forced effort, Joey began to lift his hands from his lap. When his hands were above the desk, he quickly slapped the block off the desk top.

"Joey, no!" the teacher said firmly.

As if on cue, the boy made his hand into a fist and pounded his ear repeatedly. His facial expression never changed as the teacher grabbed his wrist and placed his hand on his lap.

"No hitting," she said. Placing another red block on the desk, she repeated, "Touch red."

Again Joey started to respond, then slapped the block off the desk. Immediately he jammed the back of his hand against his mouth and began biting it.

Alone at a desk, the girl was busy placing a shiny washer on a large bolt. As she completed this action she picked up a nut and, with a quick rotation of her fingers, skillfully threaded the nut onto the bolt and placed it into a box of other similarly dressed bolts.

"Good working, Mary," her teacher complimented.

At a table in the front of the room, the teacher's aide was speaking to a handsome child who seemed to be attending closely.

"What's your name?" the aide asked.

"What's your name?" the child responded in a monotone.

"No, listen now. Tommy, what's your name?"

"Tommy, what's your name?" the child echoed.

"Okay, Tommy, let's take a break. Do you want to play?"

"Want to play?" he said, as he jumped up.

It was mid-morning and time for a break for everyone in the class.

Contributed by Jim Gilliam

Academics. Some severely disordered students are able to attain functional literacy, that is, to read, write, and compute numbers well enough to get along in society. (Estimates of functional literacy range from third-grade levels to eighth-grade levels, with many experts choosing sixth-grade as criterion level.) In very rare cases, severely disordered students are able to complete high school curriculum and maintain themselves in college. With students who are higher functioning, academic skills may constitute a feasible and separate curriculum area. (For example, a reading objective of demonstrating literal comprehension may be appropriate.) However, the majority of this population are unable to attain functional literacy and are operating at a preacademic level. For these students, academic skills are best infused into other areas of the curriculum such as vocational or self-help. (For example, a reading objective of recognition of basic sight words from a survival skills list: "Women," "Men," "Stop," "Poison," "Danger," and so forth.) In making this decision for an individual, the teacher should consider the student's age, intelligence, and language level. For adolescents who have not progressed beyond the preacademic level, it is more helpful to spend instructional time on vocational and survival skills than on isolated academic skills.

Vocational. Prevocational and vocational training are a necessity for this population if mainstreaming and deinstitutionalization are to become realities. Communication and social skills are necessary but not sufficient for severely behavior disordered adults to be able to maintain themselves independently or semi-independently in the community; some means of financial support are also necessary. The goal of vocational training is to prepare students, beginning in the elementary years, to take on job responsibilities. General skills such as complying with requests, following directions, staying on task, completing tasks, and specific skills such as using tools, sorting objects, or matching samples are common objectives of vocational training. Vocational programming for this population differs from vocational training for the mildly behavior disordered and is addressed in more detail under "Special Issues." The next section addresses points for the teacher to consider in organizing the various curricular areas and in setting priorities for individual students.

A functional curriculum. The prognosis for independent functioning for psychotic adults is quite poor; it is estimated that 75 percent of autistic adults will spend their lives in institutional placements (DeMyer, 1979) and the majority of schizophrenics will spend most of their adult lives in and out of psychiatric hospitals. If this trend of institutionalization is to be reversed, educators must prepare severely handicapped students to function as independently as possible. This goal has been dubbed the "criterion of ultimate functioning," which requires that programs for handicapped persons focus on skills that allow optimal independent functioning in the least restrictive environment (Brown, Nietupski, & Hamre-Nietupski, 1976). In other words, not only broad curricular areas but also specific instructional objectives should be selected according to plans for long-range functioning of the individual. In selecting objectives to meet the criterion of ultimate functioning, Brown et al. (1976) suggest that the following questions be answered:

(1) Why should we engage in this activity?

(2) Is this activity necessary to prepare students to ultimately function in complex hetereogeneous community settings?

(3) Could students function as adults if they did not acquire the skill?

(4) Is there a different activity that will allow students to approximate realization of the criterion of ultimate functioning more quickly and more efficiently?

(5) Will this activity impede, restrict, or reduce the probability that students will ultimately function in community settings?

(6) Are the skills, materials, tasks, and criteria similar to those encountered in real life? (p. 9)

Although such questions are vitally important for severely disordered adolescents who are nearing the end of their educational program, it is also important to consider these questions when program planning for younger and less severely handicapped students.

The concept of functional skills has been further developed by Donnellan (1980) and by McGinnis (1982). In determining future usefulness of a skill, Donnellan (1980) advocates asking the question, "If this child does not learn to perform this skill, will some one have to do it for him?" (p. 71). For instance, if a child does not learn to cut up meat at dinner or brush his teeth before bedtime, someone else will have to do it for him; however, if a child fails to recite the alphabet or sort blocks by color, no one will have to help the youngster complete the task. McGinnis (1982) cites several examples of functional and nonfunctional activities that are age-appropriate for adolescents:

NONFUNCTIONAL ACTIVITIES	**FUNCTIONAL ACTIVITIES**
a. counting pegs and blocks	counting silverware, money for a purchase
b. pointing to hands	shaking hands
c. sorting paper pieces; matching colored blocks	matching and sorting silverware into drawer tray; sorting clothing or coins; sorting materials such as nuts and bolts (needed in sheltered workshop settings)
d. placing pegs in a pegboard	placing coins in a vending machine or a washing machine at the laundry
e. reading basal text	reading bus schedules, menus, street signs, recipes, TV guides, etc.

As illustrated by the examples, functional does *not* mean nonacademic; basic academic skills such as counting and reading are very functional when applied to situations which the student encounters in everyday life. Also, tasks are not inherently functional or nonfunctional: placing pegs in a pegboard is functional if the goal is to teach the student to play a game such as cribbage.

To further clarify the concept of ultimate functioning, Brown and his colleagues (1976) and McGinnis (1982) suggest that educators consider the environmental domains in which students will be expected to function as adults. These include the home, community, vocational or work setting, and settings in which handicapped adults are expected to spend leisure time and to interact with nonhandicapped adults. Thus, skills that meet the criterion of ultimate functioning are skills that will be needed in one of these environments. For instance:

community functioning	using public transportation
	using pay telephones
	recognizing street signs
	comprehending dangerous situations
home functioning	self-help in eating and dressing
	preparing meals
	doing household chores
vocational functioning	being on time
	completing tasks
	traveling to and from work
recreational functioning	absence of self-stimulating behaviors
	interest in and ability to ride a bike, play table games, electronic games, or pinball, swim, watch TV, use books and magazines, do artwork
interacting with non-handicapped adults	greeting others
	asking appropriate questions
	dealing with frustration
	(McGinnis, 1982)

McGinnis advocates that teachers use a grid format to help develop objectives in the five curricular areas for each of the environmental domains. When using a grid, the teacher must consider the functionality of objectives before listing the domains or environments in which the skill will be useful. A grid using the five curricular areas and five domains advocated in this text is presented in Table 10–3.

TABLE 10–3.   Development of Curricular Objectives

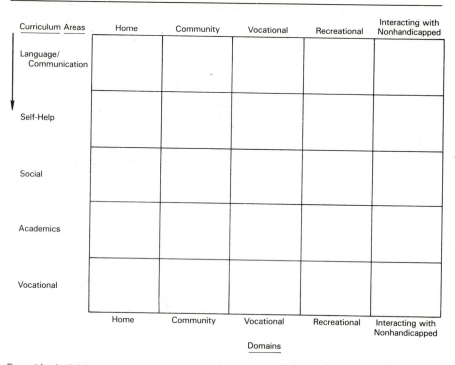

Curriculum Areas	Home	Community	Vocational	Recreational	Interacting with Nonhandicapped
Language/ Communication					
Self-Help					
Social					
Academics					
Vocational					
	Home	Community	Vocational	Recreational	Interacting with Nonhandicapped

Domains

From "An Individualized Curricula for Children and Youth with Autism," by Ellen McGinnis, 1982. In C.R. Smith, J. Grimes and J. Freilinger (Eds.). *Autism: Programmatic Considerations*, pp. 170–207. Des Moines: Iowa Department of Public Instruction. Reprinted by permission.

Deciding How to Teach

Severely disordered students require different instructional methodology from that required for the mild-moderately handicapped. It was not until the 1960s that educators and psychologists began to experience success in teaching behavioral and academic skills to the severely disordered, and it was not until the 1970s that successful model programs were established in the public schools (Koegel & Rincover, 1974; Kozloff, 1975). The success of these programs has been due largely to the increasing sophistication in applying behavioral techniques to a number of particularly difficult areas such as acquisition of language skills (Lovaas, 1966) and elimination of self-injurious behaviors (Lovaas & Simmons, 1969; Wolf, Risley, & Mees, 1964). Establishing a basic form of communication and eliminating self-injurious or self-stimulating behaviors are obvious prerequisites to learning. Because so many psychotic children experience problems in these two areas, each topic is treated separately under "Special Issues" later in this chapter.

Another important characteristic of autistic children in particular is *stimulus overselectivity.* Stimulus overselectivity is defined by Stainback and Stainback (1980) as attention to limited aspects of a task. Overselectivity has a pervasive detrimental effect on learning, as the tendency to focus on one (often irrelevant) aspect of a task (or characteristic of an object) interferes with generalization. For instance, a teacher may be attempting to teach the concept of the number five with five green blocks; while the teacher is attempting to instill an association between the word "five" and the five blocks, the student is focusing on the color green. If the materials were changed to five yellow or to multicolored blocks, the student would no longer associate the word "five" with the five blocks. In other words, the student's overselectivity caused attention to an irrelevant aspect of the task (color) and prevented learning the concept (five) and generalizing to another situation (given multicolored blocks).

The teaching of autistic students, therefore, requires that measures be taken to counteract tendencies toward overselectivity. Educators have found that varying the learning environment in systematic ways can help overcome overselectivity and promote generalization of acquired skills (Sailor & Guess, 1983). Techniques that facilitate learning in this population are reviewed in the remainder of this section: task analysis, concept analysis, discrete trial format, prompting, and suggestions for facilitating generalization.

Task analysis. Task analysis was presented in Chapter 6 as a method for assessment and instructional planning. It is reviewed here briefly: task analysis serves an assessment function when a task is broken down into its subcomponents, and the subtask that is causing difficulty for a particular student can be identified; task analysis serves an instructional function when the teacher breaks down an instructional objective or activity into smaller, teachable units. Task analysis is especially appropriate for teaching severely handicapped students because it allows the division of a larger task or a higher level skill into very small, discrete steps, which are much easier for the student to master. Task analysis can be applied to instructional objectives in all curricular areas. For example, task analysis could be applied to each of the following objectives:

communication-language	speaking sentences, signing name
self-help	brushing teeth, tying shoes
social	conversing with a peer, participating in group games
academic	writing name, adding sums under five
vocational	packaging, assembling nuts-bolts components

For a review of a complete task analysis, refer to Table 6–3.

Concept analysis. Even the most carefully planned task analysis may not be successful with some students. With autistic students who are overselective, teachers also may want to utilize concept analysis, which requires the teacher to analyze the concept to be taught to ensure that all irrelevant characteristics of the concept are varied within the teaching sequence (Dollar, 1981). Such variation helps ensure that the concept will be generalized or transferred across tasks, settings, and people. To illustrate, let us return to the example of teaching the concept of five with five green blocks. Essential characteristics of the concept are the word "five" and the presence of five objects. Irrelevant to the concept are the person who is teaching, the specific words used by the teacher, the physical presence of reinforcers for correct responses, and the use of green blocks or blocks of any color. Thus, irrelevant characteristics such as the teaching person, words that are used, type of reinforcer, and the type of objects should be varied to ensure that it is the concept of "fiveness" and not irrelevant concepts that are being learned. Other strategies for increasing generalization are presented later in this section.

Discrete trial format.   Another teaching technique that has proven successful with autistic children is the discrete trial format (Donnellan-Walsh, Gossage, LaVigna, Schuler, & Traphagen, 1976). Based on research which suggests that autistic children attain greater achievement under highly structured conditions, the discrete trial format was developed as a structured technique that can be applied to any teaching task. In discrete trial format, the teacher specifies three things: (1) the discriminative stimulus (teacher's instruction to the student), (2) the desired student response (student behavior), and (3) the consequence (teacher's behavior that follows the student response). For example:

DISCRIMINATIVE STIMULUS	STUDENT RESPONSE	CONSEQUENCE
"Do this."	imitates teacher extending hand	praise and sip of orange juice

In the example, the teacher attempts to instill a basic imitation skill, which can be built upon later to teach a variety of communication and social skills. In the initial stages, the stimulus should remain the same until the student demonstrates that the task has been learned; after competence has been demonstrated, the stimulus and consequences should be systematically varied to encourage generalization. Part of the discrete trial format is a brief interval of three to five seconds between trials which allows the teacher to record the response and reinforce the response if appropriate. The interval also provides a break that identifies each trial as discrete or separate from other trials of the same task.

Prompting.   Because of communication and language problems, psychotic children often need to be prompted to begin or to complete a task.

Instructional prompts are purposefully added to the learning situation in order to assure correct responses (McGinnis, 1982). Prompts range from demonstrating or showing the child what to do, to physically guiding the child through the activity. Dorsey (1980) outlines a hierarchy of prompts that moves from the most intrusive to the least intrusive:

full manual guidance
partial manual assistance
gesture
verbal
demonstration

For instance, a teacher using the prompt hierarchy to help a child learn the self-help skill of cutting food at mealtime might go through the following sequence:

(1) Put hands over child's hands on the utensils and manually guide the cutting.
(2) Put hands over the child's hands on the utensils and begin the motion of cutting.
(3) Gesture or pretend to cut the food.
(4) Give the direction, "Cut up your food."
(5) Actually cut up the food on own plate while child watches.

In giving prompts, teachers should always choose the least intrusive prompt that is successful and should either fade the prompt or move to a less intrusive one as soon as possible.

Facilitating generalization. Generalization of acquired skills across settings and maintenance of skills over time pose a special concern with psychotic children. Studies with these children have shown that generalization does not automatically occur unless adaptions are made in the instructional program (Koegel & Rincover, 1974; Stokes & Baer, 1977; Strain, Kerr, & Ragland, 1979). Due to characteristics including a tendency toward overselectivity, many severely handicapped students become stimulus-bound; that is, they demonstrate the skill only in one setting, in the presence of one teacher, or to a specific cue or set of directions. Therefore, in programs for psychotic children, special adaptations may be necessary that are not necessary for the mildly to moderately disordered. Some of the techniques already alluded to in this section help children generalize the skills they are taught. In addition, the following variables should be systematically varied when planning instructional programs for the severely disordered.

Setting. Instructional settings should approximate the natural setting as much as possible. For example, prevocational and vocational skills should be taught in a room that is similar to a sheltered workshop with work tables, a clock, and a similar arrangement of materials. Settings should also be varied; students should be asked to perform skills in the classroom, at home, in work or vocational settings, and in the community.

Teacher. Different people should take part in teaching and encouraging the use of acquired skills. Two or three teachers, parents, siblings and other relatives can be helpful in this role.

Content. Materials should be those the student will encounter in the natural environment (for example, matching colored samples of material instead of matching colored blocks). The same concept should be taught in different ways, with different materials, in different settings.

Instruction. Emphasis should be placed on functional skills, that is, ones the student will use in the natural environment. When reinforcement is initially used, the frequency of reinforcement should be decreased until it approximates that which is available in the natural environment. Other techniques that encourage generalization are systematic withdrawal of direct instruction and of prompts.

Small-group instruction has also been found to encourage generalization of skills. Although it was previously thought that severely handicapped students would receive maximum benefit from one-to-one instruction, this assumption has not been borne out (Brown et al., 1976). Although a one-to-one setting may be necessary for initial teaching of a concept or objective, long-term achievement has not been maximized by this arrangement. Instead, Brown et al. (1976) suggest that a one-to-one arrangement may cause students to become stimulus-bound to a particular teacher or cue and that student interaction with peers is impeded, resulting in students' malfunctioning in groups. As students are ultimately expected to function with others in group settings, group instruction in the classroom appears a more feasible approach to attaining this goal.

Koegel and Rincover (1974) developed a successful procedure for implementing group instruction with autistic children. Beginning in a one-to-one setting, the child initially was given a tangible reinforcer for each correct response, which was gradually thinned to a single reinforcer for every two correct responses. At this point, two children were paired and the reinforcement eventually was thinned to one reinforcer per three correct responses. A third child could then be introduced and the same procedure followed. Children were also reinforced for watching, listening, and taking turns.

There are some difficulties with small-group instruction such as unevenness among students in moving through the curriculum and increased difficulty in evaluating student progress; however, when the criterion of ultimate functioning is applied, it should be evident that ability to work and interact with peers in groups without one-to-one supervision is a necessity for severely behavior disordered students.

In summary, the special needs of the severely behavior disordered become apparent when their educational programs are planned. Teachers must make decisions not only about what to teach but also about how to teach this population. In deciding what to teach, educators must take into consideration special problems in communication, self-help, and social skills; along with academics and vocational training, these three areas generally constitute curricular areas for these students. When deciding how to teach, educators should be familiar with the special techniques that have proven successful with autistic and other special populations. Specific curricular objectives and activities for each individual should be applied against the criterion of ultimate functioning: will the learning of this particular objective enable the individual to function more independently in the future?

SPECIAL ISSUES

In addition to the different curricular emphases and instructional methodology required by the severely behavior disordered, there are other issues that set this population apart from the mildly and moderately disordered. Although many issues are worthy of consideration, this discussion is limited to four that are basic to the success of any educational program for the severely disordered: (1) eliminating self-stimulatory and self-injurious behavior, (2) developing language-communication skills, (3) implementing a vocational program, and (4) working with the parents of the severely disordered. This discussion is not intended as comprehensive coverage but is intended to highlight some of the questions and special problems inherent in dealing with these issues.

Self-Stimulating and Self-Injurious Behavior

Some of the most maladaptive behaviors that distinguish severely disordered children from mildly disordered children are self-stimulation and self-injurious behavior. In the past, youngsters exhibiting these conditions were often placed in physical restraints in restrictive settings such as hospitals or residential centers; with the advent of mainstreaming and increased sophistication in behavioral technology, many students exhibiting these behaviors can be found in public school programs. It is important for teachers who plan to work with this population to be aware of the special problems posed by such behaviors and to become aware of some of the behavioral techniques that have proven successful in dealing with them.

Some severely disordered students engage in self-stimulating behaviors that interfere with social contact. These repetitive, stereotypical behaviors are usually motoric (for example, hand-flapping or object-spinning) or vocal (screeching or repeating a sound such as "ah-ah-ah-ah . . .") and serve no obvious function other than sensory stimulation for the individual. However, self-stimulating behaviors have an inverse relationship to learning (Koegel & Covert, 1972) and must be replaced with more adaptive behaviors if optimal learning and social functioning are to take place.

Similar to self-stimulation, self-injurious behavior usually occurs at high rates or with high intensity, but unlike self-stimulation, it results in injury to the individual. Common examples are arm-biting, head-banging, eye-poking, hair-pulling, and slapping or scratching self. Despite the physical damage inflicted by such behavior, many individuals continue to self-injure on a daily basis.

Many researchers have attempted to identify the cause of self-injurious behavior. Carr (1977) reviewed the literature on the motivation of self-injurious behavior and formulated five major hypotheses: (1) the positive reinforcement hypothesis, which suggests that the immediate social attention received by self-injuring individuals is the motivating factor; (2) the negative reinforcement hypothesis, which suggests that individuals injure themselves to escape an unpleasant situation, such as an adult's demand; (3) the self-stimulation hypothesis, which indicates that individuals perform self-abusive acts in order to provide sensory stimulation; (4) the organic hypothesis, which states that self-injurious behavior is the product of an aberrant physiological process; and (5) the psychodynamic hypothesis, which proposes psychological causes (for example, guilt) for self-injury. From this research, it appears that self-injurious behavior is a very complex behavior with multiple causative factors, and that with any given individual, one or more of the factors could be operating. Carr (1977) offers screening guidelines to help determine whether the causes of an individual's behavior are internally or externally controlled, a determination that has implications for treatment.

Over the past two decades, a variety of behavioral techniques have been successfully applied to suppressing or eliminating self-stimulating and self-injurious behavior. Punishment—the application of aversive stimuli—has been highly successful with both types of behavior. Aversive stimuli such as electric shock, shouting, and slapping the hand or thigh have proven effective in reducing a variety of self-stimulating behaviors (Baumeister & Forehand, 1972; Bucher & Lovaas, 1968; Koegel & Covert, 1972; Lovaas & Simmons, 1969; Risley, 1968). Electric shock has also effectively eliminated self-injurious behavior in a number of severely disordered individuals (Corte, Wolfe, & Locke, 1971; Tate & Baroff, 1966; Young & Wincze, 1974). Tanner and Zeiler (1975) report the successful suppression of self-injurious behavior (face-slapping) in a young autistic woman by inducing her to smell an ammonia capsule, and Myers and Deibert (1971) report successful suppression of self-injurious behavior (head-banging) by delaying meals and withdrawing food during meals whenever the behavior occurred.

Although highly successful, the use of aversives—especially electric shock—with this population has been questioned. Proponents claim that the shock dosages are carefully controlled so as to induce small amounts of pain; they further claim that since no physiological damage is sustained, shock is not harmful and therefore is preferable to continued self-abuse (Lovaas, Schaeffer, & Simmons, 1965). However, others argue that less severe punishers and less noxious techniques or combinations of techniques can also be effective in reducing severe maladaptive behaviors. It is not likely that the use of electric shock or other severe punishers will be sanctioned in public school programs, even to prevent self-injury. Two techniques that can be used without ethical or moral repercussions are overcorrection and the combination of mild punishment with reinforcement of incompatible behaviors.

Overcorrection, a procedure developed by Foxx (1971) and Foxx and Azrin (1973), has been effective with autistic and lower functioning populations who have not responded to other forms of reinforcement or punishment. Overcorrection involves two steps: (1) correcting the environmental consequences of an inappropriate behavior (restitution), and (2) practicing an appropriate behavior that is incompatible with the inappropriate behavior (positive practice). The first step, restitution, is necessary only if the behavior has affected the environment in a negative way (for example, repeated self-induced regurgitation). Most self-injurious and self-stimulating behaviors do not have this effect on the environment and therefore only the positive practice step is implemented. For example, Kelly and Drabman (1977) reported elimination of eye-poking behavior in a visually handicapped preschooler. Each time the child poked his eye, his arms were raised and lowered repeatedly to his sides without touching his face or eyes; this positive practice was coupled with verbal praise and eventually resulted in elimination of the behavior. Other researchers reduced self-stimulating vocalizations of a severely disturbed eight-year-old in a group academic setting by having an adult place her hands over the girl's mouth for 30-second intervals (Newman, Whorton, & Simpson, 1977). In most instances of overcorrection, periods in which the maladaptive behavior does not occur are intermittently reinforced (for example, reinforcement for periods of non-eye-poking and nonverbalization). Many educators and psychologists prefer overcorrection to punishment procedures; it has the added benefit of instilling a positive behavior while decreasing a negative one.

A combination of reinforcement of incompatible behaviors with mild punishment also has been effective in reducing severely maladaptive behaviors (Repp & Deitz, 1974; Repp, Deitz, & Speir, 1974). Repp and Deitz (1974) reduced the face-scratching self-injurious behavior of a young institutionalized female by rewarding periods of non-face-scratching with candy and by giving a verbal reprimand when face-scratching did occur. These studies yield results similar to those combining reinforcement of incompatible behaviors with a time-out procedure (Ausman, Ball, & Alexander, 1974; Bostow & Bailey, 1969). In these studies, the combination of a positive technique with an aversive technique was more effective than the application of a single technique. Also, researchers are discovering that pairing punishment with reinforcement of incompatible behaviors is helpful in avoiding some of the shortcomings of punishment, such as temporary elimination of the behavior and failure to generalize.

Although punishment, overcorrection, and combinations of behavioral procedures have proven successful in eliminating self-stimulation and self-injurious behaviors, researchers are concerned about generalization and maintenance in settings other than the classroom. Many of the procedures do not generalize outside the training setting unless generalization tactics are built into the program (Kissel & Whitman, 1977). As in planning for generalization of instruction, teachers must systematically vary the settings, people, and activities with which the behavioral skills are taught. The more closely the training setting approximates the natural setting, the more generalization is facilitated.

Communication-Language Development

The majority of psychotic children have limited communication skills. Although the type and the severity of the problem differ widely from individual to individual, autistic children as a group are characterized by mutism, echolalia, and severe language delay. Schizophrenic children may create their own vocabularies or use nonsense words or sentences. Other psychotic children may have highly developed vocabularies but temporary or prolonged lapses in ability to use language to communicate with others. Some psychotic children are characterized by adequate receptive language skills but deficient expressive skills; that is, they understand what is said to them but they cannot express themselves verbally. Others, especially autistic children, may fail to attend to voices or speech sounds, which is a response found in normally developing infants at about six months of age (Kagan & Lewis, 1965). The language difficulties of these children are idiosyncratic and, as with other curriculum areas, language development programs must be tailored to fit the needs of the individual.

Echolalia and other peculiar language difficulties of autistic children were not successfully remediated until the sixties when a number of researchers began using operant conditioning techniques to teach speech to these youngsters (Hewett, 1965; Lovaas, 1966; Risley & Wolf, 1967). In most behavioral treatment programs, common speech sounds and grammatical structures were targeted and taught through imitation, reinforcement, and punishment procedures. Thus, functional language training for nonverbal children has consisted mainly of a limited number of self-help phrases that are elicited in certain contexts or in response to specific cues. As McLean and Snyder-McLean (1982) state:

> An analysis of most of our existing language treatment programs for severely handicapped students would lead one to believe that the primary functions of human communication systems are to name things, indicate desired food items or objects, and to request permission to "go bathroom." While such functions are surely included in children's communicative repertoires, they are far from adequate to represent a full appreciation of the basic function of communication in human societies. (p. 211)

Although operant conditioning of speech sounds and phrases was a definitive beginning in helping nonverbal youngsters acquire speech, many language experts believe that language therapy should focus on the individual's ability to generalize acquired language skills to other settings (Guess, Sailor, & Baer, 1978), and to use speech spontaneously for communication purposes (McLean & Snyder-McLean, 1982). Before such language programming can be accomplished, educators must clearly distinguish the concepts of speech, language, and communication. Speech is the oral or verbal production of sounds; language is the use of a symbol system that can be verbal or nonverbal; communication is the exchange of information between people, which can take any number of forms (smile, gesture, a look, writing, words, and so forth). Therefore, communication is a social tool that allows an individual to interact with others; speech and language are a means of communication, and it is the ability to communicate through whatever means that should be the focus of training in this area.

Various systems are used to teach severely disordered children to communicate, and teachers often must be proficient at alternative communication systems. Although language therapists may be responsible for designing a comprehensive language development program and may provide direct services on a routine basis, teachers obviously must be able to communicate with students as a prerequisite to teaching all other skills. Language development is therefore incorporated into all curricular areas of the program for the nonverbal or language-delayed child.

Sign language is one alternative for teaching severely disordered children to communicate. Although the usefulness of sign language in nonschool settings is being questioned, it is still taught to children who are unable to use verbal language. Two basic sign systems are used: a sign-concept system, American Sign Language (AMESLAN), and a sign-word system, Signing Exact English (SEE II). The SEE system translates into exact English, including grammatical structure components, and therefore may be better for students who have some verbal skills, who are learning to read, or who may become very proficient in signing (Marcott-Radke, 1981).

Another special education methodology borrowed from the deaf population is that of *total communication,* which includes use of speech, speech reading, a sign system, and finger spelling. The total communication system can be modified for the special language problems of the autistic. One system, the Modified for the Autistic Total Communication (M.A.T.C.) is described by Marcott-Radke (1981): M.A.T.C. consists of the simultaneous presentation of sign and verbalization, with one sign for each word plus markings for prefixes and suffixes and other meaningful units of sound. Speech reading and other strategies designed to help the hearing-impaired and deaf are excluded in modifications for the severely behaviorally disordered.

The reader who is interested in language and/or communication development is referred to McLean and Snyder-McLean (1982) and to Stainback and Stainback (1980) who raise important issues and provide conceptual frameworks for communications training for this population.

Vocational Programming

Prior to 1970, prevocational and vocational programming for the severely behavior disordered was rare if not nonexistent. However, beginning in the late sixties and continuing into the early seventies, two trends emerged that encouraged educators to begin vocational programming for this population. First was a nationwide push toward deinstitutionalization, the practice of helping handicapped adults to maintain themselves independently or semi-independently in community settings rather than in institutions. Deinstitutionalization has affected special education by requiring educators to redouble their efforts to graduate young adults who are functioning independently despite their handicaps. Vocational training has become an important part of this effort: if individuals can contribute financially to their own support by functioning in some type of sheltered workshop setting, the chances of their remaining in the community are much increased.

The second trend affecting vocational programming for this population was the development by Gold (1972, 1973) and others of successful vocational training programs for the severely retarded. By task-analyzing the component parts of tasks into small, discrete units and using reinforcement, Gold (1972) was able to teach moderately and severely retarded adults to perform such complex tasks as assembling 24-part bicycle brakes. Educators began to realize that with the proper combination of instruction and reinforcement, severely handicapped individuals are capable of learning tasks that are functional and for which they can be paid. Also, more sophisticated assessment of autistic individuals revealed a suitability for vocational training: although autistic persons generally perform poorly on abstract, symbolic, and logical tasks, they do tend to perform well on tasks requiring manipulative, visual-spatial, and short-term rote memory skills (American Psychiatric Association, 1980), all of which are helpful in performing a variety of vocational tasks.

Vocational training for the severely disordered must be designed at a much more basic level than vocational training for the mildly or moderately disordered. Motor skills such as imitation of motor movement and cognitive skills such as simple discrimination tasks may have to be taught before more formal vocational training can be effective. Social and behavioral skills such as hygiene, punctuality, and compliance also may have to be systematically taught. The remainder of this section describes the basic components of a vocational training program for autistic children and youth developed by Regan, Jones, Holzschuh, and Simpson (1982) (see Table 10–4). This overview is intended for illustrative purposes only; interested readers should refer to Regan et al. for comprehensive information on designing a vocational training program.

TABLE 10–4. Basic Components of a Vocational Program

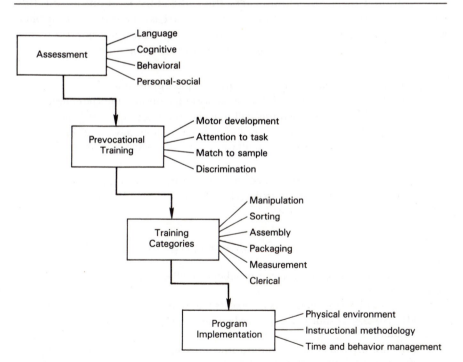

Adapted from M.K. Regan, C. Jones, R. Holzschuh, and R.L. Simpson. Autism Teacher Training Program (Kansas City, KS: Univ. of Kansas Medical Center), 1982.

Assessment. An overall profile of strengths and weaknesses of each individual should be compiled for each of the following areas: language level, cognitive-intellectual, behavioral or work habits, and personal-social. Work habits to be assessed include the ability to stay on task, to work without supervision, and to follow verbal directions. Personal-social skills include self-help skills and the ability to get along with others in a work setting.

Prevocational skills. Skills that are prerequisite to vocational performance should be assessed and taught if necessary. Regan et al. (1982) outline four areas: (1) *motor development,* including skills in grasping, wrist rotation, eye-hand coordination, and imitation of motor movement; (2) *attention to task,* preferably for five to ten minutes uninterrupted; (3) *match to sample,* making a product that matches a given sample, whether it be sorting objects or arranging objects according to a pattern or model; and (4) *discrimination,* using objects according to function, given verbal or visual cues.

Training tasks and task categories. Selecting specific training tasks for the vocational program should carry the same considerations as selecting instructional objectives in other curriculum areas: all should be applied against the criterion of ultimate functioning. The following questions may be especially helpful in selecting vocational skills to be taught:

(1)   Does the skill transfer to community job opportunities?
(2)   Will mastery of the skill facilitate assimilation into the community?
(3)   Is it feasible to teach the skill in a classroom setting?
(4)   Is it feasible to teach the skill to a given student, in view of the student's strengths, deficits, and learning potential?   (Regan et al., 1982, p. 24)

It is also helpful to organize tasks by categories so that types of tasks or skill clusters rather than isolated skills are learned. Six categories of vocational tasks are common:

(1)   *manipulation*—performing physical operations on materials, perhaps using tools

(2)   *sorting*—separating large numbers of objects according to a predetermined classification

(3)   *assembly*—putting parts of objects together, sometimes using tools

(4)   *packaging*—putting a prescribed set of materials into boxes, bags, or other containers

(5)   *measurement*—using standard units of volume, weight, and length

(6)   *clerical*—filing, alphabetizing, stuffing envelopes, stapling, collating, and other office work. (Regan et al., 1982)

Program implementation. To implement a vocational program, the teacher must set up the environment, choose appropriate instructional methodology, and manage the behavior and productivity of the students. The physical environment should approximate a work setting and should be stocked with a variety of cheap, safe, dispensable work materials. Instructional methodology is similar to that used for instruction in other curricular areas. After analyzing each specific vocational task into its component parts, the teacher may want to use one or more of the following methods: modeling, prompting, picture cues, and forward or backward chaining, which involves mastery of a single step in a hierarchy of steps toward completing a complex task. Each of the methods has advantages and disadvantages and will be better suited to certain tasks than to others.

Management strategies for a vocational training program must structure the students' time and productivity. Provisions should be made for signing in and signing out, taking breaks, recording the amount of work accomplished by each individual, and reinforcing productivity through a token system. If the token system is not understood by a student, tangible reinforcers should be paired with the token until the student learns the concept. Working for intangibles or tokens is a crucial concept for success on the job.

In summary, vocational training is a necessity for optimal functioning of the severely disordered. With proper assessment and training, many severely disordered adolescents and adults are capable of productivity in a work setting. Work habits and other prevocational skills should be assessed and taught during the elementary years, and specific vocational skills should be taught during the adolescent years as the individual nears the end of formal public school education.

Working with Parents of the Severely Disordered

Although the issue of parental involvement in education was explored in Chapter 8, parents of severely disordered students have some special needs that warrant further consideration. It is not unreasonable to suggest that the more severely disordered the child, the more stress she creates in the home. Autistic and schizophrenic children often create an unrelenting drain on their parents' time and energy. For example, many of these children have heightened activity levels and highly erratic sleeping patterns, perhaps sleeping only a couple of hours before getting up to roam about the house at night. Motivated by curiosity, they may take apart, damage, or destroy furniture, appliances, mechanical objects, and other household goods. Many psychotic children have no regard for safety and therefore cannot be left alone even for short periods of time. Thus, the sources of stress for parents of these children are real and constant. Some of the major stressors are briefly reviewed.

Managing behavior.   For obvious reasons, parents of psychotic children are concerned about compliance, that is, having their child obey their directions and instructions. For psychotic children who are nonverbal and oppositional, compliance can be a very difficult concept to teach. For children who are not safety-conscious, noncompliance can be very dangerous: they may burn, cut, or otherwise injure themselves while unattended even for a few minutes. Another major area of management is self-help skills; as psychotic children grow older, they may not naturally acquire skills in eating and dressing that are easily acquired by normally developing children. For these children, it is especially important for teachers and parents cooperatively to plan and implement behavior management programs. If behavioral programs are not carried out in both home and school settings, there is little chance that the skills will generalize to other settings or be maintained over time.

Lack of respite time.   The erratic activity levels and sleep patterns of many psychotic children can leave parents chronically exhausted. The usual respites of evenings out and vacations may not be feasible due to difficulties in acquiring baby-sitting services. Even family outings may not be possible when the child does not function well in large groups or with strangers. Such a schedule leaves parents with little time to invest in other family members or to pursue personal interests.

Disrupted family functioning.   The inordinate amounts of time and energy required by the behavior disordered child inevitably disrupt family functioning. In families that have adapted well, continuous compromises and flexibility are required of each family member. Unfortunately, many marriages do not survive the strain, as over half of the marriages of parents of handicapped children end in divorce (Raaz, 1982), as compared to about a 35 percent divorce rate in the general population.

Concerns over the future.   Even for parents who cope successfully with their child in the home and manage to maintain their child in quality educational programs, the question of the future looms large. No states are required to extend public education programs for students beyond the age of 21, and few offer adequate day or residential treatment programs for severely disordered adults which are funded from other sources, either public or private. For parents of children and adolescents who will not be able to maintain themselves independently, the question of future caretaking is burdensome. For many, institutionalization is the only feasible alternative.

The issue of institutionalization is a difficult and ever-present one. Parents who decide to place their child out of the home must deal with both their own feelings of inadequacy and guilt and with the criticisms of others. Because of these constraints, some parents wrestle with the decision for years, even when it is the best alternative for both the child and themselves. Other parents may decide upon residential or institutional placement of children who potentially could be maintained at home simply because they can no longer cope with the pressures.

Educators can play two major roles in helping ease the difficulties of these parents. The first role is advocacy for respite care programs, which include baby-sitting services, extended day care, summer educational programs, summer camps, and recreational programs or other alternative day-care programs designed to meet the needs of the severely disordered and remove the burden of caretaking from the family for a few hours. In many cases, respite care services are limited, and most state agencies do not view such services as a public responsibility. In a plea for more respite care services, Raaz (1982) cites advocate Ruth Sullivan's rationale for state provision of respite care:

> The cure for lack of respite is known, yet there is still a tremendous psychological resistance to the idea that the state has a moral responsibility to help families who need respite services.
> If we think of government as an extension of persons and families, providing for us, by our permission, what we cannot do for ourselves as efficaciously (e.g., roads, bridges, schools, parks, postal services, airport terminals), then we should have no problem in expecting government to provide to families in a crisis, no matter how long, what it does routinely for other citizens' convenience and pleasure. (Sullivan 1979, p. 114)

The second major role educators can play is that of a concerned professional who is willing to listen to parents and to offer support and guidance. In a survey of parents of autistic children in 1974, 42 percent of the parents believed that professionals were insensitive, and 79 percent felt that professionals were unwilling to listen or to share their knowledge (Salvagne, Schollenberger, & Stokes, 1974). Many parents want to be informed and involved with their child's education. According to Sullivan (1976), parents of the severely disordered want an equal role with professionals "in assigning their child's priorities and planning his future" (p. 44). Too often, educators assume that they know what is best for the child and plan the child's IEP and assign home training duties without first consulting the parents about the parents' priorities for the child. A truly successful educational program for the severely behavior disordered child combines educators' and parents' priorities for skill development and orients activities toward agreed-upon long-range goals for that child's life.

SUMMARY

The special needs of autistic and schizophrenic children and adolescents warrant educational interventions that are different from those required by mildly or moderately disordered students. Curricular areas such as self-help skills, language-communication, and vocational training must take priority for the majority of these students if they are to acquire functional skills and maintain themselves independently in the community as adults. All programming should be oriented toward helping these individuals attain maximum independence.

Teachers who work with psychotic children and adolescents should be aware of the special issues that arise. Because of the unique cognitive characteristics of this population, teachers must often employ special instructional strategies such as concept analysis, prompting, discrete trial format, and other strategies for facilitating generalization. Due to the tendency of the severely disordered toward self-stimulation and self-injurious behavior, teachers should be familiar with the pros and cons of using aversive techniques and with alternatives to aversives. Another issue arising in teaching the severely behavior disordered is institutionalization. Teachers must be aware of the special difficulties that parents face with these children and should be equipped to provide support and guidance concerning alternatives and respite care services.

KEY POINTS

(1) Schizophrenic and autistic children require special considerataions in educational programming.

(2) Although autistic children are under the rubric of "developmental disorder" rather than "emotional disturbance," they usually exhibit maladaptive behaviors that require specific behavioral interventions.

(3) Five basic curriculum areas for severely disordered students are: language-communication, self-help, social, academics, and vocational.

(4) The "criterion of ultimate functioning" should be applied to all curricular objectives (for example, Will this skill help the student to function more independently in the future?).

(5) Successful instructional strategies with this population include task analysis, concept analysis, discrete trial format, prompting, and strategies for facilitating generalization.

(6) Teachers must eliminate self-stimulatory and self-injurious behavior before optimal student learning can take place.

(7) Alternatives to punishment have been successful in eliminating self-injurious behavior.

(8) The teacher of behavior disordered students may need to become proficient at an alternative communication system in order to communicate with nonverbal students.

(9) Parents of psychotic children face difficult issues such as the lack of respite care services and the possibility of institutionalization.

ADDITIONAL READINGS

Lisa & David/Jordi, by T.I. Rubin. New York: Random House (Ballantine Books), 1962, for descriptive case studies of three schizophrenic children.

Selected chapters in *Autism: Diagnosis, instruction, management and research*. Edited by J.E. Gilliam. Springfield, IL: Chas. C Thomas, 1981, for readings on selected topics related to autism.

Criterion of ultimate functioning, by L. Brown, J. Nietupski, & S. Hamre-Nietupski. In *Hey, don't forget about me!* Edited by M.A. Thomas. Reston, VA: The Council for Exceptional Children, 1976, for a discussion of basic issues in selecting curriculum and instructing the severely handicapped.

The motivation of self-injurious behavior, by E.G. Carr. *Psychological Bulletin*, 1977, *84*, 800–811, for an article that reviews hypotheses of motivation for self-injurious behavior.

Reducing severe aggressive and self-injurious behavior: A nonintrusive, home based approach, by T.S. Woods. *Behavioral Disorders*, 1982, *7*, 180–188, for a case study reporting reduction of aggressive and self-injurious behavior.

Educating children with severe maladaptive behaviors, by S. Stainback & W. Stainback. New York: Grune & Stratton, 1980, for more comprehensive information in all areas of programming for the severely behavior disordered (including an exceptional chapter on "Teaching Language to the Nonverbal Child").

How to teach autistic and other severely handicapped children, by R.L. Koegel & L. Schreibman; *How to integrate autistic and other severely handicapped children into a classroom*, by R.L. Koegel; and *How to teach prevocational skills to severely handicapped persons*, by D.E. Mithaug, for teacher guidelines on working with autistic and severely disordered children. All three are available from Austin, TX: Pro-Ed, 1981.

NOTES

[1]Current research indicates that modeling effects with this population will not occur unless specific procedures are employed. For further information, refer to Gresham (1981), Varni, Lovaas, Koegel, and Everett (1979), and Egel, Richman, and Koegel (1981).

References

ABRAMS, J.C., & KASLOW, F. (1977). Family systems and the learning disabled child: Intervention and treatment. *Journal of Learning Disabilities, 10,* 86–90.

ACHENBACH, T.M. (1978). Psychopathology of childhood: Research problems and issues. *Journal of Consulting and Clinical Psychology, 46,* 759–776.

ACHENBACH, T.M., & EDELBROCK, C.S. (1979). The Child Behavior Profile: II. Boys aged 12–16 and girls aged 6–11 and 12–16. *Journal of Consulting and Clinical Psychology, 47,* 223–233.

AHLSTROM, W.M., & HAVIGHURST, R.J. (1971). *400 Losers.* San Francisco: Jossey-Bass.

AIELLO, B. (1976). Especially for special educators: A sense of our own history. *Exceptional Children, 42,* 244–252.

ALBERTO, P.A., & TROUTMAN, A.C. (1982). *Applied behavior analysis for teachers.* Columbus, OH: Chas. E. Merrill.

ALEXANDER, R.N., CORBETT, T.F., & SMIGEL, J. (1976). The effects of individual and group consequences on school attendance and curfew violations with predelinquent adolescents. *Journal of Applied Behavior Analysis, 9,* 221–226.

ALGOZZINE, B. (1977). The emotionally disturbed child: Disturbed or disturbing? *Journal of Abnormal Child Psychology, 5,* 205–211.

ALGOZZINE, B. & CURRAN, T.J. (1979). Teachers' predictions of children's school success as a function of their behavioral tolerances. *Journal of Educational Research, 72,* 344–347.

ALGOZZINE, R. (1981). Biophysical perspective of emotional disturbance. In R. Algozzine, R. Schmid, & C.D. Mercer (Eds.), *Childhood behavior disorders.* Rockville, MD: Aspen.

ALLYON, T., SMITH, D., & ROGERS, M. (1970). Behavioral management of school phobia. *Journal of Behavior Therapy and Experimental Psychiatry, 1,* 125–138.

ALTMAN, K.I., & LINTON, T.E. (1974). Operant conditioning in the classroom setting: A review of research. In R. Ulrich, T. Stachnik, & J. Mabry (Eds.) *Control of human behavior* (Vol. 3). Glenview, IL: Scott, Foresman.

AMERICAN ACADEMY OF NEUROLOGY. (1967). Joint executive board statement—the Doman-Delacato treatment of neurologically handicapped children. *Neurology, 17,* 637.

AMERICAN ACADEMY OF PEDIATRICS, Committee on Nutrition. (1976). Megavitamin therapy for childhood psychoses and learning disabilities. *Pediatrics, 58,* 910–912.

AMERICAN GUIDANCE SERVICE. (1964). *American study habits survey.* Circle Pines, MN: American Guidance Service.

AMERICAN PSYCHIATRIC ASSOCIATION. (1974). Task Force on Vitamin Therapy in Psychiatry. Megavitamins and orthomolecular therapy in psychiatry: Excerpts from the report of the Task Force on Vitamin Therapy in Psychiatry. *Nutrition Review, 32,* 44–74.

AMERICAN PSYCHIATRIC ASSOCIATION. (1980). *Diagnostic and statistical manual of mental disorders* (3rd ed.). Washington, DC: Author.

ANASTASI, A. (1982). *Psychological testing* (5th ed.). New York: Macmillan.

ANDERSON, C.W. (1981a). Parent-child relationships: A context for reciprocal developmental influence. *The Counseling Psychologist, 4,* 35–44.

ANDERSON, C.W. (1981b). The handicapped child's effects on parent-child relations: A useful model for school psychologists. *School Psychology Review, 10,* 82–90.

APTER, S.J. (1982). *Troubled children/troubled systems.* Elmsford, NY: Pergamon Press.

APTER, S.J., & CONOLEY, J.C. (1984). *Childhood behavior disorders and emotional disturbance.* Englewood Cliffs, NJ: Prentice-Hall.

ATWATER, E. (1983). *Adolescence.* Englewood Cliffs, NJ: Prentice-Hall.

AUSMAN, J., BALL, T.S., & ALEXANDER, D. (1974). Behavior therapy of pica with a profoundly retarded adolescent. *Mental Retardation, 12,* 16–18.

AZERAD, J., & STAFFORD, R.L. (1969). Restoration of eating behavior in anorexia nervosa through operant conditioning and environmental manipulation. *Behavior Research and Therapy, 7,* 165–171.

BAKER, A.M. (1979). Cognitive functioning of psychotic children: A reappraisal. *Exceptional Children, 45,* 344–348.

BAKER, A.M. (1980). The efficacy of the Feingold K-P diet: A review of pertinent empirical investigations. *Behavioral Disorders, 6,* 32–35.

BANDURA, A. (1965a). Behavior modifications through modeling procedures. In L. Krasner & L.P. Ullman (Eds.), *Research in behavior modification.* New York: Holt, Rinehart & Winston, 310–340.

BANDURA, A. (1965b). Vicarious processes: A case of no-trial learning. In L. Berkowitz (Ed.), *Advances in experimental social psychology* (Vol. 2). New York: Academic Press.

BANDURA, A.A. (1968). Social learning interpretation of psychological dysfunctions. In P. London & D. Rosenhan (Eds.), *Foundations of abnormal psychology.* New York: Holt, Rinehart & Winston.

BANDURA, A. (1977). *Social learning theory.* Englewood Cliffs, NJ: Prentice-Hall.

BANDURA, A., ROSS, D., & ROSS, S. (1961). Transmission of aggression through imitation of aggressive models. *Journal of Abnormal and Social Psychology, 63,* 575–582.

BANDURA, A., ROSS, D., & ROSS, S. (1963). Imitation of film-mediated aggressive models. *Journal of Abnormal and Social Psychology, 66,* 3–11.

BARKER, R.G. (1968). *Ecological psychology: Concepts and methods for studying the environment of human behavior.* Stanford, CA: Stanford University Press.

BARNETTE, S.M., & PARKER, L.G. (1982). Suspension and expulsion of the emotionally handicapped: Issues and practices. *Behavioral Disorders, 7,* 173–179.

BARTAK, L., & RUTTER, M. (1973). Special education treatment of autistic children: A comparative study. I. Design of study and characteristics of units. *Journal of Child Psychology and Psychiatry, 14,* 161–179.

BARTH, R. (1979). Home-based reinforcement of school behavior: A review and analysis. *Review of Educational Research, 49,* 436–458.

BAUMEISTER, A.A., & Forehand, R. (1972). Effects of contingent shock and verbal command on body rocking of retardates. *Journal of Clinical Psychology, 28,* 586–590.

BEAVERS, W.R. (1977). *Psychotherapy and growth: A family systems perspective.* New York: Brunner/Mazel.

BECK, T. (1972). Videotape scenes for desensitization of test anxiety. *Journal of Behavior Therapy and Experimental Psychiatry, 3,* 195–197.

BECKER, H. (1963). *Outsiders: Studies in the sociology of deviance.* New York: Free Press.

BECKER, W.C. (1964). Consequences of different kinds of parental discipline. In M.L. Hoffman & L.W. Hoffman (Eds.), *Review of child development research* (Vol. 1). New York: Russell Sage Foundation.

BEILIN, H. (1959). Teachers' and clinicians' attitudes toward the behavior problems of children: A reappraisal. *Child Development, 39,* 9–25.

BELL, R.Q. (1968). A reinterpretation of the direction of effects in studies of socialization. *Psychological Review, 75,* 81–95.

BELL, R.Q., & HARPER, L.V. (1977). *Child effects on adults.* Hillsdale, NJ: Erlbaum.

BELLAK, L., & ADELMAN, C. (1960). The children's apperception test (CAT). In A.I. Rabin & M.R. Haworth (Eds.), *Projective techniques with children.* New York: Grune & Stratton.

BELLAK, L., & BELLAK, S.S. (1949). *Children's Apperception Test.* Larchmont, NY: C.P.S., Inc.

BENDER, L. (1942). Schizophrenia in childhood. *Nervous Child, 1,* 138–140.

BENDER, L. (1946). *Bender Motor Gestalt Test.* Washington, DC: American Orthopsychiatric Association.

BENDER, L. (1954). Current research in childhood schizophrenia. *American Journal of Psychiatry, 110,* 855–856.

BENDER, L. (1968). Childhood schizophrenia: A review. *International Journal of Psychiatry, 5,* 211.

BENEDICT, R. (1959). *Patterns of culture.* Cambridge, MA: Riverside Press.

BENTZEN, F.A., & PETERSEN, W. (1962). Educational procedures with the brain-damaged child. In W.T. Daley (Ed.), *Speech and language therapy with the brain-damaged child.* Washington, DC: Catholic University Press.

BERKOWITZ, L. (1962). *Aggression: A social psychological analysis.* New York: McGraw-Hill.

BERKOWITZ, P.H. (1974). Pearl H. Berkowitz. In J.M. Kauffman and C.D. Lewis (Eds.), *Teaching children with behavior disorders: Personal perspectives.* Columbus, OH: Chas. E. Merrill.

BERKOWITZ, P.H., & ROTHMAN, E.P. (1960). *The disturbed child: Recognition and psychoeducational therapy in the classroom.* New York: New York University Press.

BERNARD, H. (1973). *Child development and learning.* Boston: Allyn & Bacon.

BERNE, E. (1965). *Games people play.* New York: Grove Press.

BESSELL, H., & PALOMARES, V. (1970). *Magic Circle/Human Development Program.* San Diego, CA: Human Development Training Institute.

BETTELHEIM, B. (1959). Joey: A mechanical boy. *Scientific American, 200,* 116–127.

BETTELHEIM, B. (1967). *The empty fortress.* New York: Free Press.

BIKLEN, D. (1976). Advocacy comes of age. *Exceptional Children, 42,* 308–313.

BLACKHAM, G.J. (1967). *The deviant child in the classroom.* Belmont, CA: Wadsworth.

BLACKWOOD, R. (1970). The operant conditioning of verbally mediated self-control in the classroom. *Journal of School Psychology, 8,* 251–258.

BLATT, B. (1972). Public policy and the education of children with special needs. *Exceptional Children, 30,* 537–543.

BLATT, M.M., & KOHLBERG, L. (1975). The effects of classroom moral discussion upon children's level of moral judgement. *Journal of Moral Education, 4,* 129–161.

BLAU, A. (1962). The nature of childhood schizophrenia. *Journal of the American Academy of Child Psychiatry, 2,* 225–235.

BLEULER, E. (1950). *Dementia praecox on the group of schizophrenics* (J. Zinkin, Trans.). New York: International University Press. (Originally published, 1911.)

BLOCK, E.E., COVILL-SERVO, J., & ROSEN, M.F. (1978). *Failing students-failing schools: A study of dropouts and discipline in New York State.* Rochester, NY: New York Civil Liberties Union.

BOLSTAD, D.D., & JOHNSON, S.M. (1972). Self-regulation in the modification of disruptive classroom behavior. *Journal of Applied Behavior Analysis, 5,* 443–454.

BOSTOW, D.E., & BAILEY, J.B. (1969). Modifications of severe disruptive and aggressive behavior using brief time-out and reinforcement procedures. *Journal of Applied Behavior Analysis, 2,* 31–37.

BOWER, E.M. (1960). *Early identification of emotionally handicapped children in school.* Springfield, IL: Chas. C Thomas.

BOWER, E.M. (1961). *The education of emotionally handicapped children.* Sacramento, CA: California State Department of Education.

BOWER, E.M. (1969). *Early identification of emotionally handicapped children in school* (2nd ed.). Springfield, IL: Chas. C Thomas.

BOWER, E.M. (1980). Slicing the mystique of prevention with Occam's razor. In N.J. Long, W.C. Morse, & R.G. Newman (Eds.), *Conflict in the classroom: The education of emotionally disturbed children* (4th ed.). Belmont, CA: Wadsworth.

BOWER, E.M. (1982). Defining emotional disturbance: Public policy and research. *Psychology in the Schools, 19,* 55–60.

BOWER, E.M., & LAMBERT, N.M. (1962). *A process for in-school screening of children with emotional handicaps.* Princeton, NJ: Educational Testing Service.

BOWER, K.B., & MERCER, C.D. (1975). Hyperactivity: Etiology and intervention techniques. *The Journal of School Health, 45,* 195–202.

BRAATEN, S. (1979). The Madison school program: Programming for secondary severely emotionally disturbed youth. *Behavioral Disorders, 4,* 153–162.

BRADLEY, C. (1937). The behavior of children receiving Benzedrine. *American Journal of Psychiatry, 94,* 577–585.

BRADY, J.P., & RIEGER, W. (1975). Behavioral treatment of anorexia nervosa. In T. Thompson & W.S. Dockens (Eds.), *Applications of behavior modification.* New York: Academic Press.

BRAGSTAD, B.J., & STUMPF, S.M. (1982). *A guidebook for teaching study skills and motivation.* Boston: Allyn & Bacon.

BRENNER, M.B. (1963). Life space interview in the school setting. *American Journal of Orthopsychiatry, 33,* 717–719.

BROLIN, D.C., & D'ALONZO, B.J. (1979). Critical issues in career education for handicapped students. *Exceptional Children, 45,* 246–253.

BROLIN, D.E., & KOKASKA, C.J. (1979). *Career education for handicapped children and youth.* Columbus, OH: Merrill.

BRONFENBRENNER, U. (1979). *The ecology of human development: Experiments by nature and design.* Cambridge, MA: Harvard University Press.

BROPHY, J.E. (1977). *Child development and socialization.* Chicago: Science Research Associates.

BROWN, L., NIETUPSKI, J., & HAMRE-NIETUPSKI, S. (1976). Criterion of ultimate functioning. In M.A. Thomas (Ed.), *Hey, don't forget about me!* Reston, VA: The Council for Exceptional Children.

BROWN, L.L. (1978). Teacher strategies for managing classroom behaviors. In D.D. Hammill & N.R. Bartel (Eds.), *Teaching children with learning and behavior problems* (2nd ed.). Austin, TX: Pro-Ed.

BROWN, L.L., & HAMMILL, D.D. (1983). *Behavior Rating Profile: An ecological approach to behavior assessment.* Austin, TX: Pro-Ed.

BROWN, L.L., & SHERBENOU, R.J. (1981). A comparison of teacher perceptions of student reading ability, reading performance, and classroom behavior. *The Reading Teacher, 34,* 557–560.

BROWN, V. (1978). Independent study behaviors: A framework for curriculum development. *Learning Disabilities Quarterly, 1,* 78–84.

BROWN, V.L., & BOTEL, M. (1972). *Dyslexia: Definition or treatment?* Bloomington, IN: Indiana University. (ERIC Document Reproduction Service No. ED 058014.)

BROWN, W.R., & McGUIRE, J.M. (1976). Current psychological assessment practices. *Professional Psychology, 7,* 475–484.

BUCHER, B., & LOVAAS, O.I. (1968). Use of aversive stimulation in behavior modification. In M.R. Jones (Ed.), *Miami symposium on the prediction of behavior, 1967: Aversive stimulation.* Coral Gables, FL: University of Miami Press.

BUDD, K.S., & LEIBOWITZ, J.M. (May 1976). *Programmed Activities for School Success (PASS): Modification of disruptive classroom behavior in young children through home-based contingencies.* Paper presented at the second annual convention of the Midwestern Association of Behavior Analysis, Chicago.

BULLOCK, L.M. (1976). *Educational interventions for children with behavioral and/or learning problems.* Gainesville, FL: Florida Educational Research and Development Council, *10.*

BULLOCK, L.M. (1981). *Basic principles for establishing programs for the seriously emotionally disturbed,* Project S.E.D. Austin, TX: Education Service Center, Region XIII.

CAMP, B.W., & BASH, M.A. (1978). *Think Aloud: Group manual* (Rev. ed.). Denver, CO: University of Colorado Medical School.

CAMP, B.W., BLOM, G.E., HEBERT, F., & VAN DOORNINCK, W.J. (1977). "Think aloud": A program for developing self-control in young aggressive boys. *Journal of Abnormal Child Psychology, 5,* 157–169.

CAMPBELL, M. (1973). Biological interventions in psychoses of childhood. *Journal of Autism and Childhood Schizophrenia, 3,* 347–373.

CAMPBELL, M. (1975). Psychopharmacology in childhood psychosis. *International Journal of Mental Health, 4,* 238–254.

CAMPBELL, S.B. (1973). Mother-child interaction in reflective, impulsive, and hyperactive children. *Developmental Psychology, 8,* 341–349.

CAMPBELL, S.B. (1975). Mother-child interaction: A comparison of hyperactive, learning disabled, and normal boys. *American Journal of Orthopsychiatry, 45,* 51–56.

CARLSON, C.F. (1967). *A neurophysiological model of early infantile autism and its therapeutic implications.* Paper presented at the American Psychological Association Symposium on Early Infantile Autism.

CARR, E.G. (1977). The motivation of self-injurious behavior: A review of some hypotheses. *Psychological Bulletin, 84,* 800–811.

CARTWRIGHT, C.A., & CARTWRIGHT, G.P. (1974). *Developing observation skills.* New York: McGraw-Hill.

CAWLEY, J.F., & WEBSTER, R.E. (1981). Reading and behavior disorders. In G. Brown, R.L. McDowell, & J. Smith (Eds.), *Educating adolescents with behavior disorders.* Columbus, OH: Chas. E. Merrill.

CHENEY, L., & MORSE, W.C. (1974). Psychodynamic interventions in emotional disturbance. In W.C. Rhodes & M.L. Tracy (Eds.), *A study of child variance* (Vol. 2). Ann Arbor, MI: The University of Michigan Press.

CHRISTENSEN, A.L. (1975). *Luria's neuropsychological investigation.* New York: Spectrum.

CLARIZIO, H.F., & McCOY, G.F. (1976). *Behavior disorders in children* (2nd ed.). New York: Thomas Y. Crowell.

CLAUSEN, J. (1968). Faulty socialization and social disorganization as etiological factors in mental disorder. In J. Zubin & F.A. Frayhen (Eds.), *Social Psychiatry, 43,* 42–55.

COATES, B. (1972). White adult behavior toward black and white children. *Child Development, 43,* 143–154.

COHEN, H.L., FILIPCZAK, J., & BIS, J. (1970). A study of contingencies applicable to special education: Case I. In R. Ulrich, T. Stachnik, & J. Mabry (Eds.), *Control of human behavior: From cure to prevention* (Vol. 2). Glenview, IL: Scott, Foresman.

COHEN, S., KEYWORTH, M., KLEINER, R., & LIBERT, L. (1971). The support of school behaviors by home-based reinforcement via parent-child contingency contracts. In E. Ramp & B. Hopkins (Eds.), *A new direction for education.* Lawrence, KS: University of Kansas, Department of Human Development.

COLEMAN, J.C. (1964). *Abnormal psychology and modern life.* Glenview, IL: Scott, Foresman.

COLEMAN, M.C. (1982). Teacher attitudes toward various dimensions of behavior exhibited by emotionally disturbed students, (Doctoral dissertation, The University of Texas, 1981). *Dissertation Abstracts International, 42,* 07A, 3103.

COLEMAN, M.C., & GILLIAM, J.E. (1983). Disturbing behaviors in the classroom: A survey of teacher attitudes. *Journal of Special Education, 17,* 121–129.

CONDRY, J., & SIMAN, M.L. (1974). Characteristics of peer- and adult-oriented children. *Journal of Marriage and the Family, 36,* 543–554.

CONGER, J.J. (1973). *Adolescence and youth: Psychological development in a changing world.* New York: Harper & Row.

CONNERS, C.K. (1969). A teacher rating scale for use in drug studies with children. *American Journal of Psychiatry, 126,* 884–888.

CONNERS, C.K. (1970). Symptom patterns in hyperkinetic, neurotic, and normal children. *Child Development, 41,* 667–682.

CONNERS, C.K., & WERRY, J.S. (1979). Pharmacotherapy. In H.C. Quay & J.S. Werry (Eds.), *Psychopathological disorders of childhood* (2nd ed.). New York: John Wiley.

COOPERSMITH, S. (1967). *The antecedents of self-esteem.* San Francisco: W.H. Freeman & Company Publishers.

CORNBLETH, C. (1974). Expectations for pupil achievement and teacher-pupil interaction. *Social Education, 38,* 54–58.

CORTE, H.E., WOLFE, M.M., & LOCKE, B.J. (1971). A comparison of procedures for eliminating self-injurious behavior of retarded adolescents. *Journal of Applied Behavior Analysis, 4,* 201–213.

COULTER, A., MORROW, H., & GILLIAM, J.E. (1979). *Emotional disturbance: Diagnostic procedures and eligibility determination* (Report to Texas Education Agency, Austin, TX).

CREAK, M., & INI, S. (1960). Families of psychotic children. *Journal of Child Psychology and Psychiatry, 3,* 501–504.

CRUICKSHANK, W.M., BENTZEN, F.A., RATZEBURG, F.H., & TANNHAUSER, M.T. (1961). *A teaching method for brain-injured and hyperactive children.* Syracuse: Syracuse University Press.

CULLINAN, D., EPSTEIN, M.H., & LLOYD, J.W. (1983). *Behavior disorders of children and adolescents.* Englewood Cliffs, NJ: Prentice-Hall.

DEARMAN, N.B., & PLISKO, V.W. (Eds.). (1979). *The condition of education: 1979 edition.* Washington, DC: U. S. Department of Health, Education, and Welfare, National Center for Educational Statistics.

DEFFENBACHER, J., & KEMPER, C. (1974). Systematic desensitization of test anxiety in junior high students. *The School Counselor, 21,* 216–222.

DELL, H.D. (1972). *Individualizing instruction.* Chicago: Science Research Associates.

DeMAGISTRIS, R.J., & IMBER, S.C. (1980). The effects of life space interviewing on academic and social performance of behaviorally disordered children. *Behavioral Disorders, 6,* 12–25.

DeMYER, M.K. (1975). The nature of neuropsychological disability in autistic children. *Journal of Autism and Childhood Schizophrenia, 5,* 109–128.

DeMYER, M.K. (1979). *Parents and children in autism.* New York: John Wiley.

DENO, E. (1968). Educational aspects of minimal brain dysfunction in children. *Proceedings of the Sixth Delaware Conference on the Handicapped Child.* 41–65. Wilmington, DE: Alfred I. Dupont Institute.

DENO, S.L., & MIRKIN, P.K. (1978). *Data-based program modification: A manual.* Reston, VA: Council for Exceptional Children.

DES JARLAIS, D.C. (1974). Mental illness as social deviance. In W.C. Rhodes & M.L. Tracy (Eds.), *A study of child variance* (Vol. 1). Ann Arbor, MI: The University of Michigan Press.

DES LAURIERS, A., & CARLSON, C.F. (1969). *Your child is asleep.* Homewood, IL: Dorsey.

DESPERT, J.L. (1965). *The emotionally disturbed child—Then and now.* New York: Robert Brunner.

DINKMEYER, D., & DINKMEYER, D., Jr. (1982). *Developing understanding of self and others—Revised.* Circle Pines, MN: American Guidance Service.

DINKMEYER, D., & McKAY, G. (1976). *STEP, systematic training in effective parenting.* Circle Pines, MN: American Guidance Service.

DOE v. KOGER, 480 F. Supp. 225, N.D. Ind. (1979).

DOLLAR, S.J. (1981). The concept of generalized imitation: Implications for developing curricula for the autistic child. In J.E. Gilliam (Ed.), *Autism: Diagnosis, instruction, management, and research.* Springfield, IL: Chas. C Thomas.

DOMAN, R., SPITZ, E.B., ZUCMAN, E., DELACATO, C., & DOMAN, G. (1960). Children with severe brain injuries. *The Journal of the American Medical Association, 174,* 257–262.

DONNELLAN, A.M. (1980). An educational perspective on autism: Implications for curriculum development and personnel development. In B. Wilcox & A. Thompson (Eds.), *Critical issues in educating autistic children and youth.* U. S. Department of Education, Office of Special Education.

DONNELLAN-WALSH, A. (1976). *Teaching makes a difference: A guide for developing successful classes for autistic and other severely handicapped children.* Administrative manual. Sacramento, CA: California State Department of Education.

DONNELLAN-WALSH, A., GOSSAGE, L.D., LaVIGNA, G.W., SCHULER, A., & TRAPHAGEN, J.D. (1976). *Teaching makes a difference: A guide for developing successful classes for autistic and other severely handicapped children.* Santa Barbara, CA: Santa Barbara Public Schools.

DORSEY, B. (1980). *Teaching the autistic child—the use of prompts.* Unpublished paper, Iowa City: The University of Iowa.

DOUGLAS, V.I., PARRY, P., MORTON, P., & GARSON, C. (1976). Assessment of a cognitive training program for hyperactive children. *Journal of Abnormal Child Psychology, 4,* 389–410.

DUNN, L. (1968). Special education for the mildly retarded—Is much of it justifiable? *Exceptional Children, 35*, 5–22.

DUNN, R., & DUNN, K. (1972). *Practical approaches to individualizing instruction.* West Nyack, NY: Parker Publishing.

DUPONT, H., GARDNER, O.S., & BRODY, D.S. (1974). *Toward affective development.* Circle Pines, MN: American Guidance Service.

DURANT, W. (1939). *The life of Greece.* New York: Simon & Schuster.

DURANT, W. (1961). *The story of philosophy: The lives and opinions of the great philosophers of the western world.* New York: Simon & Schuster.

EGEL, A.L., RICHMAN, G.S., & KOEGEL, R.L. (1981). Normal peer models and autistic children's learning. *Journal of Applied Behavior Analysis, 14*, 3–12.

EHRLICH, M.I. (1980). *Perception of primary involvement: A study of children's judgement of their family's involvement in their education.* Unpublished doctoral dissertation, University of Texas.

EHRLICH, M.I. (1981). Parental involvement in education. A review and synthesis of the literature. *Revista Mexicana de Análisis de la Conducta, 7*, 49–68.

ELARDO, P.T., & ELARDO, R. (1976). A critical analysis of social development in elementary education. *Journal of School Psychology, 14*, 118–130.

ELKIND, D. (1974). *Children and adolescents* (2nd ed.). New York: Oxford University Press.

ELLIS, A. (1962). *Reason and emotion in psychotherapy.* New York: Lyle Stuart.

ELLIS, A. (1973). *Humanistic psychotherapy: The rational-emotive approach.* New York: Julian.

ELLIS, A. (1977). The basic clinical theory of rational-emotive therapy. In A. Ellis & R. Grieger (Eds.), *Handbook of rational-emotive therapy.* New York: Springer.

ELLIS, A. (1980). An overview of the clinical theory of rational-emotive therapy. In R. Grieger & R. Boyd (Eds.), *Rational-emotive therapy.* New York: Van Nostrand Reinhold.

EPANCHIN, B.C., & DICKENS, V. (1982). Curriculum design and educational programming. In J.L. Paul & B.C. Epanchin (Eds.), *Emotional disturbance in children.* Columbus, OH: Chas. E. Merrill.

EPANCHIN, B.C., & MONSON, L.B. (1982). Affective education. In J.L. Paul & B.C. Epanchin (Eds.), *Emotional disturbance in children.* Columbus, OH: Chas. E. Merrill.

EPSTEIN, M.H., CULLINAN, C., & ROSEMIER, R.A. (1983). Behavior problems of behaviorally disordered and normal adolescents. *Behavioral Disorders, 8*, 171–175.

EPSTEIN, M., CULLINAN, D., & SABATINO, D. (1977). State definitions of behavior disorders. *Journal of Special Education, 11*, 417–425.

ERICKSON, W.D. (1984). Sexual behavior disorders in adolescents. In S. Braaten, R.B. Rutherford, Jr., & C.A. Kardash (Eds.), *Programming for adolescents with behavioral disorders.* Reston, VA: Council for Children with Behavioral Disorders.

ERICKSON, E.H. (1959). Identity and the life cycle. In G.S. Klein (Ed.), *Psychological issues.* New York: International University Press.

ERIKSON, E.H. (1968). *Identity: Youth and crisis.* New York: W.W. Norton & Co., Inc.

EYSENCK, H.J. (1973). Learning therapy and behavior therapy. In T. Millon (Ed.), *Theories of psychopathology and personality.* Philadelphia: Saunders.

FAGEN, S.A., & LONG, N.J. (1979). A psychoeducational curriculum approach to teaching self-control. *Behavioral Disorders, 4*, 68–82.

FAGEN, S.A., LONG, N.J., & STEVENS, D.J. (1975). *Teaching children self-control: Preventing emotional and learning problems in the elementary school.* Columbus, OH: Chas. E. Merrill.

FARBEROW, N.L., & LITMAN, R.E. (1970). *A comprehensive suicide prevention program.* Los Angeles: Suicide Prevention Center of Los Angeles, 1958–69. (Unpublished final report DHEW NIMH Grants No. MH 14946 and MH 00128.)

FEAGANS, L. (1974). Ecological theory as a model for constructing a theory of emotional disturbance. In W.C. Rhodes & M.L. Tracy (Eds.), *A study of child variance* (Vol. 1). Ann Arbor, MI: The University of Michigan Press.

Federal Register, Section 121a.5. (1977, August 23). Washington, DC: U. S. Government Printing Office.

FEINGOLD, B.F. (1975a). *Why your child is hyperactive.* New York: Random House.

FEINGOLD, B.F. (1975b). Hyperkinesis and learning disabilities linked to artificial food flavors and colors. *The American Journal of Nursing, 75*, 797–803.

FEINGOLD, B.F. (1977). A critique of "Controversial medical treatments of learning disabilities." *Academic Therapy, 13*, 173–183.

FENICHEL, C. (1974). Carl Fenichel. In J.M. Kauffman & C.D. Lewis (Eds.), *Teaching children with behavior disorders: Personal perspectives*. Columbus, OH: Chas. E. Merrill.

FERNALD, G. (1943). *Remedial techniques in basic school subjects*. New York: McGraw-Hill.

FITTS, W. (1964). *Tennessee Self-Concept Scale*. Nashville: Counselor Recordings and Tests.

FORER, B.R. (1957). *The Forer Structured Sentence Completion Tests*. Santa Monica, CA: Western Psychological Services.

FOWLE, A. (1968). A typical leukocyte pattern of schizophrenic children. *Archives of General Psychiatry, 18,* 666–680.

FOX, R.S. (1964). *Pupil-teacher adjustment and mutual adaptation in creating classroom learning environments. Final Report*. Michigan University. (ERIC Document Reproduction Service No. ED 068 416.)

FOXX, R.M. (1971). *The use of overcorrection procedure in eliminating self-stimulatory behavior in a classroom for retarded children*. Unpublished doctoral dissertation, Southern Illinois University.

FOXX, R.M. (1977). Attention training: The use of overcorrection avoidance to increase the eye contact of autistic and retarded children. *Journal of Applied Behavior Analysis, 10,* 489–499.

FOXX, R.M., & AZRIN, N.H. (1973). The elimination of autistic self-stimulatory behavior by over-correction. *Journal of Applied Behavior Analysis, 6,* 1–14.

FREDERICKSEN, L.W., & FREDERICKSEN, C.B. (1975). Teacher-determined and self-determined token reinforcement in a special education classroom. *Behavior Therapy, 6,* 310–314.

FREED, A.M. (1973). *T.A. for tots*. Sacramento: Jalmar Press.

FREED, A.M. (1976). *T.A. for teens*. Sacramento: Jalmar Press.

FREED, A., & FREED, M. (1977). *T.A. for kids* (Rev. ed.). Sacramento: Jalmar Press.

FREEMAN, B.J., & RITVO, E.R. (1981). The syndrome of autism: A critical review of diagnostic systems, follow-up studies, and the theoretical background of the behavior observation scale. In J.E. Gilliam (Ed.), *Autism: Diagnosis, instruction, management, and research*. Springfield, IL: Chas. C Thomas.

FRIEDMAN, R. (1973). *Family roots of school learning and behavior disorders*. Springfield, IL: Chas. C Thomas.

FROMMER, E. (1967). Treatment of childhood depression with antidepressant drugs. *British Medical Journal, 1,* 729–732.

FURSTENBERG, F. (1976). *Unplanned parenthood*. New York: Free Press.

GABLE, R. (1984). A program for prevocational instruction for adolescents with severe behavioral disorders. In S. Braaten, R.B. Rutherford, Jr., & C.A. Kardash (Eds.), *Programming for adolescents with behavior disorders*. Reston, VA: Council for Children with Behavior Disorders.

GALLAGHER, P.A. (1979). *Teaching students with behavior disorders: Techniques for classroom instruction*. Denver: Love.

GALLAGHER, T. (1974). Phenomenal growth and new problems which characterize special education. *Phi Delta Kappan, 55,* 516–518.

GARVEY, W.P., & HEGRENES, J.R. (1966). Desensitization techniques in the treatment of school phobia. *American Journal of Orthopsychiatry, 36,* 147–152.

GIBBONS, D.C. (1981). *Delinquent behavior* (3rd ed.). Englewood Cliffs, NJ: Prentice-Hall.

GILLIAM, J.E. (1981a). Crisis intervention. *Project S.E.D., Teacher Training Module*. Austin, TX: Education Service Center, Region XIII.

GILLIAM, J.E. (1981b). *Establishing and enforcing rules*. Project S.E.D., Teacher Training Module. Austin, TX: Education Service Center, Region XIII.

GILLIAM, J.E., & COLEMAN, M.C. (1981). Who influences IEP committee decisions? *Exceptional Children, 47,* 642–644.

GILLIAM, J.E., & COLEMAN, M.C. (1982). A survey of knowledge about autism among experts and caregivers. *Behavioral Disorders, 7,* 189–196.

GILLIAM, J.E., WEBBER, J., & TWOMBLY, M. (1980). *Fundamentals of identification and assessment of autism*. Austin, TX: Texas Society for Autistic Citizens.

GILLINGHAM, A., & STILLMAN, B. (1966). *Remedial training for children with specific disability in reading, spelling, and penmanship*. Cambridge, MA: Educators Publishing Service.

GLASSER, W. (1965). *Reality therapy: A new approach to psychiatry*. New York: Harper & Row.

GLASSER, W. (1969). *Schools without failure*. New York: Harper & Row.

GLAVIN, J. (1973). Follow-up behavioral research in resource rooms. *Exceptional Children, 40*, 211–213.

GLAVIN, J.P., & ANNESLEY, F.R. (1972). Reading and arithmetic correlates of conduct problem and withdrawn children. *Journal of Special Education, 5*, 213–219.

GLICK, B. (1979). Youth between the cracks. *Behavioral Disorders, 4*, 227–231.

GLYNN, E., THOMAS, J., & SHEE, S. (1973). Behavioral self-control of on-task behavior in an elementary school classroom. *Journal of Applied Behavior Analysis, 6*, 105–113.

GOETZ, E.M., & BAER, D.M. (1973). Social control of form diversity and the emergence of new forms in children's blockbuilding. *Journal of Applied Behavior Analysis, 6*, 209–217.

GOFFMAN, E. (1961). *Asylums*. New York: Doubleday.

GOLD, M.W. (1972). Stimulus factors in skill training of the retarded on a complex assembly task: Acquisition, transfer, and retention. *American Journal of Mental Deficiency, 76*, 517–526.

GOLD, M.W. (1973). Research on the vocational rehabilitation of the retarded: The present, the future. *International Review of Research in Mental Retardation* (Vol. 6). New York: Academic Press.

GOLDEN, C.J. (1981). A standardized version of Luria's neuropsychological tests: A quantitative and qualitative approach to neuropsychological evaluation. In S.B. Filskov & T.J. Bell (Eds.), *Handbook of clinical neuropsychology*. New York: John Wiley.

GOLDEN, G. (1980). Nonstandard therapies in the developmental disabilities. *American Journal of Diseases of Children, 134*, 487–491.

GOLDFARB, W. (1961). *Childhood schizophrenia*. Cambridge, MA: Harvard University Press.

GOLDFARB, W. (1964). An investigation of childhood schizophrenia. *Archives of General Psychiatry, 11*, 621–634.

GOLDSTEIN, A.P., SPRAFKIN, R.P., GERSHAW, N.J., & KLEIN, P. (1980). *Skillstreaming the adolescent*. Champaign, IL: Research Press.

GOOD, T.L. (1970). Which pupils do teachers call on? *Elementary School Journal, 70*, 190–198.

GOOD, T.L., & GROUWS, D. (1972). Reaction of male and female teacher trainees to descriptions of elementary school pupils (Tech. Rep. No. 62). Center for Research in Social Behavior, University of Missouri, Columbus.

GORDON, I. (1966). *Studying the child in school*. New York: John Wiley.

GORDON, I. (1969). Developing parent power. In E. Grotberg (Ed.), *Critical issues in research related to disadvantaged children*. Princeton, NJ: Educational Testing Service.

GORDON, R.H., & THOMAS, J.T. (1967). The effects of student characteristics on teachers' ratings. *Instructor, 77*, 51–56.

GORDON, T. (1970). *Parent effectiveness training*. New York: Wyden.

GOTTMAN, J., & McFALL, R. (1972). Self-monitoring effects in a program for potential high school drop-outs. *Journal of Consulting and Clinical Psychology, 39*, 273–281.

GRAHAM, P. (1979). Epidemiological studies. In H.C. Quay & J.S. Werry (Eds.), *Psychopathological disorders of childhood* (2nd ed.). New York: John Wiley.

GRAUBARD, P.S. (1964). The extent of academic retardation in an academic treatment center. *Journal of Educational Research, 58*, 78–80.

GRAUBARD, P.S. (1969). Utilizing the group in teaching disturbed delinquents to learn. *Exceptional Children, 35*, 267–272.

GRAUBARD, P.S. (1973). Children with behavioral disabilities. In L. Dunn (Ed.), *Exceptional children in the schools*. New York: Holt, Rinehart, & Winston.

GREENWOOD, C.R., WALKER, H.M., & HOPS, H. (1977). Issues in social interaction/withdrawal assessment. *Exceptional Children, 43*, 490–499.

GRESHAM, F. (1981). Social skills training with handicapped children: A review. *Review of Educational Research, 51*, 139–176.

GRESHAM, F. (1982). Misguided mainstreaming: The case for social skills training with handicapped children. *Exceptional Children, 48*, 422–433.

GROUP FOR THE ADVANCEMENT OF PSYCHIATRY. (1966). *Psychopathological disorders in childhood: Theoretical considerations and a proposed classification*. New York: Group for the Advancement of Psychiatry.

GUESS, D., SAILOR, W., & BAER, D. (1978). Children with limited language. In R. Schiefelbusch (Ed.), *Language intervention strategies*. Baltimore: University Park Press.

HALL, C.S. (1954). *A primer of Freudian psychology.* New York: William Collins Publishers.

HALL, C.S., & LINDZEY, G. (1970). *Theories of personality* (2nd ed.). New York: John Wiley.

HALLAHAN, D.P., & KAUFFMAN, J.M. (1976). *Introduction to learning disabilities: A psycho-behavioral approach.* Englewood Cliffs, NJ: Prentice-Hall.

HALLAHAN, D.P., LLOYD, J., KOSIEWICZ, M.M., KAUFFMAN, J.M., & GRAVES, A.W. (1979). Self-monitoring of attention as a treatment for a learning disabled boy's off-task behavior. *Learning Disabilities Quarterly, 2,* 24–32.

HALPERN, F. (1960). The Rorschach test with children. In A.I. Rabin & M.R. Haworth (Eds.), *Projective techniques with children.* New York: Grune & Stratton.

HAMMILL, D.D. (1976). Defining "learning disabilities" for programmatic purposes. *Academic Therapy, 12,* 29–37.

HAMMILL, D.D., & LEIGH, J.E. (1982). *Basic school skills inventory—diagnostic.* Austin, TX: Pro-Ed.

HANEY, B., & GOLD, M. (1973). The juvenile delinquent nobody knows. *Psychology Today,* September, 49–55.

HARING, N. (1963). The emotionally disturbed. In S. Kirk & B. Weiner (Eds.), *Behavioral research on exceptional children.* Washington, DC: The Council for Exceptional Children.

HARING, N., STERN, G., & CRUICKSHANK, W. (1958). *Attitudes of educators toward exceptional children.* New York: Syracuse University Press.

HARING, N.G., & PHILLIPS, E.L. (1962). *Educating emotionally disturbed children.* New York: McGraw-Hill.

HARRIS, D.B. (1963). *Children's drawings as measures of intellectual maturity.* New York: Harcourt, Brace Jovanovich.

HAUSER, S.T. (1972). Black and white identity formation: Aspects and perspectives. *Journal of Youth and Adolescence, 1,* 113–130.

HAWKE, W.A., & LESSER, S.R. (1977). The child with a learning disorder. In P.D. Steinhauer & Q. Rae-Grant (Eds.), *Psychological problems of the child and his family.* Toronto: Macmillan.

HAZEL, J.S., SCHUMAKER, J.B., SHERMAN, J.A., & SHELDON-WILDGEN, J. (1981). *Asset.* Champaign, IL: Research Press.

HELTON, G.B., & OAKLAND, T.D. (1977). Teachers' attitudinal responses to differing characteristics of elementary school students. *Journal of Educational Psychology, 69,* 261–265.

HERR, D., ALGOZZINE, B., & EAVES, R. (1976). Amelioration of biases held by teacher trainees toward disturbingness of behavior. *Journal of Educational Research, 69,* 261–264.

HEWETT, F. (1965). Teaching speech to autistic children through operant conditioning. *American Journal of Orthopsychiatry, 35,* 927–936.

HEWETT, F.M. (1968). *The emotionally disturbed child in the classroom.* Boston: Allyn & Bacon.

HEWETT, F.M. (1974). Frank M. Hewett. In J.M. Kauffman & C.D. Lewis (Eds.), *Teaching children with behavior disorders: Personal perspectives.* Columbus, OH: Chas. E. Merrill.

HEWETT, F.M., & TAYLOR, F.D. (1980). *The emotionally disturbed child in the classroom: The orchestration of success* (2nd ed.). Boston: Allyn & Bacon.

HICKS, D.J. (1965). Imitation and retention of film-mediated aggressive peer and adult models. *Journal of Personality and Social Psychology, 2,* 97–100.

HIRSHOREN, A., & HELLER, G. (1979). Programs for adolescents with behavior disorders: The state of the art. *Journal of Special Education, 13,* 275–281.

HOBBS, N. (1966). Helping disturbed children: Psychological and ecological strategies. *American Psychologist, 21,* 1105–1115.

HOBBS, N. (1974). Nicholas Hobbs. In J.M. Kauffman & C.D. Lewis (Eds.), *Teaching children with behavior disorders: Personal perspectives.* Columbus, OH: Chas. E. Merrill.

HOBBS, N. (1975a). *Issues in the classification of children.* San Francisco: Jossey-Bass.

HOBBS, N. (1975b). *The futures of children: Categories, labels, and their consequences.* San Francisco: Jossey-Bass.

HOBBS, N. (1982). *The troubled and troubling child.* San Francisco: Jossey-Bass.

HOFFER, A., & OSMOND, H. (1966). Nicotinamide adenine dinucleotide (NAD) as a treatment of schizophrenia. *Journal of Psychopharmacology, 1,* 79–95.

HOFFMAN, E. (1974). Treatment of deviance by the educational system: History. In W.C. Rhodes & S. Head (Eds.), *A study of child variance* (Vol. 3). Ann Arbor, MI: University of Michigan.

HOLINGER, P.C. (1979). Violent deaths among the young: Recent trends in suicide, homicide, and accidents. *American Journal of Psychiatry, 136,* 1144–1147.

HOLLISTER, L.E. (1969). Clinical use of psychotherapeutic drugs: Current status. *Clinical Pharmacology and Therapeutics, 2,* 170–198.

HOLT, J. (1967). *How children learn.* New York: Pitman.

HOMME, L. (1969). *How to use contingency contracting in the classroom.* New York: Research Press.

HORNEY, K. (1937). *The neurotic personality of our time.* New York: W.W. Norton & Co., Inc.

HOWELL, K. (1983). *Inside special education.* Columbus, OH: Chas. E. Merrill.

HOWELL, K.W., KAPLAN, J.S., & O'CONNELL, C.Y. (1979). *Evaluating exceptional children.* Columbus, OH: Chas. E. Merrill.

HOWELL, K.W., ZUCKER, S.H., & MOREHEAD, M.K. (1982). *Multilevel academic skills inventory.* Columbus, OH: Chas. E. Merrill.

HUTT, S., HUTT, C., LEE, D., & OUNSTED, C. (1964). Arousal and childhood autism. *Nature, 204,* 908–909.

HUTT, C., HUTT, S., LEE, D., & OUNSTED, C. (1965). A behavioral and electroencephalographic study of autistic children. *Journal of Psychiatric Research, 3,* 181–197.

INHELDER, B., & PIAGET, J. (1958). *The growth of logical thinking from childhood to adolescence.* New York: Basic Books.

INSTITUTE FOR PARENT INVOLVEMENT. (1980). *Strategies for effective parent-teacher interaction.* Albuquerque, NM: University of New Mexico.

JACKSON, G., & COSCA, C. (1974). The inequality of educational opportunity in the Southwest: An observational study of ethnically mixed classrooms. *American Educational Research Journal, 11,* 219–229.

JACOBS, J. (1971). *Adolescent suicide.* New York: John Wiley.

JARDIN, R.A., & ZIEBELL, P.W. (1981). Adolescent drug and alcohol abuse. In G. Brown, R.L. McDowell, & J. Smith (Eds.), *Educating adolescents with behavior disorders.* Columbus, OH: Chas. E. Merrill.

JOHNSON, D.J., & MYKLEBUST, H.R. (1967). *Learning disabilities: Educational principles and practices.* New York: Grune & Stratton.

JOHNSTON, L.D., BACHMAN, J.G., & O'MALLEY, P.M. (1980). *Highlights from student drug use in America 1975–1980.* Rockville, MD: National Institute on Drug Abuse, Division of Research.

JONES, M.C. (1924). A laboratory study of fear: The case of Peter. *Pedagogical Seminary, 31,* 308–315.

KAGAN, J. (1965). Reflection-impulsivity and reading ability in primary grade children. *Child Development, 36,* 609–628.

KAGAN, J., & LEWIS, M. (1965). Studies of attention. *Merrill-Palmer Quarterly on Behavior Development, 4,* 95–127.

KAGAN, J., PEARSON, L., & WELCH, L. (1966). Conceptual impulsivity and inductive reasoning. *Child Development, 37,* 583–594.

KAMEYA, L.I. (1974). Biophysical interventions in emotional disturbance. In W.C. Rhodes & M.L. Tracy (Eds.), *A study of child variance* (Vol. 2). Ann Arbor, MI: The University of Michigan Press.

KANNER, L. (1943). Autistic disturbance of affective contact. *Nervous Child, 2,* 217–250.

KANNER, L. (1949). Problems of nosology and psychodynamics of early infantile autism. *American Journal of Orthopsychiatry, 19,* 416–426.

KANNER, L. (1957). *Child psychiatry* (3rd ed.). Springfield, IL: Chas. C Thomas.

KANNER, L. (1962). Emotionally disturbed children: A historical review. *Child Development, 33,* 97–102.

KAUFFMAN, J.M. (1977). *Characteristics of children's behavior disorders.* Columbus, OH: Chas. E. Merrill.

KAUFFMAN, J.M. (1981). *Characteristics of children's behavior disorders* (2nd ed.). Columbus, OH: Chas. E. Merrill.

KAUFFMAN, J.M., & KNEEDLER, R.D. (1981). Behavior disorders. In J.M. Kauffman & D.P. Hallahan (Eds.), *Handbook of special education.* Englewood Cliffs, NJ: Prentice-Hall.

KAUFMAN, A.S., SWAN, W.W., & WOOD, M.M. (1979). Dimensions of problem behaviors of emotionally disturbed children as seen by their parents and teachers. *Psychology in the Schools, 16,* 207–217.

KAVALE, K.A., & FORNESS, S.R. (1983). Hyperactivity and diet treatment: A meta-analysis of the Feingold hypothesis. *Journal of Learning Disabilities, 16,* 324–330.

KAZDIN, A.E., & BOOTSIN, R.R. (1972). The token economy: An evaluative review. *Journal of Applied Behavior Analysis, 5,* 343–372.

KEDAR-VOIVODAS, G., & TANNENBAUM, A.J. (1979). Teachers' attitudes toward young deviant children. *Journal of Educational Psychology, 71,* 800–808.

KELLY, J.A., & DRABMAN, R.S. (1977). Generalizing response supression of self-injurious behavior through an overcorrection punishment procedure: A case study. *Behavior Therapy, 8,* 468–472.

KELLY, T., BULLOCK, L., & DYKES, M. (1974). *Teacher perceptions of behavioral disorders in children.* Gainesville, FL: Florida Educational Research and Development Council.

KENNARD, M. (1965). Application of EEG to psychiatry. In W. Wilson (Ed.), *Applications of electroencephalography in psychiatry.* Durham, NC: Duke University Press.

KESSLER, J.W. (1966). *Psychopathology of childhood.* Englewood Cliffs, NJ: Prentice-Hall, 1966.

KINGSLEY, R. (1967). Prevailing attitudes toward exceptional children. *Education, 87,* 426–430.

KISSEL, R.C., & WHITMAN, T.L. (1977). An examination of the direct and generalized effects of a play-training and overcorrection procedure upon the self stimulatory behavior of a profoundly retarded boy. *AAESPH Review, 2,* 131–146.

KLEPSCH, M., & LOGIE, L. (1982). *Children draw and tell: An introduction to the projective uses of children's human figure drawings.* New York: Brunner/Mazel.

KNOBLOCK, P. (1983). *Teaching emotionally disturbed children.* Boston: Houghton Mifflin.

KNOPP, F. (1982). *Remedial intervention in adolescent sex offenses: Nine program descriptions.* Syracuse, NY: Safer Society Press.

KOEGEL, R.L., & COVERT, A. (1972). The relationship of self-stimulation to learning in autistic children. *Journal of Applied Behavior Analysis, 5,* 381–387.

KOEGEL, R.L., & RINCOVER, A. (1974). Treatment of psychotic children in a classroom environment: Learning in a large group. *Journal of Applied Behavior Analysis, 7,* 45–49.

KOHLBERG, L., & TURIEL, E. (1971). Moral development and moral education. In G. Lesser (Ed.), *Psychology and educational practice.* Glenview, IL: Scott, Foresman.

KOLSTOE, O. (1981). Career education for the handicapped: Opportunities for the '80s. *Career Development for Exceptional Individuals, 4,* 3–12.

KONOPKA, G. (1983). Adolescent suicide. *Exceptional Children, 49,* 390–394.

KOPPITZ, E.M. (1968). *Psychological evaluation of children's human figure drawings.* New York: Grune & Stratton.

KOZLOFF, M. (1975). *Educating children with learning and behavior problems.* New York: John Wiley.

KOZLOFF, M.A. (1973). *Reaching the autistic child: A parent training program.* Champaign, IL: Research Press.

KRAGER, J., & SAFER, D. (1974). Type and prevalence of medication used in the treatment of hyperactive children. *New England Journal of Medicine, 291,* 1118–1120.

KROTH, R.L. (1975). *Communicating with parents of exceptional children.* Denver, CO: Love.

KROTH, R.L., & SIMPSON, R.L. (1977). *Parent conferences as a teaching strategy.* Denver, CO: Love.

KUHN, D., & ANGELEV, J. (1976). An experimental study of the development of formal operational thought. *Child Development, 47,* 696–706.

KUNZELMANN, H., COHEN, M., HULTEN, W., MARTIN, G., & MINGO, A. (1970). *Precision teaching.* Seattle, WA: Special Child Publications.

LAMBERT, N.M., HARTSOUGH, C.S., & BOWER, E.M. (1979). *Pupil Behavior Rating Scale.* Monterey, CA: CTB/McGraw-Hill.

LAMKIN, J.S. (1980). *Getting started: Career education activities for exceptional students (K–9).* Reston, VA: The Council for Exceptional Children.

LANEVE, R.S. (1979). Mark Twain School: A therapeutic educational environment for emotionally disturbed students. *Behavioral Disorders, 4,* 183–192.

LA NUNZIATA, L.J., HILL, D.S., & KRAUSE, L.A. (1981). Teaching social skills in classrooms for behaviorally disordered students. *Behavioral Disorders, 6,* 238–246.

LARSEN, L.A. (1976). Deinstitutionalization. In M.A. Thomas (Ed.), *Hey, don't forget about me!* Reston, VA: The Council for Exceptional Children.

LATEN, S., & KATZ, G. (1975). *A theoretical model for assessment of adolescents: The ecological/behavioral approach.* Madison, WI: Madison Public Schools, Special Educational Services.

LAVOIE, R., & ADAMS, L. (1974). *The chosen ones: A study of the effects of children's conduct, sex, and facial attractiveness on teacher expectations.* (ERIC Document Reproduction Service No. ED 08873.)

LAWRENCE, T.S., & VELLEMAN, J.D. (1974). Correlates of drug use in a suburban high school. *Psychiatry, 37,* 129–136.

LEFKOWITZ, M.M., & BURTON, N. (1978). Childhood depression: A critique of the concept. *Psychological Bulletin, 85,* 716–726.

LEWIS, D.C. (1975). Drug education and prevention. In H.D. Thornburg (Ed.), *Contemporary adolescence: Readings* (2nd ed.). Monterey, CA: Brooks/Cole.

LEWIS, D.O., Shanok, S.S., & Pincus, J.H. (1979). Juvenile male sexual assaulters. *American Journal of Psychiatry, 136,* 1191–1196.

LINDSLEY, O. (1971). Precision teaching in perspective. *Teaching Exceptional Children, 3,* 114–119.

LIPPETT, R. (1968). Improving the socialization process. In J. Clausen (Ed.), *Socialization and society.* Boston: Little, Brown, 321–374.

LLOYD, J. (1980). Academic instruction and cognitive behavior modification: The need for attack strategy training. *Exceptional Education Quarterly, 1,* 53–63.

LOCKWOOD, A.L. (1978). The effects of values clarification and moral development on curricula of school-age subjects: A critical review of recent research. *Review of Educational Research, 48,* 325–364.

LONG, N.J., MORSE, W.C., & NEWMAN, R.G. (1965). *Conflict in the classroom: The education of emotionally disturbed children.* Belmont, CA: Wadsworth.

LONG, N.J., MORSE, W.C., & NEWMAN, R.G. (1976). Conceptual models of emotional disturbance. *Conflict in the classroom: The education of emotionally disturbed children* (3rd ed.). Belmont, CA: Wadsworth.

LONG, N.J., MORSE, W.C., & NEWMAN, R.G. (Eds.). (1980). Editors' commentary in *Conflict in the classroom: The education of emotionally disturbed children* (4th ed.). Belmont, CA: Wadsworth.

LONG, N.J., & NEWMAN, R.G. (1965). Managing surface behavior of children in school. In N.J. Long, W.C. Morse, & R.G. Newman (Eds.), *Conflict in the classroom: The education of emotionally disturbed children.* Belmont, CA: Wadsworth.

LOVAAS, O.I. (1966). Program for establishment of speech in schizophrenic and autistic children. In J.K. Wing (Ed.), *Early childhood autism: Clinical, educational, and social aspects.* London: Pergamon Press.

LOVAAS, O.I. (1977). *The autistic child.* New York: Irvington.

LOVAAS, O.I., KOEGEL, R., SIMMONS, J., & STEVENS, J. (1972). Some generalizations and follow up measures on autistic children in behavior therapy. *Journal of Applied Behavior Analysis, 34,* 17–23.

LOVAAS, O.I., SCHAEFFER, B., & SIMMONS, J.A. (1965). Experimental studies in childhood schizophrenia: Building social behaviors by use of electric shock. *Journal of Experimental Studies in Personality, 1,* 99–109.

LOVAAS, O.I., & SIMMONS, J. (1969). Manipulation of self-destruction in three retarded children. *Journal of Applied Behavior Analysis, 2,* 143–157.

LOVITT, T.C. (1975). Applied behavior analysis and learning disabilities. Part I: Characteristics of ABA, general recommendations, and methodological limitations. *Journal of Learning Disabilities, 8,* 432–443.

LOW, B. (1928). *Psychoanalysis and education.* New York: Harcourt Brace Jovanovich.

MACCOBY, E. (1966). *The development of sex differences.* Stanford, CA: Stanford University Press.

MACK, J.H. (1980). *An analysis of state definitions of severely emotionally disturbed.* Reston, VA: Council for Exceptional Children Policy Research Center. (ERIC Document Reproduction Service No. ED 201 135.)

MAHLER, M.S. (1952). On child psychosis and schizophrenia. *Psychoanalytic Studies of the Child, 7,* 286–305.

MAIN, G.C., & MUNRO, B.C. (1977). A token reinforcement program in a public junior-high school. *Journal of Applied Behavior Analysis, 9,* 25–30.

MARCOTT-RADKE, A. (1981). A multipurpose communication system: Modified for the autistic total communication (M.A.T.C.). In J.E. Gilliam (Ed.), *Autism: Diagnosis, instruction, management, and research.* Springfield, IL: Chas. C Thomas.

MARSHALL, A.E., & HEWARD, W.L. (1979). Teaching self-management to incarcerated youth. *Behavioral Disorders, 4,* 215–226.

MARTIN, B. (1975). Parent-child relations. In F.D. Horowitz (Ed.), *Review of child development research* (Vol. 4). Chicago: University of Chicago Press.

MASLOW, A.H. (1954). *Motivation and personality.* New York: Harper & Row.

MASLOW, A.H. (1967). A theory of metamotivation: The biological rooting of the value life. *Journal of Humanistic Psychology, 7,* 93–127.

MATTES, J.A. (1983). The Feingold diet: A current reappraisal. *Journal of Learning Disabilities, 16,* 319–323.

McCARTHY, J.M., & PARASKEVOPOULOS, J. (1969). Behavior patterns of learning disabled, emotionally disturbed, and average children. *Exceptional Children, 36,* 69–74.

McDOWELL, R.L. (1981). Adolescence. In G. Brown, R.L. McDowell, & J. Smith (Eds.), *Educating adolescents with behavior disorders.* Columbus, OH: Chas. E. Merrill.

McDOWELL, R.L., & BROWN, G.B. (1978). The emotionally disturbed adolescent: Development of program alternatives in secondary education. *Focus on Exceptional Children, 10,* 1–15.

McGHIE, A., & CHAPMAN, J. (1961). Disorders of attention and perception in early schizophrenia. *British Journal of Medical Psychology, 34,* 103–116.

McGINNIS, E. (1982). An individualized curriculum for children and youth with autism. In C.R. Smith, J.P. Grimes, & J.J. Freilinger (Eds.), *Autism: Programmatic considerations.* Des Moines, IA: State Department of Public Instruction.

McKENZIE, H.S., ENGER, A.N. KNIGHT, M.F., PERELMAN, P.F., SCHNEIDER, B.M., and GARVIN, J.S. (1970). Training consulting teachers to assist elementary teachers in the management of handicapped children. *Exceptional Children, 37,* 137–143.

McKINNEY, J.A. (1975). *The development and implementation of a tutorial program for parents to improve reading and mathematics achievement of their children.* (ERIC Document Reproduction Service No. ED 113 703.)

McKINNON, J.W. (1976). The college student and formal operations. In J.W. Renner, D.G. Stafford, A.E. Lawson, J.W. McKinnon, F.E. Friot, & D.H. Kellogg, *Research, teaching, and learning with the Piaget model.* Norman, OK: University of Oklahoma Press.

McLAUGHLIN, T.F. (1976). Self-control in the classroom. *Review of Educational Research, 46,* 631–663.

McLEAN, J.E., & SNYDER-McLEAN, L.K. (1982). Communication: New perspectives on assessment and treatment. In C.R. Smith, J.P. Grimes, & J.J. Freilinger (Eds.), *Autism: Programmatic considerations.* Des Moines, IA: State Department of Public Instruction.

McLOUGHLIN, J.A., & LEWIS, R.B. (1981). *Assessing special students.* Columbus, OH: Chas. E. Merrill.

MEDWAY, F.J., & SMITH, R.C. (1978). An examination of contemporary elementary school affective education programs. *Psychology in the Schools, 15,* 260–269.

MEEHL, P. (1969). Schizotaxia, schizotypy, schizophrenia. In A. Buss (Ed.), *Theories of schizophrenia.* New York: Lieber-Atherton, 21–46.

MEICHENBAUM, D., & CAMERON, R. (1974). The clinical potential of modifying what clients say to themselves. In M.J. Mahoney & C.E. Thoresen (Eds.), *Self-control: Power to the person.* Monterey, CA: Brooks/Cole.

MEICHENBAUM, D., & GOODMAN, J. (1971). Training impulsive children to talk to themselves: A means of developing self-control. *Journal of Abnormal Child Psychology, 77,* 115–126.

MESSER, S. (1970). Reflection-impulsivity: Stability and school failure. *Journal of Educational Psychology, 61,* 487–490.

MILLER, J.P. (1975). Suicide and adolescence. *Adolescence, 10,* 11–24.

MILLER, L.C. (1980). Dimensions of adolescent psychopathology. *Journal of Abnormal Child Psychology, 8,* 161–173.

MILLER, T., & SABATINO, D. (1978). The evaluation of the teacher consultant model as an approach to mainstreaming. *Exceptional Children, 45,* 86–91.

MILLON, T., & MILLON, R. (1974). *Abnormal behavior and personality*. Philadelphia: Saunders.

MINUCHIN, S. (1970). The use of an ecological framework in the treatment of a child. In J.E. Anthony & C. Koupernik (Eds.), *The child in his family*. New York: John Wiley.

MIZE, G. (1977). *The influence of increased parental involvement in the educational process of their children*. Technical Report No. 418, Wisconsin University. (ERIC Document Reproduction Service No. ED 151 661.)

MONTGOMERY, M.D. (1982). Educational services for emotionally disturbed children. In J.L. Paul & B.C. Epanchin (Eds.), *Emotional disturbance in children: Theories and methods for teachers*. Columbus, OH: Chas. E. Merrill.

MOONEY, C., & ALGOZZINE, R. (1978). A comparison of the disturbingness of behaviors related to learning disability and emotional disturbance. *Journal of Abnormal Child Psychology, 6*, 401–406.

MORSE, W.C. (1965). The crisis teacher. In N.J. Long, W.C. Morse, & R.G. Newman (Eds.), *Conflict in the classroom: The education of emotionally disturbed children*. Belmont, CA: Wadsworth.

MORSE, W.C. (1969a). Preparing to teach the disturbed adolescent. In H.W. Harshman (Ed.), *Educating the emotionally disturbed: A book of readings*. New York: Thomas Y. Crowell.

MORSE, W.C. (1969b). Training teachers in life space interviewing. In H. Dupont (Ed.), *Educating emotionally disturbed children: Readings*. New York: Holt, Rinehart & Winston.

MORSE, W.C. (1980). The crisis or helping teacher. In N.J. Long, W.C. Morse, & R.G. Newman (Eds.), *Conflict in the classroom: The education of emotionally disturbed children* (4th ed.). Belmont, CA: Wadsworth.

MORSE, W.C. (1982). Reactions to certain of Rhodes' predictions. *Behavioral Disorders, 7*, 249–254.

MORSE, W.C., CUTLER, R.L., & FINK, A.H. (1964). *Public school classes for the emotionally handicapped: A research analysis*. Reston, VA: The Council for Exceptional Children.

MOTTO, J.J., & WILKINS, G.S. (1968). Educational achievement of institutionalized emotionally disturbed children. *Journal of Educational Research, 61*, 218–221.

MURRAY, H.A. (1943). *Thematic Apperception Test*. Cambridge: Harvard University Press.

MYERS, J., & DEIBERT, A. (1971). Reduction of self-abusive behavior in a blind child by using a feeding response. *Journal of Behavior Therapy and Experimental Psychiatry, 2*, 141–144.

MYERS, P.I., & HAMMILL, D.D. (1982). *Learning disabilities: Basic concepts, assessment practices, and instructional strategies*. Austin, TX: Pro-Ed.

NATIONAL INSTITUTE ON DRUG ABUSE. (1980). *Review of evidence on effects of marijuana use*. Washington, DC: U. S. Government Printing Office.

NEEL, R. (1979). Autism: Symptoms in search of a syndrome. In F. Wood & C. Lakin (Eds.), *Disturbing, disordered, or disturbed?* Minneapolis: Department of Psychoeducational Studies, University of Minnesota.

NEIL, A.S. (1960). *Summerhill*. New York: Hart.

NEIMARK, E.D. (1975). Intellectual development during adolescence. In F.D. Horowitz (Ed.), *Review of child development research* (Vol. 4). Chicago: University of Chicago Press.

NELSON, C.M., & KAUFFMAN, J.M. (1977). Educational programming for secondary school age delinquent and maladjusted pupils. *Behavioral Disorders, 2*, 102–113.

NEWCOMER, P.L. (1980). *Understanding and teaching emotionally disturbed children*. Boston: Allyn & Bacon.

NEWMAN, R.G. (1980). Treatment groups. In N.J. Long, W.C. Morse, & R.G. Newman (Eds.), *Conflict in the classroom: The education of emotionally disturbed children* (4th ed.). Belmont, CA: Wadsworth.

NEWMAN, R., WHORTON, D., & SIMPSON, R.L. (1977). The modification of self-stimulatory verbalizations in an autistic child through the use of an overcorrection procedure. *AAESPH Review, 2*, 157–163.

NIAID STUDY GROUP. (1981). *Sexually transmitted diseases: 1980 status report*. Washington, DC: U. S. Government Printing Office (NIH Publications No. 81–2213).

NUTRITION FOUNDATION (1975). *National Advisory Committee on Hyperkinesis and Food Additives, Report to the Nutrition Foundation*, New York.

O'LEARY, K.D. (1975). Behavioral assessment: An observational slant. In R.A. Weinberg &

F.H. Wood (Eds.), *Observation of pupils and teachers in mainstream and special education settings: Alternative strategies.* Reston, VA: The Council for Exceptional Children.

O'LEARY, K.D., & DRABMAN, R. (1971). Token reinforcement programs in the classroom: A review. *Psychological Bulletin, 75,* 379–398.

O'LEARY, S., & SCHNEIDER, M. (1977). Special class placement for conduct problem children. *Exceptional Children, 44,* 24–31.

OLSON, J., & MERCER, C.D. (1981). Public school programs for emotionally handicapped students. In R. Algozzine, R. Schmid, & C.D. Mercer (Eds.), *Childhood behavior disorders.* Rockville, MD: Aspen.

ORNITZ, E. (1978). Neurophysiologic studies. In M. Rutter & E. Schopler (Eds.), *Autism: A reappraisal of concepts and treatment.* New York: Plenum.

ORNITZ, E.M., & RITVO, E. (1968). Neurophysiological mechanisms underlying perceptual constancy in autistic and schizophrenic children. *Archives of General Psychiatry, 19,* 22–27.

PALARDY, J. (1969). What teachers believe—what children achieve. *Elementary School Journal, 69,* 370–374.

PARISH, T., DYCK, N., & KAPPES, B. (1979). Stereotypes concerning normal and handicapped children. *The Journal of Psychology, 102,* 63–70.

PATTERSON, G.R. (1975). The aggressive child: Victim and architect of a coercive system. In E.J. Mash, L.A. Hamerlynck, & L.C. Handy (Eds.), *Behavior modification in families.* New York: Brunner/Mazel.

PATTERSON, G.R., & COBB, J.A. (1973). Stimulus control for classes of noxious behavior. In J.S. Knutson (Ed.), *The control of aggression: Implications from basic research.* Chicago: Aldine.

PAULING, L. (1968). Orthomolecular psychiatry. *Science, 160,* 265–271.

PECK, H., RABINOVITCH, R., & CRAMER, J. (1969). A treatment program for parents of schizophrenic children. *American Journal of Orthopsychiatry, 19,* 592–598.

PETERS, L.J. (1965). *Prescriptive teaching.* New York: McGraw-Hill.

PETERSON, R.L. (1982). Theory z child variance. *Behavioral Disorders, 7,* 243–249.

PHILLIP PRATT V. BOARD OF EDUCATION OF FREDERICK COUNTY, 501 F. Supp. 232, D.D. Md. (1980).

PIAGET, J. (1972). Intellectual evolution from adolescence to adulthood. *Human Development, 15,* 1–12.

PIERS, E., & HARRIS, D. (1969). *The Piers-Harris Children's Self-concept Scale.* Nashville: Counselor Recordings and Tests.

POWERS, H.W.S., Jr. (1977). A reply to Robert L. Sieben's critique. *Academic Therapy, 2,* 197–203.

PREMACK, D. (1965). Reinforcement theory. In D. Levine (Ed.), *Nebraska Symposium on Motivation.* Lincoln: University of Nebraska Press.

QUAY, H.C. (1966). Personality patterns in pre-adolescent delinquent boys. *Educational and Psychological Measurement, 26,* 99–110.

QUAY, H.C. (1972). Patterns of aggression, withdrawal and immaturity. In H.C. Quay & J.S. Werry (Eds.), *Psychopathological disorders of childhood.* New York: John Wiley.

QUAY, H.C. (1975). Classification in the treatment of delinquency and antisocial behavior. In N. Hobbs (Ed.), *Issues in the classification of children* (Vol. 1). San Francisco: Jossey-Bass.

QUAY, H.C., MORSE, W.C., & CUTLER, R.L. (1966). Personality patterns of pupils in classrooms for the emotionally disturbed. *Exceptional Children, 32,* 297–301.

QUAY, H.C., & PARSONS, L.B. (1970). *The differential behavioral classification of the juvenile offender.* Morgantown, WV: Robert F. Kennedy Youth Center.

QUAY, H.C., & PETERSON, D.R. (1967). Manual for the Behavior Problem Checklist. Champaign, IL: Children's Research Center. Mimeographed.

QUAY, H.C., & PETERSON, D.R. (1983). *Revised Behavior Problem Checklist.* Coral Gables, FL: University of Miami.

RAAZ, N. (1982). Working with parents of students with autism. In C.R. Smith, J.P. Grimes, & J.J. Freilinger (Eds.), *Autism: Programmatic considerations.* Des Moines, IA: Iowa Department of Public Instruction.

RABKIN, L., & SUCHOSKI, J. (1967). Teachers' views of mental illness: A study of attitudes and information. *Journal of Teacher Education, 18,* 36–41.

RANDALL, D., & WONG, M.R. (1976). Drug education: A review. *Journal of Drug Education, 6,* 1–21.

RANKIN, P.T. (1967). *The relationship between parent behavior and achievement of inner city elementary school children.* (ERIC Document Reproduction Service No. ED 017 550.)

RAPP, D.J. (1978). Does diet affect hyperactivity? *Journal of Learning Disorders, 11,* 383–389.

REDL, F. (1959a). The concept of a therapeutic milieu. *American Journal of Orthopsychiatry, 29,* 721–734.

REDL, F. (1959b). The concept of the life space interview. *American Journal of Orthopsychiatry, 29,* 1–18.

REDL, F. (1965). The concept of the life space interview. In N.J. Long, W.C. Morse, & R.G. Newman (Eds.), *Conflict in the classroom: The education of emotionally disturbed children.* Belmont, CA: Wadsworth.

REDL, F. (1966). *When we deal with children.* New York: Free Press.

REDL, F., & WINEMAN, D. (1957). *The aggressive child.* New York: Free Press.

REEVE, R., & KAUFFMAN, J. (1978). The behavior disordered. In N.G. Haring (Ed.), *Behavior of exceptional children* (2nd ed.). Columbus, OH: Chas. E. Merrill.

REGAN, M.K., JONES, C., HOLZSCHUH, R., & SIMPSON, R.L. (1982). *Autism teacher training program: Vocational training for autistic children/youth.* Kansas City, KS: University of Kansas Medical Center.

REILLY, M.J., IMBER, S.C., & CREMINS, J. (1978). *The effects of life space interviews on social behaviors of junior high special needs students.* Paper presented at 56th International Council for Exceptional Children, Kansas City, MO.

REINERT, H.R. (1976). *Children in conflict.* St. Louis: C.V. Mosby.

REINERT, H.R. (1980). *Children in conflict* (2nd ed.). St. Louis: C.V. Mosby.

RENNER, J.W., & STAFFORD, D.G. (1976). The operational levels of secondary school students. In J.W. Renner, D.G. Stafford, A.E. Lawson, J.W. McKinnon, F.E. Friot, & D.H. Kellogg, *Research, teaching, and learning with the Piaget model.* Norman, OK: University of Oklahoma Press.

REPP, A.C., & DEITZ, S.M. (1974). Reducing aggressive and self-injurious behavior of institutionalized children through reinforcement of other behaviors. *Journal of Applied Behavior Analysis, 7,* 313–325.

REPP, A.C., DEITZ, S.M., & SPEIR, N.C. (1974). Reducing stereotypic responding of retarded persons by the differential reinforcement of other behavior. *American Journal of Mental Deficiency, 79,* 279–284.

REYNOLDS, M.C. (1962). Framework for considering some issues in special education. *Exceptional Children, 28,* 367–370.

REZMIERSKI, V., & KOTRE, J. (1974). A limited review of theory of the psychodynamic model. In W.C. Rhodes & M.L. Tracy (Eds.), *A study of child variance* (Vol. 1). Ann Arbor, MI: The University of Michigan Press.

RHODES, W.C. (1967). The disturbing child: A problem of ecological management. *Exceptional Children, 33,* 449–455.

RHODES, W.C. (1970). A community participation analysis of emotional disturbance. *Exceptional Children, 36,* 309–314.

RHODES, W.C. (1979). Beyond theory and practice: Implications in programming for children with emotional disabilities. *Iowa Perspectives.* Iowa Department of Public Instruction. *4,* 1–6.

RHODES, W.C. (1982). The future. *Behavioral Disorders, 7,* 226–234.

RHODES, W.C., & TRACY, M.L. (Eds.) (1974). *A study of child variance* (3 vols.). Ann Arbor, MI: The University of Michigan Press.

RICH, D., VAN DIEN, J., & MATTOX, B. (1979). *Families as educators of their own children.* Washington, DC: Home and School Institute.

RICH, H.L. (1979). Classroom interaction patterns among teachers and emotionally disturbed students. *Exceptional Child, 26,* 4–40.

RIMLAND, B. (1964). *Infantile autism: The syndrome and its implications for a neural theory of behavior.* Englewood Cliffs, NJ: Prentice-Hall.

RIMLAND, B. (1971). The effect of high dosage levels of certain vitamins on the behavior of children with severe mental disorders. In D.R. Hawkins and L. Pauling (Eds.), *Orthomolecular psychiatry.* San Francisco: W.H. Freeman & Company Publishers.

RIMLAND, B. (1983). The Feingold diet: An assessment of the reviews by Mattes, by Kavale and Forness and others. *Journal of Learning Disabilities, 16*, 331–333.

RIMLAND, B., CALLAWAY, E., & DREYFUS, P. (1978). The effect of high doses of vitamin B₆ on autistic children: A double-blind crossover study. *American Journal of Psychiatry, 135*, 472–475.

RISLEY, T., & WOLF, M. (1967). Establishing functional speech in echolalic children. *Behavior Research and Therapy, 5*, 73–88.

RISLEY, T.R. (1968). The effects and side effects of punishing the autistic behaviors of a deviant child. *Journal of Applied Behavior Analysis, 1*, 21–34.

RIST, R. (1970). Student social class and teacher expectation: The self-fulfilling prophecy in ghetto education. *Harvard Educational Review, 40*, 411–451.

RITVO, E., & FREEMAN, B.J. (1977). National Society for Autistic Children: Definition of autism. *Journal of Pediatric Psychology, 4*, 146–148.

RITVO, E., RAHM, K., YUWILER, A., FREEMAN, B.J., & GELLER, E. (1978). Biochemical and hematologic studies: A critical review. In M. Rutter & E. Schopler (Eds.), *Autism: A reappraisal of concepts and treatment*. New York: Plenum.

ROBBINS, M., & GLASS, G. (1969). The Doman-Delacato rationale: A critical analysis. In J. Hellmuth (Ed.), *Educational therapy* (Vol. 2). Seattle, WA: Special Child Publications.

ROBIN, A.L., ARMEL, S., & O'LEARY, K.D. (1975). The effects of self-instruction on writing deficiencies. *Behavior Therapy, 6*, 178–187.

ROBINSON, J.P., & SHAVER, P.R. (1973). *Measures of social psychological attitudes* (2nd ed.). Ann Arbor, MI: The University of Michigan Press.

ROGERS, C. (1959). A theory of therapy, personality, and interpersonal relationships, as developed in the client-centered framework. In S. Kock (Ed.), *Psychology: A study of a science* (Vol. 3). New York: McGraw-Hill.

ROGERS, C. (1969). *Freedom to learn*. Columbus, OH: Chas. E. Merrill.

ROHRKEMPER, M.M., & BROPHY, J.E. (April 1979). *Classroom strategy study: Investigating teacher strategies with problem students*. Paper presented at the annual meeting of the American Educational Research Association, San Francisco.

RORSCHACH, H. (1921). *Psychodiagnostics: A diagnostic test based on perception*. New York: Grune & Stratton.

ROSE, T. (1978). The functional relationship between artificial food colors and hyperactivity. *Journal of Applied Behavior Analysis, 11*, 439–446.

ROSENBLATT, R. (1980, August 18). New York, N.Y., It's a . . . *Time Magazine*, p. 19.

ROSENSTOCK, H.A., & VINCENT, K.R. (1979). Parental involvement as a prerequisite for successful adolescent therapy. *Journal of Clinical Psychiatry, 40*, 132–134.

ROSS, M., & SALVIA, J. (1975). Attractiveness as a biasing factor in teacher judgments. *American Journal of Mental Deficiency, 80*, 96–98.

ROTTER, J.B., & RAFFERTY, J.E. (1950). *The Rotter Incomplete Sentences Blank*. New York: The Psychological Corp.

RUBIN, R.A., & BALOW, B. (1971). Learning and behavior disorders: A longitudinal study. *Exceptional Children, 38*, 293–299.

RUBIN, R.A., & BALOW, B. (1978). Prevalence of teacher identified behavior problems: A longitudinal study. *Exceptional Children, 45*, 102–111.

RUBIN, T.I. (1962). *Lisa & David/Jordi*. New York: Random House.

RUSS, D.F. (1974). A review of learning and behavior theory as it relates to emotional disturbance in children. In W. Rhodes & M.L. Tracy (Eds.), *A study of child variance* (Vol. 1). Ann Arbor, MI: The University of Michigan Press.

RUTTER, M. (1965). The influence of organic and emotional factors on the origins, nature, and outcome of childhood psychosis. *Developmental Medicine and Child Neurology, 7*, 518–528.

RUTTER, M. (1978). Language disorder and infantile autism. In M. Rutter & E. Schopler (Eds.), *Autism: A reappraisal of concepts and treatment*. New York: Plenum.

RUTTER, M., BARTAK, L., & NEWMAN, S. (1971). Autism: A central disorder of cognition and language? In M. Rutter (Ed.), *Infantile autism: Concepts, characteristics, and treatment*. London: Churchill.

S-1 v. TURLINGTON, 635 F. Supp. 342, rev'd. No. 79-2742, 5th Cir. (January 26, 1981).

SAFER, D.J. (1982). Varieties and levels of interventions with disruptive adolescents. In D.J. Safer (Ed.), *School programs for disruptive adolescents*. Baltimore: University Park Press.

SAFER, D.J., & ALLEN, R.P. (1976). *Hyperactive children: Diagnosis and management.* Baltimore: University Park Press.

SAFER, D.J., & HEATON, R.C. (1982). Characteristics, school patterns, and behavioral outcomes of seriously disruptive junior high school students. In D.J. Safer (Ed.), *School programs for disruptive adolescents.* Baltimore: University Park Press.

SAGOR, M. (1974). Biological bases of childhood behavior disorders. In W.C. Rhodes & M.L. Tracy (Eds.), *A study of child variance* (Vol. 1). Ann Arbor, MI: University of Michigan Press.

SAILOR, W., & GUESS, D. (1983). *Severely handicapped students: An instructional design.* Boston: Houghton Mifflin.

SALVAGNE, B., SCHOLLENBERGER, G., & STOKES, K. (1974). *Research into the needs of parents of autistic children as perceived by the parents.* Unpublished manuscript, Cambridge, MA: Harvard University.

SALVIA, J., & YSSELDYKE, J.E. (1981). *Assessment in special and remedial education* (2nd ed.). Boston: Houghton Mifflin.

SANTOGROSSI, D.A., O'LEARY, K.D., ROMANCZYK, R.G., & KAUFMAN, K.F. (1973). Self-evaluation by adolescents in a psychiatric hospital training program. *Journal of Applied Behavior Analysis, 6,* 277–287.

SCHAEFER, C.E., & MILLMAN, H.L. (1977). *Therapies for children.* San Francisco: Jossey-Bass.

SCHEFF, T.J. (1966). *Being mentally ill: A sociological theory.* Chicago: Aldine.

SCHLECHTY, P.C., & PAUL, J.L. (1982). Sociological theory and practice. In J.L. Paul & B.C. Epanchin (Eds.), *Emotional disturbance in children.* Columbus, OH: Chas. E. Merrill.

SCHLOSSER, L., & ALGOZZINE, B. (1979). The disturbing child: He or she? *The Alberta Journal of Educational Research, 25,* 30–36.

SCHMID, R., & SLADE, D. (1981). Adolescent programs. In R. Algozzine, R. Schmid, & C.D. Mercer (Eds.), *Childhood behavior disorders: Applied research and educational practice.* Rockville, MD: Aspen.

SCHREIBER, D. (1963). Juvenile delinquency and the school dropout problem. *Federal Probation, 27,* 15–19.

SCHULTZ, E., SALVIA, J., & FEINN, J. (1974). Prevalence of behavioral symptoms in rural elementary school children. *Journal of Abnormal Child Psychology, 1,* 17–24.

SELIGMAN, M.E.P. (1975). *Helplessness: On depression, development, and death.* San Francisco: W.H. Freeman & Company Publishers.

SHORES, R.E. (1981). *Environmental consistency.* Project S.E.D., Teacher Training Module. Austin, TX: Education Service Center, Region XIII.

SHOTEL, J., IANO, R., & McGETTIGAN, J. (1972). Teacher attitudes associated with the integration of handicapped children. *Exceptional Children, 39,* 677–683.

SIEBEN, R.L. (1977). Controversial medical treatments of learning disabilities. *Academic Therapy, 2,* 133–147.

SIEBEN, R.L. (1983). Medical treatment of learning problems: A critique. In *Interdisciplinary voices in learning disabilities and remedial education.* Society for Learning Disabilities and Remedial Education. Austin, TX: Pro-Ed.

SIGEL, I. (1960). The application of projective techniques in research with children. In A.I. Rabin & M.R. Haworth (Eds.), *Projective techniques with children.* New York: Grune & Stratton.

SILBERMAN, M.L. (1969). Behavioral expression of teachers' attitudes toward elementary school students. *Journal of Educational Psychology, 60,* 402–407.

SILBERMAN, M.L. (1971). Teachers' attitudes and actions toward their students. In M.L. Silberman (Ed.), *The experience of schooling.* New York: Holt, Rinehart & Winston.

SIMON, S.B., HOWE, L.W., & KIRSCHENBAUM, H. (1978). *Values clarification* (Rev. ed.). New York: Hart.

SIMPSON, R.L. (1982). *Conferencing parents of exceptional children.* Rockville, MD: Aspen.

SIMPSON, R.L., & COMBS, N.N. (1978). *Parenting the exceptional child: A workshop manual.* (Developed under federal contract 300–75–0309 with the Bureau of Education for the Handicapped) Washington, DC: U. S. Office of Education, Department of Health, Education and Welfare.

SKINNER, B.F. (1953). *Science and human behavior.* New York: Macmillan.

SMITH, C.R. (1979). Identification of emotionally disabled pupils: An overview. In *The identi-*

fication of emotionally disabled pupils: Data and decision making. Des Moines, IA: Iowa Department of Public Instruction.

SMITH, M.B. (1970). To educate children effectively . . . we must involve parents. *Instructor, 80,* 118–121.

SMITH, M.L., & GLASS, G.V. (1977). Meta-analysis of psychotherapy outcome studies. *American Psychologist, 32,* 752–760.

SOCIAL RESEARCH GROUP. (1975). *The status of children—1975.* Washington, DC: George Washington University.

SORENSON, R.C. (1973). *Adolescent sexuality in contemporary America.* New York: World Publishing.

SPIVACK, G., & SPOTTS, J. (1966). *The Devereux Child Behavior Rating Scale.* Devon, PA: Devereux Foundation.

SPIVACK, G., SPOTTS, J., HAIMES, P.E. (1967). *The Devereux Adolescent Behavior Rating Scale.* Devon, PA: Devereux Foundation.

SPIVACK, G., & SWIFT, M. (1967). *The Devereux Elementary School Behavior Rating Scale.* Devon, PA: Devereux Foundation.

SPRING, C., & SANDOVAL, J. (1976). Food additives and hyperkinesis: A critical evaluation of the evidence. *Journal of Learning Disabilities, 9,* 560–569.

SROUFE, L.A. (1975). Drug treatment of children with behavior problems. In F.D. Horowitz (Ed.), *Review of child development research* (Vol. 4). Chicago: University of Chicago Press.

STAINBACK, S., & STAINBACK, W. (1980). *Educating children with severe maladaptive behaviors.* New York: Grune & Stratton.

STEPHENS, T.M. (1977). *Teaching skills to children with learning and behavior disorders.* Columbus, OH: Chas. E. Merrill.

STEPHENS, T.M. (1978). *Social skills in the classroom.* Columbus, OH: Cedars Press.

STEVENS, D. (1973). *The Self-Control Curriculum Project, 1972–1973.* Report to the Eugene and Agnes Meyer Foundation, Washington, DC.

STEVENS-LONG, J. (1973). The effects of behavioral context on some aspects of adult disciplinary practice and affect. *Child Development, 44,* 476–484.

STOKES, T.F., & BAER, D.M. (1977). An implicit technology of generalization. *Journal of Applied Behavior Analysis, 10,* 349–368.

STONE, F., & ROWLEY, V.N. (1964). Educational disability in emotionally disturbed children. *Exceptional Children, 30,* 423–426.

STRAIN, P.S., KERR, M.M., & RAGLAND, E.U. (1979). Effects of peer-mediated social initiations and prompting/reinforcement procedures in social behavior of autistic children. *Journal of Autism and Developmental Disorders, 9,* 41–54.

STRAUSS, A.A., & LEHTINEN, L.E. (1947). *Psychopathology and education of the brain-injured child.* New York: Grune & Stratton.

STRUB, R.L., & BLACK, F.W. (1977). *The mental status examination in neurology.* Philadelphia: F.A. Davis.

SULLIVAN, R.C. (1976). The role of the parent. In M.A. Thomas (Ed.), *Hey, don't forget about me!* Reston, VA: The Council for Exceptional Children.

SULLIVAN, R.C. (1979). The burnout syndrome. *Journal of Autism and Developmental Disorders, 1,* 113–114.

SZASZ, T. (1961). *The myth of mental illness.* New York: Hoeber-Harber.

SZUREK, S. (1956). Childhood schizophrenia symposium: Psychotic episodes and psychotic maldevelopment. *American Journal of Orthopsychiatry, 25,* 519.

TANNER, B.A., & ZEILER, M. (1975). Punishment of self-injurious behavior using aromatic ammonia as the aversive stimulus. *Journal of Applied Behavior Analysis, 8,* 53–57.

TATE, B.G., & BAROFF, G.S. (1966). Aversive control of self-injurious behavior in a psychotic boy. *Behavior Research and Therapy, 4,* 281–287.

TELFORD, C.W., & SAWREY, J.M. (1981). *The exceptional individual* (4th ed.). Englewood Cliffs, NJ: Prentice-Hall.

TERMAN, L.M., & MERRILL, M.A. (1972). *Stanford-Binet Intelligence Scale.* Boston: Houghton Mifflin.

THOMAS, A., & CHESS, S. (1977). *Temperament and development.* New York: Brunner/Mazel.

THOMAS, A., CHESS, S., & BIRCH, H. (1969). *Temperament and behavior disorders in children.* New York: New York University Press.

THOMPSON, J.M., & SONES, R.A. (1973). *Education Apperception Test.* Los Angeles: Western Psychological Services.

THORNDIKE, E.L. (1932). *The fundamentals of learning.* New York: Teacher's College.

THURLOW, M.L., & YSSELDYKE, J.E. (1980). *Factors influential on the psychoeducational decisions reached by teams of educators* (Research Report No. 25). Minneapolis: University of Minnesota Institute for Research on Learning Disabilities.

TOWNS, P. (1981). *Educating disturbed adolescents: Theory and practice.* New York: Grune & Stratton.

TREVOR, W. (March 1975). *Teacher discrimination and self-fulfilling prophecies.* Paper presented at the annual meeting of the American Educational Research Association.

TRIPPE, M. (1966). *Educational therapy.* Seattle, WA: Special Child Publications.

TURNBULL, H.R. (July 1977). Recent federal legislation on educating the handicapped. *School Law Bulletin,* Chapel Hill, NC: Institute of Government, University of North Carolina, Volume 3, No. 3.

U. S. BUREAU OF THE CENSUS. (1980). *Statistical abstract of the United States: 1980* (101st ed.). Washington, DC: U. S. Government Printing Office.

U. S. SENATE SUBCOMMITTEE TO INVESTIGATE JUVENILE DELINQUENCY. (1975). *Our nation's schools.* Washington, DC: U. S. Government Printing Office.

USHAKOV, G.K. (1971). Anorexia nervosa. In J.G. Howells (Ed.), *Modern perspectives in adolescent psychiatry.* New York: Brunner/Mazel.

VAAC, N.A., & KIRST, N. (1977). Emotionally disturbed children and regular classroom teachers. *Elementary School Journal, 77,* 309–317.

VADEN, T.B. (1972). *An evaluation of a psychoeducational approach to the concept of self-control.* Unpublished doctoral dissertation, University of Virginia.

VANDERKAMP, H. (1966). A biochemical abnormality in schizophrenia involving absorbic acid. *International Journal of Neuropsychiatry, 2,* 204–206.

VAN HASSELT, V.B., HERSEN, M., WHITEHILL, M.D., & BELLACK, A.S. (1979). Social skills assessment and training for children: An evaluative review. *Behavior Research and Therapy, 17,* 413–437.

VAN PRAAG, H.M. (1977). The vulnerable brain: Biological factors in the diagnosis and treatment of depression. In V.M. Rakoff, H.C. Stancer, & H.B. Kedward (Eds.), *Psychiatric diagnosis.* New York: Brunner/Mazel.

VARNI, J.W., LOVAAS, O.I., KOEGEL, R.L., & EVERETT, N.L. (1979). An analysis of observational learning in autistic and normal children. *Journal of Abnormal Child Psychology, 7,* 31–43.

WALKER, H.M. (1979). *The acting-out child: Coping with classroom disruption.* Boston: Allyn & Bacon.

WALKER, H.M., & BUCKLEY, N.K. (1973). Teacher attention to appropriate and inappropriate classroom behavior: An individual case study. *Focus on Exceptional Children, 5,* 5–11.

WALKER, H.M., & BUCKLEY, N.K. (1974). *Token reinforcement techniques: Classroom applications for the hard to teach child.* Eugene, OR: E-B Press.

WALKER, H.M., MCCONNELL, S., HOLMES, D., TODIS, B., WALKER, J., & GOLDEN, N. (1983). *The Walker Social Skills Curriculum: The ACCEPTS Program.* Austin, TX: Pro-Ed.

WALKER, H.M., & RANKIN, R. (1980). Assessment for Integration into Mainstream Settings (AIMS). Social Behavior Survival Project, Center on Human Development, Eugene, OR.

WALKER, J.E., & SHEA, T.M. (1976). *Behavior modification: A practical approach for educators.* St. Louis: C.V. Mosby.

WALLACE, G., & LARSEN, S.C. (1978). *Educational assessment of learning problems: Testing for teaching.* Boston: Allyn & Bacon.

WATSON, J.B., & RAYNOR, R. (1920). Conditioned emotional reactions. *Journal of Experimental Psychology, 3,* 1–14.

WEBBER, J., & GILLIAM, J.E. (1981). *Working with parents.* Project S.E.D. Teacher Training Module. Austin, TX: Education Service Center, Region XIII.

WECHSLER, D. (1974). *Wechsler Intelligence Scale for Children—Revised.* New York: Psychological Corp.

WEINER, I.B. (1980). Psychopathology in adolescence. In J. Adelson (Ed.), *Handbook of adolescent psychology.* New York: John Wiley.

WEINSTEIN, G., & FANTINI, M.D. (1970). *Toward humanistic education: A curriculum of affect.* New York: Praeger.

WENZ, F.V. (1979). Self-injury behavior, economic status and the family anomie syndrome among adolescents. *Adolescence, 14,* 387–398.

WERRY, J., & QUAY, H.C. (1971). The prevalence of behavior symptoms in younger elementary school children. *American Journal of Orthopsychiatry, 41,* 136–143.

WHELAN, E. (1978). *Preventing cancer.* New York: W.W. Norton & Co., Inc.

WICKMAN, E.K. (1928). *Children's behavior and teachers' attitudes.* New York: Commonwealth Fund.

WIEDERHOLT, J., HAMMILL, D.D., & BROWN, V.L. (1983). *The resource teacher: A guide to effective practices* (2nd ed.). Austin, TX: Pro-Ed.

WILLENBERG, E.P. (1971). Policy statements: Call for response. *Exceptional Children, 37,* 421–434.

WILLIAMS, R., & ALGOZZINE, B. (1977). Differential attitudes toward mainstreaming: An investigation. *Alberta Journal of Educational Research, 23,* 207–212.

WING, L. (Ed.) (1967). *Early childhood autism.* Oxford, UK: Pergamon Press.

WINN, C. (1969). Adolescent suicidal behavior and hallucinations. In G. Caplan & S. Lebovici (Eds.), *Adolescence: Psychosocial perspectives.* New York: Basic Books.

WOLF, M., RISLEY, T., & MEES, H. (1964). Application of operant conditioning procedures to the behavior problems of an autistic child. *Behavior Research and Therapy, 1,* 305–312.

WOLPE, J. (1958). *Psychotherapy by reciprocal inhibition.* Stanford, CA: Stanford University Press.

WOLPE, J. (1964). Behavior therapy in complex neurotic states. *British Journal of Psychiatry, 110,* 28–34.

WOLRAICH, M.L. (1977). Stimulant drug therapy in hyperactivity: Research and clinical implications. *Pediatrics, 60,* 512–518.

WONG, M.R. (1979). Drug abuse prevention and the special education student. In D. Cullinan & M.H. Epstein (Eds.), *Special education for adolescents.* Columbus, OH: Chas. E. Merrill.

WOOD, F., NELSON, C.M., GILLIAM, J. SHORES, R., and BULLOCK, L. (1979). Competency model for teachers of the seriously emotionally disturbed. Working papers, Project S.E.D., Education Service Center, Region XIII, Austin, TX.

WOOD, F.H. (1979). Defining disturbing, disordered, and disturbed behavior. In F.H. Wood & K.C. Lakin (Eds.), *Disturbing, disordered or disturbed? Perspectives on the definition of problem behavior in educational settings.* Minneapolis: Advanced Training Institute, University of Minnesota.

WOOD, F.H. (1982). The antithesist vision of William Rhodes. *Behavioral Disorders, 7,* 234–243.

WOOD, M.M. (Ed.) (1975). *Developmental therapy.* Baltimore: University Park Press.

WOOD, M.M., & SWAN, W.W. (1978). A developmental approach to educating the disturbed young child. *Behavioral Disorders, 3,* 197–209.

WOODCOCK, R.W. (1967). *Peabody rebus reading program.* Circle Pines, MN: American Guidance Service.

WOODY, R.H. (1969). *Behavioral problem children in the schools.* New York: Appleton-Century-Crofts.

WORKMAN, E., & DICKINSON, D. (1979). The use of covert positive reinforcement in the treatment of a hyperactive child: An empirical case study. *Journal of School Psychology, 17,* 57–73.

WORKMAN, E., & DICKINSON, D. (1980). The use of covert conditioning with children: Three empirical case studies. *Education and Treatment of Children, 2,* 24–36.

WORKMAN, E., & HECTOR, M. (1978). Behavior self-control in classroom settings: A review of the literature. *Journal of School Psychology, 16,* 227–236.

WORKMAN, E.A. (1982). *Teaching behavioral self-control to students.* Austin, TX: Pro-Ed.

WORKMAN, E.A., HELTON, G.B., & WATSON, P.J. (1982). Self-monitoring effects in a four year old child: An ecological behavior analysis. *Journal of School Psychology, 20,* 57–64.

WYATT, R.J., TERMINI, B.A., & DAVIS, J. (1971). Biochemical and sleep studies of schizophrenia: A review of the literature, 1960–1970. *Schizophrenia Bulletin, 4,* 9–66.

WYLIE, R.C. (1974). *The self concept: A review of methodological considerations and measuring instruments* (Vol. 1, Rev. ed.). Lincoln: University of Nebraska Press.

YOUNG, J.A., & WINCZE, J.P. (1974). The effects of the reinforcement of compatible and incompatible alternative behaviors on the self-injurious and related behaviors of a profoundly retarded female adult. *Behavior Therapy, 5,* 614–623.

YSSELDYKE, J.E. (1979). Issues in psychoeducational assessment. In G.D. Phye & D. Reschly, *School psychology: Perspectives and issues.* New York: Academic Press.

YSSELDYKE, J.E., & ALGOZZINE, B. (1982). *Critical issues in special and remedial education.* Boston: Houghton Mifflin.

ZIONTS, P. (1985). *Teaching disturbed and disturbing students.* Austin, TX: Pro-Ed.

Index